T0190456

Lecture Notes in Computer Science　12434

More information about this series at http://www.springer.com/series/7409

Minhua Ma · Bobbie Fletcher ·
Stefan Göbel · Jannicke Baalsrud Hauge ·
Tim Marsh (Eds.)

Serious Games

Joint International Conference, JCSG 2020
Stoke-on-Trent, UK, November 19–20, 2020
Proceedings

 Springer

Editors
Minhua Ma ⓘ
Falmouth University
Penryn, UK

Bobbie Fletcher ⓘ
Staffordshire University
Stoke-On-Trent, UK

Stefan Göbel ⓘ
Multimedia Communications Lab - KOM
TU Darmstadt
Darmstadt, Germany

Jannicke Baalsrud Hauge ⓘ
KTH
Royal Institute of Technology
Södertälje, Stockholms Län, Sweden

Tim Marsh ⓘ
Griffith University
Brisbane, QLD, Australia

ISSN 0302-9743   ISSN 1611-3349   (electronic)
Lecture Notes in Computer Science
ISBN 978-3-030-61813-1   ISBN 978-3-030-61814-8   (eBook)
https://doi.org/10.1007/978-3-030-61814-8

LNCS Sublibrary: SL3 – Information Systems and Applications, incl. Internet/Web, and HCI

This Springer imprint is published by the registered company Springer Nature Switzerland AG
The registered company address is: Gewerbestrasse 11, 6330 Cham, Switzerland

Preface

Serious games operate on the interdisciplinary interactions of art, design, computer science, electronic engineering, entertainment, human computer interaction, psychology, education, and numerous application domains. The Joint Conference on Serious Games (JCSG) aims to bring together game designers and developers, researchers and practitioners, from diverse backgrounds relating to serious games.

We present the conference proceedings of JCSG 2020, an event that marked the 15th edition of JCSG and its predecessors GameDays and SGDA. The conference merged the GameDays conference and the Conference on Serious Games Development and Applications (SGDA) in 2015. Both conferences were founded in 2010 and have been running for over a decade in Derby, UK (2010), Lisbon, Portugal (2011), Bremen, Germany (2012), Trondheim, Norway (2013), Berlin, Germany (2014), Huddersfield, UK (2015), Brisbane, Australia (2016), Valencia, Spain (2017), Darmstadt, Germany (2018), and Arequipa, Peru (2019).

We initially planned to host the JCSG 2020 at Staffordshire University, Stoke-on-Trent, UK. Due to the COVID-19 pandemic and the UK government requirements of social distancing, the conference could not take place physically, and so it was held virtually this year.

After a robust peer-review process, we selected 22 papers, including 10 serious games (3 desktop games, 2 virtual reality games, 2 augmented reality games, 1 LEGO Serious Play, 1 escape room, and 1 tabletop game); 4 game design papers discussing the pay-to-win aspects, motivation tools, participatory design, and design games for solving wicked problems; 3 papers on games for learning; 3 papers on debriefing; 1 paper on effects of esports on positive behavioural change; and 1 paper on serious game controls.

We would like to thank the members of the Program Committee, without whom the conference would not have been possible. The JCSG 2020 Program Committee is composed of 29 experts from 10 countries, comprising a unique representation of the global serious games communities. The importance and credibility of these proceedings are sustained by the competence and dedication of these experts.

The conference program was further enriched by keynote speakers Prof. Dr. Sylvester Arnab of Coventry University, UK, and Eric Treske of Intrestik, Germany.

September 2020

Minhua Ma
Bobbie Fletcher
Stefan Göbel
Jannicke Baalsrud Hauge
Tim Marsh

Organization

General Chairs

Minhua Ma	Falmouth University, UK
Bobbie Fletcher	Staffordshire University, UK

Steering Committee

Minhua Ma	Falmouth University, UK
Stefan Göbel	Technical University of Darmstadt, Germany
Jannicke Baalsrud Hauge	BIBA - Bremen Institute for Production and Logistics, Germany, and KTH, Sweden
Manuel Fradinho Oliveira	SINTEF, Norway
Tim Marsh	Griffith University, Australia

Program Chairs and LNCS Volume Editors

Minhua Ma	Falmouth University, UK
Bobbie Fletcher	Staffordshire University, UK
Stefan Göbel	Technical University of Darmstadt, Germany
Jannicke Baalsrud Hauge	BIBA - Bremen Institute for Production and Logistics, Germany, and KTH, Sweden
Tim Marsh	Griffith University, Australia

Program Committee

Bobbie Fletcher	Staffordshire University, UK
David White	Staffordshire University, UK
Erik van der Spek	TU Eindhoven, The Netherlands
Esteban Clua	Fluminense Federal University, Brazil
Guenter Wallner	Eindhoven University of Technology, The Netherlands
Heinrich Söbke	Bauhaus University Weimar, Germany
Helmut Hlavacs	University of Vienna, Austria
Jannicke Baalsrud Hauge	BIBA - Bremen Institute for Production and Logistics, Germany, and KTH, Sweden
Jose Luis Soler	Aumentaty, Spain
Josep Blat	Pompeu Fabra University, Spain
Jun Hu	Eindhoven University of Technology, The Netherlands
Manuel Contero	Polytechnic University of Valencia, Spain
Manuel Fradinho Oliveira	SINTEF, Norway
Marc Cavazza	University of Greenwich, UK
Mariano Alcañiz	Polytechnic University of Valencia, Spain

Miguel Angel Teruel	Castilla La Mancha University, Spain
Minhua Ma	Falmouth University, UK
Paul Grimm	Fulda University of Applied Sciences, Germany
Pascual Gonzalez	Castilla La Mancha University, Spain
Peter Henning	Karlsruhe University of Applied Sciences, Germany
Petros Lameras	Coventry University, UK
Polona Caserman	Technical University of Darmstadt, Germany
Ralf Dörner	RheinMain University of Applied Sciences, Germany
Sebastiaan Meijer	KTH Royal Institute of Technology, Sweden
Sobah Abbas Petersen	Norwegian University of Science and Technology, Norway
Stefan Göbel	Technical University of Darmstadt, Germany
Tanya Krzywinska	Falmouth University, UK
Tim Marsh	Griffith University, Australia
Thomas Tregel	Technical University of Darmstadt, Germany

Contents

Games for Learning

Game Design and Study

Game Debriefing

Virtual and Augmented Realities

StreetConqAR: Augmented Reality Anchoring in Pervasive Games

Thomas Tregel$^{(\boxtimes)}$ (iD), Tim Dutz, Patrick Hock, Philipp Niklas Müller,
Philipp Achenbach, and Stefan Göbel

Multimedia Communications Lab - KOM,
Technical University of Darmstadt, Darmstadt, Germany
`thomas.tregel@kom.tu-darmstadt.de`

Abstract. Pervasive games have increased in popularity with the rise of location-based games, but their content quality varies based on the area it is played in. We present a system of anchoring street signs into an approach based on augmented reality, allowing a game being played in all rural and urban areas without the need for custom content creation. By using publicly available map data, we allow for gameplay across city and country borders. Our approach identifies and augments street signs on a player's camera feed. It then automatically creates an AR challenge, based on the classical game Mastermind, for the player to capture the virtual street. The virtual streets are integrated into one game world where players can conquer and take virtual ownership of whole blocks, districts, or cities. We achieve correct augmentation rates of 84.7% with initial delays of one second and continuous fluent augmentation.

Keywords: Pervasive games · Augmented reality · Mobile gaming

1 Introduction

In contrast to classical video games, pervasive games integrate smoothly into their player's everyday activities. A motivation for pervasive games amongst others is to create a deeper gaming experience, which is usually pursued by combining reality and virtuality, making them mixed reality games. In particular, they are often designed as augmented reality (AR) games blending visually virtual elements and the real world. Another motivation for pervasive games is to bring more physical movement and social interactivity into video games while still utilizing the benefits of computing and graphical systems [15]. Physical activity is addressed, for instance, in many location-based games, which make the player move to different places in the real world while playing the game. In urban games, for instance, the city is used as the game board. The game context changes depending on the position of the player inside the city, which is usually retrieved by GPS.

M. Ma et al. (Eds.): JCSG 2020, LNCS 12434, pp. 3–16, 2020.
https://doi.org/10.1007/978-3-030-61814-8_1

Combining both AR and location awareness in pervasive games was attempted in different approaches. Human Pacman, for instance, is an AR urban game that transcribes the video game Pacman to a real city [8]. Some of the most popular location-based games are Ingress [19] and Pokémon GO [29], which are available for mobile devices. Although Ingress claims to be an AR game, it neither blends virtual and real-world elements nor includes real-world objects directly into the gameplay. Location-based games overlay the virtual world not everywhere to the physical but anchor these overlays at specific locations. Anchors have the advantage that information is persistently tethered to their location. However, they also have the drawback that they usually limit the game as they can not be found everywhere. Either designers place them at specific locations, which makes the game not cover all areas, or users have to place them in a specific game area that needs a long setup of the game.

2   Background and Related Work

A pervasive game blurs the boundaries between itself and the real world. According to Nieuwdorp [20], there are two perspectives on pervasive games: the technological and the cultural ones. The technological perspective regards pervasive games especially to input devices used: the game depends on "pervasive technology and nonstandard input devices" [7]. Cheok et al. published Human Pacman in 2004 [8], which translates the video game classic Pacman to real-world streets. Today the genre evolved to today's popular Location-based Augmented Reality Games like Ingress [19] or Pokémon GO [29], which have been accounted for positive health effects [1,33]. Game areas in these games are typically semistructured [16], which combine the advantages of structured game areas where all game locations are defined [23] with unstructured game areas without any fixed locations [2,4,25].

The cultural perspective of pervasive games discussed by Nieuwdorp includes the following characteristics, among others: its gameplay interacts with or is related to elements of the real world [20], and it has an omnipresent gaming world that lets players connect with the game anywhere and anytime [23].

These requirements cannot be met for purely structured game areas when only pre-defined locations are valid game locations, which has shown to be a problem even in popular Location-based AR Games [9,32].

3   Requirements for Real-World Anchoring

To use real-world objects in a pervasive urban AR game, we have to overcome some drawbacks that can be found in many pervasive location-based AR games, especially if they are designed as perpetual, unlimited games. We identified the following drawbacks during related work analysis:

– Although the game design proposes that the game area is unlimited most games are not playable everywhere.

– Anchors are not integrated into the games logically, which leads to a lack of smooth transition between reality and virtuality.
– Non-vision based AR is used, which does not allow a precise and realistic augmentation. If vision-based AR is used, typically, markers have to be placed within the game area before playing.

Out of these drawbacks we deduced a list of concrete requirements:

1. *Objects can be found everywhere in populated areas and are accessible* By creating anchors automatically based on the environmental circumstances, the game is not limited to certain areas. The use of recurring real-world objects can make a pervasive game playable everywhere, as they can be found in any populated area. Traffic signs e.g. usually are standardized within a country which means that each unique sign must be stored only once in a database. They can be used as anchors in cities as well as in small villages. However, traffic signs might not be the best choice for anchors in a pervasive game since they often are not accessible for pedestrians and can endanger people attempting to capture the sign. These security risks have to be considered, as well as privacy aspects. Benford et al. [5] note that including bystanders could violate their privacy when players are starting to track them down or enter their private property. Trespassing, in general, has been reported in other games as a central problem [6,17]. However, the availability of content plays a central role [28].

2. *Objects are related logically to the game* If players associate real-world objects to the virtual game and if they have to find these tangible objects to progress within the game, the need for physical movement in the real-world is comprehensible for them. To create a deeper coalescence between virtuality and reality, real-world objects should be logically related to the gameplay or the narrative. A game that uses manhole covers as real-world objects, for instance, could have a narrative related to water that could be used as entries to secret passages underground. This implies that the meaning of an object must be known by game designers to relate the object to game content. Recurring real-world objects have the advantage that they can be created once and be reused in different places.

3. *Objects can be used for vision based AR without placing tracking markers and are persistently present* Vision based AR is therefore preferred to be used in pervasive games [3]. However, placing markers before playing does not apply to these games, as players should not need to do time-consuming preparations to be able to play. However, to place a virtual object precisely into a natural scene, the object's model must be known beforehand and needs to not change positions.

4   Using Real-World Objects as AR Anchors

To meet the requirements listed in the previous Section, several types of objects come into consideration.

- Statues are not applicable as they are different in shape and size.
- Logos or advertisement posters could be used in areas where they are densely distributed. Depending on the game details, a model of each supported object would be required.
- Public buildings could be used as anchors, as they are present in all urban areas. However, similar to statues, they are not generic.
- Manhole covers have a similar appearance, and therefore can be used as natural markers for vision-based AR. However, the positions of manhole covers in the real world are, to the best of our knowledge, not known in public data, which leads to problems when generating content.
- Post boxes have an uniform appearance, and therefore could be recognized from a vision based algorithm.
- Bus stop signs and public transport signs, in general, are also uniform in appearance and could be used as an anchor, with a decreasing number of available locations in rural areas.
- Street name signs have the advantage that their positions are known by game designers based on public map data. Additionally, they are equally distributed within a city and rural areas as well. Although the exact position of a street name sign is usually not available, the fact that street name signs are placed in the corresponding street should be sufficient in most scenarios.

4.1   StreetConqAR

StreetConqAR is designed as an unlimited pervasive game. Unlimited in this case means, being playable everywhere in an urban environment, at any time, and with any number of players. In StreetConqAR players get motivated to physically move in an urban environment trying to conquer streets, districts,

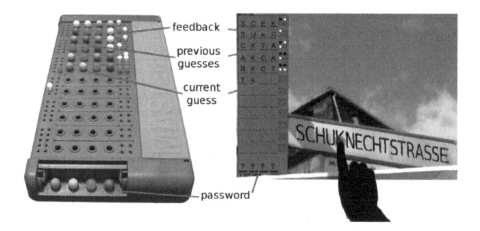

Fig. 1. Original Mastermind game and game concept adaptation for street signs. (Color figure online)

and whole cities. To conquer a street players have to find a street name sign, and capture it using their smartphone camera. The sign is augmented by a riddle, which is related to the street name. When the riddle gets solved, the player successfully conquers the street and becomes its "owner". Subsequently, owning the most streets in a district, a city, or a region awards the respective owner a title and increases the player's score. In challenges of varying difficulty, players receive a set of street riddles to conquer over a limited time period, for a respective reward in points.

The riddle was designed analog to the board game Mastermind invented in 1970. In Mastermind, one player has to find out a code consisting of four pegs with each peg have any out of six different colors. After each guess he code creator gives feedback on the guess by telling the player the amount of pegs with (1) correct color and correct position and (2) correct color and wrong position. Based on the given feedback, the player can improve his guess in each round until he finds the code or the maximum number of rounds has been reached, as shown in Fig. 1. Other types of riddles we explored have been a permutation riddle, where players are to bring the letters in the correct order, and a riddle based on the idea of "Wheel of fortune". We decided against those concepts, as the Mastermind game allowed us to provide a big challenge, which is unlikely to be solved by pure guessing.

On the right side of Fig. 1 our word adaptation of the original game is conceptualized. A code is generated by the system out of the current street name. A letter can be added to the current guess by touching it on the screen. This leads to a much higher number of possible code combinations c than in the original game with a street name of n letters:

$$c = \frac{n!}{(n-4)!} \tag{1}$$

This is addressed by coloring the same letters in the riddle with the same color reducing n to the number of unique letters in a street name, as shown in Fig. 2. Additionally, individual letters cannot be used multiple times.

In the game's conquer mode, the user sees a map of his surroundings, including the current street game data, as shown in Fig. 3a. Players can freely explore and conquer nearby streets. Thereby, streets identified by OpenStreetMap are colorized according to the current virtual owner.

In the challenge mode players are tasked to capture a number of streets within a given time limit. A difficulty can be selected, which influences both the estimated game length and the expected route distance. The street are then selected automatically. Players might be challenged to conquer a specific amount of streets out of a larger selection, giving him the freedom of choice, where to go. To estimate the expected duration of their trip during challenge generation and also during gameplay, a route planning approach, like the orienteering problem [12], can be used. This approach can adapt to their current performance and dynamically change the challenge for struggling players, so their goal location can be reached in time for a reduced reward [30,31].

Fig. 2. A screenshot while playing the Mastermind riddle, with same letters having same colors. Black dots indicate correct letters and correct positions. White dots indicate correct letters at wrong positions. (Color figure online)

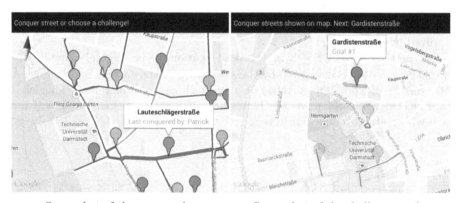

Screenshot of the map mode.   Screenshot of the challenge mode.

Fig. 3. Screenshot of the two different available game modes.

4.2   Sign Recognition and Augmentation

In order to recognize and augment street signs on a mobile device, we use a five-step approach described below, which are inspired by the TranslatAR algorithm [11]. The approach is thereby designed to not put a strain on the mobile device in terms of computation requirements, as the user selects the street sign in the augmented game mode. This allows for a local analysis of the selected area rather than a global continuous search for each input frame.

Our approach uses mainly vision-based techniques like geometric, affine and perspective transformation [13], image features [22,24], image binarization [21], text extraction in the form of the TranslatAR algorithm [11], as well as optical character recognition (OCR) [26].

Estimation and Binarization of Sign Area. First, to correctly augment the street sign, the sign area needs to be extracted. Due to the application scenario, the approach needs to address the following possible challenges: distance to the sign leading to too small or big letters, perspective-based distortion due to the angle of the image, sunlight leading to low contrast or shadows and unexpected occlusion of parts due to vegetation or dirt.

By using the user's selected position as a starting point, we use TranslatAR's gradient threshold approach, which uses an up- and down-moving line to find the text boundaries. After the vertical center is found, the area can be extracted, as street signs are expected to be rectangular with respect to camera distortion. A histogram analysis is then used to isolate the background in a localized approach to attribute for possible artifacts. The result is shown in Fig. 4a.

To improve the results of the upcoming OCR the image must be binarized, and adaptive thresholding image equalization is performed, to stretch the histogram. Afterward, a fixed threshold value can be used, considering the assumption that the area covered by text is smaller than the area covered by background, as shown in Fig. 4b.

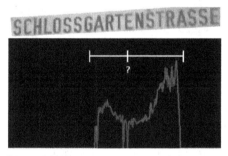

The sign area image is binarized. The inaccuracy of the previous step are yet ignored.

Histogram of possible output after area estimation when the sign is dirty. An accurate threshold value cannot directly be extracted as there is no clear separation in the histogram.

Fig. 4. Street sign binarization.

Street Name Recognition. To recognize the street name in the image, we first perform Tesseract's OCR without providing a dictionary to identify singular letters (Fig. 5a). Afterward, these letters need to be combined into a real street name. Eligible street names are extracted by using the player's current position requesting street data of OpenStreetMap over the Overpass API in a bounding box around the coordinates. For name recognition, these eligible street names are compared with the OCR results, finding the best match, and deciding whether the match is good enough to continue. This is relevant as non-street signs could be used as an input that needs to be rejected. Additionally, a bad match would lead to incorrect positioning of the remaining letters in the later augmentation step. The matching is done using the Smith-Waterman algorithm [27] (Fig. 5b) because it allows us to ignore edit operations at the beginning and the end of the word. Thereby, we can cut off artifacts at the sides of each street sign. Other popular algorithms like the Levenshtein algorithm [18] or computing the longest common subsequence do not allow for this in its basic form.

SCHUKNECHTSTRASSE   13
LIEBFRAUENSTRASSE   6
ECKHARDTSTRASSE   6
BARKHAUSSTRASSE   6
FRIEDRICH-EBERT-PLATZ 2

Output of the OCR steps, with letters in green being true positives.

Match scores with Smith-Waterman algorithm.

Fig. 5. Street name recognition selecting most similar street name in vicinity.

Calculate Homography. To apply an augmentation to the video frame captured from the smartphone camera, we create a model containing each letter's position and measures (width, height). The signs are not expected to be parallel to each other, and the points of the sign are transformed to the screen by a non-affine transformation [13]. Therefore we can specify the relation between the position of a latter in the model to its position on the screen by a perspective transformation [13] (homography). To find the homography it is sufficient to relate four points from the model to the scene, because of a sign's rectangular shape. Using the RANSAC algorithm [10], we identify the homography, finding an estimation with a high degree of accuracy even if a significant number of outliers are present. Afterward, we can directly map positions, and thereby letters, in the camera image to the model by using the inverse of the homography.

Replace Original Letters. Now that letters can be identified by screen touch position, we can start augmenting the image and individual virtual letters. However, if the calculated homography is not accurate wrong letters would be identified with virtual letters overlapping original letters at a wrong position. To overcome this problem all original letters are removed and replaced by reconstructed letters at their calculated position. This also attributes for the challenge that would require us to identify the street sign font in use.

We delete the letters by constructing a clear background using the color information gained during image binarization and a mask on the sign area. To achieve a more natural look, we create a smooth gradient between the colors at the borders of the mask as shown in Fig. 6a. The font color is similarly extracted from the image binarization allowing us to reconstruct the whole sign as depicted in Fig. 6b.

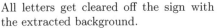

All letters get cleared off the sign with the extracted background.

Letters are reconstructed on the now blank background

Fig. 6. Street sign is cleared and letters are reconstructed again. (Color figure online)

Retaining Optical Flow During Movement. So far the algorithm is only applied to a singular frame, which includes costly calculations including, sign area estimation, OCR, and tracking, which can lead to a noticeable delay when rendering the initial frame.

To increase the frame rate to an acceptable level, we apply a less time-consuming approach to the following frames, which still ensure the accurate visualization of the virtual letters and the identification of letters by screen touch position. This is a common and well-examined problem and is solved by tracking the street name sign and updating the virtual objects' transforms accordingly.

Fig. 7. Results of the multi-scale Lucas-Kanade algorithm on a street sign.

To track the sign area from $frame_i$ to $frame_{i+1}$, the optical flow needs to be calculated, which requires a set of points to be tracked. There are different methods to find the best features, e.g. like proposed by Shi and Tomasi [24], which are calculated only within the area of the sign text mask. The transformation from $frame_i$ to $frame_{i+1}$ can be found by using the Lucas-Kanade algorithm [14], which receives the gray-scale images and a set of points resulting in the transformed set of points as shown in Fig. 7. After obtaining the new letter positions, the homography is updated, and letters are replaced, as described in steps three and four.

This approach is required constantly because while holding the smartphone in his hands, the player will always slightly move it, due to hand or walking movement, or during display interaction.

5   Evaluation of Recognition Quality

To be able to test and adjust the recognition stage algorithm was not only included into the Android application but also compiled in a standalone application running on a desktop computer. Instead of using real-time captured video frames, we recorded a video file for testing and balancing parameters. From the video, we selected 50 frames containing 15 different street name signs under differing conditions (e.g. different angles). The frames were selected so that exceptional circumstances (e.g. shadows, dirt, occlusion) were acceptable, whereas the assumption was made that acceptable means that maximal two letters are affected by these circumstances. We used a second video as a test set to evaluate how accurate the algorithm recognized the street names using the algorithm parameters identified in the training step.

These parameters include resolutions the image gets scaled to, thresholds for sign area identification as well as letter and name identification, and maximum height derivation rates for identified boxes addressing too high distortion.

We achieved a recognition rate of 92% with 4 signs out of 50 being not recognized as a sign. No recognized signs were matched wrong, with a candidate street name pool of 30 elements. As shown in Table 1, we achieved an accuracy of 84.7% on the test set. However, the recognition rates are difficult to compare to other publications. The TranslatAR algorithm, for instance, according to Fragoso et al. [11], recognized only 45.6% correctly but used more complex images as input including strong exceptional gradients and the dictionary with which the OCR result had to be compared was much bigger than the set of 30 names used in this evaluation.

Table 1. Recognition rates on training and test data

Sign data	Training (n = 50)		Training (n = 150)	
	Amount	Ratio	Amount	Ratio
Correct	46	0.92	127	0.847
Failed	4	0.08	18	0.12
Wrong	0	0	5	0.033

5.1 User Evaluation

In the user experience evaluation 16 people of age between 22 and 32 years participated, with each participant being asked to play the game for a period of at least five to ten minutes. Eleven participants were supervised and guided in detail, and the other five participants were given detailed instructions but could choose the game anywhere they wanted. The eleven participants played in the city of Darmstadt next to University in an area with little traffic but some pedestrians.

Our goal was to examine how the use of real-world objects supports the blur of virtuality and the real environment in a game, as well as the players' perception of the environment during gameplay: Does the player feel embarrassed when bystanders watch him, or does he see himself potentially in danger when playing games next to streets where traffic passes?

While accompanying the players when conquering streets, much information could be gathered by observing them. Many users were enthusiastic when they first touched the sign and saw the appearance of colored letters and the corresponding riddle. This positive feeling changed when they realized that they had to keep their hands above the shoulders for a while as they got exhausted after a short time. Most of the players had problems keeping their hands steady for a long period of time while aiming at the sign.

We initially made the assumption that players would be able to solve 2 or 3 riddles in less than 10 min. During a playing time of 310 min 23 streets were conquered, which means that players needed approximately 13.4 min per riddle to solve it. This was also because most users did not know Mastermind before playing, resulting in more required time to solve it, which was hard due to the strain on the arms holding the camera up and steady. Taller players were subjectively faster and had fewer problems with the recognition not working due to worse angles. By improving the detection quality for distorted images and zoom quality, these problems can be reduced.

Problems in street sign detection could be identified when players selected areas far outside of the street sign, as the sign could not be identified due to the local search approach described in Sect. 4.2.

The answers given in the questionnaire, on a scale from one to five, approved most information achieved during observation. The uncomfortable position strongly decreased the gaming experience for most users, as they became exhausted. Most users (12 of 16) proposed the option to scan the sign once and then being able to solve the riddle in a different position, which defeats the idea of continuous AR integration but would be a good compromise to lessen the burden on the arms.

Presence in a public environment did not affect players negatively while playing. They neither felt embarrassed (*was embarrassing*: $\bar{v} = 1.56$), nor endangered by traffic or else (*was dangerous*: $\bar{v} = 2.33$).

Players found the game being integrated into every day life (*was integrated*: $\bar{v} = 4.14$), especially caused by AR (*integration AR*: $\bar{v} = 4.21$) supported by street signs (*integration signs*: $\bar{v} = 3.75$), and because it played in a real city (*integration city*: $\bar{v} = 3.67$). Although the recognition rate was much lower than expected, players rate the detection as being mostly correct (*was correct*: $\bar{v} = 3.93$) with acceptable response times (*was slow*: $\bar{v} = 2.27$).

The reactions of players to the game were predominantly positive, especially if they were guided. They liked the concept of integrating city data into the game, especially "the idea to conquer my district". The perception of streets was found positive and indicated that the integration of real-world objects support the game experience.

6   Discussion and Final Remarks

We analyzed how pervasive urban games can integrate real-word objects and vision-based augmented reality into its gameplay. By integrating street name signs into a pervasive urban AR game, the approach can be used in rural areas as well, in contrast to current location-based games. In the user experience study, the immersive effect was perceived positive, however, it was not convenient to use the vision-based approach, including tracking the object during gameplay. The detection rate for street signs was good under conditions of mostly stable device handling. Due to the exertion factor of holding the arms stable above the head the full desired game experience could not be achieved. As users suggested, this could be addressed by using only snapshots of street signs. Another option would be to integrate other recurrent objects from the urban environment like license number plates. These could be augmented in a similar approach but would need a different game approach, as they are not stationary.

Due to the street conquering aspect the game can be used as a basis for evaluating collaboration and social interactivity: although neither of the aspects was included in the evaluation, users reported it to be motivating to conquer streets from friends and asked for the possibility to post high scores and trophies on social networks and to be able to conquer suburbs together with friends.

References

1. Althoff, T., White, R.W., Horvitz, E.: Influence of Pokémon GO on physical activity: study and implications. J. Med. Internet Res. **18**(12), 1–14 (2016)
2. Anastasi, R., et al.: Can you see me now? A citywide mixed-reality gaming experience. In: Proceedings of the UbiComp 2002. Springer (2002)
3. Azuma, R.T.: A survey of augmented reality. Presence: Teleoper. Virtual Environ. **6**(4), 355–385 (1997)
4. Benford, S., et al.: Can you see me now? ACM Trans. Comput.-Hum. Interact. (TOCHI) **13**(1), 100–133 (2006)
5. Benford, S., et al.: The frame of the game: blurring the boundary between fiction and reality in mobile experiences. In: Proceedings of the SIGCHI Conference on Human Factors in Computing Systems, CHI 2006, pp. 427–436. ACM, New York (2006). https://doi.org/10.1145/1124772.1124836
6. Bhattacharya, A., et al.: Group interactions in location-based gaming: a case study of raiding in Pokémon GO. In: Proceedings of the 2019 CHI Conference on Human Factors in Computing Systems, pp. 1–12. ACM (2019)

7. Chalmers, M., Bell, M., Brown, B., Hall, M., Sherwood, S., Tennent, P.: Gaming on the edge: using seams in ubicomp games. In: Proceedings of the 2005 ACM SIGCHI International Conference on Advances in Computer Entertainment Technology, ACE 2005, pp. 306–309. ACM, New York (2005). https://doi.org/10.1145/1178477.1178533

8. Cheok, A.D., et al.: Human Pacman: a mobile, wide-area entertainment system based on physical, social, and ubiquitous computing. Pers. Ubiquit. Comput. **8**(2), 71–81 (2004). https://doi.org/10.1007/s00779-004-0267-x

9. Colley, A., et al.: The geography of Pokémon GO: beneficial and problematic effects on places and movement. In: Proceedings of the 2017 CHI Conference on Human Factors in Computing Systems, pp. 1179–1192. IEEE (2017)

10. Fischler, M.A., Bolles, R.C.: Random sample consensus: a paradigm for modelfitting with applications to image analysis and automated cartography. Commun. ACM **24**(6), 381–395 (1981)

11. Fragoso, V., Gauglitz, S., Zamora, S., Kleban, J., Turk, M.: TranslatAR: a mobile augmented reality translator. In: 2011 IEEE Workshop on Applications of Computer Vision (WACV), pp. 497–502 (2011). https://doi.org/10.1109/WACV.2011.5711545

12. Golden, B.L., Levy, L., Vohra, R.: The orienteering problem. Naval Res. Logist. (NRL) **34**(3), 307–318 (1987)

13. Jähne, B.: Digitale Bildverarbeitung. Springer, Berlin (2010)

14. Lucas, B.D., Kanade, T.: An iterative image registration technique with an application to stereo vision. In: Proceedings of the 7th International Joint Conference on Artificial Intelligence, IJCAI 1981, San Francisco, CA, USA, vol. 2, pp. 674–679 (1981)

15. Magerkurth, C., Cheok, A.D., Mandryk, R.L., Nilsen, T.: Pervasive games: bringing computer entertainment back to the real world. Comput. Entertain. **3**(3), 4 (2005). https://doi.org/10.1145/1077246.1077257

16. Matyas, S.: Playful geospatial data acquisition by location-based gaming communities. IJVR **6**(3), 1–10 (2007)

17. Motsinger, K.: Pokémon Go away: augmented reality games pose issues with trespass and nuisance. San Diego L. Rev. **54**, 649 (2017)

18. Navarro, G.: A guided tour to approximate string matching. ACM Comput. Surv. (CSUR) **33**(1), 31–88 (2001). https://doi.org/10.1145/375360.375365

19. Niantic, Inc., Ingress. Game [Android, iOS]. Google, Menlo Park, United States of America (2013)

20. Nieuwdorp, E.: The pervasive discourse: an analysis. Comput. Entertain. **5**(2), 13 (2007). https://doi.org/10.1145/1279540.1279553

21. Nobuyuki, O.: A threshold selection method from gray-level histograms. IEEE Trans. Syst. Man Cybern. **9**(1), 62–66 (1979). https://doi.org/10.1109/TSMC.1979.431007

22. Rosten, E., Drummond, T.: Fusing points and lines for high performance tracking. In: Proceedings of the Tenth IEEE International Conference on Computer Vision - ICCV 2005, vol. 2, pp. 1508–1515, IEEE, Washington, DC (2005). https://doi.org/10.1109/ICCV.2005.104

23. Schlieder, C., Kiefer, P., Matyas, S.: Geogames: designing location-based games from classic board games. IEEE Intell. Syst. **21**(5), 40–46 (2006). https://doi.org/10.1109/MIS.2006.93

24. Shi, J., Tomasi, C.: Good features to track. In: Proceedings of IEEE Conference on Computer Vision and Pattern Recognition, pp. 593–600(1994). https://doi.org/10.1109/CVPR.1994.323794

25. Six to Start: Zombies, Run! Game [Android, iOS, Windows Phone]. Six to Start, London, United Kingdom (2012)
26. Smith, R.: An overview of the tesseract OCR engine. In: Proceedings of the Ninth International Conference on Document Analysis and Recognition, ICDAR 2007, vol. 2, pp. 629–633. IEEE, Washington, DC (2007)
27. Smith, T.F., Waterman, M.S.: Identification of common molecular subsequences. J. Mol. Biol. **147**(1), 195–197 (1981). https://doi.org/10.1016/0022-2836(81)90087-5
28. Söbke, H., Hauge, J.B., Stefan, I.A.: Prime example ingress reframing the pervasive game design framework (PGDF). Int. J. Serious Games **4**(2), 1–20 (2017)
29. The Pokémon Company, Nintendo, and Niantic, Inc., Pokémon GO. Game [Android, iOS]. Niantic, San Francisco, United States of America (2016)
30. Tregel, T., Möller, P.N., Göbel, S., Steinmetz, R.: Where's Pikachu: route optimization in location-based games. In: 10th International Conference on Virtual Worlds and Games for Serious Applications (VS-Games), pp. 1–8. IEEE (2018)
31. Tregel, T., Müller, P.N., Göbel, S., Steinmetz, R.: Looking for Charizard: applying the orienteering problem to location-based games. Vis. Comput. **2019**, 1–15 (2019). https://doi.org/10.1007/s00371-019-01737-z
32. Tregel, T., Raymann, L., Göbel, S., Steinmetz, R.: Geodata classification for automatic content creation in location-based games. In: Alcañiz, M., Göbel, S., Ma, M., Fradinho Oliveira, M., Baalsrud Hauge, J., Marsh, T. (eds.) JCSG 2017. LNCS, vol. 10622, pp. 212–223. Springer, Cham (2017). https://doi.org/10.1007/978-3-319-70111-0_20
33. Xian, Y., et al.: An initial evaluation of the impact of Pokémon GO on physical activity. J. Am. Heart Assoc. **6**(5), e005341 (2017)

Immersive Storytelling in Augmented Reality: Witnessing the Kindertransport

Yunshui Jin[1] ⓘ, Minhua Ma[2] ⓘ, and Jiachen Li[1(✉)] ⓘ

[1] College of Arts and Media, Tongji University, Shanghai, China
{jinyunshui,lijiachen1666}@tongji.edu.cn
[2] Falmouth University, Cornwall, UK
m.ma@falmouth.ac.uk

Abstract. Although hardware and software for Augmented Reality (AR) advanced rapidly in recent years, there is a paucity and gap on the design of immersive storytelling in augmented and virtual realities, especially in AR. In order to fill this gap, we designed and developed an immersive experience based on HoloLens for the National Holocaust Centre and Museum in the UK to tell visitors the Kindertransport story. We propose an interactive narrative strategy, an input model for Immersive Augmented Reality Environment (IARE), a pipeline for asset development, the design of character behavior and interactive props module and provide guidelines for developing immersive storytelling in AR. In addition, evaluations have been conducted in the lab and in situ at the National Holocaust Centre and Museum and participants' feedback were collected and analysed.

Keywords: HoloLens · Serious game · Museum · Augmented reality · Interactive narrative · Immersive storytelling · The Kindertransport · The holocaust

1 Introduction and Background

According to Reggio Emilia's concept of the 'third teacher', the physical learning environment and space, such as a museum, play a particularly important role in modern learning, can act as primus inter pares (first among equals) and create a direct communication with the young learners. However, many museums traditionally have perpetuated the "primacy of the ocular", where they have supported visitors looking at objects, but discouraged them from actually handling or experiencing objects through different sensory modalities [1]. Though it was found that some museums were using innovative techniques and multi-sensory approach to augment children's learning experience, there is still much to do to create compelling education for the young generation.

Narratives are proved to be a powerful method for empathy such as perspective taking and emotional engagement [2]. Many researchers claim positive association between empathy and prosocial behaviors [3–5].

The National Holocaust Centre and Museum (NHCM) is one of the few museums employing the narrative technique to unveil the history and enable young generations

© Springer Nature Switzerland AG 2020
M. Ma et al. (Eds.): JCSG 2020, LNCS 12434, pp. 17–33, 2020.
https://doi.org/10.1007/978-3-030-61814-8_2

to carefully examine, commemorate and learn from the tragedy of the Holocaust. *The Journey*, one of its permanent exhibitions, tells the story using environment storytelling technique through the eyes of a fictional Jewish boy Leo who survived the Holocaust and came to the UK via the *Kindertransport*[1]. Six rooms are restored to show how Jewish's life look like including Leo's family living room, Leo's classroom in his school, the street after Night of Broken Glass, the tailor's shop of Leo's family, a train carriage for *Kindertransport* and refuge in the UK. In each room, audience can watch a short video of Leo giving a monologue of what he saw, heard, experienced and felt at that time [6]. The visitors can experience the complete story gradually by going through each room, interacting with objects and watching videos.

NHCM devotes to make the exhibition more compelling and accessible. With the invention of HoloLens [7], a Head Mounted Display (HMD) for Augmented Reality (AR), a new form and media for narratives and exhibition has emerged. This new AR device differs from the previous hand-held devices (e.g. mobile phone) or VR because it overwhelms participants sense by filling the space with virtual holograms and spatial sound through the HMD, but still keeping them connected with the real world. HoloLens can be considered as a new media which creates the unique Immersive Augmented Reality Environment (IARE) where virtually holographic characters and objects can be mixed into real-world space seamlessly while participants observe, walk and interact with things in the real-world environment. IARE enables people to navigate and interact with a physical space freely while watching a performance of holographic characters. In a word, HoloLens offers a new possible solution for museums conveying stories and a fully-immersive experience to the audience.

2   A Review of Immersive Storytelling in VR and AR

There are two distinct properties of HMD AR as well as HMD VR compared with other media. *Presence* is one of them, which refers to a subjective user experience of being in the virtual or mixed-reality environment rather than the actual physical locale [8]. Different from the flat screen, HMD is a binocular device which can not only help user perceive the accurate size of an object, but also cover the large part of user's vision to generate an overwhelming sensory feeling.

The other feature is *agency*, which refers to the ability to "do something" in the experience—to interact or react rather than simply perceive. Agency is the core of VR/AR experience because virtual environment (VE) within headset gives the audience the native agency of looking [9]. In other words, IARE has the built-in nature of interaction as audience would like to have more ability to interact with the environment rather than looking.

Due to the lack of theory and barrier of the technical issues, though there were a few VR narrative animations/films on the market, such as works from Oculus Story Studio like *Lost* (2016), *Henry* (2016) and *Dear Angelica* (2017), works from Google

---

[1] Kindertransport was the title for historical events that British government made efforts to bring Jewish children out of Nazi Germany, occupied Austria and Czechoslovakia before the outbreak of World War II. During a nine-month period, 10,000 Jewish children aged between 1 and 17 were transported to the UK.

Spotlight like *Rain & Shine (2016)*, *Buggy Night(2016)*, *Pearl* (2017), *Back to the Moon* (2018), *Scoring Age of Sail* (2019), VR documentary like *Nomads* (2016) and VR feature film *Manslaughter* (2015). These visual carnivals have achieved great successes from the market and *Pearl* even won an Oscar nomination. Yet most of them are timid and unimaginative in respect of screen grammar, employing either a complete static shot or a continuous long take. The only two creative films namely *Pear* explores the teleportation across the space and *Dear Angelica* explores collision of intensive color and abstract shapes to elicit emotions. There was also very few immersive AR narrative work, fortunately, *Fragments*, a suspense & adventure narrative experience of HoloLens developed by Asobo Studio [10], is a pioneer exploration as an AR narrative experience. The success of Fragments further revealed potential for narratives in IARE.

IARE is probably effective for narratives of serious purpose rather than suspense or adventure types. IARE can involve hologram of virtual characters that enable the richness and more possibilities of a profound storytelling suitable for adults. Further, IARE can also adapt easily to a new real-world space and projects the virtual characters, furniture and object into the new one. Lastly, the experience of narrative in IARE aligns with the experience of video games and immersive theatre, which is affable and approachable for young adults.

3   Design

The aim of the project is to develop an AR application, creating an innovative experience for museum which focuses on fostering children's moral development. The objectives of this AR application are as follows:

1. engaging young generation to learn more details about this history;
2. fostering sensibilities to the principles of equality and justice for historical-political learning.

The design process followed 4-phases procedurals proposed by Hartmut Koenitz [11], starting with *paper phase* (Stage 1) to create the general outline of events and use a flow diagram to visualize sequencing and choice point of a Jewish boy Leo's Kindertransport experience. In the *prototype phase* (Stage 2), the interaction design was examined without assets, and redundant narrative elements were removed and feasibility of interactions with characters and props was checked. The *production phase* (Stage 3) included the development and integration of final assets, such as modeling, texturing, animation, programming, audio and music. In the *testing phase* (Stage 4), the AR app was published and evaluated in the lab, and the app was revised according to user feedback to be ready for final experiment in situ.

3.1   Interactive Narrative Design

The first step was to develop an interactive narrative strategy for this AR app. In order to ensure historical accuracy, the script and dialogue need to be rewritten based on an existing script from a parallel project of the virtual journey app [12] in collaboration with a historian at the NHCM. One influential narrative approach taken in *Facade* allows for users to influence the story through natural language conversations established with the main characters, thus influencing its outcome [13]. However, considering the dialogues and plots of this app were required to be designed based on survivors' testimonies and facts of the past, the narrative approach used in *Facade* can't work in our case. In other words, the theme of the story should be clear and chain of events were limited to history facts.

Koenitz and Chen [14] summarized a model of interactive narrative strategy (see Fig. 1). Based on this model, the narrative strategy used in our AR app is illustrated as solid lines in Fig. 1.

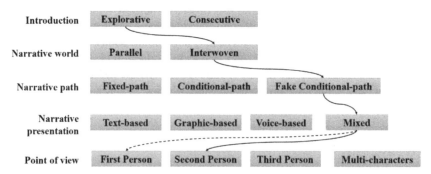

Fig. 1. A model of interactive narrative strategy

- As IARE has the built-in nature that allows the audience to walk within a real-world space and touch, interact with real-world or virtual props and objects, an *explorative introduction* was chosen, audience need to find their own ways into the narrative world instead of having a clear guide.
- As the purpose of *The AR Journey* is Holocaust education and the story of Leo's escape from Germany through Kindertransport should be conveyed clearly, *interwoven world* type was chosen, in which an overarching narrative instead of several sub-narratives exists.
- *Conditional-path* means consequences of choices are influence by audience's decision made through the story rather than entirely pre-determined by the author (fixed-path), meanwhile, conditional-path also involves more asset development. Therefore, a technique named *fake conditional-path* was used, which utilized a fixed narrative path under the hood, but letting the audience have an illusion that they can influence the plot.
- In order to maximize the display capability of HoloLens, a mixed presentation was made, including virtual character animation, graphic, dialogue, music and text.
- Point of View (POV) is an interesting topic for narrative in IARE. Since the audience and the virtual characters are in the same space—the augmented reality real-world space, the audience aren't able to view as an omniscient viewer but an invisible observer (*third person view*). Audience could also act as one of the characters in the

story (*first person view*) or act as a visible observer (*second person view*). If audience is a visible observer, the virtual character could "see and interact" with the audience, making the audience easier to empathy with them. Thus, in this project, either first person view or second person view could be a good choice. In this case, *second person view* is selected as the POV of the narrative.

The level design and scriptwriting were based on the above narrative strategy. Figure 2 shows the main story of Level 1 in a branch structure, using the *fake conditional-path* technique. The main story focused on a debate between Leo's parents taking place in the living room and questions are raised to the audience whose opinion they agree with.

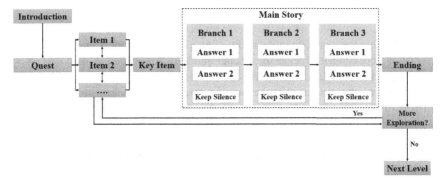

Fig. 2. Flow diagram of Level 1

Level 1 is designed based on the real-world living room scene of *the Journey* exhibition. When wearing HoloLens in the living room, audience are introduced by an off-screen of a narrator's voice that they are equipped with supernatural power to explore invisible materials and they need to find a submerged story inside this room. The user can interact with several objects in the room, such as telephone, radio, a suite case, a newspaper and a gramophone (see Fig. 3). Through these items, audience can find fragments of information like Nuremberg Race Laws, Nazi government propaganda radio broadcasting, and Leo's parents' happy life in the past. When finding Leo's diary (key item in the Fig. 2), vivid virtual holographic characters of Leo and his parents appears in the room (Fig. 3 right), talking and debating with each other. At the decision point of branches, audience can help Leo to make decisions including supporting mother or father, attitude towards equality, raising questions to parents. Whatever the audience's answers given to the branch 1, 2 & 3, the plot outcomes always lead to the same point (Fig. 2). However, as an on-site experience at NHCM, majority of the audience are supposed to have a one-time experience rather than repeating the experience several times. Therefore, the fake conditional path design can be possibly effective. After the main story ends, audience can explore more items or real-world props in the room or move to the next room/level to continue the story.

Level 2 is designed based on real-world classroom scene of the exhibition. As the Fig. 4 showed, Level 2 also uses a branched structure for the main story, and allows audience to have more interaction to find more fragments of the story. Leo talks about his

Fig. 3. Concept image for the *AR Journey* in living room at NHCM (right) and layout of some props (left)

distaste of going to school at the end of main story of Level 1, players then enter into the real-world classroom scene where the reason for Leo's soreness can be explained. Audience could trigger the reenactment by finding Leo's diary and witness the uncomfortable conversation between Mr. Becker the teacher and Leo. Audience can help Leo answer Mr. Becker's challenge (see Fig. 5). Besides, if audience help Leo to find his favorite missing drawing, the virtual wallpaper will be mapped into the real-world classroom, consisting of floating text and pictures on walls. Audience can read and interact with the virtual wallpaper as well as the human figure icon placed on the desk (see Fig. 5). By activating the icon one by one to hear Leo's classmates' voice talking about their attitude, understanding and behavior towards Leo and Jewish people, it is like a virtual interview. Finally, audience are asked to write down their comprehension for the initial question on a sticky note and put it on the blackboard.

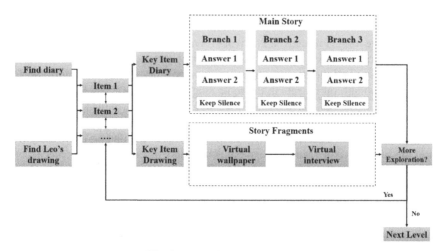

Fig. 4. Flow diagram of Level 2

Level 3 is designed based on real-world tailor's shop scene of the exhibition. Level 3 is climax of the story and use the same narrative structure as Level 1 but with more branches. It has two parts which are Night of Broken Glass and family's discussion on sending Leo to the UK via the Kindertransport. Audience can witness the mess after

Fig. 5. Concept image for the reenactment of school scene

Night of Broken Glass and the sad family conversation. They can help Leo comfort his mother, find the missing item during the riot, decide which item to pack into the suitcase, decide how to spend the final day in Berlin (Fig. 6).

Fig. 6. Players need to decide which item Leo should package into the small suitcase to take along with him (left), concept image for 'white rose' scene (right)

Level 4 is designed based on the real-world exhibition room where audience is encouraged to brace up Leo by leaving a voice message that turns into a swaying white rose in the air (Fig. 6). Audience can pick up a white rose of others to hear their message. In this way, players share their interpretation and memories of this AR Journey.

3.2 Input Strategy for HoloLens

The interaction design includes three parts: the HoloLens' input mechanism, the character interaction system and the props interaction system. Storytelling with HoloLens is triggered by user input and the user needs to choose a branch of the story using HoloLens' interface. The current available input for IARE, which consists of input type and input model, is analysed. The input type refers to fundamental genres of input in IARE including gaze, gesture, clicker and voice command. Audience can perform the same type using different apparatus, e.g. the action of gaze can be performed via head (head gaze) or eyes (eye gaze), the action of pointing and manipulation can be executed via hand gesture or a controller. It is important to understand that different input types can be combined or used alone with their own conventions to form an input model, which are listed as followings [15]:

– *Direct manipulation* is an input model that involves touching holograms/real world objects directly with one's hands or controllers. (Hololens 2 only)
– *Point and commit* is a 'far' input model that enables users to target, select and manipulate 2D content and 3D objects that are out of reach using hand gestures or controllers.
– *Gaze and commit* is a far input model using eye/head gaze and commit action via hand gesture, a controller or voice command.
– *Gaze and dwell* is a hand free input model. The user keeps gazing (with their head or eyes) at the target and lingers there for a moment to activate it.
– *Voice input* is a hand free input model by using one's voice to command and control an interface, e.g. the user can read a button's name out to activate it

As HoloLens 2 is still not available in the consumer market and the motion controllers are too large to eliminate the gap between virtual and real worlds, input models of direct manipulation and point & commit are out of the question. Eye gaze is excluded because it is only available for HoloLens 2. Voice input is infeasible as Chinese voice input is poorly supported and hand gestures have proved problematic in our preliminary study. In summary, there are two possible paths of interaction left for the *AR Journey*, which are head gaze & commit with a HoloLens clicker[2] and head gaze & dwell (Fig. 7). To be more specifically, audience are able to use their head gaze to active the choice and confirm the choice via the clicker or gazing for a certain amount of time; audience can pick the gramophone using head gaze and perform "play music" action via the clicker or dwelling the gazing for a whole. Both interaction methods aim at virtual targets and lead to output in virtual world.

As Coleridge stated that Narrative pleasure requires 'willing suspension of disbelief' [16], which refers to the willingness of the audience to overlook the limitations of a medium, making an essential contribution to the positive narrative experience. Murray addressed that the 'active creation of belief' in video game can be a substitute for 'suspension of disbelief' [17]. Therefore, to make the environment more convincible subjectively, secondary interactions and interactions with straightforward feedback should be included. This straightforward feedback, such as switching light, opening the curtain, pulling the drawer, etc., can be treated as active action to confirm the authenticity of the mixed-reality world. On the other side, narrative understanding describes how viewers make sense of or understand the narrative [2]. Story fragments and pieces of events are able to construct the narrative understanding.

---

[2] The HoloLens Clicker (clicker for short) is the peripheral device built specifically for HoloLens 1 & 2. It is a miniature controller that lets the user click on whatever he or she is looking at and there is a motion sensor inside to check the clicker's up, down, left, and right.

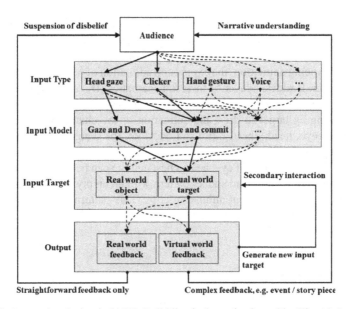

Fig. 7. Interaction design in IARE (Solid line is the path adopted by *The AR Journey*)

4 Development

4.1 Coding

The programing was developed in the Unity3D game engine. HoloToolKit[3] is used as the HoloLens SDK for Unity3D. The main challenge for coding was to develop the behaviours of characters and interactive props. There are two existing animation systems in Unity3D, the *timeline* system and the *animator* system. The timeline system, which is easy to cut, edit, and match different animation clips together with audio, is suitable for non-interactive character animation. The animator system, a finite state machine that contains different animation clips (states) and switches between different clips if the predefined conditions are satisfied, is suitable for interactive character animation. There are a lot of complicated non-interactive characters animations, e.g. Leo hugging his parents, and interactive character animations e.g. Leo finding and walking towards the user, and making eye contact with him/her. Therefore, it is important to combine the timeline and animator system. As Fig. 8 shows, a character behavior module was designed, mixing the timeline and finite state machine. The main idea was to put timeline animation and the finite state machine animation into three channels, known as *playables* in Unity3D, and use an animation mixer to mix the three *playables* with adjustable weight. The three *playables* are two timeline playables, which can dynamically load timeline animation assets and blend from one to the other seamlessly by animating the weight value, and a playable of animation layer mixer, which is the output result of the

---

[3] HoloToolKit is a collection of scripts and components for Unity3D to develop AR application for HoloLens. It contains the features, such as hand gesture input, voice recognition, spatial Mapping, spatial Sound, and spatial anchor management [27].

finite state machine animation. For the finite state machine part, a separate control of upper body, lower body and expression was achieved with *avatar mask* in Unity3D. In this way, the system can extract the lower body part of a walk cycle animation, the upper body part of a dancing animation, the expression animation of a greeting animation, and put them together. Besides, a layer of Inverse Kinematics (IK) animation with a weight value is added before the final output of the finite state machine part, which allows using a real-time changing target to drive the animation of the character. There are six IK goals including eye, head, chest, hip, hand and foot, the weight values of which can be assigned separately. In order to achieve a natural eye contact gazing animation of a character, the IK weight value of eye, head, chest and hip can be set to 100%, 70%, 40% and 20%. Moreover, the 'hub and spoke' pattern with an empty hub node is used as the main pattern to connect different animation clips. This pattern design can seamlessly blend any two animation clips of all the clips.

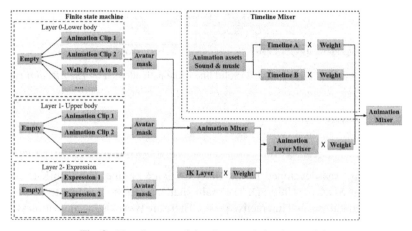

Fig. 8. The diagram of the character behavior module

Props interaction is a crucial part for the overall user experience and storytelling, and there are many different kinds of user interaction, such as opening a virtual newspaper or picking up the receiver of a virtual telephone. In order to develop and manage the interactive props efficiently, a general module for interactive props was developed (see Fig. 9). In general, there are four states for interactive props: inactive, standby, active, activated. Inactive state is the default state to avoid false triggering. The standby state can only be entered when the distance between the prop and the user is less than a threshold and the prop is targeted by the user gaze. In standby state, hint animations are shown including glowing highlight, floating text and sound effects. The active state can be entered if the user further performs an action on the prop. In the active state, the prop animations like unfolding newspaper, rotating vinyl of a gramophone, opening a suitcase, accompanied by audio. Meanwhile, it may also trigger secondary animations including character animation and special effects. For example, after the gramophone begins playing music, Leo can turn to the audience and talk about his parents dancing in the living room with the music in the old days. When all the animations end, the prop automatically enters into the activated state. In this state, a new interface may emerge, e.g. headline news on the newspaper are displayed after the newspaper is spread; a new prop may show, e.g. a diary appears when the suitcase is open; or it may trigger the close animation automatically or manually and set the state back to inactive.

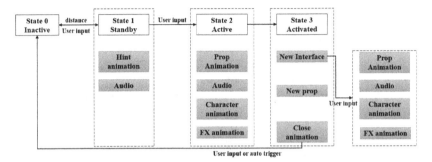

Fig. 9. The diagram of the interactive prop's module

4.2 Asset Development

There are four characters, 40 min full-body character animation, 15 props and their associated animations, several special effects and 20 UI elements required to be created for this AR app. The visual asset development follows the same rule as script development with regard to historical accuracy. Most references came from the National Holocaust Center and Museum and the online United States Holocaust Memorial Museum.

Character model and animation are the biggest part of asset development in this project. The character asset development is consisted of model part, animation part, sound design part and real-time asset part (see Fig. 10). The model part follows the latest Physically Based Rendering (PBR) pipeline in the game industry, including collecting reference, sculpting in Zbrush, re-topology in Wrap 3, cloth modeling in Marvelous Designer, normal map baking with Zbrush and Xnormal, texture painting in Substance Painter, and finally adjusting material in Unity3D (see Fig. 11). This pipeline is accessible and effective. It separates the shaping process into two independent steps, sculpting and topology instead of mixing them together as traditional way does. Moreover, Wrap 3 can efficiently complete the topology task as it can map a standard-topology character model onto the sculpting model instead of retopology manually. Cloth with natural folds is important to make a character visually believable and Marvelous Designer is the best tool which can precisely create cloth folds in a quick way. Substance painter is the most popular PBR texture painting tool, however, skin shader is different between Substance Painter and Unity3D. Standard material in Unity3D doesn't support Subsurface Scattering (3S) effect and some third-party materials like LUX 3S material is not supported by Hololens hardware. Consequently, in order to make the skin as natural as possible, extra tweaking and adjustment need to be done for standard material in Unity3D.

Full body animation was capture with Vicon Mocap System in the Mocap Lab at Tongji University where we restored the layout of the rooms in Holocaust Center

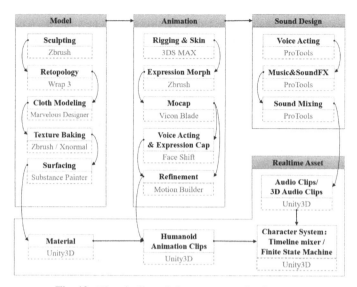

Fig. 10. The pipeline of character asset development

Fig. 11. Pipeline of Leo's model creation

to ensure the holographic virtual character could dovetail the real-world space (see Fig. 12). The facial expression capture has been implemented with PrimeSense 1.0, a depth camera and Faceshift software. In order to use Faceshift, 51 expression morphers need to be made to meet the requirement of the internal expression manager of Faceshift (see Fig. 13). Students from the acting department of the university performed for facial motion capture to match the existing body animation.

Fig. 12. Motion capture for scene 1(left), concept composition of mocap animation and living room (right)

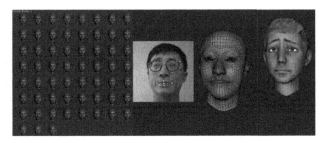

Fig. 13. Using Faceshift to perform facial expression capture

As to spatial sound, Hololens headphone can achieve spatial sound via Head Related Transfer Function (HRTF) technology, making the position and direction of an audio source recognizable in a real-world space. Spatial sound can strengthen the fidelity and direction of the sound effect, character's voice and sound of props. Built-in 3D sound module in Unity3D and Microsoft HRTF Spatializer plugin can deliver the audio into headphones of HoloLens as spatial sound.

4.3 Lessons Learned

Key lessons learned from the development phase are as follows:

– Character animation merging and refinement issues. Motion Builder is the key tool to process the Mocap data. Motion Builder is optimized for rendering and modifying real-time character animations. For example, Motion Builder can easily handle a 15-min shot containing 3 characters' animation and over 100,000 keyframes, which may lead other software crash or stuck. Besides, its built-in story mode can edit multiple character animation clips together with audios using a layered track structure as film editing software. Position and rotation of different animation clips can be re-aligned automatically based on the same bone, such as hip, foot, hand, etc., and animation clips can be blended by overlapping with each other on the track. Therefore, Motion Builder can merge and match the expression animation and body animation and voice acting quickly. Lastly, Motion Builder has a better integrated Forward Kinematics (FK) and Inverse Kinematics (IK) character rigging system, which can make the adjustment of the animation faster.
– Interactive path finding issue. Path finding is a common demand for interactive character. In this project, protagonist Leo need to find the audience and talk to them face to face. Unity3D has a *Navmesh* module for pathfinding, which can dynamically generate a ground surface for navigation based on the 3D scanning data from HoloLens, and character can avoid the obstacles and find the target on the generated ground surface. Though navmesh offers good result, it's not a perfect solution as it requires extra computing. In order to save computing power, a simplified pathfinding module was developed using *animator*. It consisted of turning into the target, walking towards the target, and stopping in front of the target.
– Real-time shading issue. Due to Covid-10 pandemic, it is infeasible to conduct in-situ evaluation on site, thus we had to create the environment to facilitate an alternative

evaluation off-site. And Fig. 15 shows the real environment and the real-time photo-realistic rendering used for evaluation remotely. As HoloLens has limited computing power, it's impossible to use complicated shader for interior scene and props. However, it doesn't mean realistic image can't be achieved with simplified shaders that only have diffuse and specular. Lighting, baked global illumination and post-process like bloom effect can help to build a realistic atmosphere with a simple diffuse shader (see Fig. 14).

Fig. 14. A photograph of the physical exhibition room in the museum (left); real-time photorealistic rendering in Unity3D (right)

– Stabilization of the hologram in HoloLens issue. Hologram's stability is a common issue in AR. Microsoft has developed and defined several terminologies to describe the hologram's instability, including jitter, judder, drift, jumpiness, swim and color separation. In order to avoid the above issues, frame rate and frame-rate consistency is the first pillar of hologram stability. 60 FPS is the ideal and maximum frame rate for HoloLens, and 30 FPS or below can lead to obvious drifting or jitter issue according to our tests. Besides, a constantly fluctuating framerate is a lot more noticeable to a user than running consistently at lower frame rates. Furthermore, it's important to choose the right spatial coordinate systems: Stationary Frame of Reference (SFoF) and spatial anchors. SFoF is a single rigid coordinate system suitable for a small room scale experience within 5-m diameter or moving objects like walking characters and floating UI. Spatial anchors are a multiple coordinate system suitable for world-scale experiences beyond 5 m, which can mark the important point in the real-world and each anchor stays precisely where it was placed relative to the real-world. In this project, spatial anchors coordinate system are used to stabilize the hologram, and these anchors can be persistent, which are stored and loaded back even when HoloLens restarts. Lastly, HoloLens performs a sophisticated hardware-assisted holographic stabilization technique known as reprojection. For HoloLens 1, *Automatic Planar Reprojection* technology is usually used to set a stabilization plane using information in the depth buffer. On Unity, this is done with the "Enable Depth Buffer Sharing" option in the Player Settings pane.
– Optimization for FPS issues. There are many possible reasons to slow down the program. The most effective treatments during our development include: 1) use release mode to deploy the program instead of debug; 2) set blend weight of skin to 2 bones if possible; 3) keep pixel shader as simple as possible (avoid to use standard shader)

and use unit or vertex lit if possible; 4) use prebaked textures for shadows and lights instead of real-time; 5) keep texture size under 2048 and generate mipmaps; 6) turn off anti-aliasing and use bilinear filtering; 7) use instancing when ring multiples of the same mesh.

5   Interview and Discussion

After the development of the alpha version was completed, 9 people were invited to participant in the testing and interview. The testing was held in the Lab in Staffordshire University and the National Holocaust Center and Museum (see Fig. 15).

Fig. 15.   The Lab for testing in university lab (left), the exhibition room for testing at the National Holocaust Center and Museum (right)

The interview questions were as follows:

- Q1: Do you notice the characters or environment are unnatural? If so, what aspect is unnatural?
- Q2: Do you feel the interaction are uncomfortable? If so, what aspect is uncomfortable?
- Q3: How do you like the experience? Please describe it and give some examples.
- Q4: How do you dislike the experience? Please describe it and give details.

The main findings according to the common feedback from the participants include:

- The gaze & dwell input model is difficult to use for selection, as there is an issue of "observation vs. commit". Because the FOV is narrow in HoloLens, users tend to put the choice in the middle of the view to read, which would accidently trigger the choice while reading. This is the reason why we prefer gaze & commit input model.
- The low framerate (<30 FPS) caused discomfort for 2 participants while others haven't noticed this issue.
- 4 participants said that ambient sounds like raining, noise, street cars were too distracting and sometimes they couldn't hear the characters' dialog.
- 6 participants felt the FOV of HoloLens was too narrow and the edge of the display could be identified. It was strange to see the virtual character was trimmed by the edge of the display.

- One participant thought it was much more interesting to interact with virtual character like greeting and having eye contact other than watching a branched story.
- All participants thought it was interesting to have this mixed reality experience and to see these holograms of characters in a real environment.
- Several participants noticed that Leo can have eye contact with them and they thought it was interesting.

In summary, the feedback of the alpha version met our initial expectations. According to the interview, we could conclude that the overall experience was interesting even if the narrow FOV limitation was annoying. Moreover, gaze and commit were used as the input model other than gaze and dwell. Framerate was improved above 50 fps in accordance with official guidelines [18] and suggestions from the developer community [19]. The pitch of Leo's voice acting was modified to make the voice younger, and it was later noticed that girls or women could perform a good job for a young boy's voice acting if the boy actor of the right age couldn't be found. A new sound manager module, which can adjust the ambient sound dynamically based on audience's attention, was developed to solve the issues that ambient sound was sometimes too loud to hear the actors' voice. It is also reasonable infer that characters' full-body animation is more important than their material and textures according to the interview result. Therefore, it is important to assign more time to animation other than modeling and surfacing. Lastly, it is interesting that the narrow FOV can sometimes hide problems, e.g. audience usually tend to focus on Leo's head and upper body while any problem of lower body is ignored as it's usually out of the HoloLens display.

6   Conclusion and Future Work

The author developed an AR interactive narrative experience based on HoloLens and evaluated the programme with a small group of people. The overall feedback was positive. Besides, the development pipeline, interactive narrative strategy, input strategy, the design of the character and props module and AR related technologies were summarised. However, the evaluation was done with a small group via interview, more rigorous evaluation including quantitative methods with more subjects should be considered. Moreover, AR technologies are advancing very fast recently, during the development, HoloLens 2 has already published on the market while this study used HoloLens 1 to develop and evaluate. HoloLens 2 has great improvement in terms of FOV and input methods, which should be further studied in the future. Lastly, due to the lack of narrative work in the field of HMD-based AR, more empirical studies and explorations for interactive narrative in AR should be made in both industry and academia.

Acknowledgement. This work was jointly funded by the National Key Research and Development Program of China (2018 YFB1004903) and Staffordshire University in the UK. We would also like to acknowledge the support from Jake Lynch for script development and the support from Elinor Rosa Williams, Zhang Nan, Zhang Zian, Yu Guodong for motion capture.

References

1. Kiberd, D.: Learning in museums. In: Keynote Address Symposium, Learning in the Context of Irish Museums Friday, 1st November 2002, pp. 3–14 (2002)
2. Busselle, R., Bilandzic, H.: Measuring narrative engagement. Media Psychol. **12**(4), 321–347 (2009)
3. Hoffman, M.L.: Interaction of affect and cognition in empathy. In: Emotions, Cognition, and Behavior, pp. 103–131 (1984)
4. Saarni, C., Crowley, M.: The development of emotion regulation: effects on emotional state and expression. In: Emotions and the Family: For Better or for Worse, pp. 53–73 (1990)
5. Jin, Y., Ma, M., Hua, D., Coward, S.: Games for mental and moral development of youth: a review of empirical studies. In: Alcañiz, M., Göbel, S., Ma, M., Fradinho Oliveira, M., Baalsrud Hauge, J., Marsh, T. (eds.) JCSG 2017. LNCS, vol. 10622, pp. 245–258. Springer, Cham (2017). https://doi.org/10.1007/978-3-319-70111-0_23
6. Brondi, R., et al.: Evaluating the impact of highly immersive technologies and natural interaction on player engagement and flow experience in games. In: Chorianopoulos, K., Divitini, M., Hauge, J.B., Jaccheri, L., Malaka, R. (eds.) ICEC 2015. LNCS, vol. 9353, pp. 169–181. Springer, Cham (2015). https://doi.org/10.1007/978-3-319-24589-8_13
7. Hololens 1 Hardware Specification. https://docs.microsoft.com/en-us/hololens/hololens1-hardware,last. Accessed 31 Jan 2020
8. Witmer, B.G., Singer, M.J.: Measuring presence in virtual environments: a presence questionnaire. Presence **7**(3), 225–240 (1998)
9. Newton, K., Soukup, K.: The storyteller's guide to the virtual reality audience. The Standford D School (2016)
10. Introduction for Fragments from Asobo Studio. https://www.asobostudio.com/games/fragments. Accessed 22 Aug 2020
11. Koenitz, H.: Towards a theoretical framework for interactive digital narrative. In: Aylett, R., Lim, M.Y., Louchart, S., Petta, P., Riedl, M. (eds.) ICIDS 2010. LNCS, vol. 6432, pp. 176–185. Springer, Heidelberg (2010). https://doi.org/10.1007/978-3-642-16638-9_22
12. Malbos, E., Rapee, R.M., Kavakli, M.: Behavioral presence test in threatening virtual environments. Presence: Teleoper. Virtual Environ. **21**(3), 268–280 (2012). https://doi.org/10.1162/pres_a_00112
13. Mateas, M., Stern, A.: Integrating plot, character and natural language processing in the interactive drama Façade. In: Proceedings of the 1st International Conference on Technologies for Interactive Digital Storytelling and Entertainment, TIDSE 2003 (2003)
14. Koenitz, H., Chen, K.-J.: Genres, structures and strategies in interactive digital narratives – analyzing a body of works created in ASAPS. In: Oyarzun, D., Peinado, F., Young, R.M., Elizalde, A., Méndez, G. (eds.) ICIDS 2012. LNCS, vol. 7648, pp. 84–95. Springer, Heidelberg (2012). https://doi.org/10.1007/978-3-642-34851-8_8
15. Mixed Reality Interaction Models Documentation from Microsoft. https://docs.microsoft.com/en-us/windows/mixed-reality/interaction-fundamentals. Accessed 31 Jan 2020
16. Coleridge, S.T.: Biographia Literaria, or, Biographical Sketches of My Literary Life and Opinions. Princeton University Press, Princeton (1984)
17. Murray, J.H., Murray, J.H.: Hamlet on the Holodeck: The Future of Narrative in Cyberspace. MIT Press, Cambridge (2017)
18. Microsoft Mixed Reality Documentation. https://docs.microsoft.com/en-us/windows/mixed-reality/understanding-performance-for-mixed-reality. Accessed 31 Jan 2020
19. Hololens Forum. https://forums.hololens.com/discussion/409/low-fps-in-hololens-app. Accessed 31 Jan 2020

Become a Scrum Master: Immersive Virtual Reality Training to Learn Scrum Framework

Polona Caserman$^{(\boxtimes)}$ⓘ and Stefan Göbelⓘ

Multimedia Communications Lab - KOM,
Technical University of Darmstadt, Darmstadt, Germany
{polona.caserman,stefan.gobel}@kom.tu-darmstadt.de

Abstract. Serious games are digital games that have an additional goal beyond entertainment, e.g., educational games can be a motivational tool for teaching or training players. Among other things, educational games can also be used in IT companies to convey approaches of agile software development. Such learning environments can improve the player's skills in software development processes to reduce risks of schedule delays or incurred cost overruns. In particular, educational games should provide an effective and motivating learning environment for the players and should include hands-on activities to reinforce learning. To this end, we have developed an immersive virtual reality educational game to teach the Scrum framework. This game aims to efficiently train complex processes and improve the player's skills in agile process management. In the virtual environment, players can go through a software development process to discover different activities, such as daily Scrum and sprint planning. The presented paper introduces a game design, results of initial user testings, and subsequent re-design of the early state educational game. The evaluation results of a user study show that the developed game can indeed teach the basics of the Scrum framework to players with little knowledge. However, the game scenario needs to be improved to make it more engaging and immersive for experienced players.

Keywords: Educational games · Serious games · Computer-based training · Scrum framework · Agile development · Business process management · Immersed virtual reality

1 Introduction

Serious games are created with the intention to entertain and need to achieve at least one additional goal, e.g., improve learning outcomes [6]. They aim to

Electronic supplementary material The online version of this chapter (https://doi.org/10.1007/978-3-030-61814-8_3) contains supplementary material, which is available to authorized users.

M. Ma et al. (Eds.): JCSG 2020, LNCS 12434, pp. 34–48, 2020.
https://doi.org/10.1007/978-3-030-61814-8_3

accomplish this twofold mission, i.e., achieve intended effects without compromising the player experience and engagement. Recent studies already proved the suitability of the simulation-based serious games as a learning tool to optimize business processes in a company [24], to efficiently use the healthcare resources in a hospital emergency unit [18], or to manage a university [15]. Additionally, serious games can also enhance player's skills, such as team and communication skills [16] or project management skills [19].

Thus, serious games seem to be useful to simulate scenarios of the real world to optimize processes and to manage companies efficiently. They allow players to experience situations that are not possible in the real world due to too high costs, too high time requirements, or insufficient safety [4]. Players can use such simulator-based serious games to run through different scenarios to develop required skills while facing different challenges. Slater and Sanchez-Vives [21] further point out that immersive virtual reality is particularly suitable in education because it gives the players an opportunity to get hands-on experience. Thus, one should employ immersive virtual reality applications so that the players can explore and experiment to enhance motivation to learn and improve learning outcomes.

Particularly during a development process, it is important to use appropriate methods to handle the challenges of managing complex projects. It is crucial to optimize development processes by identifying tasks, managing time effectively, and setting-up teams [11]. For example, Scrum and Kanban are the two most commonly used approaches to improve and optimize the development processes and are often used to manage work on complex products. Scrum framework describes several events and the team needs to run through a specific sequence of activities (a sprint) to ensure that the entire development process runs smoothly and efficiently [20]. On the contrary, Kanban imposes fewer constraints and does not contain sprints [10]. Kniberg and Skarin [10] furthermore suggest using both methods to combine the best of both.

This paper presents an immersive virtual reality educational game that addresses the main elements of the Scrum framework. In the game, the player should continuously improve the virtual product and help the team maintain the rules, as defined in the Scrum guide [20]. This work focuses on teaching the player the basics of the Scrum framework while he or she faces various challenges and needs to perform the tasks of a Scrum master. For example, the player needs to communicate with virtual characters to learn about the roles. Furthermore, he or she needs to participate in various activities to learn about different artifacts. To review the player performance, the serious game includes various multiple-choice tests, which are integrated into the gameplay. The aim of this paper is to evaluate the preliminary design and to verify if the current game scenario is suitable for teaching players the fundamentals of agile development.

The remainder of the paper is organized as follows. In Sect. 2, we present the literature review and in Sect. 3.1, we introduce the design of the developed game. Section 4 describes the evaluation and Sect. 5 presents the research findings. In Sect. 6, we discuss the results and conclude in Sect. 7.

2   Related Work

2.1   Learning and Training in Immersive Virtual Reality

Many recent studies have shown the benefits of immersive virtual reality over traditional learning and training methods, e.g., enhanced motivation in mathematics education, contributing to more efficient learning and understanding [5]. Furthermore, the work of Papanastasiou [16] shows that virtual reality applications provide a useful tool to enhance learning, in particular, improving 21st-century skills, e.g., creative thinking, communication, collaboration, and problem-solving ability. On the contrary, other studies suggest that immersive virtual reality may overload and distract learners, resulting in poorer learning outcomes [13]. Similarly, reduced learning effects in immersive virtual reality compared to a desktop application (a PowerPoint presentation) have also been found in a study by Parong and Mayer [17].

However, immersive virtual reality can be advantageous because it supports "doing" rather than just observing [21]. Studies have shown that players can transfer the knowledge and skills to a real-life situation if the training occurs in a realistic virtual environment, e.g., virtual training for police officers [1,14] or simulations to learn survival skills applicable during an earthquake [12]. Further scenarios suggest collaborative training for firefighters [7]. That is to say, if experiences in a virtual learning environment resemble the real situation in which the skills are going to be used, this can increase the chances for a successful learning transfer.

2.2   Serious Games About Business Process Management

Many studies explored the potential of serious games for educational or training purposes. *INNOV8*, developed by IBM, is a serious game that provides a learning environment for IT and business professionals to learn the fundamentals of business process management.[1] In this simulation-based game, players can interact with other virtual employees and can participate in their daily activities to learn about business process management and how to optimize the company's business process [2]. The study by Tantam et al. [24] evaluated the effectiveness of the *INNOV8* game and concluded that the serious game indeed increases learning outcomes and flow.

Another serious game that teaches and simulates business processes was developed by Ribeiro et al. [18]. In the game *ImPROVE*, players need to model a business process underlying the hospital emergency unit to protect human lives, efficiently use the healthcare resources, and uphold fairness. An additional example to learn business processes modeling is covered in [15]. In this serious game, the players are required to manage a virtual university, particularly choosing the appropriate strategy to improve educational quality. Furthermore, Strecker and

---

[1] https://www.ibm.com/developerworks/library/ws-bpm-innov8/, last visited on April 14th, 2020.

Rosenthal [22] present a cooperative game to familiarize players with the intricacies of the manufacturer's tender process. Moreover, Herzberg and Kunze [8] aim to gamify a business process to engage users, to support them in achieving their goals, and to improve their skills.

2.3   Agile Development

One of the most common agile project management approaches is Scrum, whereas Kanban also became very common in recent years. Kniberg and Skarin [10] describe in their book the strengths and limitations of Scrum and Kanban. Both approaches seem to be useful for teams doing agile software development. Scrum and Kanban's main objective is to optimize the development process by identifying the tasks, managing time more effectively, and setting-up teams [11].

Scrum was first introduced in 1986 by Takeuchi and Nonaka [23]. The authors describe a new approach for product development that would increase speed and flexibility. Based on this approach, many researchers adopted new process frameworks. Among others, in the early 1990s, Sutherland and Schwaber presented a Scrum framework for developing, delivering, and sustaining complex products [20]. Scrum strength lies in small teams that are highly flexible and adaptive. The team selects high priority items that the development team can commit in a single sprint. Due to the iterative approach, product management and work techniques can be optimized to reduce risks of schedule delays or incurred cost overruns. The prescribed events and artifacts make sure to discover problems quickly and to adapt or replan the work if necessary.

In addition to Scrum, also Kanban is a very effective Agile project management approach. Lei et al. [11] suggest that both, Scrum and Kanban, lead to the development of a successful project; however, Kanban can be better than Scrum in managing a project schedule. The work of Kniberg and Skarin [10] indicates that Scrum and Kanban are very similar, e.g., they are both lean and agile, can break down the work into smaller pieces, have self-organizing teams, focus on delivering releasable software early and often, and both use pull scheduling. One of Scrum and Kanban's most crucial aspects is the necessity of a feedback loop (also called Retrospective) so that the teams can quickly improve or adapt the process.

3   Design

3.1   Game Scenario

In the educational game, the player should learn the fundaments of agile project management, especially the Scrum framework. Players should get to know different roles, events, artifacts, and rules, as defined in the Scrum guide [20]. Therefore, they need to run through multiple Scrum sprints and should ensure that the Scrum team follows the rules during the development of an Arcade game. Thus, players learn the basics of Scrum by communicating with various characters and participating in different activities.

Arcade Game. The aim of the game is to successfully complete a virtual project (an Arcade game) by using the Scrum principles. The development team needs to design and implement a simple Jump'n'Run game, as shown in Fig. 1. In this Arcade game, the player controls an astronaut and needs to explore the planet to collect the reward (rare stones). Additionally, the astronaut must defend himself against the enemy aliens with a raygun.

To successfully implement the game, the development team needs to complete five tasks: create (1) graphic assets and (2) background music as well as sound effects. Additional tasks include the implementation of different kinds of movements: (3) running, (4) jumping, and (5) shooting. Scrum team uses a whiteboard with sticky notes, where all tasks are described so that everybody in the team can see what has been done so far and what still needs to be done.

In each Scrum planning, the development team selects one of these tasks and implements it in the subsequent sprint. In the sprint review, the player then needs to review if the tasks have been achieved. The player can turn on the Arcade by pushing the red button, jump with the blue button, and shoot with the yellow button. Furthermore, the joystick is used to move the character left or right. After all tasks have been developed in the last sprint, the player can play the game without restriction, i.e., move the character, jump from one platform to the next, and shoot the enemies.

(a) Arcade   (b) Game design

Fig. 1. Arcade Jump'n'Run game (Color figure online)

Virtual Characters. The virtual guide in the game (a hologram dragon), gives the player important instructions and background information about the Scrum framework, e.g., maximal duration of different activities and responsibilities of the Scrum team members. The player can always require help by extending the right palm (see Fig. 2a). When the player rotates the hand, the hologram appears above the controller and suggests what the player should do, e.g., tells the player to go to the conference room to meet the team.

In addition to the virtual guide, the player can interact with multiple non-player characters (NPCs), e.g., product owner and the development team (see

(a) Hologram   (b) Product owner

Fig. 2. Interaction with the virtual guide and product owner

Fig. 2b). To speak with NPCs, the player needs to enable the controller's laser pointer and point at the virtual character (see Fig. 3b). The team members have specialized skills and areas of focus that are necessary to develop all the features of the Arcade game. The data in Table 1 shows the associated role and expertise of individual characters. While the Scrum team is self-organizing (the members choose how best to accomplish their job, rather than being assigned by others outside the team), they should still know the roles of the other team members. Thus, to learn the different roles in Scrum, the player has to interact with different NPCs.

Fig. 3. The main characters

Furthermore, to access the player performance, the virtual characters ask the player questions about the Scrum rules. These multiple-choice tests are provided so that the player can reflect the acquired knowledge. The tests are carried out randomly between the Scrum activities. When the player answers a question incorrectly, the NPC will give the player a hint.

Table 1. Team responsibilities

Character	Role	Expertise
Joe	Product owner	Project management
Elizabeth	Environment artist and animator	Graphic assets and character animations
Kate	Animator	Character animations
Lewis	Programmer	Gameplay and sound programming
Malcom	Game designer and sound engineer	Designs gameplay and rules, generates audio elements
Suzie	Game designer and sound engineer	Designs gameplay and rules, generates audio elements

Activities. There are different activities and artifacts the player can discover during the gameplay. The player needs to go through the process of agile software development to review the main elements of the Scrum framework. The development team itself is responsible for the delivery of a successful outcome at each sprint and the main focus of the player is to safeguard this process. The game consists of five sprints in order to successfully develop the Arcade game. Figure 4 shows a Scrum sprint phase the player needs to go through to learn the roles, events, artifacts, and the rules.

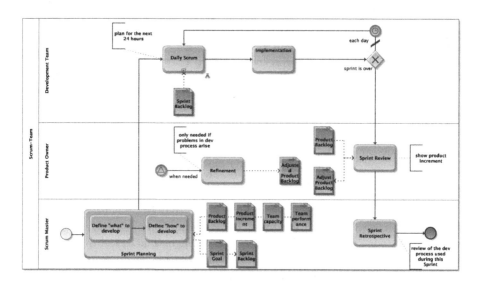

Fig. 4. Scrum sprint phase

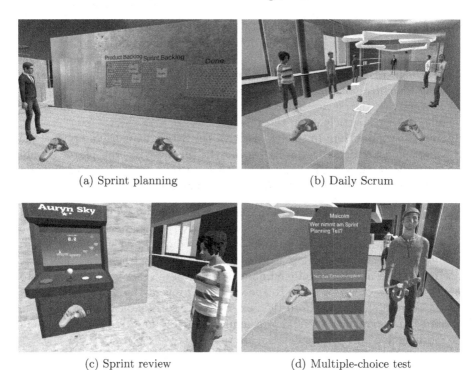

(a) Sprint planning

(b) Daily Scrum

(c) Sprint review

(d) Multiple-choice test

Fig. 5. Game activities

In general, there exist four formal events for inspection and adaptation:

Sprint planning: In the beginning, the product owner defines the features of the Arcade game. The development team then decides which tasks from the product backlog should be implemented in the coming sprint. Therefore, the player must choose a task from the product backlog, drag it across the whiteboard, and drop it into the sprint backlog (see Fig. 5a). In this activity, the player should learn how to efficiently develop the Arcade game in small and short increments. Furthermore, in a multiple-choice test, the player needs to answer the question about the primary goal of sprint planning, who participates in this event, and its maximum duration (see Fig. 5d).

Daily Scrum: In a short meeting, the development team discusses their work and progress. The player needs to ensure that daily Scrum takes place every day in the same meeting room and that the prescribed times are respected, i.e., max 15 min. Figure 5b shows the development team in a meeting room during a daily Scrum. During this meeting, the player's knowledge is examined in a multiple-choice test. The player should learn who needs to take place at the daily Scrum, what the involved members should discuss, and what is the maximum duration.

Sprint Review: The responsible NPC presents the player with the result of the last sprint. The player can directly play the Arcade game to review if the requested task has been successfully developed (see Fig. 5c). If the development team addressed the customer's requirement, the player can drag the corresponding task from the sprint backlog into the increment. In this activity, the player should learn when the sprint review takes place and who needs to participate in this meeting.

Sprint Retrospective: In the last activity, the Scrum team should review the development process of the last sprint. In this activity, the player should learn the primary goal of the sprint retrospective, when this event should occur, who should be present, and its maximum duration.

The player decides when he or she wants to do something. The hologram and the product owner give instructions on what activity should occur, though the player decides what she or he wants to do in one day and when to move on to the next day. While the development team is implementing the game, the player can freely move in the virtual environment and can interact with the NPCs to check the status of the project. To speed up the process, the player can push a button below a clock, to skip to the next day. The clock indicates if it is in the morning, afternoon, or evening. For example, daily Scrum takes place always in the morning and sprint review in the afternoon.

3.2 Hardware

The game was designed to be used with an omnidirectional treadmill, i.e., Cyberith Virtualizer[2], to enable full movement in virtual environments. This treadmill allows the players to naturally walk and run on a low-friction surface to explore infinitely sized virtual environments [3]. In contrast to teleportation, which is one of the most common locomotion techniques in virtual reality, treadmills keep players stationary while aiming to provide the full gait cycle. Furthermore, to enable immersive virtual reality experience, we initially developed a serious game to be used with HTC Vive Pro[3].

However, in order to enable the broadest possible usage (e.g., at different universities) without requiring the treadmill, we could expand the game through teleportation. In this case, we would still provide an immersive experience with HTC Vive head-mounted display without restricting the player's interaction with the virtual world.

4 Evaluation

We conducted an early user study, to evaluate the preliminary game design and to gain further insights. In particular, we wanted to find out if the current

---

[2] Cyberith Virtualizer: https://www.cyberith.com, last visited on May 26th, 2020.

[3] HTC Vive pro: https://enterprise.vive.com/us/product/vive-pro/, last visited on May 26th, 2020.

game design is suitable for teaching the players the fundaments of the Scrum framework. However, due to coronavirus COVID-19 pandemic, we could not invite students to the university to evaluate the current game as desired. As already mentioned in Sect. 3.2, the current prototype requires HTC Vive Pro and Cyberith Virtualizer. To enable evaluation in a safe home environment, we needed to adjust the controls to play the game without special hardware requirements. Therefore, we used a simulator that allows the players to use a keyboard and mouse to control the HTC Vive controllers and move through the virtual environment.

4.1   Method

Participants. We initially recruited 37 participants. However, due to low-end hardware (the participant's computer did not always meet the minimum hardware requirements), not all participants were able to complete it. Thus, 14 participants were excluded from the analysis due to incomplete responses. Finally, we included the data of 23 participants (6 females, 17 males), aged between 19 and 31 years old ($M = 23.4, SD = 2.7$). The previous knowledge about Scrum framework was balanced: Eight participants had fairly or extremely previous knowledge, whereas seven participants had no or only slight knowledge. Similarly, one-third of the participants ($n = 8$) had moderate knowledge (see Fig. 6).

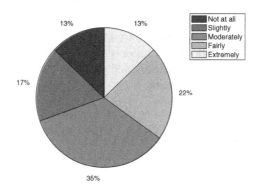

Fig. 6. Prior knowledge about Scrum framework

Procedure. In the beginning, the participants were asked to look at a video (2.87 min), explaining the game's purpose and mechanics. We furthermore provided a short instruction, summarizing the keyboard functions, e.g., use WASD keys to move in the virtual environment and M to enable the laser pointer of a controller. These shortcuts were furthermore visible during the gameplay on the top left corner (the participants could toggle the instruction using F1).

The participants then independently played the game until the Scrum team developed all five tasks. Thus, to complete the game, the players needed to ensure that all tasks in the product backlog get done. Afterward, the players were asked to fill out the online questionnaire.

Measures. As the primary goal of the developed serious game was to teach players the Scrum framework, we asked them about their Scrum knowledge before and after playing. We hypothesize that players with only slight prior or even without any prior Scrum knowledge will learn the principles. We furthermore applied the Game Experience Questionnaire (GEQ) that contains 33 questions to evaluate *competence, sensory and imaginative immersion, flow, tension/annoyance, challenge, negative,* and *positive affect* [9]. Each question could be responded on a five-point scale, from 0 ("not at all") to 4 ("extremely"). For each component, we calculate the median value (MED) and interquartile distance (IQR) as well as minimum and maximum value.

5   Results

5.1   Learning Outcomes

Self-reported ratings on learning outcomes confirm that players with no or little prior knowledge about the Scrum framework thought that they were learning. In contrast, participants with fairly or extreme prior knowledge reported that they did not learn something new. Figure 7 shows the relationship between prior and post-knowledge. We furthermore calculated the Spearman correlation between prior and post-knowledge and found an only weak negative correlation ($r(21) = -0.23, p = 0.3$). Nevertheless, the developed game seems to be suitable to teach players about the Scrum fundaments.

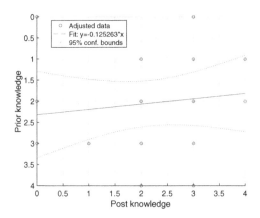

Fig. 7. Correlation between knowledge before and after playing the game

5.2   Game Experience

Overall, as listed in Table 2, the results show only low scores for the game experience. As already mentioned in Sect. 3.2, we were not able to evaluate the current game as desired. Thus, we believe that these poor results arise from the fact that the simulator's game controls were not very easy to use. The participants often noted that they were frustrated due to complicated controls, i.e., using mouse and keyboard to control both HTC Vive controllers individually. Some participants also mentioned that they think that the game may be fun to play using real HTC Vive controllers.

Table 2. GEQ results

Component	MED (IQR)	Min	Max
Competence	1.83 (0.48)	1.43	2.35
Sensory and Imaginative Immersion	1.59 (0.37)	1.17	1.74
Flow	0.91 (0.26)	0.52	1.96
Tension/Annoyance	1.96 (0.46)	1.13	2.04
Challenge	0.78 (0.17)	0.35	0.87
Negative affect	1.96 (0.90)	1.04	2.57
Positive affect	1.65 (0.09)	1.35	1.91

6   Discussion

The results of the first user testing provided important insights into targeting group preferences and wishes. The results (see Sect. 5.1) show that the game is suitable especially for players with little knowledge on Scrum; however, for a more immersive experience, the game mechanics need to be improved and the game scenario needs to be expanded. To improve the game for more experienced players, we need to vary the level of difficulty. For example, to enhance the current scenario, we want to add "troublemakers" who then prevent the development team from delivering the tasks. In this case, experienced players would need to interfere in order to solve the problem and, in particular, overcome unexpected problems.

The results furthermore show that participants had difficulties with the navigation mechanisms of the game and could not effortlessly control the game. Difficult controls also caused frustration in the participants. During the gameplay, some of the participants asked for instruction (via Skype or email), because they did not know how to complete specific tasks, e.g., turn on an Arcade. Currently, the product owner or the hologram give instructions. However, the evaluation results revealed that sometimes more instructions are needed. To better support the players in the future, we want to add more instructions so that they can independently complete the game. Another possibility would be to develop a multiplayer scenario, where the second player can monitor the progress of the trainee and support as well as guide him or her.

Based on the participants' feedback and wishes, we also want to improve the current game scenario. We came up with a second level, in which the participants also learn the Kanban principles. Therefore, players can then deploy the acquired skills to combine Scrum and Kanban while supporting the team and safeguarding the development of the product. This task of combining different frameworks would increase the level of difficulty of the educational game and would also challenge players with good Scrum knowledge.

7 Conclusion

In this paper, we present a design for an educational game to teach players the fundaments of the Scrum framework. The proposed game scenario allows the players to actively participate in various hands-on activities rather than only observe the development process. The aim of the serious game is to provide opportunities to simulate certain situations and encourage players to engage actively in practical activities.

To enable an immersive experience, the serious game was initially designed and implemented to be used with HTC Vive Pro and Cyberith Virtualizer treadmill to allow players to naturally walk and run on a low-friction surface to explore the virtual environment. However, due to coronavirus COVID-19 pandemic, we could not evaluate the current game as desired and thus used a simulator. Although the evaluation results show poor results on game engagement, which we believe arise due to complicated simulator controls, the self-reported ratings on learning show that it is suitable to teach players about Scrum fundaments.

In future work, we want to combine Scrum and Kanban framework. Furthermore, we want to deploy a multiplayer mode, where the role of the second player may vary between the monitoring, supporting, and guiding. Moreover, we want to conduct an additional user study using HTC Vive Pro and Cyberith Virtualizer to access the player engagement.

Acknowledgment. This work has been co-funded by the German Federal Ministry of Education and Research (BMBF) within the framework of the Software Campus project "TargetVR" [01|S17050]. The authors would like to thank Sabrina Schüssler for the design of the virtual environment. The authors would also like to thank Steffen Schäfer, Tamara Ihlefeld, Till Fritz-Vietta, and Amien Al-Abed for the implementation of the game as part of their studies at the Technical University of Darmstadt.

References

1. Bertram, J., Moskaliuk, J., Cress, U.: Virtual training: making reality work? Comput. Hum. Behav. **43**, 284–292 (2015). https://doi.org/10.1016/j.chb.2014.10.032
2. Bulander, R.: A conceptual framework of serious games for higher education: conceptual framework of the game INNOV8 to train students in business process modelling. In: 2010 International Conference on e-Business (ICE-B), pp. 1–6, July 2010
3. Cakmak, T., Hager, H.: Cyberith Virtualizer: a locomotion device for virtual reality. In: ACM SIGGRAPH 2014 Emerging Technologies, SIGGRAPH 2014. Association for Computing Machinery, New York (2014). https://doi.org/10.1145/2614066.2614105
4. Corti, K.: Games-based learning; a serious business application. Informe de Pixel-Learning **34**(6), 1–20 (2006)
5. Demitriadou, E., Stavroulia, K.-E., Lanitis, A.: Comparative evaluation of virtual and augmented reality for teaching mathematics in primary education. Educ. Inf. Technol. **25**(1), 381–401 (2019). https://doi.org/10.1007/s10639-019-09973-5
6. Dörner, R., Göbel, S., Effelsberg, W., Wiemeyer, J.: Serious Games: Foundations, Concepts and Practice. Springer, Cham (2016). https://doi.org/10.1007/978-3-319-40612-1
7. Eller, C., Bittner, T., Dombois, M., Rüppel, U.: Collaborative immersive planning and training scenarios in VR. In: Smith, I., Domer, B. (eds.) EG-ICE 2018. LNCS, vol. 10863, pp. 164–185. Springer, Cham (2018). https://doi.org/10.1007/978-3-319-91635-4_9
8. Herzberg, N., Kunze, M.: The business process game. In: ZEUS, pp. 26–32 (2015)
9. IJsselsteijn, W., De Kort, Y., Poels, K.: The Game Experience Questionnaire, pp. 3–9. Technische Universiteit Eindhoven, Eindhoven (2013)
10. Kniberg, H., Skarin, M.: Kanban and Scrum: Making the Most of Both. InfoQ (2010)
11. Lei, H., Ganjeizadeh, F., Jayachandran, P.K., Ozcan, P.: A statistical analysis of the effects of Scrum and Kanban on software development projects. Robot. Comput.-Integr. Manuf. **43**, 59–67 (2017). https://doi.org/10.1016/j.rcim.2015.12.001. Special Issue: Extended Papers Selected from FAIM 2014
12. Li, C., Liang, W., Quigley, C., Zhao, Y., Yu, L.: Earthquake safety training through virtual drills. IEEE Trans. Visual. Comput. Graph. **23**(4), 1275–1284 (2017). https://doi.org/10.1109/TVCG.2017.2656958
13. Makransky, G., Terkildsen, T.S., Mayer, R.E.: Adding immersive virtual reality to a science lab simulation causes more presence but less learning. Learn. Instr. **60**, 225–236 (2019). https://doi.org/10.1016/j.learninstruc.2017.12.007
14. Moskaliuk, J., Bertram, J., Cress, U.: Impact of virtual training environments on the acquisition and transfer of knowledge. Cyberpsychol. Behav. Soc. Netw. **16**(3), 210–214 (2013). https://doi.org/10.1089/cyber.2012.0416. pMID: 23363227
15. Mouaheb, H., Fahli, A., Moussetad, M., Eljamali, S.: The serious game: what educational benefits? Proc. - Soc. Behav. Sci. **46**, 5502–5508 (2012). https://doi.org/10.1016/j.sbspro.2012.06.465. 4th World Conference on Educational Sciences (WCES-2012) 02–05 February 2012 Barcelona, Spain
16. Papanastasiou, G., Drigas, A., Skianis, C., Lytras, M., Papanastasiou, E.: Virtual and augmented reality effects on K-12, higher and tertiary education students' twenty-first century skills. Virtual Real. **23**(4), 425–436 (2018). https://doi.org/10.1007/s10055-018-0363-2

17. Parong, J., Mayer, R.E.: Learning science in immersive virtual reality. J. Educ. Psychol. **110**(6), 785–797 (2018). https://doi.org/10.1037/edu0000241
18. Ribeiro, C., Fernandes, J., Lourenço, A., Borbinha, J., Pereira, J.: Using serious games to teach business process modeling and simulation. In: Proceedings of the International Conference on Modeling, Simulation and Visualization Methods (MSV), pp. 1–7. The Steering Committee of The World Congress in Computer Science, Computer Engineering and Applied Computing (WorldComp) (2012)
19. Riedel, J.C.K.H., Hauge, J.B.: State of the art of serious games for business and industry. In: 2011 17th International Conference on Concurrent Enterprising, pp. 1–8, June 2011
20. Schwaber, K., Sutherland, J.: The Scrum GuideTM. The definitive guide to scrum: The rules of the game, pp. 1–19 (2017)
21. Slater, M., Sanchez-Vives, M.V.: Enhancing our lives with immersive virtual reality. Front. Robot. AI **3**, 74 (2016). https://doi.org/10.3389/frobt.2016.00074
22. Strecker, S., Rosenthal, K.: Process modelling as serious game: design of a role-playing game for a corporate training. In: 2016 IEEE 18th Conference on Business Informatics (CBI), vol. 01, pp. 228–237, August 2016. https://doi.org/10.1109/CBI.2016.33
23. Takeuchi, H., Nonaka, I.: The new new product development game. Harv. Bus. Rev. **64**(1), 137–146 (1986)
24. Tantan, O.C., Lang, D., Boughzala, I.: Learning business process management through serious games: feedbacks on the usage of INNOV8. In: 2016 IEEE 18th Conference on Business Informatics (CBI), pp. 248–254, August 2016. https://doi.org/10.1109/CBI.2016.35

Social MatchUP: Collaborative Games in Wearable Virtual Reality for Persons with Neurodevelopmental Disorders

Francesco Vona$^{(\boxtimes)}$ ⓘ, Silvia Silleresi ⓘ, Eleonora Beccaluva ⓘ,
and Franca Garzotto ⓘ

Department of Electronics, Information and Bioengineering, Politecnico di Milano, Milan, Italy
{francesco.vona,silvia.silleresi,eleonora.beccaluva,
franca.garzotto}@polimi.it

Abstract. Our research explores game play in Wearable Collaborative Virtual Environments (WCVEs) to provide new forms of treatment for persons with Neurodevelopmental Disorders (NDD) that complement traditional methods of intervention. We investigate this issue using the *Social MatchUP (SMUP)* application as a case study. SMUP provides a set of games in WCVEs that have been co-designed with NDD experts and aim at improving communication skills. In SMUP, multiple users wearing a Virtual Reality visor play together to accomplish collaborative tasks that take place in shared virtual environments and require talking to each other to be completed. The paper presents an exploratory empirical study devoted to evaluate the potential of SMUP games for persons with NDD to improve their speech-based conversational capability. We organized participants (24 persons with NDD) in 2 groups, one playing a game in SMUP and one playing a similar game in the real world, and assessed likability, usability, and a number of conversational performance metrics. Our results indicate that the game experience in SMUP was usable and enjoyable, and boosted higher conversational skills with respect to its counterpart in the physical setting.

Keywords: Collaborative immersive virtual environment · Wearable virtual reality · Serious game · Neurodevelopmental disorders · Communication skill

1 Introduction

Our research explores the potential of serious games in collaborative virtual environments for a specific target group: persons with Neurodevelopmental Disorders (NDD). NDD is an umbrella term for a group of disorders (including, among others, Autism Spectrum Disorders, Intellectual Disability, and Communication Disorders) that are associated primarily with the functioning of the neurological system and brain [1]. According to the Diagnostic and Statistical Manual of Mental Disorders (DSM-5 [1]), individuals with NDD typically display co-occurring developmental impairments that very frequently affect social and communication skills, such as the inability to initiate and sustain reciprocal interaction and to apply language and speech to engage in conversations with others effectively. Traditional interventions typically involve one-to-one, clinician-directed

© Springer Nature Switzerland AG 2020
M. Ma et al. (Eds.): JCSG 2020, LNCS 12434, pp. 49–65, 2020.
https://doi.org/10.1007/978-3-030-61814-8_4

interactions or group sessions that use different approaches to promote the development of linguistic skills, e.g., storytelling, "social stories", role-play, or collaborative board games [2], which stimulate active engagement and social interaction, create situations that motivate the conversation, and support their generalization to real-life contexts.

More innovative, but still exploratory, approaches use game-based interactive technologies to complement traditional interventions. In this arena, play activities in Collaborative Virtual Environments (CVEs) [23] are thought to be particularly promising and to provide a context for investigating new therapeutic practices. By allowing multiple users to play together within a shared virtual space, CVEs offers a stimulating and engaging environments that seem to promote alternative ways of social learning among individuals with NDD [5, 28].

Most existing studies focus on CVE-based play for improving collaboration capability of this target group. Relatively few studies look at these game experiences as means to practice and enhance communication skills [4, 7, 8]. Our research addresses this latter aspect, focusing on *speech-based conversational* skills. In addition, we consider a subclass of CVE technology, namely, CVEs on *wearable* head mounted displays, hereinafter referred to as *Wearable Collaborative Virtual Environments*, or *WCVEs*.

We explore the potential of WCVE-based games for persons with NDD using a case study - *Social MatchUP* (*SMUP* for short). SMUP is a set of multiplayer serious games that take place in various wearable virtual environments and have been co-designed by a mixed team of therapists and engineers with the specific aim of creating opportunities of spontaneous communication during WCVE collaborative play.

To evaluate the effectiveness of SMUP, we performed an exploratory empirical study that involved *24 persons with NDD* and was devoted to answer the following main research question: *"Does SMUP games enhance conversational skills in individuals with NDD more than analogous games in real-life?"*

Our results indicate that the game experience in SMUP was usable and enjoyable, and boosted higher conversational skills with respect to its counterpart in the physical setting, highlighting that properly designed play activities in WCVE could be adopted for NDD interventions in the communication area.

The rest of the paper is organized as follows: in Sect. 2 we discuss the related work concerning CVEs and WCVEs technologies in research, clinical practice and special education for individuals with NDD. After describing SMUP (Sect. 3), Sects. 4 and 5 present the research methodology of the empirical study and its main results. Sections 6 and 7 discuss the contribution of our research and outline future research directions.

2   State of the Art

Since more than two decades researchers have been investigating how Collaborative Virtual Environments (CVEs) and Wearable Virtual Reality (WVR) can provide means to develop new forms of treatment for various impaired populations, particularly persons with Neurodevelopmental Disorder (NDD) [10–13].

CVEs provide shared virtual spaces for multiple individuals to interact with one another and/or with virtual items, and have witnessed a growing interest for supporting social skills in individuals with NDD, particularly autism [22]. CVEs are especially suitable for simulating collaboration tasks and group work among patients in a safe and controlled environment; they provide opportunities for situational learning where behaviors and responses can be practiced and built upon in a context that provides minimal modification across similar scenes, stimulating generalization and mitigating the cognitive rigidity that often characterizes this target group [18, 25, 26]. CVEs seem to provide an efficient and beneficial means of fostering communication skills particularly among populations with language and emotion impairments [24], reducing the potential stress of face-to-face conversations, prompting communicative production and dialogues better than regular interventions [8, 27, 28], and engaging individuals for longer periods of time [29]. Some studies provide preliminary evidence that students and adults with autism respond socially to virtual characters supporting conversations and nonverbal cues in the CVE better than to humans, suggesting that these shared digital environments could offer useful platforms for intervention in the social and communication area.

In the past, the technological weaknesses of first-generation virtual reality headsets (e.g., poor viewing angles, high latency, and weight) and their high cost prevented the adoption of Wearable Virtual Reality (WVR) in educational or therapeutic interventions. Today's HMD displays are much more comfortable and often commercially available at an affordable cost, and a number of studies show that they are well accepted by persons with NDD. Experiences in WVR typically provide realistic or imaginary settings for practicing practical and social skills [14–18]. Thanks to their high degree of immersiveness, interactivity, and immediate feedback, they are thought to be useful to reduce behavioral problems, improve autonomy, and mitigate phobias. Regarding communication skills, WIVR technologies have been successfully used to encourage children in hospitals to interact with other children who have common conditions or disorders [19, 20]. Play experiences in WIVR seem to stimulate the hospitalized child to explore different scenarios and adopt different identities, which helps them to divert the attention from their health condition, also providing a safe environment in which they feels more comfortable to communicate with peers [21].

Despite the fact that both CVE and WVR technologies proved to have several advantages for individuals with communication deficits, there is a noted lack of CVEs applications that are expressly tailored for wearable devices and are targeted to people with NDD and their communication needs and impairments. These are the two main characteristics of Social MatchUP (SMUP), the game kit presented in this paper. The general game logic of SMUP is simple and mimics existing real-life games. Still, the play experience in SMUP has been explicitly designed to stimulate speech-based conversational skills: Play tasks require a mutual exchange of information between the participants to be completed and involve speech communication among players as a prerequisite for proceeding in the game, which is expected to improve conversational skills. The current version of SMUP extends the one presented in a previous paper [9] (where no evaluation activity was reported) and comprises a larger number of games (four), as discussed in the next session.

3 Smup

3.1 General Features

SMUP is a set of collaborative virtual reality games that are used on smart phones inserted in Google Cardboards. Google Cardboard is composed of two biconvex lenses mounted on a plastic or cardboard structure available in different colors and shapes. The smart phone set inside the visor displays the visual contents, splitting them into two near-identical bi-dimensional images. The illusion of 3D depth and immersion is created by the stereoscopic effect generated by the viewer lenses and the human visual system. The lenses map the up-close display to a wide field of view while also providing a more comfortable distant point of focus. The human brain combines the two images and gives the perception of a single planar representation. Interaction is based on gazing, i.e., looking at virtual objects or areas in the virtual world or changing gaze direction generates (possibly multimedia) effects. Gaze orientation and gaze focus are extrapolated from head position and movements detected by the sensors embedded in the smart phone. This technology has been chosen for two main reasons: low-cost and simplicity of the interaction mode. Smart phones are widely available and Google cardboard costs a few euros. The native interaction mode of this technology involves head movements and gaze control only, which is simpler to learn compared to interaction based external controllers, and more accessible to people with motor impairments or limited motor control.

In each SMUP game, two players share the virtual environment populated with virtual objects, and see each other as avatars. To activate an object, the user must look at it in such a way that the small visual "pointer" in the middle of the screen overlaps with it; After few seconds, the object changes color and can be "grasped" and "moved".

3.2 Games

The current version of SMUP includes four games: Matching Up the Pairs, Fixing, Collaborative Puzzle, and Sorting (Fig. 1). The games were designed in collaboration with NDD therapists from a local care center who collaborated with us in previous Virtual Reality projects, and are inspired to some concepts at the basis of well-known psychometric tests used in clinical practice (the Wechsler Adult Intelligence Scale-IV or WAIS) [33]. "Matching up the Pairs" was designed on the basis of the Symbol Search subtest of WAIS, "Fixing" on the Figure completion subtest, and "Puzzle" on the Visual Puzzle subtest. "Sorting" is the "sort by colors" version of the Sorting task. Play rules are defined keeping in mind an intrinsic characteristic of WCVEs, i.e., the users' *co-presence in the virtual environment,* as well as some additional requirements:

- Users play in pairs (collaboration within a larger group would be too complex) and perform a goal-driven tasks that can completed only by mutually sharing information, initially hold by one of the two players only; each user must therefore speak with his/her companion in order to proceed.
- The objects in the virtual reality space are familiar to the players, i.e., represent common objects that use in regular play (e.g., balls) or in therapy (e.g., picture cards), so that users do not need to understand what these objects are and can focus on what to do with them.

- There is no predefined, temporally rigid turn-taking: each user has the freedom to try a task as many times as she or he desires and has all needed time to execute it and to negotiate turns with the companion;
- Games can be personalized (at different degrees) by both the patient and the caregiver, in order to make the experience more engaging and more appropriate to the players' characteristics. For examples, users can choose their own avatars and caregiver can set the complexity level (depending on the game, e.g., number of objects and their shape).
- With respect to the intellectual and motor skills required to play, games are "easy yet challenging": tasks involve actions similar to those that users would perform with physical objects in the real work, but have features (e.g., configurable constraints) that introduce complexity and challenges.

"Matching up the Pairs" Game

The game goal is to discover pairs of identical images (one image per player) and remove them from the scene. Each player has a set of images around him or her and cannot see the other player's set. The number of images is configurable and is the same for each player. Each image is surrounded by a colored aura (red for one player and blue for the other). Players have to look simultaneously at the same image for 5 s to make it disappear (which also generate a cheerful "pop" sound). In order to look at the same image, the players need to communicate with each other and describe the image they are looking at. The game ends when there are no more images in the scene.

"Fixing" Game

Players cooperate to "fix" some broken parts in a complex object. To do so, one player has to look at the broken object (e.g., a bike without a wheel), while the other one has to select at the corresponding "fixing" element (e.g., the bike wheel). Communication is needed in order to identify the missing element in the broken object.

"Collaborative Puzzle" Game

Players cooperate to complete a puzzle. One user sees the complete picture, while the other places the puzzle pieces on a grid that has configurable dimensions (sized min 3 × 3, max 10 × 10). The player selecting a piece must tell the characteristics of the piece to the other player. Th player looking at the puzzle must describe to the companion where to place the piece in the grid.

"Sorting" Game

Each player is in front of a table giving their back to the other player, and can grasp and move a set of balloons that have different colors and are initially located on the ground. The set of balloons is the same - for number of items, size and color of balloons - for each player. The goal of the game is to place all balloons on each table so that the sequence is the same on both tables. The players cannot see change view perspective, i.e., they cannot turn and see the other player's table. To complete the task, they must mutually describe the position of each balloon and negotiate the movements to perform.

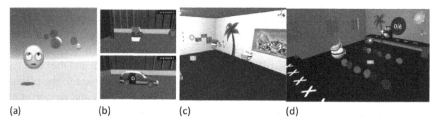

Fig. 1. The four games in SMUP: (a) Matching up the pairs; (b) Fixing; (c) Collaborative Puzzle; (d) Sorting

4 Exploratory Study

4.1 Research Method

We performed an empirical study to explore whether SMUP can enhance conversational skills in individuals with NDD. The research was designed as a controlled study where we compared the improvement of conversational skills in two groups of participants with NDD, respectively playing the Sorting Game in SMUP (*"VR group"; n = 12*) and a similar game in the physical context (*"Physical group"; n = 12*). Moreover. We also evaluated the likability and usability of the SMUP game, using a questionnaire submitted to all participants in the VR group.

4.2 Research Variables

To evaluate *conversation skills*, we adopted specific metrics for linguistic production that are theoretically grounded on Sack's conversational analysis method [34], and considered the following *measures of linguistic performance*:

1. *Length of the conversation*, in which we distinguished two sub-variables:

   a. Time where both players did not speak during the game (*silences*)
   b. Time where at least one player did speak during the game (*speaking time*)

2. *Total number of words* produced during the game
3. *Total number and types of utterances produced*, distinguishing a number of sub-variables:

   a. Total number of *single lexical words* produced (e.g. "yellow")
   b. Total number of *interrogative clauses* (e.g., "Where did you put the balloon?")
   c. Total number of *declarative clauses* (e.g., "I put the yellow balloon on the first spot on the left")

4. *Total number of turn takings* (calculated as the number of times a participant start speaking after the other participant has finished his/her turn of conversation).

The quantitative data to measure to the above variables were extracted by a researcher in linguistics analyzing the video recording of each session. The results were later compared inter-group (VR group vs Physical group) to investigate the potential communication benefits of game-based activities in virtual reality with respect to analogous plat in physical sessions.

Concerning *Likability* and *Usability* of the SMUP game, we used a survey method. Participants in the VR group were asked to complete two questionnaires (reported in Annex): one comprising a set of questions investigating how much they enjoyed the SMUP game, and one focusing on the ease of use of the different actions required by the game. Each questionnaire (see Appendix) consisted in a set of 10 questions, each one associated to a 7 points scale [35] (7 being the highest value, 1 the lowest one). In both surveys some questions asked about positive attitudes towards the application (e.g., "Was the game fun"?) while others investigated negative attitudes towards the application (e.g., "Was the game boring?").

4.3 Participants

Twenty-four adults with NDD (10 females) aged 20–50 years old (mean $= 29;3$, SD $=$ 7.7) were recruited from two local non-profit associations. The diagnosis of NDD was based on diagnostic assessment by a psychiatrist and confirmed by the DSM-5 criteria. Among the diagnosis of NDD we acknowledged individuals with Autism Spectrum Disorder, with Intellectual Disability, with motor disorders, with other "not otherwise specified" neurodevelopmental disorders. All the participants were monolingual Italian-speaking. They were randomly assigned to one the experimental conditions (SMUP game and physical game). In each group we randomly created 6 pairs of players. Groups' characteristics are reported in Table 1, showing that there is no significant difference between the two groups on age (U (23) $= 64.5$, $p = .685$).

Table 1. Characteristics of the two groups of participants

Group	Mean Age (y;m) and range	Gender
VR	29;1 (22;0–25;5)	F (n $= 6$) M (n $= 6$)
Physical	29;4 (20;9–50;9)	F (n $= 4$) M (n $= 8$)

4.4 Apparatus and Materials

The Game

We selected the *Sorting Game* to achieve the highest level of similarity in the two experimental conditions, in terms of objects, environment set-up, and play rules.

Both the virtual and the real environments for game play have the following characteristics: The space was a simple room with no furniture except two big tables in front of which the players are located; The room was symmetric (squared), in order to give players the same exact points of reference in the space (Fig. 2); Each table was marked with white crosses at equally distant positions to identify where objects could be placed; All users had six balloons to manage (a size that therapists suggested to be the appropriate level of complexity for the profile of participants); The two players had to maintain the front view of their table, giving their back to the other player. In the virtual version, the application prevented "by design" each player to turn and see the other player. In the physical version, users were instructed to maintain the front positing and were reminded to follow the rule by their caregivers.

In the virtual version, the player could: grab a balloon by staring at it for a few seconds; drag it with the gaze by moving the head in a given direction, and release it on one of the available positions by stopping there for few seconds. Visual and audio feedbacks were produced when a balloon was successfully grabbed and placed on any free position. A victory sound effect (people clapping) was produced when both players positioned the balloons in the same mutual order.

In physical play, the user grasped the blown-up balloons with their hands and moved them to the different positions (a sticky strip was used to keep the balloon in place), receiving a "bravo!" greeting from the caregiver (otherwise silent, and clapping only at the game completion) (Fig. 3).

Fig. 2. A session of the Sorting Game in SMUP   **Fig. 3.** Preparing the room for the physical Sorting Game

4.5 Procedure

The study was performed within the therapeutic centers' ordinary schedule, to ensure that the research would not impact the normal flow of participants' activities. All individuals signed a consent form authorization to perform the study following the research protocol. The study received the approval from the Ethical Committee of our University.

Each pair of players was involved in one session and played the game in the assigned modality (either VR or Physical) until they completed the game. Both in the VR and the physical condition, the game was explained to each user before the session. The members of the VR group were trained on Wearable VR before the study, using a "tutorial" application designed for users to learn the gaze-based interaction mechanism. At least one caregiver was present in each session to maintain a high level of focus and a schedule that was appropriate for all participants. Each session was video-recorded. All participants in the VR group filled the two questionnaires (on Likeability and Usability – see Appendix) at the end of the session.

5 Results

5.1 Linguistic Performance

Due to the non-normal distribution of the data (which was confirmed by the Shapiro–Wilk test), our analyses were conducted using non-parametric tests, with ANOVA by ranks (Kruskal–Wallis test) in order to reveal group effects, the Mann–Whitney test for inter-group comparisons, and the Wilcoxon test for intra-group comparisons, associated with Spearman's rank correlations. Results were considered significant at $p < .05$.

Session duration ranged between 3:15 min to 13:40 min. Our findings indicate that the VR group took more time to complete the task than the Physical group, with an average time of 08:24 min of VR sessions against 06:34 min in Physical sessions (Fig. 4). As mentioned in Sect. 5.2, in the analysis of play time we distinguished between the periods during which the participants communicated with each other (*Speaking Time*) and the periods when participants did not communicate (*Silences*).

Speaking Times were similar in the VR group (5:48 min) and the Physical group (5:21 min), while Silences were longer in the VR group (2:36 min) than in the Physical group (1:13 min). Nonetheless, Mann–Whitney inter-group comparisons showed that differences between the two groups were not significant on average time spent playing the game ($U(23) = 98, p = .259$), on speaking time ($U(23) = 22, p = .588$) and on silences ($U(23) = 26, p = .225$).

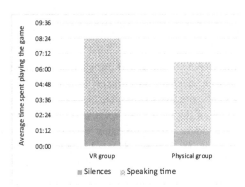

Fig. 4. Average time (silences and speaking time) spent playing the game by each group.

Concerning the *verbalization* produced by the players (Fig. 5), the results show that the average number of exchanged words in the virtual reality play context (*average produced words* = 82.4) was *significantly higher* than the one obtained by players in physical sessions (average produced words = 51) ($U(23) = 104.5, p = .047$) indicating that the players in the VR group were more engaged in mutual communication than the players in the Physical group, and had a bigger linguistic production.

It is worth considering these findings also in light of the absence of correlation ($r_s =$ .297, $p = .158$) between the number of words produced and the amount of time spent by each player communicating with their companion during the game. Figure 6 shows that individuals with NDD who played the Sorting game in VR were more prone to communicate with each other than individuals who played in the physical environment, *even when the "speaking time" was the same in the two conditions.*

Concerning the *number of turn takings*, the value of this variable was significantly higher in the VR group than in the Physical sessions ($U (23) = 111, p = .024$).

Taken together, these findings suggest that for individuals with NDD, game activities in wearable VR environments might be more effective to stimulate conversational skills that physical play in a real environment.

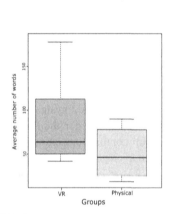

Fig. 5. Mean rate of words produced by the VR group and the Physical group on the Sorting task

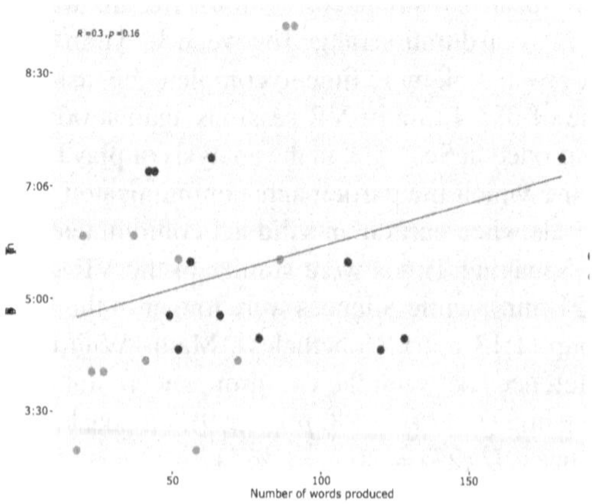

Fig. 6. Comparison between number of words produced and speaking time in minutes for each individual in the VR group and in the Physical group

Regarding the *type of utterances* emerged during the conversation, *75%* of the production of the VR group were *declarative clauses*, 12% were *interrogative clauses* and 13% single lexical words. The production of utterances types for the Physical group was distributed as follows: 93% of declarative clauses, 6% of interrogative clauses and 1% of single lexical words. A tendency to significance emerged between the two groups on declarative clauses ($U (23) = 102.5, p = .081$) and single lexical words ($U (23) = 105$, $p = .056$), while no difference emerged on interrogative clauses ($U (23) = 93.5, p = .195$).

5.2   Likeability and Usability

The results of likeability that emerge from the survey (see Appendix– Table 2) showed a general positive attitude toward the VR game: the overall likeability on items investigating positive attitude towards the application was around 89% of positive responses, with five people who exclusively assigned scores in the range between 6 and 7 points of the Likert scale. Results on the three control items (3, 5, 8) of the questionnaire, investigating whether the participants perceived the game as boring or annoying, showed a general disagreement. In particular, the results confirmed a good degree of engagement of the game task (Fig. 7), with a nearly unanimous high vote on the questions relative to how fun and engaging was to play the game (Items 1, 4, 6, 10). In addition, results showed a general curiosity and attraction toward games in Virtual Reality, with a mean of 6.4 points to question 9: "would you like to play other game with the headset?". Results emerging from the usability questionnaire (see Appendix– Table 3) were also positive, with a majority of the population who gave an overall score equal or greater than 5 points on the Likert scale, which indicates the effective ease of use of the SMUP game (Fig. 8). Further confirmation was given by the answers to items 5 and 10, which excluded possible negative effects of VR. Comments given by participants with motor disorders pinpointed two critical points in the experience that may affect usability for this population: the difficulty in reaching some objects with the gaze and some uncomfortable feeling in wearing the VR headset.

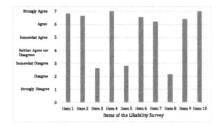

Fig. 7. Questionnaire results: Likeability

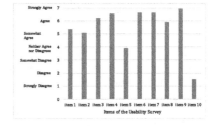

Fig. 8. Questionnaire results: Usability

6   Discussion

The findings of the study seem to suggest that when compared on the same game (Sorting Game) played in wearable virtual reality and in the real world, individuals with NDD were more prone to communicate with each other in the former environment. This evidence emerged from the significantly higher number of words and turn-takings produced by the VR group with respect to the Physical group. Crucially, the amount of speaking time in the two groups was very similar, indicating that playing the task in virtual environments did not lead to a longer amount of time spent conversing, but to a richer conversation between players (in terms of number of words produced).

Quantitative analysis on the types of utterances produced showed no significant result. Nonetheless, some considerations can be made from a qualitative point of view. Declarative clauses (e.g., "I put the yellow balloon on the first spot on the left") were the most frequently produced utterances in both modalities, indicating that players usually communicate with each other with the aim of describing the exact position of the objects on the tables. Interrogative clauses, particularly "Wh-questions" (e.g., "Where did you put the balloon?", "Which color is the balloon?") were more frequent in the VR group than in the Physical group. This may be due to the fact that wearing headsets and being immersed in a shared virtual space never seen before was an unprecedent situation for the participants. This may have led in turn to a higher number of questions to the other player in order to confirm the position or the color of the balloon in the virtual space.

In this vein, we can interpret also the higher mean rate of lexical words (e.g. "yellow") produced in the virtual environment: these single words were usually used as answers to questions. The higher percentage of interrogative clauses in the VR condition w.r.t. the physical condition (the value is doubled in VR) is an interesting finding also from a social interaction perspective. Interrogative clauses are those utterances that – more than declarative clauses – trigger linguistic production between two interlocutors and characterize the "relational" dimension of the conversation and its "dialogic" nature; indeed, dialogue etymologically means "speech through", i.e., an "exchange of speech acts" between two actors).

In general, the results of our research are consistent with previous studies showing the potentiality of wearable VR and CVEs in enhancing communication and social skills in individuals with communication deficits [29–32, 3, 6]. SMUP allowed players to perform the game task in a more controlled and ecological modality, which in turn seemed to prompt and enhance linguistic production and dialogues more than physical play. Even the fact that the time spent playing the game was longer (even tough not significant) in VR than in real-life session could indicate that the use of SMUP engaged individuals for longer periods of time. A deeper morphosyntactic, semantic and pragmatic analyses of the production of persons with NDD during play in the two experimental conditions (planned, but not yet performed) may provide further insights on the differences in linguistic performance level between VR and physical settings.

In summary, our findings indicate that wearable CVEs could be introduced in therapeutic activities, alongside traditional methods, with the specific aim to support communication reinforcement in individuals with NDD.

Still, our empirical study is explorative and has a number of limitations; its results are preliminary, and should be interpreted as early indications. Analogous exploratory studies should be run with the entire game kit of SMUP as well with other games in wearable CVRs to test the validity of the results. Moreover, the size of the groups of participants was comparable to most studies in the field of interactive technology for NDD persons, but is still too small to enable us generalize the benefits of VR game play to the entire population with a similar profile. A higher number of participants would be needed to lead to more statistically significant results. Finally, even if the study procedure and the data analysis protocol were well defined before performing the study, we had to face, as it is common in most empirical studies, some technical issues during the interaction in the VR mode (e.g., network connection issues) that may have biased our results.

7 Conclusions and Future Work

In a society where social and communication disorders are amongst the most frequent co-occurring conditions worldwide [36], it is important to investigate the use of innovative technologies, such as wearable collaborative immersive virtual environments, for individuals with conversational impairments. Our research explores the potential of Wearable Collaborative Virtual Environments (WCVEs) to enhance conversational skills in individuals with NDD (who very often have social and communication impairments). In this paper, we have addressed this issue using a case study: SMUP - a set of WCVE games designed specifically for this target group. Specifically, we have explored whether SMUP can be a suitable and engaging medium with respect to traditional interventions that exploit play activities in physical settings, in order to improve linguistic production capability.

In order to answer to this question, we ran an exploratory study involving two groups of individuals with NDD who played a Sorting Game in SMUP and in a physical setting respectively. We applied domain-specific measures of the linguistic production during conversation (speaking times, silences, turn takings, number of words and utterances) in order to see whether players who completed the activity in the VR were more prone to communicate than players who completed the game in physical settings. Finally, we assessed likability and usability of the SMUP game using two structured surveys submitted to the participants who played in SMUP.

To the best of our knowledge, our research is unique in the current state of the art for a number of reasons. None of the studies in the current literature: i) have verified the effectiveness – for persons with NDD - of playing in wearable collaborative virtual environment by comparing its benefits against the ones of playing the same game in real life; ii) have analyzed the conversational outcome of the activity played in the two situations (WCVE and physical setting) using theoretically grounded linguistic metrics; (2) have involved individuals with forms of NDD other than Autism Spectrum Disorder.

Our study indicates that SMUP is a suitable medium for enhancing conversational skills of people with NDD. This evidence emerged both from results on linguistic production (significantly higher in the VR experience) and from positive findings on the two surveys on likability and usability.

More generally, our study sheds a light on the potential of game play in wearable collaborative virtual environments to provide new forms of interventions for individuals with communication impairments, offerings a means that is engaging and affordable (in term of costs and duration) and might even be more effective than play in traditional physical settings.

There are several items in our future research agenda. We will run a similar experimental study using the other three games of SMUP. We will explore the use of SMUP with other populations, particularly people with specific language disorders (e.g., pragmatic language impairment or stuttering) and persons with NDD from other countries and continents (notably Asia), in order to investigate whether the presence of specific disorders or cultural differences would impact on the linguistic production findings associated to SMUP. Finally, we are working on technological aspects in order to simplify the work of therapists and researchers. We are integrating in SMUP some new features to support automatic data gathering and (at some degree) automatic assessment of linguistic metrics based on the analysis of speech-to-text transcriptions.

Acknowledgments. We thank all the participants of our empirical study, their families and their therapists This research is partially supported by EIT Digital - Project 19283 "Letssay".

Appendix

Table 2. Survey on Likeability

Items	Questions[a]
Item 1	How much did you like the game?
Item 2	Is the game good?
Item 3	Is the avatar annoying?
Item 4	Is the game fun?
Item 5	Is it bad to play with the avatar?
Item 6	Did you have fun playing the activity?
Item 7	Is the environment nice?
Item 8	Was the game boring?
Item 9	Would you like to play other game with the headset?
Item 10	Was the game engaging?

[a]Each question must be answered on a 7 points scale

Table 3. Survey on Usability

Items	Questions[a]
Item 1	How easy was the game for you?
Item 2	How comfortable was to wear the headset?
Item 3	Is it easy to play?
Item 4	Is it fun to look for the balloons?
Item 5	Is it annoying to keep the headset on?
Item 6	Could you clearly see what was shown by the headset?
Item 7	Was it clear what you had to do?
Item 8	Was it simple to understand where the avatar was
Item 9	Was it simple to find the objects indicated?
Item 10	Was the game too tiring?

[a]Each question must be answered on a 7 points Scale

References

1. American Psychiatric Association: Diagnostic and statistical manual of mental disorders (5th ed.) (2013)
2. Timler, G.: Social communication: a framework for assessment and intervention. ASHA Leader. **13**, 10–13 (2008)
3. Pantelidis, V.S.: Reasons to Use Virtual Reality in Education and Training Courses and a Model to Determine When to Use Virtual Reality. 12
4. Parsons, S., Cobb, S.: State-of-the-art of virtual reality technologies for children on the autism spectrum. Eur. J. Spec. Needs Educ. **26**, 355–366 (2011). https://doi.org/10.1080/08856257.2011.593831
5. Bellani, M., Fornasari, L., Chittaro, L., Brambilla, P.: Virtual reality in autism: state of the art. Epidemiol Psychiatr Sci. **20**, 235–238 (2011). https://doi.org/10.1017/S2045796011000448
6. Mitchell, P., Parsons, S., Leonard, A.: Using virtual environments for teaching social understanding to 6 adolescents with autistic spectrum disorders. J. Autism Dev. Disord. **37**, 589–600 (2007). https://doi.org/10.1007/s10803-006-0189-8
7. Millen, L., et al.: Collaborative technologies for children with autism. In: Proceedings of the 10th International Conference on Interaction Design and Children - IDC 2011, Ann Arbor, Michigan, pp. 246–249. ACM Press (2011)
8. Pares, N., Masri, P., van Wolferen, G., Creed, C.: Achieving dialogue with children with severe autism in an adaptive multisensory interaction: the "MEDIATE" project. IEEE Trans. Visual Comput. Graphics **11**, 734–743 (2005). https://doi.org/10.1109/TVCG.2005.88
9. Loiacono, T., Trabucchi, M., Messina, N., Matarazzo, V., Garzotto, F., Beccaluva, E.A.: Social MatchUP -: a memory-like virtual reality game for the enhancement of social skills in children with neurodevelopmental disorders. In: Extended Abstracts of the 2018 CHI Conference on Human Factors in Computing Systems - CHI 2018, Montreal QC, Canada, pp. 1–6. ACM Press, Montreal (2018)
10. Bryant, L., Brunner, M., Hemsley, B.: A review of virtual reality technologies in the field of communication disability: implications for practice and research. Disability and Rehab. Assistive Technol. 1–8 (2019). https://doi.org/10.1080/17483107.2018.1549276
11. Etchart, M., Caprarelli, A.: A wearable immersive web-virtual reality approach to remote neurodevelopmental disorder therapy. In: Proceedings of the 2018 International Conference on Advanced Visual Interfaces - AVI 2018, Castiglione della Pescaia, Grosseto, Italy, pp. 1–3. ACM Press (2018)
12. Maskey, M., : Using virtual reality environments to augment cognitive behavioral therapy for fears and phobias in autistic adults. Autism Adulthood **1**, 134–145 (2019). https://doi.org/10.1089/aut.2018.0019
13. Ravindran, V., Osgood, M., Sazawal, V., Solorzano, R., Turnacioglu, S.: Virtual reality support for joint attention using the floreo joint attention module: usability and feasibility pilot study. JMIR Pediatr Parent. **2**, e14429 (2019). https://doi.org/10.2196/14429
14. Garzotto, F., Gelsomini, M., Gianotti, M., Riccardi, F.: Engaging children with neurodevelopmental disorder through multisensory interactive experiences in a smart space. In: Soro, A., Brereton, M., Roe, P. (eds.) Social Internet of Things. IT, pp. 167–184. Springer, Cham (2019). https://doi.org/10.1007/978-3-319-94659-7_9
15. Garzotto, F., Gelsomini, M., Occhiuto, D., Matarazzo, V., Messina, N.: Wearable immersive virtual reality for children with disability: a case study. In: Proceedings of the 2017 Conference on Interaction Design and Children - IDC 2017, pp. 478–483. ACM Press, Stanford (2017)
16. Gelsomini, M.: An affordable virtual reality learning framework for children with neurodevelopmental disorder. In: Proceedings of the 18th International ACM SIGACCESS Conference on Computers and Accessibility - ASSETS 2016, Reno, Nevada, USA, pp. 343–344. ACM Press (2016)

17. Gelsomini, M., Garzotto, F., Matarazzo, V., Messina, N., Occhiuto, D.: Creating social stories as wearable hyper-immersive virtual reality experiences for children with neurodevelopmental disorders. In: Proceedings of the 2017 Conference on Interaction Design and Children - IDC 2017, Stanford, California, USA, pp. 431–437. ACM Press (2017)

18. Morina, N., Ijntema, H., Meyerbröker, K., Emmelkamp, P.M.G.: Can virtual reality exposure therapy gains be generalized to real-life? A meta-analysis of studies applying behavioral assessments. Behav. Res. Ther. **74**, 18–24 (2015). https://doi.org/10.1016/j.brat.2015.08.010

19. Hirose, M., Taniguchi, M., Nakagaki, Y., Nihei, K.: Virtual playground and communication environments for children. IEICE transactions on Information and Systems. **77**, 1330–1334 (1994)

20. Stephenson, J.: Sick kids find help in a cyberspace world. J. Am. Med. Assoc. **274**, 1899–1901 (1995)

21. Bricken, M.: Virtual worlds: no interface to design. Virtual Worlds 14

22. Newbutt, N., Sung, C., Kuo, H.-J., Leahy, M.J., Lin, C.-C., Tong, B.: Brief report: a pilot study of the use of a virtual reality headset in autism populations. J. Autism Dev. Disord. **46**(9), 3166–3176 (2016). https://doi.org/10.1007/s10803-016-2830-5

23. Benford, S., Greenhalgh, C., Rodden, T., Pycock, J.: Collaborative virtual environments. Commun. ACM **44**, 79–85 (2011)

24. Reynolds, S., Bendixen, R.M., Lawrence, T., Lane, S.J.: A pilot study examining activity participation, sensory responsiveness, and competence in children with high functioning autism spectrum disorder. J. Autism Dev. Disord. **41**, 1496–1506 (2011). https://doi.org/10.1007/s10803-010-1173-x

25. Nararro-Haro, M.V., et al.: The use of virtual reality to facilitate mindfulness skills training in dialectical behavioral therapy for borderline personality disorder: a case study. Front. Psychol. 7 (2016). https://doi.org/10.3389/fpsyg.2016.01573

26. Schmidt, C., Schmidt, M.: Three-dimensional virtual learning environments for mediating social skills acquisition among individuals with autism spectrum disorders. In: Proceedings of the 7th international conference on Interaction design and children - IDC 2008, Chicago, Illinois, p. 85. ACM Press (2008)

27. Kuriakose, S., Kunche, S., Narendranath, B., Jain, P., Sonker, S., Lahiri, U.: A step towards virtual reality based social communication for children with Autism. In: 2013 International Conference on Control, Automation, Robotics and Embedded Systems (CARE), Jabalpur, India, pp. 1–6. IEEE (2013)

28. Parsons, S., Mitchell, P.: The potential of virtual reality in social skills training for people with autistic spectrum disorders: autism, social skills and virtual reality. J. Intellect. Disabil. Res. **46**, 430–443 (2002). https://doi.org/10.1046/j.1365-2788.2002.00425.x

29. da Silva, C.A., Fernandes, A.R., Grohmann, A.P.: STAR: speech therapy with augmented reality for children with autism spectrum disorders. In: Cordeiro, J., Hammoudi, S., Maciaszek, L., Camp, O., Filipe, J. (eds.) ICEIS 2014. LNBIP, vol. 227, pp. 379–396. Springer, Cham (2015). https://doi.org/10.1007/978-3-319-22348-3_21

30. Zhang, L., Weitlauf, A.S., Amat, A.Z., Swanson, A., Warren, Z.E., Sarkar, N.: Assessing social communication and collaboration in autism spectrum disorder using intelligent collaborative virtual environments. J. Autism Dev. Disord. **50**(1), 199–211 (2019). https://doi.org/10.1007/s10803-019-04246-z

31. Dhamodharan, T., et al.: Cognitive rehabilitation for autism children mental status observation using virtual reality based interactive environment. In: Ahram, T., Karwowski, W., Vergnano, A., Leali, F., Taiar, R. (eds.) IHSI 2020. AISC, vol. 1131, pp. 1213–1218. Springer, Cham (2020). https://doi.org/10.1007/978-3-030-39512-4_185

32. Halabi, O., Abou El-Seoud, S., Alja'am, J., Alpona, H., Al-Hemadi, M., Al-Hassan, D.: Design of immersive virtual reality system to improve communication skills in individuals with autism. Int. J. Emerg. Technol. Learn. **12**, 50 (2017). https://doi.org/10.3991/ijet.v12i05.6766

33. Weschler, D.: Wechsler adult intelligent scale - IV. San Antonio (2008)

34. Sacks, H., Schegloff, E.A.., Jefferson, G.: A simplest systematics for the organization of turn-taking for conversation. Language, **50** 696–735 (1974)

35. Muffels, R.: Labor markets and underemployment. In: Michalos, A.C. (ed.) Encyclopedia of Quality of Life and Well-Being Research, pp. 3483–3486. Springer, Dordrecht (2014)

36. Jijo, P.M., Sreeraj, K., Sandhya, K., Preethi, M., Rashmi, P.: Prevalence and causes of communication disorders- a retrospective study from Northern Karnataka. Clinical Epidemiol. Global Health **8**, 138–141 (2020). https://doi.org/10.1016/j.cegh.2019.06.002

Serious Play

Cookie Mania: A Serious Game for Teaching Internet Cookies to High School and College Students

John Dominic S. Diez[✉] and Edward F. Melcer[✉]

University of California Santa Cruz, Santa Cruz, CA 95064, USA
{jdiez,eddie.melcer}@ucsc.edu

Abstract. Internet cookies are data storage tools that collect information from a platform's users to inform various aspects of the platform such as marketing and recommendations systems. Notably, there is a lack of understanding around what internet cookies are and how they work, which spans from adolescents to adults. This can lead to major misunderstandings of how consenting information works in online mediums, and results in negative outcomes and effects for users by default. To help increase understanding of internet cookies and address these issues, we have developed a serious game called *Cookie Mania*. Our game aims to develop knowledge of internet cookies and related ethical issues through an interactive narrative, as well as foster additional engagement through cookie-focused minigames. In this demonstration paper, we discuss the design and development of *Cookie Mania*—highlighting how the various design choices target learning objectives for internet cookies and their underlying ethical issues.

Keywords: Internet cookies · Media literacy · Ethics · Interactive narrative · Game-based learning · Serious game

1   Introduction

In this modern age, knowing how to use technologies such as computers and phones is an essential skill. Individuals are now exposed to the internet at even younger ages [4, 30], and many begin interacting with smart phones and tablets from almost the moment they are born [30]. For instance, approximately 85% of children under 6 use some sort of technology device within the U.S [22]. With a growing dependence at younger ages on such technologies comes a growing need to teach technology and media literacy, especially with respect to internet cookies. Specifically, internet cookies are widely misunderstood, and most individuals (from children to adult) do not fully understand how they work or what they even do [21]. This is especially problematic for adolescents and young adults since they are particularly susceptible to the erosion of privacy due to social media and internet search engines [8, 30].

Electronic supplementary material The online version of this chapter (https://doi.org/10.1007/978-3-030-61814-8_5) contains supplementary material, which is available to authorized users.

© Springer Nature Switzerland AG 2020
M. Ma et al. (Eds.): JCSG 2020, LNCS 12434, pp. 69–77, 2020.
https://doi.org/10.1007/978-3-030-61814-8_5

One tool which has been demonstrated to effectively enhance learning outcomes of knowledge and ethical issues are serious games, especially ones that incorporate an interactive narrative [2, 20]. While there are serious games that teach important related topics such as responsible conduct of research [20, 21], social anxiety [26], and ethics [9], to name a few, to our knowledge there has not been a game created to teach concepts focusing on internet cookies. In this demonstration paper, we discuss the design of *Cookie Mania*—a serious game created to develop knowledge of internet cookies and underlying ethical issues through an interactive narrative.

2 Background

The origins of internet cookies date back to Lou Montello when he gave the internet the ability to have a memory and coined the term "magic cookie" [5]. Magic Cookies were small files that would track what a person's computer did in a specific website and allowed that information to be transferred from one computer to another, effectively allowing memory and actions to be stored in a computer. However, these magic cookies also resulted in newfound issues of privacy, secured information, and laws [18, 25]. While the function of cookies today remains the same and can be utilized to provide the convenience benefit of storing important information like passwords, preferred website settings, and so forth, cookies still present huge problems of privacy and consent—namely due to their ability to store sensitive information for a long period of time without secure servers or proper protections [16, 27].

While internet cookies may only have a simple function, their real dangers lie in how companies utilize different forms of cookies and if/how users perceive this usage. For instance, once individuals started deleting regular cookies from their browsers, flash cookies were developed to maintain preferences such as volume and language while being harder to delete [27]. However, these new cookies also enabled transfer of data between websites with no expiration date. This in turn allowed more direct tracking of users and the websites they visited, giving marketing companies access to even more unprotected data for prediction and recommendation [4, 8]. Unfortunately, many more types of cookies and related tools (such as web beacons) have similarly been created with good intentions, but are ultimately abused. E.g., in the case of web beacons, they allow tracking of user interactions to improve website design [18], but this is done with a severe lack of awareness from the user that their data is being collected [4, 23, 30].

Ultimately, criticisms of internet cookies have been brought up since their creation, leading to studies highlighting their confusing nature to users [3, 7, 12] and loss of privacy/internet protections [9, 23, 24]. These issues recently pushed the EU to pass *The General Data Protection Regulation (GDPR)*—providing user protections through consent or other specific exceptions [7, 12]. Although this change was only done in the EU, it has had a global impact due to most countries hosting websites that attract EU users. However, even with these important steps towards properly informing and protecting users, there is still a large majority of individuals who misunderstand cookies as well as websites that make it difficult to protect personal data [17]. This led to the development of our game in order to teach players how their data is collected/used.

3 Game Design

We developed *Cookie Mania* to focus not only on teaching players what internet cookies are, but also how internet cookies are affecting their very lives. We do this through a linear 5-month storyline in which players become a website manager for a major technology company. Throughout gameplay, players are introduced to several major NPC characters which they can interact with through dialogue choices. Their interactions with these NPCs contain both teaching moments and moral decisions that mirror ethical issues which have arisen in the real world. This implementation of moral decision-making is important in that it can increase engagement and retention [10, 14, 20], as well as help players develop better moral reasoning and critical thinking skills [14, 20, 27, 28, 31]. In between the segments of interactive narrative, learners will also play cookie-based minigames designed to further increase player engagement and motivation. These minigames act as set milestones throughout the narrative and are necessary to advance the story.

3.1 Learning Outcomes

Based on the many ethical issues surrounding internet cookies as well as their current applications and relevance, we determined 5 key learning outcomes that were critical for players to learn through gameplay. Since the game covers a timeline of five months, we have ordered these learning outcomes by the in-game month they are taught to the player. These month-by-month progressions also allow us to make the storyline more fluid, making the jumps between learning each outcome coherent within the storyline. For example, by the time the player reaches to the final month where they learn how to protect themselves and others with data consent, they would have experienced a data breach, viruses, different types of cookies used by companies, and general knowledge of how cookies are used in their everyday lives. The learning outcomes are as follows:

- (MONTH 1) Understand the definition of internet cookies and the different types of cookies that are implemented within websites [1, 28].
- (MONTH 2) Reinforce cookie knowledge by using real world context and scenarios including laws and large events related to the topic [7, 12].
- (MONTH 3) Help players understand how companies use different types of cookies and how they work internally through basic lessons on ML, AI, and marketing [26].
- (MONTH 4) Teach players how cookies are related to virus and malware spread, as well as how to prevent it [8, 24, 26].
- (MONTH 5) Provide players with real world actions and guidance for how to act regarding sharing information to cookies and consenting to it [14, 23].

3.2 Game Characteristics

From the beginning, we wanted to teach the learning outcomes through an interactive narrative game. Prior work has suggested that effective ways to enable educational games to address learning outcomes is the incorporation of a convincing and interactive narrative [21], scaffolding and proximal growth for development [19], and also to appeal to players from different ethnic, social, and individual backgrounds [25]. The gameplay loop for *Cookie Mania* draws from this, providing a linear story that spans 5 different "months" (learning outcomes) with branching paths that change various dialogue as well as the ending. After each month is completed in the narrative, the learner then plays a minigame to unlock the next month. Each learning outcome will be taught through the narrative, as well as through special events within the minigames.

Moral Choices. To tackle the interactive narrative portion, we have implemented ethical decision-making where parts of the game require players to make moral choices. This is done to help players understand how cookies are utilized by companies/people and the corresponding the results of these actions, e.g., [28, 29, 32]. These choices lead to different endings, but more importantly they demonstrate how such choices affect both the consumer and the provider. This helps put more weight on player actions and can foster further investment and care from the player towards the interactive narrative [23, 27, 31].

Table 1. A subset of the different types of cookies that appear in *Cookie Mania*.

Type of Cookie	Function and implications
HTTP/Magic Cookie	First iteration of internet cookies. Its main function was to store units of information, effectively providing the internet with memory.
Flash Cookies	Stored user preferences such as volume and language but was harder to delete and more permanent. Used by viruses and malware to collect and steal data and hack into accounts.
Beacons	Tracks user interactions on websites. Very subtle and the user is even more naïve in what specifically is being collected.

Teaching Through Gameplay Representation. Enemies are specifically designed to represent their corresponding internet cookie types visually. Table 1 illustrates different types of cookies taught in the game and their memorable visual representations. To improve engagement and applicability to the real world [25], we made sure that the events and moral choices within the game mirrored events that occurred in real life, specifically focusing on different scandals from big tech companies' problems with cookie and recommendation algorithms. For example, Cambridge Analytica was a major scandal in the United States where Facebook user's data were taken without consent by Cambridge Analytica, causing major discussions on privacy and user rights [30]. Using this event, we implemented a storyline within the game that mimicked the events of

Cambridge Analytica, with moral decision making and repercussions for whether to include consent at the player's company.

Personalization. Serious and educational games need to be accessible to a range of individuals [25], which is why we designed our game to make it adaptable to different individuals and their skills/preferences in order to increase engagement and playability. Specifically, we used gender neutral language throughout the game, and also included character and gameplay customization options to help players identify with their character and the company (see Fig. 1)—as this can help maintain player motivation [12].

Fig. 1. Screenshot of cookie customization screen. Players can customize their cookie character, company name, and main art styles for development.

3.3 Gameplay

Office Scenes and Desktop Scenes. Players will go between two main game screens during the game. One section will be in the offices (see Fig. 2), while the other will be in the desktop scene where they would take on their role as a manager. While some learning of different cookie types is implemented in the minigames, most moral decisions and lessons will occur in these scenes through office dialogue and pop-up emails.

Fig. 2. The boss's office (left) and the main office (right) represent the main story setting in which the player interacts with other NPCs through dialogue to learn cookie related material.

Minigames. The minigames provide extrinsic motivation to play the game and can be selected through the Desktop scene (see Fig. 3). Most progression in *Cookie Mania* lies with playing minigames multiple times, collecting points for upgrades and unlocking the next month. Currently, there are two minigames that can be unlocked—i.e., the marketing minigame and the security minigame. In the marketing minigame, players are instructed to jump to different platforms to avoid malicious cookies and collect good ones for the company. The collection of these cookies allows players to gain upgrades and improve their website's data collection. In the security minigame, players are instructed to protect their customer's data by destroying viruses and zombie cookies from reaching the data. Destroying these enemies also yields points for upgrades.

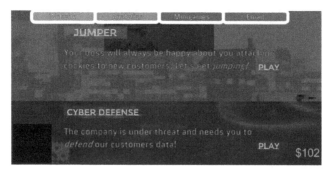

Fig. 3. The figure represents the desktop "tab" in which players can collect resources by choosing to play one of the two main video games. The Jumper game represents our marketing minigame where players collect cookies to improve their website, while cyber defense represents security for the website.

Analytics Page. The analytics page provides players with a growing knowledge set of how cookies work and what they provide in the "website manager" context. The screen visually shows how many websites use these cookies and what information they collect.

Upgrade System. Once players' finish the minigames, they will have points that they have accumulated to spend on upgrades. These upgrades improve gameplay throughout the course of the game and add additional information to the analytics page. Both the analytics page and upgrade system are designed to scaffold learning through the gradual introduction of upgrades that match what is newly learned as the player progresses [19].

Email Tab. The email tab provides narrative related information and moral decision making. Players can also use this tab to replay tutorials, reread specific events and dialogue, or explore additional information on what they are learning in that month.

4   Conclusion and Future Work

Cookie Mania is a serious game created to develop knowledge of internet cookies and underlying ethical issues through an interactive narrative. In this paper, we described the design of *Cookie Mania* and its core target learning outcomes. *While Cookie Mania is still a work in progress game, we are close to completing it and conducting an initial evaluation of its efficacy.* Due to the nature of a 1-h game, players may not have a large retention rate, so we hope to conduct a longitudinal study as well.

Acknowledgements. This research was supported in part by a CITRIS Tech for Social Good award from CITRIS and the Banatao Institute. We also want to formally thank the team who is continually working on Cookie Mania. This could not have been done without them:

Game Developers: Mia King, Matthew Stevens, Jacob Wynd

Researcher Assistants/Script Writers: Jacob Brinneman, Sanyukta Kamath Ahn-tu Pham

Artists: Cole Cota, Delong Du, Miriam Perez, Amber Vo

References

1. Cahn, A., Alfeld, S., Barford, P., Muthukrishnan, S.: An empirical study of web cookies. In: Proceedings of the 25th International Conference on World Wide Web, WWW 2016, pp. 891–901. International World Wide Web Conferences Steering Committee, Republic and Canton of Geneva, Switzerland (2016). https://doi.org/10.1145/2872427.2882991
2. Camingue, J., Melcer, E.F., Carstensdottir, E.: A (Visual) novel route to learning: a taxonomy of educational visual novels. In: Proceedings of the 15th International Conference on the Foundations of Digital Games, FDG 2020, Malta. ACM (2020)
3. Abt, C.C.: Serious Games. The Viking Press, New York (1970)
4. Crocco, M.S., Segall, A., Halvorsen, A.-L., Stamm, A., Jacobsen, R.: "It's not like they're selling your data to dangerous people": internet privacy, teens, and (non-)controversial public issues. J. Soc. Stud. Res. **44**, 21–33 (2020). https://doi.org/10.1016/j.jssr.2019.09.004
5. Djaouti, D., Alvarez, J., Jessel, J.-P., Rampnoux, O.: Origins of serious games. In: Ma, M., Oikonomou, A., Jain, Lakhmi C. (eds.) Serious Games and Edutainment Applications, pp. 25–43. Springer, London (2011). https://doi.org/10.1007/978-1-4471-2161-9_3
6. Englehardt, S., et al.: Cookies that give you away. In: Proceedings of the 24th International Conference on World Wide Web - WWW 2015 (2015). https://doi.org/10.1145/2736277.274 1679
7. European Commission: Adequacy of the protection of personal data in non-EU countries (2018). https://ec.europa.eu/info/law/law-topic/data-protection/data-transfers-outside-eu/ade quacy-protection-personal-data-non-eu-countries_en
8. Ha, V., Inkpen, K., Shaar, F.A., Hdeib, L.: An examination of user perception and misconception of internet cookies. In: CHI 2006 Extended Abstracts on Human Factors in Computing Systems - CHI EA 2006. https://doi.org/10.1145/1125451.1125615
9. Hodhod, R., Kudenko, D., Cairns, P.: AEINS: adaptive educational interactive narrative system to teach ethics. In: AIED 2009: 14 th International Conference on Artificial Intelligence in Education Workshops Proceedings, p. 79 (2009)
10. Holl, E., Bernard, S., Melzer, A.: Moral decision-making in video games: a focus group study on player perceptions. Hum. Behav. Emer. Technol. **2**, 278–287 (2020). https://doi.org/10.1002/hbe2.189
11. Homer, B.D., et al.: Moved to learn: the effects of interactivity in a Kinect-based literacy game for beginning readers. Comput. Educ. **74**, 37–49 (2014). https://doi.org/10.1016/j.compedu.2014.01.007
12. International dimension of data protection. In: European Commission - European Commission. https://ec.europa.eu/info/law/law-topic/data-protection/international-dimension-data-protection_en. Accessed 7 July 2020

13. Isbister, K., Schwekendiek, U., Frye, J.: Wriggle: an exploration of emotional and social effects of movement. In: CHI 2011 Extended Abstracts on Human Factors in Computing Systems, pp. 1885–1890. ACM, May 2011

14. Khoo, A.: Video games as moral educators? Asia Pacific J. Educ. **32**, 416–429 (2012). https://doi.org/10.1080/02188791.2012.738638

15. Kim, N.Y.: The effect of ad customization and ad variation on internet users' perceptions of forced multiple advertising exposures and attitudes. J. Interact. Advert. **18**, 15–27 (2018). https://doi.org/10.1080/15252019.2018.1460225

16. Kulyk, O., Hilt, A., Gerber, N., Volkamer, M.: "This Website Uses Cookies": users' perceptions and reactions to the cookie disclaimer. In: Proceedings 3rd European Workshop on Usable Secur. (2018). https://doi.org/10.14722/eurousec.2018.23012

17. Lomas, N.: Europe's top court says active consent is needed for tracking cookies. In: TechCrunch (2019). https://techcrunch.com/2019/10/01/europes-top-court-says-active-consent-is-needed-for-tracking-cookies/. Accessed 7 July 2020

18. Martin, D., Wu, H., Alsaid, A.: Hidden surveillance by Web sites. Commun. ACM **46**, 258 (2003). https://doi.org/10.1145/953460.953509

19. Mayer, R.E.: Computer Games for Learning: An Evidence-Based Approach. MIT Press, Cambridge (2014)

20. Melcer, E.F., et al.: Getting academical: a choice-based interactive storytelling game for teaching responsible conduct of research. In: Proceedings of the 15th International Conference on the Foundations of Digital Games. FDG 2020, Malta. ACM (2020)

21. Melcer, E.F., et al.: Teaching responsible conduct of research through an interactive storytelling game. In: Extended Abstracts of the 2020 CHI Conference on Human Factors in Computing Systems (2020). https://doi.org/10.1145/3334480.3382973

22. New Research from the TEC Center at Erikson Institute • TEC Center. In: TEC Center. https://teccenter.erikson.edu/publications/tec-parent-survey/. Accessed 6 July 2020

23. Peacock, S.E.: How web tracking changes user agency in the age of Big Data: the used user. Big Data Soc. (2014). https://doi.org/10.1177/2053951714564228

24. Pierson, J., Heyman, R.: Social media and cookies: challenges for online privacy. Info **13**, 30–42 (2011). https://doi.org/10.1108/14636691111174243

25. Plass, J., Homer, B., Kinzer, C.: Playful Learning: An Integrated Design Framework (2014). https://doi.org/10.13140/2.1.4175.6969

26. Sanchez, A.Y.R., Kunze, K.: Flair: towards a therapeutic serious game for social anxiety disorder. In: Proceedings of the 2018 ACM International Joint Conference and 2018 International Symposium on Pervasive and Ubiquitous Computing and Wearable Computers - UbiComp 2018 (2018). https://doi.org/10.1145/3267305.3267558

27. Schmaling, K.B., Blume, A.W.: Ethics instruction increases graduate students' responsible conduct of research knowledge but not moral reasoning. Accountabil. Res. **16**, 268–283 (2009). https://doi.org/10.1080/08989620903190323

28. Schrier, K.: Designing games for moral learning and knowledge building. Games Cult. **14**, 306–343 (2017). https://doi.org/10.1177/1555412017711514

29. Sipior, J.C., Ward, B.T., Mendoza, R.A.: Online privacy concerns associated with cookies, flash cookies, and web beacons. J. Internet Commerce **10**, 1–16 (2011). https://doi.org/10.1080/15332861.2011.558454

30. Schwartz, J.: Giving web a memory cost its users privacy. In: The New York Times (2001). https://www.nytimes.com/2001/09/04/business/giving-web-a-memory-cost-its-users-privacy.html. Accessed 7 Jul 2020

31. Staines, D.: Videogames and moral pedagogy. Advances in Game-Based Learning Ethics and Game Design 35–51 (2010). https://doi.org/10.4018/978-1-61520-845-6.ch003

32. Stephen, C., Edwards, S.: Digital technology use and uptake by young children. Young children playing and learning in a digital age, pp. 95–108 (2017). https://doi.org/10.4324/978131 5623092-9

33. Wong, J.C., Lewis, P., Davies, H.: How academic at centre of Facebook scandal tried – and failed – to spin personal data into gold. In: The Guardian. https://www.theguardian.com/news/2018/apr/24/aleksandr-kogan-cambridge-analytica-facebook-data-business-ventures. Accessed 12 July 2020

Proposal of a Beer Distribution Game Considering Waste Management and the Bullwhip Effect

Mizuho Sato[1]([✉]) [iD], Masaru Nakano[2] [iD], Hajime Mizuyama[3] [iD], and Christoph Roser[4] [iD]

[1] Department of Food Environment Economics, Tokyo University of Agriculture, 1-1-1, Sakuragaoka, Setagaya-ku, Tokyo 156-0054, Japan
ms207184@nodai.ac.jp
[2] Graduate School of System Design and Management, Keio University, 4-1-1 Hiyoshi, Kohoku-ku, Yokohama, Kanagawa 223-8526, Japan
[3] Department of Industrial and Systems Engineering, Aoyama Gakuin University, 5-10-1 Fuchinobe, Chuo-ku, Sagamihara-shi, Kanagawa 252-5258, Japan
[4] Karlsruhe University of Applied Sciences, Moltkestr. 30, 76133 Karlsruhe, Germany

Abstract. The beer distribution game is a role-playing board game that also helps people learn about the importance of supply chain management. However, the game does not include the major difficulties in managing food and beverages supply chains. Food and beverages are assigned expiration or best-before date. If these goods cannot be sold within the period of the expiration or best-before date, they are wasted. Therefore, the purpose of this study is to extend the beer distribution game for incorporating these issues and to investigate the effects of the issues with playing the refined game. So, we set a time limit for products in the beer distribution game and include a rule that the products will be considered wasted after the time limit. We subsequently examined the effect of the time limit on food supply chain management. As a result of a preliminary game experiment, we find that the back order is highest at the distributors. Stock is the largest at the factory. Wholesalers and factories cause excessive waste. If the expiration date has passed, delivery is not possible, and the items will therefore be wasted. Furthermore, items will not reach the end consumer. In addition, higher inventory and waste are generated upstream. This result reflects the actual situation in the real world food and beverage industry.

Keywords: Beer distribution game · Bullwhip effect · Supply chain management · Food waste

1 Introduction

The beer distribution game is a role-playing game developed at the Sloan School of Management at the Massachusetts Institute of Technology (MIT) in the 1960s [1]. The beer distribution game outlines the process from production to retail across four roles

© Springer Nature Switzerland AG 2020
M. Ma et al. (Eds.): JCSG 2020, LNCS 12434, pp. 78–84, 2020.
https://doi.org/10.1007/978-3-030-61814-8_6

(factory, distributor, wholesaler, and retailer). Beer is produced by the factory and delivered from the factory to the retail outlet through the wholesaler and the distributor. It is important for each role to control inventory because there is a time lag between the order and the delivery. The most important rule in the beer distribution game is that there must be no communication among players. Decision making is performed while mutually experiencing pressure from the other members who are in similar situations. While the original goal of the simulation game was to research the effect of systems structures on people's behavior ("structure creates behavior"), it subsequently came to be used to demonstrate the benefits of information sharing and the importance of supply chain management.

The beer distribution game also teaches people about the bullwhip effect [1]. When demand information sails up a supply chain from the final customer to the factory, the upstream roles of the supply chain receive a bigger fluctuation of demand. Therefore, the manufacturer needs safety stock of a larger size to cover the big demand fluctuation. If the organization of the downstream increases the volume of the order, the demand of upstream organization is increased. When the organization of the downstream side decreases the volume of the order, the upstream organization demand decreases or stops. Every single step the demand information sails up the supply chain, the fluctuation is amplified. This is known as the bullwhip effect.

Improving the bullwhip effect also leads to solving supply chain management issues. Lee et al. [2] points out that production (demand signal processing), inventory, order units, and price fluctuations in response to customers' demand have a significant impact on supply chain management. In addition, simulation experiments demonstrate that the bullwhip effect can be improved by adjusting the number of orders, reducing delivery delays, providing downstream inventory information to the upstream, sharing point-of-sale (POS) information, and reducing lead time [3–6]. On the other hand, online beer games have demonstrated that human behavior amplifies the bullwhip effect, and that communication alone does not improve the bullwhip effect, and that vague human behavior affects the supply chain [7, 8]. In Roser et al. [9], in addition to beer, wine and schnapps were also used to examine the effects of changes in demand and the presence or absence of communication on the supply chain management. Decision making becomes difficult when there are multiple products, but it is relatively easy to make decisions if the player knows the maximum number of orders in advance. However, it is difficult to reduce the bullwhip effect without knowing whom to communicate with. Amoni et al. [10] also examined the educational effects of supply chain management using the beer distribution game. The team that played the game twice and fully understood the rules of the beer distribution game improved the performance of the second run from the first by giving the factory initiative and shortening the lead time. In this manner, real supply chains are imagined using the beer distribution game, and simulations including human behavior—such as improvement methods, and educational effects—have been studied.

In actual supply chain management, manufacturers strive to properly manage production volume, delivery volume, inventory volume, however these are difficult to control perfectly. Products such as food and beverage have set expiry dates or best-before dates, so if they cannot be sold within the duration of the expiry date or the best-before-date, they are considered to be wasted. In Japan's food and beverage industry, the one-third rule is often raised as one of the leading causes of food loss. Under this rule, each food and drink must be sold by the corresponding selling time limit, which is set as two-thirds of the time from its production to the best-before date. If goods remain unsold when the selling time expires, a wastage of goods occurs. It is difficult to control the food and beverage supply chain, because production volume, order volume, inventory volume, must be determined considering the one-third rule. In addition, if there is a back-order at some point of the chain, orders to the point cannot be fulfilled immediately, and therefore, the lead time will become longer than usual. This then makes the inventory level higher. In addition, rather than one item, multiple items are manufactured, delivered, and sold, which makes supply chain management more difficult.

Therefore, we set a sales expiration date for the beer distribution game and decided to discard the beer after its expiration date, and subsequently examined its effect on supply chain management.

2 Contents of Beer Distribution Game Considering Waste Management

Our study was based on the general rules of the beer distribution game [1]. This game is a role-playing board game. We divided participants into four teams as per the four roles (factory, distributor, wholesaler, and retailer), which corresponded with the process of beer distribution from production to supply. The game is played over a span of a 52 weeks, where each week was counted as one round (Fig. 1). As actual beer could not be used in the game, it was played using crown caps of beer bottles. At the beginning of the game, there are 12 crown caps in the current inventory of each role except for the factory, four crown caps in shipping delay ① and four in shipping delay ②. Similarly, at the factory, there are 12 caps in the current inventory, four caps in the production delay ①, and four in the production delay ②. The number of orders from customer is four. The game starts in this situation. Each role except for the factory moved the crown caps at "Shipping delay ②" to "Inventory" and the crown caps at "Shipping delay ①" to "Shipping delay ②". The factory moved the ingredients at "Production delay ②" to "Inventory" and those at "Production delay ①" to "Production ②". Then each player confirms the order from the customer, the immediately downstream role, and ships crown caps to fulfill the order. The order from the final customer increases to eight at a point and remains at eight after that. If the stock is less than the number of orders, it will result in a back order. If the goods remain in the inventory area, they will be in stock. Then, players think about the next order independently, and place an order, that is, write the number of goods necessary in the corresponding "order placed" cell in the Fig. 1. This is the process of one round (one week). Communication between roles is not possible.

In a normal beer distribution game, all products flow from upstream to downstream in the supply chain. However, the expiration date is set for food and beverage, and if the date passes, the goods will be wasted and cannot flow further downstream. Thus, in this game, after shipping the goods to the customer (i.e. the immediately downstream role), the crown caps remaining in the inventory are turned over (Fig. 2). If they cannot be shipped within the next two weeks, they will be wasted. Customers who received the flipped goods treat them as normal products. Generally, the period that the products can

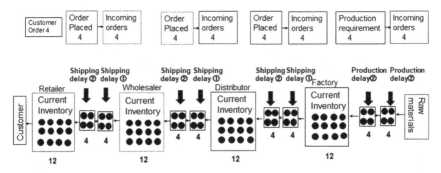

Fig. 1. The flow of the standard beer distribution game

be used by the downstream role should be shorter, but this rule was adopted not to make the rule too complicated. In addition, the evaluation method was 0.5 €/piece/week for inventory cost, 1.0 €/piece/week for order backlog, and 0.7 €/piece/week for disposal.

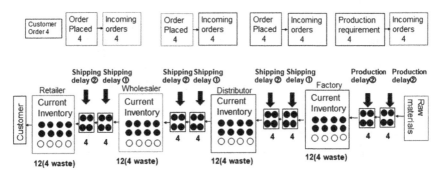

Fig. 2. The flow of the proposed beer distribution game considering waste

3 Experiment

The experiment was conducted at Keio University Hiyoshi Campus on October 4, 2018 (14:00–17:00). The participants were individuals who were actually developing products in the company and had never experienced a basic beer distribution game. In this experiment of playing the proposed beer distribution game considering waste, the total cost was 15,972 € (40 weeks), and the cost per week was 399.3 €. On the other hand, the total cost of a regular beer distribution game played at Keio University Graduate School was approximately 1500–2500 € (24–35 weeks), which is between 42.6 and 74.8 € a week. The cost in the proposed game is about five to nine times higher than that of the standard game. Thus, the bullwhip effect is very large in this game (Fig. 3). A time limit was set for the experiment and the lecture. The time used for playing the game was approximately two hours.

Table 1 shows the back order, stock, and waste for each role. The distributor had the highest number of back-order goods. The factory had the highest inventory, while

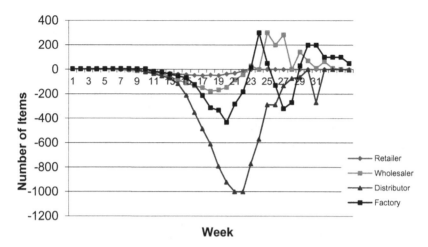

Fig. 3. The back order and inventory

wholesaler and factory had high levels of waste. After the expiration date, goods could not be delivered, were wasted, and failed to reached to the final consumer.

Table 1. Each player's score in the beer distribution game

	Retailer	Wholesaler	Distributor	Factory	Sum
Backorder	530	1328	8177	2800	12,835
Stock	11	560	14	702	1287
Waste	86.1	796	226	742	1850

4   Discussion

In this paper, we implemented a waste beer distribution game. The results indicated that the bullwhip effect is greater than in a regular beer distribution game. The back order is highest at the distributor, at 8177. The factory is higher in both inventory and waste. Some products are delivered to the distributor but not to the end customer. In addition, higher inventory and waste are generated upstream (factory). In the actual food and beverage industry as well, there are situations wherein food is manufactured at the factory but is not delivered to the customer and products are wasted. In fact, Japan's food industry reportedly has the highest amount of food waste in the food supply chain [11].

In this rule, when turned over crown cups (old products) were moved to next process (factory, distributor, wholesaler, and retailer), they were treated as normal goods. In other words, when moving to the next process, the deadline is reset. Originally, the expiration date should be managed from the factory to the final consumer, therefore, it is more realistic to count from the manufacturing date (factory) and waste the goods past the expiration date. The idea is to prepare crown cups of different number of colors equivalent to that of the length until the expiration date (for example, six colors for six days), proceed with the game, and when the expiration date comes, the crown cups of the corresponding color get wasted. We intend to consider this aspect in a future study.

5 Conclusions

The following conclusions were drawn from this study:

1) We developed a waste beer distribution game and played it between members of individuals working in a company. The bullwhip effect was larger than the normal beer distribution game. In addition, as the factory's stock and waste were both higher, the results accurately reflected real society.
2) The expiration date was set in each process (factory, distributor, wholesaler, and retailer), and was reset when moving on to the next process. It is necessary to play the game where the expiration date is set from the factory to the final consumer.
3) It is necessary to verify the bullwhip effect improvement method (production volume, order volume, stock volume, lead time, communication method) in the supply chain with the expiration date. For this purpose, we intend to play the game repeatedly and verify it with the simulation.
4) Sato et al. developed a game based on the milk supply chain utilizing the one-third rule [12]. The players take the roles of the supermarket and the milk manufacturer and their aim is to increase profit as they decide the order, production volumes, sales volumes, and sales price while simultaneously considering customers' behavior. Since these decisions will impact the bullwhip effect, comparing this game with the beer distribution game considering waste management will be also an interesting topic.

Acknowledgements. The authors are grateful to the participants of the game experiment.

References

1. Forrester, J.W.: Industrial dynamics. a major breakthrough for decision makers. Harvard Bus. Rev. **36**(4), 37–66 (1958)
2. Lee, H., Padmanabhan, V., Whang, S.: Information distortion in a supply: the bullwhip effect. Manage. Sci. **43**(4), 546–558 (1997)
3. Steckel, J.H., Gupta, S., Banerji, A.: Supply chain decision making will shorter cycle times and shared point-of -sale information necessarily help? Manage. Sci. **50**(4), 458–464 (2004)
4. Croson, R., Donohue, K.: Behavioral causes of the bullwhip effect and the observed value of inventory information. Manage. Sci. **52**(3), 323–336 (2006)
5. Croson, R., Donohue, K.: Impact of POS data sharing on supply chain management: an experimental study. Prod. Oper. Manag. **12**(1), 1–11 (2003)

6. Boute, R.N., Disney, S.M., Lambrecht, M.R., Van Houdt, B.: A win-win solution for the bullwhip problem. Prod. Plann. Control **19**(7), 702–711 (2008)
7. Nienhaus, J., Ziegnbein, A., Schoensieben, P.: How human behavior amplifies the bullwhip effect. A study based on the beer distribution game online. Prod. Plann. Control **17**(6), 547–557 (2006)
8. Wu, Y.D., Katok, E.: Learning, communication, and bullwhip effect. J. Oper. Manage. **24**, 839–850 (2006)
9. Christoph, R., Sato, M., Nakano, M.: Would you like some wine? introducing variants to the beer game. Prod. Plann. Control, 1–9, March 19, 2020
10. Antonio, K., Lau, W.: Teaching supply chain management using a modified beer game: an action learning approach. Int. J. Logistics Res. Appl. **18**(1), 62–81 (2015)
11. Ministry of Agriculture, Forestry and Fisheries, 2016 fiscal year food waste and recycling. https://www.maff.go.jp/j/tokei/kekka_gaiyou/loss/jyunkan_h29/index.html. Accessed 30 Mar 2020
12. Sato, M., Mizuyama, H., Nakano, M.: How different commercial rules affect actors and waste in milk supply chain. In: The International Simulation and Gaming Association, Congress Proceedings, Thailand, pp. 528-535 (2018)

Design and Implementation of a Serious Game to Make Construction Workers Aware of Exposure to Silica Dust in the Workplace

Sorelle Audrey K. Kamkuimo[1]($\boxtimes$) ⓘ, Benoît Girard[2], Patrick Lapointe[3], and Bob-Antoine J. Menelas[1] ⓘ

[1] Department of Computer Sciences and Mathematics, University of Quebec at Chicoutimi, Quebec, Canada
{sorelle-audrey.kamkuimo-kengne1,bamenela}@uqac.ca
[2] La Futaie Therapy Center, Boulevard Tadoussac, Saint-Fulgence, Quebec, Canada
beni.girard@gmail.com
[3] Integrated University Health and Social Services Centres of Saguenay–Lac-Saint-Jean, Chicoutimi, QC, Canada
patrick.lapointe.asss@ssss.gouv.qc.ca

Abstract. Silicosis is a lung disease due to the inhalation of crystalline silica dust. In the province of Quebec in Canada, it is the third pulmonary occupational disease recognized by the Committee on Standards, Equity, Health and Safety at Work. To date, lung transplantation is the only proven curative treatment. Consequently, prevention remains the best way to fight against silicosis. This requires that workers, at risk of exposure, have adequate training on the subject. For this, passive slide-based training is generally used. The goal of this paper is to operate a Serious Game to facilitate the training of construction workers on the prevention of silicosis and the protection of health in the workplace. We are interested in exploiting this media because we see in these types of games an active and situated problem-solving with probably some social interactions. They can transmit knowledge while entertaining the user in diversified activities. In this article, we report the development project and preliminary evaluation of a serious game in which the player is faced with different situations that involve exposure to silica. The aim is to train and make the player aware of silica, its risks, and its consequences. The results show the ability of this serious game to transmit knowledge about silica dust, the risk that it represents for health, the risk tasks and the protective measures in the workplace, and finally the consequences of the inhalation of silica dust.

Keywords: Serious games · Learning · Training · Action · Silica dust · Silicosis

1 Introduction

Silicosis is a lung disease caused by the inhalation of crystalline silica dust [1]. It is an occupational hazard to workers of multiple industries such as mining, pottery, oil and

© Springer Nature Switzerland AG 2020
M. Ma et al. (Eds.): JCSG 2020, LNCS 12434, pp. 85–98, 2020.
https://doi.org/10.1007/978-3-030-61814-8_7

gas and construction, among others, making it one of the most important occupational diseases worldwide [2]. Silicosis destroys lung tissue that can continue to develop even when the worker is no longer exposed to silica dust [3]. In Canada, in the province of Quebec, it was the third pulmonary occupational disease recognized by the Committee on Standards, Equity, Health and Safety at Work (CNESST) [4]. As lung transplantation is the only proven cure [1, 5], prevention remains the best way to fight the disease. The National Institute of Occupational Safety and Health (NIOSH) recommends four main categories of measures that help to control the development of silicosis [6]: (1) Dust Control which consists of canalizing the dust to prevent its propagation in the air; (2) Personal Hygiene which includes responsible worker behaviour to minimize the risk of inhalation of silica dust; (3) Protective Clothing such as a work uniform for workers to use, maintain and store properly; and (4) Air Monitoring which alerts workers to potential dangers so that they may take appropriate measures to limit their exposure to silica dust.

All of these recommendations require the worker to make informed choices based on the configuration of the environment and the controlling factors (e.g. ventilation and humidity). The fight against silicosis, therefore, requires that workers at risk of exposure have adequate training on the subject. Passive slide-based training is generally used for this purpose [7]. In Quebec, such training is provided by Occupational Safety and Health workers in the public health network. In the construction sector, the high mobility of labour and businesses and the lack of a permanent employment link for almost all workers create barriers to disease prevention. Our goal is to operate a serious game (SG) to facilitate the training of construction workers on the prevention of disease and the protection of health.

We are interested in exploiting SG because these types of games require active and situated problem-solving with likely social interaction [8, 9]. Moreover, SGs allow for a learner approach [10] while creating a meaningful environment for learning [11, 12]. By doing so, they can address both cognitive and affective dimensions of learning [13]. Indeed, learning can be defined as 'an enduring change in behaviour, or in capacity to behave in a given fashion, which results from practise or other forms of experience' [14]. It is a process of promoting learners' engagement in activities of knowledge acquisition or behaviour modification [15]. As learning theories have evolved, several researchers have established that action-oriented learning in a specific context would allow for better changes in the learner than passive learning [14–16]. They subsequently proposed factors that would facilitate the acquisition of knowledge through the interactions between the subject and the environment: learning content, learning context, practice, corrective feedback, manipulation of information, and physical and mental activity of the learner, among others [14]. These factors are even more important to consider when using SGs. We are particularly interested in SGs because of their ability to transmit information while entertaining the user in diversified activities through interactions. In the health sector, they can be used for several purposes including training, information, education and awareness.

In this article, we report the project development and preliminary evaluation of an SG in which the player is faced with different situations that involve exposure to silica. Our goal in using this game is that the player becomes well informed of the various means of prevention to limit the risks of inhalation of silica particles and that he develops an awareness of the consequences that negligence could have on his health and life.

2 Materials and Methods

2.1 Presentation and Objectives

We named the developed tool 'The Four Aces'. It is an SG of four missions to educate construction workers about silica dust. This concept was selected as a result of the average age of the target population [17]. The game environment is a worksite in summer during the day. It is divided into four missions, each associated with an ace from a deck of 52 cards. The goal of the game is to collect all four aces: spade, diamond, club and heart. Each ace thus constitutes the reward for a fully completed mission. Each mission contains only cards of the same colour. Points are awarded to the player for each card won. To be able to move to the next mission, the player must earn at least half of the points (06/12). A time parameter is associated with each mission to stimulate the player's concentration and commitment.

As the goal is to educate workers without frustrating them, we based the game design on the GameFlow model of Sweetser and Wyeth [18]. The principle is to ensure the player a better experience during the game and keep him in a psychological area free from boredom and anxiety. We first ensured that there was a good balance between the challenges of the in-game tasks and the skills of the player. To accomplish this, the tasks given to the players in the game are all associated with construction jargon. Moreover, the game interface and gameplay are made as simple as possible, and controls are easy. Mission goals are clearly defined, and the player receives immediate feedback on his actions in the game. The player does not receive punishment for error. Instead, he is allowed to retry as many times as necessary, as long as there is time left for the mission. At the end of each mission, a summary is given to the player. For players who missed certain cards, correction images are given to them in this summary so that they can still consider their failures and the right answers. So, regardless of whether the player has won the ace[1], he proceeds to the next mission, having learned what was presented to him in the previous one.

For the first three missions, each card is associated with a specific task, action or situation that can be found on a construction site. In the fourth mission, each card is associated with an effect of silicosis. There is, therefore, a total of forty-eight situations of identification, elimination, protection, and awareness regarding silica dust in a worksite.

2.2 Devices and Mechanics

The game must be installed on a desktop computer with a Windows 64-bit operating system to run correctly. Since workers are not necessarily familiar with computer technologies, the operations are simple and consist of simple clicks or click-and-drag with the mouse. For a quick start to the game, an interactive tutorial is presented to the player

---

[1] The ace is won if the score is 12/12, and the player can even go to next mission with a score of 06/12 without winning the ace.

at launch (See Fig. 1). This approximately two-minute tutorial constitutes learning by action. It assembles all the manipulations and forms of instructions that the player will have to use throughout the game.

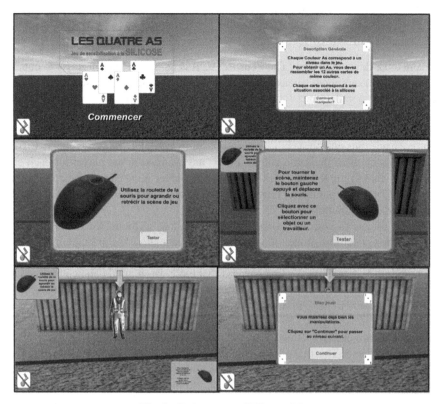

Fig. 1. Serious game (SG) tutorial

2.3   Missions of the Game

The four missions of the game are described below.

Ace of Hearts – Identification: Identify the Risks of Inhaling Silica Dust

This mission lasts at most ten minutes and is associated with heart suit cards. In this mission, the player is invited to identify situations in which one is likely to inhale silica dust in the worksite. For this, the player must go through the virtual worksite and find the twelve workers who do not meet workplace safety standards. Each situation found allows the player to obtain a heart card with which the tool or the situation concerned is associated on the site. To do this, the player must select a card by clicking on it in the upper part of the screen, browse the virtual worksite by clicking and drag with the mouse to find and click on the "non-standard" worker associated with the image engraved on the card.

The order in which the player resolves this mission is not important (he can start with any card). The different risk situations for inhaling silica dust, and the corresponding cards are as follows: 2 of hearts – aspiration without a protective mask; 3 of hearts –sweeping that raises dust without a protective mask; 4 of hearts – bush-hammering without a protective mask; 5 of hearts – concrete mixing without a protective mask; 6 of hearts – inactive standing worker without a protective mask in a dusty area; 7 of hearts – abrasive jet without a protective mask; 8 of hearts – demolition of the slab using a jackhammer without a protective mask; 9 of hearts – grinding without a protective mask; 10 of hearts – cleaning the tool with a sandblast without a protective mask; jack of hearts – perforation of a wall without a protective mask; queen of hearts – concrete sawing without a protective mask; and king of hearts – blowing without a protective mask. Figure 2 shows some of the situations within this mission.

Fig. 2. Some situations of mission 1 in the SG

Ace of Spades – Elimination: Eliminate the Risk of Inhaling Silica Dust

This mission lasts at most height minutes and is associated with spade suit cards. The player must resolve twelve situations associated with ways to eliminate the risk of inhalation of silica dust on a work site. The situations are presented in a scrolling fashion with an average duration of forty seconds each. In each situation presented to him, the player must use the indicative text to click on the action to be performed to eliminate the risk of inhaling silica dust. These situations and the associated cards are as follows: 2 of spades – general aspiration; 3 of spades – delimitation of the work area; 4 of spades

– agglomeration of the cement; 5 of spades – aspiration at the source; 6 of spades – humidification of the area; 7 of spades – suction instead of sweeping; 8 of spades – use of a filtration hood; 9 of spades – use of an automated crushing arm in the filtering cabin; 10 of spades – sandblasting with non-siliceous materials; jack of spades – humidification at the source; queen of spades – choice of the right tool between a saw with an integrated vacuum cleaner and a saw without an integrated vacuum cleaner; and king of spades - change of cabin filters. Figure 3 shows some situations within this mission.

Fig. 3. Some situations of mission 2 in the SG

Ace of Diamonds – Individual and Collective Protection Measures: Protect Yourself and Others from the Risks of Inhaling Silica Dust
This mission lasts at most height minutes and is associated with diamond suit cards.

The aim of this mission is to compel the player to acquire individual and collective protective measures against silica dust in twelve situations, as follows: 2 of diamonds – before working, dress in the protective uniform (wear your work clothes); 3 of diamonds – shave the beard to seal the mask; 4 of diamonds – wear at least one disposable respiratory mask in case of low exposure; 5 of diamonds – wear a respiratory mask in case of strong exposure; 6 of diamonds – wear a respiratory suit in case of very intense exposure; 7 of diamonds – avoid excessive physical effort in a dusty environment; 8 of diamonds – avoid smoking in the workplace; 9 of diamonds – clean the mask; 10 of diamonds – store the mask; jack of diamonds – vacuum all the dust present on the work equipment; queen of diamonds – store work clothes; and king of diamonds – attend safety training.

The manipulations in this mission are the clicks for the situations corresponding to cards 2, 4, 5, 6, 7, 8, 9, queen and king, and the click-and-drag for those corresponding to cards 3, 10 and jack. In these last three situations, clicking and dragging allow the player to perform actions as in real life. Figure 4 shows some of the situations within this mission.

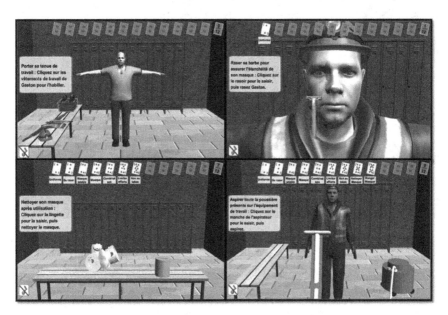

Fig. 4. Some situations of mission 3 in the SG

Ace of Clubs – Sensitization: Consideration of Silicosis Effects on the Worker's Life

This mission lasts at most two minutes and is associated with club suit cards. The aim is to make the player aware of the consequences of silicosis. With a simple click of the mouse, the player could browse the various clubs' cards and inquire about the information presented to him concerning the consequences of silicosis. This information is presented in the form of animated images. The different situations are as follows: 2 of clubs – degradation of the lungs; 3 of clubs – decline in breathing capacity; 4 of clubs – risk of lung cancer; 5 of clubs – difficulty breathing; 6 of clubs – physical weakness; 7 of clubs – loss of work capacity; 8 of clubs – early retirement; 9 of clubs – financial problems; 10 of clubs – inability to participate in spare-time activities; jack of clubs – loss of family activities; queen of clubs – awareness of the fact that there is no treatment for silicosis; and king of clubs – reduced life expectancy. Figure 5 shows some of the situations within this mission.

At the end of the game, an end scene is presented to the player to congratulate him on what he has just accomplished (Fig. 6).

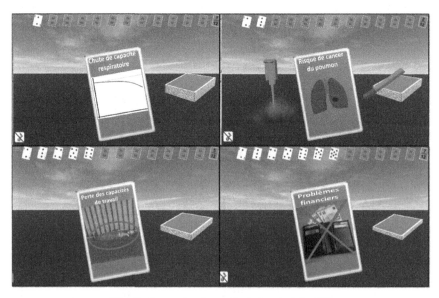

Fig. 5. Some situations of mission 4 of the SG

Fig. 6. Congratulations scene after the SG

3   Preliminary Evaluation and Results

In this section, we present the preliminary results of the test we conducted to assess the usability of this game. We focused on the ease of use of the mechanics, the ease of learning the knowledge we desired to communicate, and the average time taken by the participants to finish the game while having acquired the expected learning.

3.1 Participants

Participants were five community health student interns from the Faculty of Medicine and Health Sciences at the University of Sherbrooke. They were not familiar with the construction sector.

3.2 Procedure

To better appreciate the effectiveness of this SG, we compared the participants to themselves to solve the problem linked to the absence of a control group. To do this, the participants completed the evaluation questionnaire for the first time one month before the game test. This period allowed us to limit the bias linked to the reproduction of the responses when they must complete the same questionnaire for the second time, after the game test. The questionnaire was divided into three sections, and the type of question proposed was diverse, including multiple-choice questions and open-ended questions.

3.3 Results

We report here the results of this preliminary assessment. Notably, for all the participants, the maximum time spent to complete the game was fifteen minutes.

The First Section of the Questionnaire

The first section concerned the participants' personal information, such as their educational level and their experience with the building sector.

Before the completion of the participation questionnaire, none of the participants had already received training on the risks of silica.

The Second Section of the Questionnaire

The second section concerned a personal estimate of the degree of danger posed by silica dust.

- This section primarily evaluated the knowledge of the participants on silica dust and its health effects. Among other things, participants responded that silica dust could be found in sand, concrete, stone and metal. This last element, which is not entirely correctly designated as containing silica, was underlined by 40% of the participants before playing the game. After playing the game, to this same question, all participants (100%) answered sand, concrete and stone. This answer reflects the fact that the game allowed participants to learn precisely about the elements that could contain silica dust.
- Before playing the game, the participants estimated the level of risk of silica dust on health at an average of 84%. After the game, this average increased to 96%, indicating that participants understood that silica dust could be even more dangerous than they had previously imagined.

The Third Section of the Questionnaire

This section of the questionnaire concerned general knowledge of measures to prevent the inhalation of silica dust on a work site.

- Before the game, participants estimated that wearing a mask could protect workers from silica dust by an average of 84%. After the game, this average increased to 94%, reflecting the extent to which the game helped participants to understand the importance of protection from inhaling silica dust.
- Before the game, participants rated the importance of a workplace silica prevention program at 82%. After playing the game, this was estimated at 96%, reflecting the participants' awareness of training that workers must complete.
- Participants were also asked to identify five tasks that could significantly expose people to silica in the workplace. According to their general personal cultures before the game, the participants listed sanding, drilling, cutting stones, working in the ground, making concrete, renovating, working in mines, working near a conveyor, sawing of stone, being in a factory manufacturing stone, maintenance of such a factory, welding, laying of concrete and laying of sand, among others. After the game, the participants' knowledge seemed to be better circumscribed because their responses were more precise, with appropriate terms such as sanding, sawing concrete, pouring concrete, sweeping with a broom, drilling walls, making holes in the ground with a jackhammer, abrasive jet, sweeping, sawing, being near a source, polishing, grinding stone, casting concrete and sweeping concrete. Once again, knowledge had been successfully transmitted.
- Another point of the questionnaire was for the participants to name five methods to eliminate the production of silica dust at the source. The answers to this question before the game were to use appropriate tools, good ventilation, masks, equipment with protective measures, maximum exposure time, use of alternative material, distance when using the equipment, humidify the stone, adequate ventilation, work outside, vacuum dust, reduce dust production and do not use certain rocks, stones or metals. Once again, after the game, the participants' responses were much more circumscribed, clear and with appropriate terms and expressions such as the use of a filtering cabin, aspirating at the source, humidifying the environment, vent hood, delimiting the workspace, putting a hood, the tool must contain a vacuum cleaner, vacuuming the suits, using other material without silica, humidification at the source, use of a concrete agglomeration, cabin with filter, use of a substrate with low silica concentration and alternative sand.
- Participants were asked to name three steps required to ensure the effectiveness of the filter mask. Before the game, the participants' answers were among others: waterproofness, good use, well adjusted, must not be too wet or soiled, check that there is no break, adjust the mask, wear the mask at the appropriate times, respect the expiration dates, wear the correct size of mask and wear a clean mask. After the game, as for the two previous questions, the answers were more precise: tightness, good use, stored well, shaved the beard well, clean the mask and store it, make sure the mask is properly adjusted, change the cartridges, and use of correct size and model depending on the intensity. Shaving, cleaning, and storage are terms that were mentioned many times.

- The next question aimed to consider the views of participants regarding the need for training to ensure the effectiveness of a respiratory protection program. Before and after the game, the participants were unanimous in answering 'totally'.
- On the last question of the form, participants had to identify 3 possible consequences for workers exposed to silica. Before the game, the answers were: silicosis, lung cancer, asthma, pulmonary silicosis, eye inflammation, pulmonary adenocarcinoma and pulmonary fibrosis. After the game, the participants' responses were more diverse and generalized: silicosis, lung cancer, asthma, lung damage, breathing difficulties, deterioration in the quality of life, lung neoplasia, decrease in life expectancy, financial costs, loss of physical capacity, increased risk of lung cancer, pulmonary silicosis, use of sick leave and loss of functional capacity. This multitude of responses after the game is partly linked to the fourth mission of the game, which presented the consequences of silica dust. However, certain consequences listed by the participants were not part of the content of this mission. We must, therefore, assume that as they were health students, from all that they learned about silica throughout the game, they were able to associate other diseases they knew about with the information that they learned about silica dust.

4   Discussion

4.1   Active Learning Favours the Satisfactory Transmission of Information

The analysis of these results shows the capacity of an SG of 30 min to train and raise peoples' awareness of silica, its risks and its consequences. Indeed, between the evaluation results before and after playing the game, we can observe that the general knowledge of the participants had evolved. We can also see how the participants' answers are "imprecise" before the game and much clearer, more precise and with appropriate terms after the game. This clarity in the responses can be associated with the actions performed to solve the game, and with textual and graphic indications which were used in the game to guide the player. We can find terms and expressions such as abrasive jet and filtering cabin, which are reported exactly as presented in the game. In addition, certain game scenarios such as shaving the beard, cleaning the mask, storing the mask and vacuuming the dust on the coveralls involved an action performed with the mouse as it would be done in real life. To shave the beard, the player had to grab the razor by clicking on it and make shaving movements on the face of the avatar until all the beard was removed. To clean the mask, the player had to take a wipe by clicking on it and simulate cleaning movements on the mask until all the dust was removed. To store the mask, the player had to grab it by clicking on it, and move it to his box, and then move the box containing the mask to the canteen. To vacuum the dust on the work suit, the player had to grab the vacuum cleaner by clicking on it and perform aspiration movements on the avatar suit until all the dust was vacuumed. In participants' responses after playing the game, these scenarios came up repeatedly.

Given that the game aims to raise awareness and, therefore, to transmit new learning and new behaviours to the player, the participants' results confirm the effectiveness of active learning. Indeed, according to the study of the evolution of learning theories, the subject acquires knowledge better and this permanently when he builds it through an autonomous activity [15]. Already at the base, as we underlined in the introduction, the objective of making an SG for the training and education of workers on the dangers of silica is to be able to transfer this concept of learning into training for a respiratory protection program for workers in the workplace. Thus, all the scenarios of the game 'The Four Aces' involve the worker's activity (identify, select, eliminate). So, interactivity makes this game a different type of media from the slide-based training routinely given to workers.

Another notable result is the response of the participants after the game to the question concerning the consequences of silica dust is that eight of the twelve situations presented in mission 4 were reported as presented in the game. One of the participants had just cited "silicosis" before the test. After the test, he gave three much more elaborate answers, all present in mission 4 of the game: reduced physical capacity, increased risk of lung cancer and development of silicosis. It should be noted that in this game mission, the descriptive text of the consequence was accompanied each time by an animated image. This way of presenting information allowed the participant to integrate knowledge easily.

Finally, all of the answers before and after the game show that this SG had the expected effect on the participants: the ability to identify and eliminate the risks of inhaling silica dust, applying measures of protection against silica dust, and the awareness of the danger that this dust can have on health and human life.

4.2   Participants' Involvement and Observable Behaviours

During the game, we were able to observe the substantial involvement of the participants. For most of the participants, manipulations were very intuitive; it was easy for them to make the association between the input device (mouse) and the tasks they had to perform in the game world, demonstrating a good balance between the tasks, the manipulations, and the skills of the participants.

4.3   Suggestions Made by Participants

At the end of the game, the participants were debriefed, to provide their comments and suggestions for improvement. The positive points noted by the participants were as follows: good tutorial, good graphics, the possibility of going back and correcting mistakes, the scores favoured enjoyment, and the manipulations were easy. However, they suggested adding informational tips to accompany the player better and adding background sound to improve the game feel for the player. They also suggested that the timer be more highlighted for the player. Indeed, some participants did not notice the presence of a "timer" in each mission and were slightly anxious because they did not know how long they had to complete the game. They still completed the game in a much shorter time than what was normally offered to them.

These suggestions have been implemented in the current version of the game. To the suggestion of a background sound, we downloaded free sound effects and integrated them into the game. The informational tips were dynamically added to the game; through the user's manipulations, we detect when the user is incorrect and we inform him, in an informational tip, of what to do. These tips are also used to give positive feedback to the player when he succeeds in an action. The timer is also more highlighted in the current version of the game.

4.4 Transferability of These Results to the Target Group

This game could produce similar results with construction workers. Indeed, the target audience will have the advantage of knowing the tasks and tools used in the workplace, which could ease the expected learning of good habits that prevent silicosis. However, we have some reservations at the technological level because we cannot attest to their familiarity with computers. Even though we anticipated this by offering the player simplistic in-game mechanics, we could still expect some difficulty in getting started for those people who rarely deal with computers. Nevertheless, these preliminary tests that we conducted reveal a reliable advantage. Indeed, the participants, who are an audience that can be considered technologically skilled, completed the game in less than 15 min while it is intended to be played in 30 min. This margin allows us to hypothesize that those less familiar with the technologies in the target group could still be able to play the game within 30 min and acquire the targeted skills. Therefore, we could consider the possibility of adapting the time allocated to each section of the game to the evolution of the player. In the future, we will study the differences in results between this test group and the target group. We will also be interested in the technological impact on the possible differences that may exist between the two groups. If we realize that there are difficulties for the target group, we could add additional stages to the game to best assist the player.

5 Conclusion

Despite the limitation in the number of participants to this study, this preliminary evaluation allowed us to see that the SG "The Four Aces" was able to effectively transmit learning to people with almost no basic knowledge of silica dust. So, it helps us understand that this could be an effective way to educate workers in the building sector. This game is scheduled to be played in 30 min to comply with the duration of the standard slide-based training. In contrast to the slide-based training, the participant's activity during the game could allow him to better acquire the knowledge by maintaining concentration and motivation.

The project is a SG that should be used by construction companies to train and educate workers on the dangers of silica dust and the protective measures to be observed in the workplace. Thus, just as for the 30 min slide-based training courses that are currently provided, the player must complete this 30 min game during his working hours and will, therefore, be paid during this training. It should also be noted that bosses may need to monitor the performances of their workers in this game, which they could add as a parameter to assess their ability to observe good protective reflexes in the workplace. So, to make the project easily exploitable by these bosses, we have created a data structure in a JSON file, allowing for storage of the player's information as well as his achievements for each game mission. For the next version, we will use the information in this file to provide a graphical interface for managers to track the achievements of their workers during this SG training. Replayability is, therefore, an important point to underline. If necessary, a copy of the game can be given to employees so that they can practice more at home.

References

1. Leung, C.C., Yu, I.T.S., Chen, W.: Silicosis. The Lancet **379**(9830), 2008–2018 (2012)
2. Greenberg, M.I., Waksman, J., Curtis, J.: Silicosis: a review. Dis. Mon. **53**(8), 394–416 (2007)
3. Ziskind, M., Jones, R.N., Weill, H.: Silicosis. Am. Rev. Respir. Dis. **113**(5), 643–665 (1976)
4. CNESST, Committee on Standards, Equity, Health and Safety at Work 2016–2020
5. Mao, W.-J., et al.: Lung transplantation for end-stage silicosis. J. Occup. Environ. Med. **53**(8), 845–849 (2011)
6. NIOSH: Preventing silicosis and deaths in construction (2014)
7. NIOSH: A Safety & Health Training for Young Workers (2018)
8. Iten, N., Petko, D.: Learning with serious games: is fun playing the game a predictor of learning success? Br. J. Educ. Technol. **47**(1), 151–163 (2016)
9. Menelas, B.-A.J., Benaoudia, R.S.: Use of haptics to promote learning outcomes in serious games. Multimodal Technol. Interact. **1**(4), 31 (2017)
10. Menelas, B.-A.J., Otis, M.J.-D.: Design of a serious game for learning vibrotactile messages. In: 2012 IEEE International Workshop on Haptic Audio Visual Environments and Games (HAVE 2012) Proceedings, pp. 124–129. IEEE (2012)
11. Djaouti, D., et al.: Origins of serious games. In: Ma, M., Oikonomou, A., Jain, L.C. (eds.) Serious Games and Edutainment Applications, pp. 25–43. Springer, London (2011). https://doi.org/10.1007/978-1-4471-2161-9_3
12. Stapleton, A.J. Serious games: serious opportunities. In: Australian Game Developers Conference, Academic Summit, Melbourne (2004)
13. O'Neil, H.F., Wainess, R., Baker, E.L.: Classification of learning outcomes: evidence from the computer games literature. Cirriculum J. **16**(4), 455–474 (2005)
14. Ertmer, P.A., Newby, T.J.: Behaviorism, cognitivism, constructivism: comparing critical features from an instructional design perspective. Perform. Improv. Q. **6**(4), 50–72 (1993)
15. Prince, M.: Does active learning work? a review of the research. J. Eng. Educ. **93**(3), 223–231 (2004)
16. Kamkuimo Kengne, S.A., et al.: Action-centered exposure therapy (ACET): a new approach to the use of virtual reality to the care of people with post-traumatic stress disorder. Behav. Sci. **8**(8), 76 (2018)
17. Sokas, R.K., Dong, X.S., Cain, C.T.: Building a sustainable construction workforce. Int. J. Environ. Res. Public Health **16**(21), 4202 (2019)
18. Sweetser, P., Wyeth, P.: GameFlow: a model for evaluating player enjoyment in games. Comput. Entertainment (CIE) **3**(3), 3 (2005)

Needs Analyses with LEGO® SERIOUS PLAY®

Tanja Kranawetleitner(✉) ⓘ, Heike Krebs ⓘ, Nina Kuhn ⓘ, and Marietta Menner ⓘ

University of Augsburg, Universitaetsstrasse 1a, 86159 Augsburg, Germany
tanja.kranawetleitner@amu.uni-augsburg.de

Abstract. In the development of companies, innovative methods, including game-based approaches, can support change management. Within the project "Education 4.0 for SMEs", LEGO® SERIOUS PLAY® (LSP) is used in small and medium-sized enterprises as a needs analysis based on the gamification approach. LSP is a methodology that stimulates free communication. It opens access to those types of knowledge that are otherwise difficult to reach or to express, like personal attitudes or values. Constructions using LEGO® bricks help to visualise this knowledge and to make abstract ideas tangible. Hence, it is a particularly suitable method for needs analysis in times of digitalisation. The paper presents first data collected using LSP in the business context, providing a first impression of the possibilities, limitations, and applications of this method.

Keywords: LEGO® SERIOUS PLAY® · Needs analysis · Digitalisation · SMEs

1 Introduction

In the past decades, large companies have increasingly used game-based methods for their strategic development. Gradually, however, small and medium-sized enterprises (SMEs) are also dealing with gamification approaches as an innovative tool for designing change processes, personnel development or product training [1]. Gamification elements can be applied to increase the motivation to deal with tasks that are unrelated to the game [2]. Using these elements, Game-Based-Learning can occur because "learning – or a flow of information – takes place [...] through gaming overall" [3].

The LEGO® SERIOUS PLAY® (LSP) gamification approach described below is a possibility of motivating employees to engage intensively with the development of the company. It can especially be used to identify possible fears and inhibitions about change and visualise these with the help of LEGO® bricks.

2 LEGO® SERIOUS PLAY® – in Theory

LSP, developed in 1996 by Johan Roos and Bart Victor within the LEGO® Company and released for public use in 2010, is a method for solving problems and developing ideas [4]. The initial thought was to support managers to more easily scrutinise their own view of the company and thus to optimise their performance [4]. Ideas and opinions are exchanged more easily using LSP – whether in groups or individual coaching sessions.

© Springer Nature Switzerland AG 2020
M. Ma et al. (Eds.): JCSG 2020, LNCS 12434, pp. 99–104, 2020.
https://doi.org/10.1007/978-3-030-61814-8_8

Discussion and finding a solution are also encouraged [5]. In LSP, participants work manually with the bricks and describe as well as reflect their constructions afterwards. This enables a special form of creativity that leads to completely different perspectives. Besides, the representation of one's ideas by a self-created object simplifies and improves mutual understanding [4].

LSP relies on a theoretical framework described by four elements: Papert's theory of *constructionism* is based on Piaget's constructivism, but goes beyond it: "Constructionism is a way of making formal, abstract ideas and relationships more concrete, visible, tangible, manipulative and therefore easier to understand" [6]. Secondly, *play* always serves a certain purpose, is voluntary, structured and limited [6]. In play and thus in LSP, metaphors and storytelling are important aspects. The telling of stories does not only illustrate hopes and fears more clearly, but in an organizational context, it also serves a better resolution of conflicts, the socialization of new members and identification with the company. Metaphors are essential for understanding the opposite party better [6]. In addition, playing can cause a flow effect. This describes the immersion in a task, which is combined with enjoyment and forgetting oneself and the outside world [7]. *Imagination* is an interplay of describing, creating and questioning something. Different forms of imagination enable not only to represent and relate what is visible, including discovering new facets of known aspects, but also to develop something fundamentally new [6]. Finally, *identity* means self-image and self-understanding and points to the individual note of LSP [8].

3   LEGO® SERIOUS PLAY® – in Practice

LSP can be used in various areas, for example, in coaching, idea development, team building or product innovation. The construction work is carried out in different stages. It ranges from individual to shared, and system models [4]. Ordinarily, a workshop takes between three hours and one day [5]. The process includes not only the cycles of building, but also the subsequent phases of reflection and thus collaborative learning. Therefore, it should not only be applied as an icebreaker at the beginning or for convincing others of a certain opinion. Instead, one's own thoughts, ideas and attitudes should be presented, which are given a frame by the LEGO® bricks [5]. Moreover, LSP helps the participants immerse themselves in a topic, whether in personal or team development tasks or complex challenges in business contexts [9]. Nevertheless, according to The LEGO® Group itself, facilitators should check if the method is appropriate for the occasion before using it, as it might not be useful in all cases [5].

4   LEGO® SERIOUS PLAY® – an Exploratory Study

Talking about the future of work often includes considering new, possibly virtual or virtually augmented, spaces and the increasing use of digital tools. However, current studies show that the situation of companies concerning digitalisation is largely dependent on their size and branch [10]. Especially small and medium sized enterprises are lacking physical and personal resources for this digital transformation, although in principle, employees are interested in developing their knowledge [11].

This situation is the starting point of the project "Education 4.0 for SMEs". It aims at finding out more about possible support for SMEs in Germany in their digitalisation challenges, especially in terms of knowledge transfer. In order to increase the digital competences of staff and equip SMEs with suitable tools, a first step consists of a detailed assessment of the companies' requirements and the staff's need of support.

4.1 Needs Analysis in the Project "Education 4.0 for SMEs"

For this purpose, the project carries out a needs analysis after a preliminary discussion with the management, in which initial starting points have already been identified. The needs analysis intends to reify the discrepancy between the desired and the actual situation and thus has the aim of "analysing deficits in education, promotion and organisational development at the strategic, operational and individual level" [12].

The needs analysis focuses on the knowledge and attitudes of the employees concerning digitalisation. In addition to factual knowledge, especially experiential and implicit knowledge take centre stage. "These types of knowledge denote the hidden knowledge content, which knowledge carriers are largely unconscious of" [13], and which is difficult to express [14].

Apart from the collection of this evasive knowledge, it is important to find out about unspoken and critical issues, like reservations, difficulties, and obstacles at the personal and structural basis. From individual to organizational levels, the needs analysis should also uncover shortcomings of intentions (motivation), lack of abilities or competences (qualifications), and obstacles concerning access or permission (organizational development) [12]. All of those three, motivation, qualification and organizational development are part of the project "Education 4.0 for SMEs".

4.2 LSP Methodology in the Project "Education 4.0 for SMEs"

In the LSP workshop, the employees start with a warm-up exercise, building a simple model like a walrus according to original LEGO® instructions. Then they transform this model to include features associated with a digitalised company (Fig. 1). After the individual presentations, which should not be interrupted for the benefit of an open atmosphere, further models show the staff's ideas of their departments after a success-ful process of digitalisation (Fig. 2). These constructions are classified as "individual models" [4]. Only in the last step, the departments literally grow together and by dis-cussing the individual parts and priorities, the participants jointly construct their ideal digital company ("shared and system model" [4]). During the whole workshop, each participant uses the same number and type of bricks (LSP Starter Kit).

Considering that using LSP as a method of inquiry is unprecedented in the area described, one main aspect is to find out more about the suitability of the method itself. Regarding the topic of digitalisation, three aims can be pursued, whereas this paper focuses on (2) and (3) in order to show the potential of LSP as a game-based approach: (1) Collect factual knowledge about participants; (2) Provoke individual expressions of attitudes and emotions; (3) Engender individual reflections of one's needs.

In addition to the data collection by means of LSP in the field of digitalisation, at the end the participants fill in a questionnaire in which they evaluate the experienced

LSP workshop (9 items with 5-point Likert scale ranging from "totally agree" to "totally disagree"). In order to gain as broad an insight as possible, the participants ($n = 21$) consist of heterogeneous representatives of the workforce of each participating SME (age, gender, education, part-time or full-time, department and company hierarchy).

Fig. 1. Example of a modified walrus   **Fig. 2.** Building a digitalised department

4.3 Preliminary Results

First and foremost, LSP serves to elicit attitudes and emotions with the aim of finding out more about personal needs. This information is obtained by participants' explicit descriptions as well as their reflection and interpretation of their models, which are quoted in the following. For instance, a digitalised walrus might include wheels, a transparent "shield" in front of its eyes and might be built with or without a "driver" (quotations refer to the participants' presentations). Usually, the description goes along with the builder's own interpretation. Diversity appears not only due to varying types of construction (e.g. a "pillar" for "stability" instead of wheels for "speed, agility, flexibility"), but also by individual readings of the same materials: The mentioned "shield", for instance, was understood as a way of "protection" against the dangers of digitalisation or as a type of "glasses" to "see through". Whereas the former idea can indicate a possible reservation towards the challenges of digitalisation, the latter might suggest a less critical stance. Based on identical sets of bricks, the participants also build different constructions whose interpretation is similar. For example, the association of "speed" was embodied not only by wheels but also by a helicopter or plane. Individual interpretations (e.g. the figure of a driver who "steers" the digitalised company, or the co-presence of other figures showing that it is important for managers "to take their staff along") lead to the overt discussion of the employees' needs, values and attitudes – personal statements, not usually mentioned thoughtlessly in an ordinary meeting.

4.4 Evaluation of the Method in the Project "Education 4.0 for SMEs"

The evaluation of using LSP in a business context for an assessment of the staff's attitudes and requirements concerning digitalisation in their company shows first implications for the further development of the method. The majority of those questioned ($n = 21$) did not know and had not used the method before. Therefore, possible reservations against using LEGO® were ruled out from the beginning. One of the main tenets of the method, namely its playfulness and enjoyable nature, were confirmed by a clear majority (90%). Even more importantly, the method helped the employees to become aware of practical implications of digitalisation (86%), and some even learned something new by participating (76%). Only some employees found the method helpful to understand digitalisation in a company in general (38%). The items about the communication of knowledge by the method point to the suggested low relevance of collecting factual knowledge (aim 1, see Sect. 4.2).

4.5 Discussion

From a purely quantitative perspective, the small number of participants is problematic. However, although findings from the collected data can only count as indications rather than robust results, they clearly show the potential of LSP. For a comprehensive outcome, it should also be considered that most participants verbalise their thoughts and feelings already during the process of building. Therefore, the documentation or recording (obeying the rules of privacy protection) should span the whole workshop.

In addition, it is essential to discuss problems of accessibility. The participants may feel uncomfortable if they have little or no experience in playing with LEGO®. Moreover, LSP uses "new" types of bricks. This could lead to confusion and the necessity of more time to get to know the unknown bricks and thus to build with them.

Another aspect to mention is the diversity of the participants, starting with the risk that it may be difficult for people to structure their thoughts manually and to articulate their ideas metaphorically in retrospect. Besides, building with small LEGO® bricks might prove an obstacle for people with certain impairments, which could lead to their exclusion. Finally, especially in the corporate context some could also consider the method too "playlike", and for this reason do not take it seriously.

5 Conclusion and Perspectives

Concluding, LSP has yielded promising results for the collection of individual assessments of possibly controversial topics. Additionally to the business context, the LSP approach has already been tested with students aged 13 and above. Apart from building the digitalised school of the future, their workshop tackled topics of Industry 4.0, such as the loss of jobs due to the use of robots, artificial intelligence, and others.

For the future, the project "Education 4.0 for SMEs" is planning to include further target groups. This will provide the opportunity to analyse the method itself in greater depth. Moreover, a transfer of LSP into the digital space is intended, raising the question how the lack of haptics of virtual LEGO® bricks influences the results. Finally, the use of LSP for learning will be tested. As the game-based learning approach can not only be applied to the "flow of information" [3] as in the present case, but also offers the possibility to generate learning itself, this might be a promising undertaking. In this vein, LSP can also be used for further qualification or other areas of application.

Acknowledgements. The Project "Bildung 4.0 für KMU" ("Education 4.0 for SMEs", Grant number 01PA17014) is funded by the German Federal Ministry of Education and Research and the European Social Fund for Germany.

References

1. Niedermeier, S., Müller, C.: Game-Based-Learning in Aus- und Weiterbildung – von der Idee zur Umsetzung. In: Wachtler, J., et al. (eds.): Digitale Medien: Zusammenarbeit in der Bildung, pp. 190–200. Waxmann, Münster, New York (2016)
2. Deterding, S., Khaled, R., Nacke, L.E., Dixon, D.: Gamification: toward a definition. Vancouver, British Columbia: ACM (2011). http://gamification-research.org/wp-content/uploads/2011/04/02-Deterding-Khaled-Nacke-Dixon.pdf. Accessed 19 June 2020
3. Wilms, M.: Serious Games – Anwendung digitaler Spiele, insbesondere in den Bereichen Training, Bildung und HealthCare. GRIN, Munich (2009). [Quotes translated]
4. Blair, S., Rillo, M.: Serious Work: Meetings und Workshops mit der Lego® Serious Play®-Methode moderieren. Verlag Franz Vahlen GmbH, Munich (2019)
5. The LEGO® Group: LEGO® Serious Play™. Open-Source/ <Introduction to LEGO® Serious Play™> . The LEGO® Group (2010). https://www.dropbox.com/s/8n2drwvqq5tzqdl/LSP_Open_Source.pdf?dl=0. Accessed 13 OCT 2020
6. The LEGO® Group: LEGO® Serious Play™. Die Wissenschaft von LEGO® Serious Play™. Spiel. Konstruktion. Imagination. The LEGO® Group (2002). [Quotes translated]
7. Csikszentmihalyi, M., Csikszentmihalyi, S.: Optimal Experiences: Psychological Studies of Flow in Consciousness. Cambridge University Press, New York (1988)
8. Arnold, R., Nolda, S., Nuissl, E.: Wörterbuch Erwachsenenbildung, 2nd edn. Verlag Julius Klinkhardt, Bad Heilbrunn (2010)
9. Kristiansen, P., Rasmussen, R.: Building a Better Business using the LEGO® SERIOUS PLAY® Method. John Wiley & Sons Inc, Hoboken (2014)
10. Techconsult, Deutsche Telekom (eds.): Digitalisierungsindex 2019/2020, https://www.digitalisierungsindex.de/wp-content/uploads/2019/11/techconsult_Telekom_Digitalisierungsindex_2019_GESAMTBERICHT.pdf. Accessed 16 June 2020
11. Taapken, N., Luh, K.: Wie digital-fit sind Deutschlands Arbeitnehmer? The better the question. The better the answer. The better the world works. Eine EY Studie aus Mitarbeitersicht. EY (2019)
12. Becker, M.: Personalentwicklung. Bildung, Förderung und Organisationsentwicklung in Theorie und Praxis. Schäffer-Poeschel, Stuttgart (2013). [Quotes translated]
13. Liebscher, J., Schubert, J., Nakhosteen, C.B.: Informelles Wissen durch E-Portfolios sichtbar machen. In: Weiterbildung - Zeitschrift für Grundlagen, Praxis und Trends 2011, Nr.1, S.35–39 (2011). [Quotes translated]
14. Klappacher, C., Rasmussen, R.: Implizites Wissen und Intuition. Warum wir mehr wissen, als wir zu sagen wissen: die Rolle des Impliziten Wissens im Erkenntnisprozess. VDM Verlag Müller, Saarbrücken (2006)

The Development and Testing of a Self-designed Escape Room as a Concept of Knowledge Transfer into Society

Julia Thurner-Irmler$^{(\boxtimes)}$ ⓘ and Marietta Menner ⓘ

University of Augsburg, Universitaetsstr. 1a, 86159 Augsburg, Germany
julia.thurner@amu.uni-augsburg.de

Abstract. In the last years, knowledge transfer has played a more and more important role, especially between the academic field and society. But to offer a low-threshold access to scientific topics, new procedures have to be examined. Based on Game-Based Learning, Escape Rooms are a contemporary format of knowledge transfer, due to their possibility of easy and playful approaches towards different topics. To investigate if this format is accepted by the targeted group, a self-concepted and designed Escape Room was tested twice through observations, talks and an evaluation. The results show that this concept is perceived as an interesting and approved method for the intended purpose.

Keywords: Knowledge transfer · Game-based learning · Escape room · STEM

1 Introduction

Knowledge transfer between science and economy has gained great interest in the last years, especially regarding the transfer of information and technology in favor of development, products or innovations [1]. But this perception is merely referring to technology committal. Today, knowledge transfer claims to exist between academia, economy and society. Closely connected is the discussion about the 'Third Mission' of universities and academic institutions, which addresses social tasks and responsibilities next to their core duties teaching ('First Mission') and researching ('Second Mission') [2]. But knowledge transfer into society faces various challenges, e.g. digitalization, technology – or even only word choices. The dilemma of science is that it has to communicate the restrictions and limits of scientific knowledge towards a society, which demands clarity [3].

The initial point to engage within this field is a project about knowledge transfer into society around the subjects of Industry 4.0, digitalization, technology, science and researching. Timidity and barriers should get dismantled. In this context, different transfer instruments and formats are investigated and tested to be able to address a large part of society. But how can topics like science or technology be refined to offer a low-threshold, understandable and interesting access and introduction for everyone, especially young people and adults? The work at hand focuses on the contemporary and playful concepts

© Springer Nature Switzerland AG 2020
M. Ma et al. (Eds.): JCSG 2020, LNCS 12434, pp. 105–116, 2020.
https://doi.org/10.1007/978-3-030-61814-8_9

of 'Escape Rooms' as a possible approach to answering this research question. Respecting the Game-Based Learning approach, an Escape Room can be applied as a Serious Game.

This paper examines a first try to design and install an Escape Room as a possible concept and format of knowledge transfer about academical topics into society. Requirements and decisions will be illustrated as well as features like riddle organization and dependencies, followed by an exemplification of two performances of the self-developed Escape Room. A presentation of observations, conversations and results of an evaluation helps to depict first assessments of the targeted group about the suitability and acceptance of an Escape Room as a format of scientific knowledge transfer.

2   Escape Room as a Serious Game

When the term 'Serious Game' is mentioned, many people think about (digital) learning games, which one can play on a computer, but are often not as entertaining as commercial video games. That is, because not the fun, but the "carefully thought-out educational purpose" [4] is the main goal in Serious Games. Nevertheless, one cannot neglect the entertainment during the education, because there are a lot of areas, which overlap and where players can benefit from each other to reach the learning target [5].

However, in the last years, a new entertaining concept became popular, which can also function as Serious Games and/or support Serious Gaming: Escape Rooms. These are "live-action team-based games where players discover clues, solve puzzles, and accomplish tasks in one or more rooms in order to accomplish a specific goal (usually escaping from the room) in a limited amount of time" [6]. The first kinds of Escape Rooms were concepted and designed by Takao Kato, an employee of the Japanese company SCRAP. He filled bars and clubs with objects, riddles and codes, and visitors had a specific amount of time to 'escape' from the location [7]. Since then, commercial Escape Rooms have spread around the world.

If an Escape Room is created "for an educational specific aim" [8], you may also designate it as a Serious Game. There are already some (Educational) Escape Rooms available around the globe, for examples with topics such as history, geography, chemistry, literature, cultural theme, etc. [6]. Some challenges appear when constructing an Escape Room as a Serious Games, because "the hedonic nature of the game is highlighted in escape rooms" [8], whereas in Serious Games, this feature is less important. However, in Serious Games as well as in Escape Rooms, the method of Game-Based Learning plays an important role. In general, the term 'Game-Based learning' is used when learning – or a flow of information – takes place through computer applications or through gaming overall [9]. Gaming types are not only restricted to digital learning games. Commercial off-the-shelf games from the entertainment industry can also be provided if they are thematically suited for reaching the learning goal [10] – just like Escape Rooms, which can be especially designed for achieving a specific learning task, too.

But even if an Escape Room is not specifically designed to be a Serious Game, Serious Gaming and Game-Based Learning can happen through various elements. For example, when players are in a room as a team with diverse puzzles at different places, communication and teamwork are essential to solve riddles together [6, 11, 12]. In this context one may be able to develop new soft skills like tolerance and acceptance towards other people, as well as their own approaches and activities towards difficult settings. Also, the use of your knowledge and skills while working on complicated puzzles and situations under time pressure can be trained [11]. During the process of solving the riddles, you may gain a new ability, e.g. like learning a few words from an unknown language or decoding [6]. Escape Rooms can even be used to get confronted with fears in a safe and controlled room and framing, like in cases to temper claustrophobia [8].

3 Concept Development of a STEM-Escape Room

STEM contains a broad field of engineering science (like architecture, engineering, electrical engineering, computer sciences, manufacturing systems engineering, etc.) and mathematical and natural sciences (like biology, chemistry, geoscience, mathematics, physics, pharmacy, etc.) [13]. The word STEM summarizes all the diverse topics in the umbrella terms Science, Technology, Engineering and Mathematics. To bring these subjects into the broad society is necessary, because the mathematical, nature and computer science-related performances of young people have been dropping continuously since the past years [14]. Therefore, it was decided to create a STEM-Escape Room to increase the awareness and interest in STEM.

3.1 Requirements and First Decisions

The target group of the STEM-Escape Room is the society, ranged from young individuals to adults and elderly people. Since the Escape Room should be provided during different events as part of a social program, the time required for this experience should not exceed 30 min. About six to eight people are planned to be in one team.

After clarifying basic requirements, a learning goal of the Escape Room has to be set. Since the target group contains a great variety of different people and it is supposed that many of them probably have not been in contact with STEM-related subjects, the main aim was set to get to know what STEM is and which fields it encompasses. The visitors should also be able to gain first-hand experiences in each of the four sectors. The acronym 'STEM' is taken literally as it was planned to create four puzzles, one for each area. A decision was also made towards a pure open riddle organization: each puzzle is presented individually. The solution of these four riddles leads to one big meta-puzzle. Problems with this kind of organization are the progression and development of difficulty as well as the usage of experiences from earlier puzzles, compared to e.g. sequential or a path-based organization, in which solutions lead to other riddle(s) before reaching the meta-riddle [6] (see Fig. 1). But respecting the available time and possible differences within the target group, an open approach seemed the best way to work simultaneously on riddles following one's own interests and strengths. However, communication and teamwork still play a leading role to solve the four puzzles and finally the meta-riddle together.

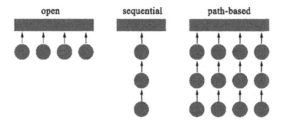

Fig. 1. Different kinds of (fundamental) riddle organizations [3]

3.2   Process and Riddles of the STEM-Escape Room

The Escape Room visiting team is greeted outside the room. The person explains the procedure of an Escape Room, and that different puzzles have to be solved to 'escape' the room. It is emphasized that communication and teamwork are essential, since the people probably meet for the first time. More information is explained, e.g. the usage of mobile phones is not allowed in the Escape Room and that the gamemaster is in the room to introduce them to the story and help them if there are troubles. But a hint or a helping item is only provided if they find one of four special 'hint-objects' hidden in the room.

It was decided to let the gamemaster be in the same room because it offers flexibility to room and technical arrangements during different events the Escape Room will be featured in. The gamemaster can react to current situations and problems, too, as he/she knows the status quo of all riddle progressions and is prepared with diverse hints for each possible constellation. Also, the concept of exchanging an object for a tip or an item was used to provide hints, but not unlimited or only one in a specific time limit.

After the reception, the team is guided into the Escape Room. They are awaited by the gamemaster who sets the atmosphere and starts the story as well as the story goal: The setting is a few hours before the ongoing event. A certain URL, which should be provided to the guests, has gone missing. There is a tablet available and handed out to the visitors, who play the role as the staff of the event, but it is locked by an unknown code. However, the code has to be somewhere in the room. The details of the story (e.g. where the URL is leading to) can be adapted and changed individually for each activity.

The setting of the Escape Room is an open-plan office, or a work or study room. Overall, there are six different (working/learning) areas, each equipped with decorative elements like books, papers, writing pads, cups, and pencils. In addition, each of the four stations contains a puzzle for one of the STEM sections:

- Science: understanding the mechanism of a Magic Cup (thermochromism)
- Technology: decoding a Morse code message
- Engineering: completing an electrical circuit (electrical conductivity)
- Mathematics: calculating a rule of three (percentage)

The stations are marked with a customized color and a poster (Fig. 2), on which the addressed STEM subject is explained and general information are presented. Hints are placed at each riddle section to support the process of solving the puzzle, like the poster, postcards with written words, notes on papers or writing pads, and marked sections/texts in books (Fig. 2 and Fig. 3).

Fig. 2. Arrangement of a section poster and a postcard as a hint to solve the puzzle

Fig. 3. Arrangement of the station containing the mathematical riddle

Yet the riddles are not complete on each location. Required objects or parts are sited on other stations. For example, at the puzzle for the Technology field, a word written in Morse code is hidden inside a book thematically related to computer programming, but there is no decoding key. It can be found at the station of the mathematical task in another coding book, although some parts are ripped apart. If using one of the hidden 'hint-objects', one can demand the missing part of the key from the gamemaster if necessary. When a player is not able to connect the Morse code riddle to the technology sector, the poster hints that decoding is a part of this field, can assist. In a riddle flow and dependencies chart (Fig. 4), the puzzles, hints on each station, and the placement of required objects at other areas are visible. Each block represents one station in the setting, jointly leading all together to the meta-riddle and finally the story goal.

After solving each puzzle, the Escape Room visitors receive a number. If all four are collected, the meta-riddle needs to be solved to unlock the tablet and to gain the URL. The numbers have to be ordered correctly considering the term STEM: number of the Science, then Technology, Engineering and finally the Mathematical riddle. At the sixth station, a 3D-printed QR-code is placed in a 3D printer. With the unlocked tablet, the team is now able to scan the code, which leads directly to the requested URL. The story goal is fulfilled. The gamemaster thanks the visitors as he/she accepts the tablet and sees the players off. This text also has to be customized and adapted to the situation and event.

There is no direct 'escape' from the room. The feature of escaping is not actually essential for an Escape Room. Reaching a goal, saving someone, or create something together as a team are also possible endings in Escape Rooms, even in the non-educational sector [6].

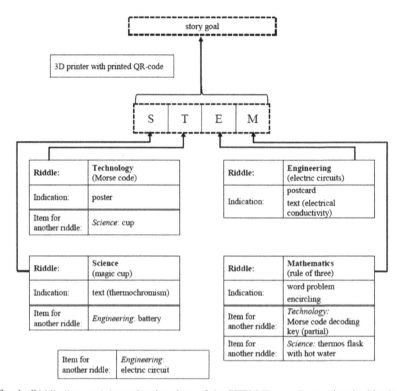

Fig. 4. Riddle flow and dependencies chart of the STEM-Escape Room (inspired by [15])

3.3 Pretest

All experiments, poster, postcards and decorations were self-made or collected. One week before the first execution, a pretest with six work colleagues (five females, one male) took place. The colleagues had knowledge of the Escape Room, but were not aware of the topic or the riddles. The goal of the pretest was to examine the difficulty of the puzzles and the meta-puzzle as well as the designated time frame.

The group needed 27 min to solve the STEM-Escape Room. This is a little bit longer than the intended time slot, given that in real conditions, the room needs to be reset for the next group. In the discussion after the pretest, no one perceived the riddles to be too easy or too difficult. However, they lost a lot of time due to some distractions, which are often part of Escape Rooms [6]. For example, in the corner of a blackboard, a small equation was scribbled as part of the decoration of the room with no ulterior motive. This equation drew more attention than the actual task, which was written in big letters in the middle of the blackboard. Also, an unintended tic-toc-toe doodled on one of the writing pads was considered to be a hidden message. Because of time management, it was noticed to be careful when decorating and enliven the Escape Room.

Another problem was the order of the code of the meta-puzzle. Even hints asked for by the participants did not helped. It had to be explained, how the digits have to be arranged. Therefore, some adjustments were conducted: The locked screen of the tablet was replaced through a self-designed background picture with the message "STEM is the answer". The four letters of the term STEM corresponded with the color of the poster of the four sections. Also, the gamemaster should emphasize in her/his introduction to the story – while (s)he hands over the tablet – that the visitors need S-T-E-M to solve the riddle.

4 Executions of the STEM-Escape Room

4.1 First Performance

In the area of Augsburg, there are plenty of offerings to create an interest in STEM for all different age groups. To give an overview over all these offers, a brochure was published, which should be introduced at a special evening. As part of the social program, the STEM-Escape Room was tested for the first time. About 60 to 70 people at the age over 18 years were expected to register for this event, mainly from fields like politics, press, the education sector, university students, and other interested individuals. It was assumed that not everyone joining the evening has an interest in visiting the Escape Room. In the two hours frame of the social program, a maximum of 40 people was planned to be able to experience the Escape Room.

In total, five different groups visited the STEM-Escape Room. The teams finished the experience in 22 min on average. During all visits, no one required a helping item through a found 'hint-object'. Overall, a (spoken) hint from the gamemaster was requested in six cases. One time, the wrong number was picked at a riddle, which was hinted at by the gamemaster after the question. In another case, the Morse code puzzle could not be related to the correct field of STEM. Only one group did not need any clue to find the correct order of the code of the meta-riddle. The newly added picture as the locking screen has not had the desired effect and also unspecific hints from the gamemaster, which did not address the solution directly, could not lift the difficulties.

4.2 Second Performance

At another event, in which pupils of different kinds of schools and grades took part, the Escape Room was offered a second time as a part of the social program. All together 120 disciples participated in the event, and 53 were able to join the STEM-Escape Room. Every visitor filled out a printed, self-designed and voluntary survey after the attendance to be able to express their acceptance or disapproval towards this kind of format. Among them, there were 25 females and 23 males (diverse: 0, no statement: 5). 16 pupils stated that they visit a secondary modern school, 34 a grammar school. Of the 48 disciples who made statements about their grade, the average age was 15.8 years.

The execution of the Escape Room happened without any incidents. Only one team requested a helping item (the missing part of the Morse code decoding key) through a 'hint-object'. There have been several problems again with the ordering of the from the riddle received numbers. Just one group was able to solve the meta-riddle without specific hints from the gamemaster.

During the survey, other than demographic questions, the pupils were also asked to assess their Escape Room experience by rating statements at a five-point scale, ranging from "do completely agree" to "do not agree at all" (with a possibility of choosing "no statement"). Also, open-ended questions about positive and negative elements of the Escape Room were answered to spot potential improvements preferred by the target group.

5   Results of the Executions of the STEM-Escape Room

5.1   Observations and Conversations at the First Performance

The interest towards the STEM-Escape Room was greater than expected. For the very first execution of the Escape Room, already more than 20 people lined up. The people in charge had to distribute time tickets and raise the size of the team to up to ten visitors per Escape Room experience to meet the sudden rush. The performance was perceived as energy-sapping, especially the gamemaster sensed two hours of extreme liability in this short time, because she/he had to adapt to all the different situations, people and questions. Also, the team responsible for the event outside of the Escape Room often had trouble handling all the requests. This shows the large existing interest from the society towards this format.

In general, a lot of positive feedback was received from the visitors. Because of the time pressure and the extreme rush, only observations and random single conversations were possible to execute. In these talks, most guests admitted that they had not been to an Escape Room before. Therefore, they were excited and motivated to join the experience, since they have had no imagination of the content and process of a STEM-Escape Room. They also mentioned that they see the possible applicability of these kinds of Escape Rooms not only in STEM, but also in other subjects, especially as an introduction, repetition or application of new or/and already learnt substances. Everybody agreed that they are now able to answer the question, what STEM means and which fields this term contains.

From people who had already visited (commercial) Escape Rooms before, the replies were also very affirmative. However, some people criticized elements like the independencies of the puzzles and the short amount of time compared to other non-educational Escape Rooms.

5.2   Evaluation Results from the Second Performance

Compared to the first execution of the STEM-Escape Room, the target group of the second performance were still pupils under the age of 18. 26 of them answered that they had not visited an escape room before. 13 disciples had already attended one, and eight students two Escape Rooms. Six people did not answer this question.

The visitors were asked to rate the statement "I liked the visit in the STEM-Escape Room" (Fig. 5). 81.3% of the consulted disciples agreed, that they liked or liked the visit in the Escape Room very much, whereas 15.1% saw this statement neutral. Two people (3.8%) disagreed.

A similar result was received to the statement "I had fun in the STEM-Escape Room" (Fig. 6), which once again 81.13% of the questioned students approved of. Compared

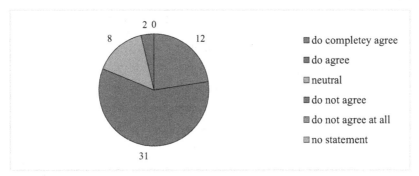

Fig. 5. Overview of the ratings towards the statement "I liked the visit in the STEM-Escape Room."

to the first question, seven more pupils agreed completely than only consented with this proposition. Also, eight people (15.1%) held a neutral attitude again; there was one (1.9%) disagreement and one (1.9%) abstention.

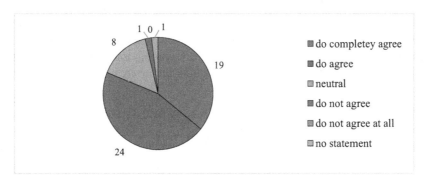

Fig. 6. Overview of the ratings towards the statement "I had fun in the STEM-Escape Room."

73.6% (17 totally agree, 22 agree) stated that the teamwork functioned well. However, 5.7% (do not agree: 2, do not agree at all: 1) disapproved this statement, the same amount of people who valued this declaration neutral. One person did not want to rate. The proposition "I was able to include myself in the solving process of the riddle" was rated a little bit more in a negative way which probably can be related to the increased team size: 71.7% agreed (38 people), 17% (nine people) kept a neutral attitude and 9.4% (five people) disagreed or disagreed totally. Once again there was one abstention. Nevertheless, 39 (73.6%) of 53 people would recommend a visit in the STEM-Escape Room, 12 pupils (22.6%) rated it neutral. There was one disapproval and one abstention.

At the open-ended question "What appealed to you specifically?", 37 answers were received. In these replies, various statements were brought up, which are listed in the following table regarding the frequency of their references (Table 1).

In summary, all four puzzles were mentioned at least once. Especially the experiment in the science sector, the riddle about the magical thermochromic cup, was brought up

Table 1. References to the question "What appealed to you specifically?"

"What appealed to you specifically?"	Mentions
Science experiment ("magic cup")	7
Engineering experiment ("electrical circuit")	6
Many topics/riddles in a short amount of time	5
Working together with other people	5
Technology experiment ("Morse code")	4
Practice	3
Searching and finding things	2
Understandable and solvable tasks	2
Working with digital tools	2
Mathematical riddle ("rule of three")	1
Pens	1
Time pressure	1

seven times, followed by the engineering experiment with seven votes (technology: four votes, mathematic: one vote). Also, the aspect of working together as a team and the variety of topics and riddles in this short amount of time were brought up five times by

Table 2. References to the question "What did you miss?"

"What did you miss?"	Mentions
Nothing	6
Dependency of the riddles	4
More rooms	2
Result	2
Action	1
Difficulty	1
More distinct instructions	1
More exciting setting	1
More riddles	1
My friends	1
Teamwork	1
The feeling of 'escaping'	1
Time	1
Too many people	1

the pupils. Other answers referred to e.g. the first-hand experiences (practice), puzzle types (search and find) or the handling with digital devices.

In addition, the consulted students answered the question "What did you miss?" 21 times. 14 different mentions were received (Table 2). Some people did not miss anything, and the independency of the riddles/the open riddle organization was criticized the most with four mentions. Another annotation was a request for more rooms. One answer mentioned the missing feeling of having to 'escape' – which could be attributed to the lack of having to change rooms, and which does not exist and is not intended in this first concept of the STEM-Escape Room. Furthermore, the goal of finding the URL, was not a satisfying story goal for two students. More elements people missed were e.g. a tangible setting, more action, more tasks, or a more complex difficulty.

6 Discussion and Conclusion

This paper examines the first attempt to concept, build, and test a self-designed STEM-Escape Room as a possible format of knowledge transfer to the society.

Because of the time management and the time pressure during the first execution of the STEM-Escape Room, a more quantitative evaluation was not possible and therefore only observations and conversations of and with the visitors of the first test are available. The second performance – with another part of the targeted group – demonstrates interesting information and assessments.

Due to various conditions, decisions of the riddle organization, puzzle number, game setting and role of the gamemaster have had to be made. These choices were partially criticized by the second tested part of the target group. Building an Escape Room that satisfies the preferences of the society through all age groups will face many challenges, especially in terms of the setting, story goal, riddle design, puzzle organization and difficulty. A more adaptive setting design and/or different kinds of (riddle) complexity could be taken into account, depending on the compilation of the target group, their previous knowledge towards the addressed topic and maybe preexisting experiences in other Escape Rooms. As an important step to offer the Escape Room more independently, a digitalization of the gamemaster is already planned.

Considering the positive feedback from the first test and the evaluation results of the second execution, a self-made Escape Room – resting upon the concept of Game-Based learning – seems to be perceived by the target group as an accepted format of possible scientific knowledge transfer into society.

References

1. Rauter, R.: Interorganisationaler Wissenstransfer. Zusammenarbeit zwischen Forschungsein-richtungen und KMU. Springer, Wiesbaden (2013). https://doi.org/10.1007/978-3-658-009 27-4
2. Kanning, H., Meyer, C.: Verständnisse und Bedeutungen des Wissenstransfers für Forschung und Bildung im Kontext einer Großen Transformation. In: Abassiharofteh, M., et al. (eds.) Räumliche Transformation: Prozesse, Konzepte, Forschungsdesigns, pp. 9–28. Verlag der ARL-Akademie für Raumforschung und Landesplanung, Hannover (2019)

3. Weitze, M.-D, Heckl, W.M.: Wissenschaftskommunikation – Schlüsselideen, Akteure, Fall-beispiele, 1st edn. Springer Spektrum, Heidelberg (2016). https://doi.org/10.1007/978-3-662-47843-1

4. Abt, C.: Serious Games. University Press of America, Boston (1987)

5. Michael, D.R., Chen, S.L.: Serious Games – Games That Educate, Train, and Inform. Course Technology, Mason (2006)

6. Nicholson, S.: The state of the escape: escape room design and facilities. Paper Presented at Meaningful Play 2016. Lansing, Michigan (2016). http://scottnicholson.com/pubs/stateofescape.pdf. Accessed 03 Apr 2020

7. Corkill, E.: Real Escape Game brings its creator's wonderment to life. The Japan Times Online (2009). https://www.japantimes.co.jp/life/2009/12/20/general/real-escape-game-brings-its-creators-wonderment-to-life/#.Xocyd0pCQ2x. Accessed 03 Apr 2020

8. Bakhsheshi, F.F.: Serious games and serious gaming in escape rooms. In: International Serious Games Symposium (ISGS), pp. 42–47 (2019)

9. Wilms, M.: Serious Games – Anwendung digitaler Spiele, insbesondere in den Bereichen Training, Bildung und HealthCare. GRIN, Munich (2009)

10. Le, S., Weber, P., Ebner, M.: Game-based learning. Spielend lernen? In: Ebner, M., Schön, S. (eds.) Lehrbuch für Lernen und Lehren mit Technologien, 2nd edn., pp. 219–228. epubli GmbH, Berlin (2013)

11. Glavaš, A., Staščik, A.: Enhancing positive attitude towards mathematics through introducing Escape Room Games. In: Kolar-Begovic, Z., Kolar-Super, R., Jukic Matic, L. (eds.) Mathematics Education as a Science and Profession, pp. 201–294. Faculty of Education, Department of Mathematics (2017)

12. Hermanns, M., et al.: Using an 'Escape Room' toolbox approach to enhance pharmacology education. J. Nurs. Educ. Pract. **8**(4), 89–95 (2017)

13. Komm mach MINT: Das zählt zu MINT. https://www.komm-mach-mint.de/service/mint-datentool/das-zaehlt-zu-mint. Accessed 14 May 2020

14. acatech, Körberstiftung (eds.): MINT Nachwuchsbarometer. Gutenberg Beuys Feindruckerei, Hannover (2020)

15. Borrego, C., Fernández, C., Blanes, I., Robles, S.: Room escape at class: escape games activities to facilitate the motivation and learning in computer science. J. Technol. Sci. Educ. **7**(2), 162–171 (2017)

Bridging the Cyber Security Skills Gap: Using Tabletop Exercises to Solve the CSSG Crisis

Giddeon N. Angafor[1]($\boxtimes$) (iD), Iryna Yevseyeva[1] (iD), and Ying He[2] (iD)

[1] De Montfort University, Leicester, UK
giddeon.angafor@my365.dmu.ac.uk
[2] Nottingham University, Leicester, UK

Abstract. Recent breaches like the WannaCry ransomware attack in 2017 are evidence of the rapidly evolving cyber security threat landscape. They demonstrate the ability of cybercriminals to take down individuals and businesses efficiently. This is an indication that few companies can sustain these challenges due to a shortage of professionals with essential specialist cyber security skills. It puts into perspective the urgent need to train and nurture new graduates who possess the minimum qualifications and aptitudes required in the cyber security profession. This study investigates the current cyber security skills gap (CSSG). It observes that cyber security skills are high in demand, yet short in supply, with employers facing problems attracting skilled personnel to fill the ever-growing cyber security roles within their businesses. The study noted that while there are some attempts to address the CSSG through education and training, some recruiting managers held that many cyber security graduates lacked essential business sustaining skills. It observed that graduates focused more on technical skills like hacking while ignoring critical, practical, hands-on abilities. The study identified 5 features of the CSSG and argued that they can be addressed through a serious games (SGs) training approach. This method makes use of SG elements like tabletop exercises (TTXs) which nurture and enhance practical hands-on skills. TTXs enhance the development of skills like problem-solving, communication, teamwork and business processes understanding thereby enabling cyber security incident teams (CSIRTs) to conduct their daily activities unperturbed.

Keywords: Cyber security · Cyber security skills gap · Serious games · Game-based learning · Tabletop exercises · Tabletop serious games

1 Introduction

Cybercrimes, including breaches of data and attacks on critical national infrastructure, are growing in number and sophistication. However, there are not enough people with the right skills needed to defend against these transnationals and continually evolving threats. The global shortage of skilled cyber security professionals, otherwise referred to as the CSSG has enormous consequences on individuals, enterprises, and nation-states [1]. Reference [2] ascertains that the cyber security workforce gap is bound to reach 1.8 million by 2022, a 20% increase from the predictions in 2015. With the inability to recruit

© Springer Nature Switzerland AG 2020
M. Ma et al. (Eds.): JCSG 2020, LNCS 12434, pp. 117–131, 2020.
https://doi.org/10.1007/978-3-030-61814-8_10

and retain skilled cyber personnel, many organisations are left exposed to cyber threats of all sorts. There are many attempts to find solutions to these dilemmas. Government agencies, education institutions and training providers are advocating for more uptake of college and university courses in cyber security-related disciplines. However, [3] and [4] argue that current teaching methods are too traditional, often out of date and not focusing on the right skills. Some organisations within the industry are pushing for cyber security certifications as a minimum requirement for candidates and new graduates into the cyber security profession. Despite that, [5] and [6] contend that cyber security certifications are mostly theory-oriented and are often too costly, especially for small and medium-sized enterprises. They also do not equip new entrants into the profession with the essential skills required for employability. Given these challenges, there is a need for an urgent and affordable solution to filling the CSSG. Such a solution should be balanced and cost-effective, with a possibility to respond to some of the challenges raised in this background statement, but also open for improvement.

The answer to such a challenge according to [7] could be found in serious games SGs or game-based learning (GBL) and training. SGs are games that are not primarily focused on entertainment, enjoyment, or pure fun [8]. They are games designed and used for education or training. Studies indicate that the intentional use of games as learning tools is not new. For example, study [9] held that non-digital games have previously been used for learning social, physical, and psychological skills, such as coping with the emotions, learning the ground rules for appropriate behaviours amongst others. Reference [10] elaborate that SGs and GBL are varied and wide-ranging, they include but are not limited to simulations, role-playing games, board games, TTXs, and other exercises, in both digital and non-digital formats. SGs and GBL approaches have been used as effective teaching and learning tools. Study [9] noted that SGs are used widely outside of formal education systems. They observed that SGs are utilised by the military, as well as within the transport and in the health and commerce sectors. They hold that SGs and GBL are interactive and engaging, making use of immersive activities which enthuse and motivate trainees far beyond classroom learning. Similarly, [7] argue that SGs are particularly effective in promoting skill acquisition, helping with knowledge retention, and supporting the understanding of new concepts and ideas. According to reference [11], SGs also help in shaping behaviours and improving context-based problem-solving. Reference [12] argues that GBL programs are good for education because they provide good staging grounds where students or participants can safely experiment without being afraid, should they get it wrong. This suggests that SGs, like TTXs, have the potential to be deployed as effective teaching and learning tools to help solve the CSSG crisis.

The motivation for the study is to conduct a general review of the CSSG to understand what it is and highlight its main features or manifestations. The study also explores the concept of SGs, with an emphasis on TTXs which are one category of SGs. It will elaborate on how TTXs, which are otherwise referred to as tabletop serious games (TTSGs) offer viable solutions for education and training within academia and the cyber security industry and have the potential to help reduce the CSSG. They are called TTXs or TTSGs because those involved in the exercises sit at or gather around a table to participate. Reference [13] holds that SGs such as TTXs are a common phenomenon in education, corporate training, military training, healthcare, public management training amongst others as they encourage problem-solving abilities.

This paper makes the following contributions: It reviews and categorises the CSSG challenge into five distinct topic areas, namely: a problem of global cyber personnel shortage, obsolete or inadequate training, skills mismatch, finance, and diversity of gender and race. It introduces the concept of SGs and gives a brief overview of TTXs or TTSGs, which are a subset of SGs and outlines how they have the potential to provide a practical, low-cost solution to the CSSG crisis.

The rest of the paper is structured as follows: Sect. 2 provides a discussion of the literature search criteria employed in the study. In Sect. 3, there is an overview of the CSSG, including its main features and some challenges it poses for the security industry. Section 4 introduces the concept of SGs and elaborates on TTXs. Section 5 explains how TTX or TTSGs can contribute to bridging the CSSG. Finally, Sect. 6 concludes the study.

2   Literature Search Method

The main aim of the research is to find out what the CSSG is and how to it can be addressed. It seeks to establish whether SGs programs like TTXs can provide solutions to the CSSG crisis. The specific questions which this paper seeks to answer are as follows:

1. RQ1: What is the cyber security skills gap?
2. RQ2: How is the cyber security skills gap manifested?
3. RQ3: What are TTSGs, and what contribution can they make in the CSSG crisis?

To find answers to these questions, a literature search was conducted in May 2020 using the SCOPUS academic database and a generic Google search. The searches targeted articles published in English using the search criteria of 'Cyber security Skills Gap', 'Cyber security Workforce Shortage' and 'Cyber security Skills Challenge'. The SCOPUS database search returned 842 articles related to the search criteria. Once all duplicates and irrelevant articles were removed, the authors were left with 122 articles. These papers were reviewed by title and abstract, and those that were not clear, and further understanding was required were considered in full. After the review, the researchers established that 90 articles were not explicitly related to the subject of cyber security skills or workforce shortage. We reviewed the remaining 32 articles and found that 6 were related to general cyber security awareness, while 7 dealt with the theme of skills tests and assessments. This evaluation left us with 19 articles, of which 15 discussed the cyber security skills or workforce gap to a reasonable degree. All items included in the study had to treat the subject matter of outlet in the search criteria to a considerable depth. The relevant articles from the search highlighted what the CSSG is and its 5 key themes or features which are discussed in the proceeding sections.

3   What Is the CSSG?

Many studies have attempted to define the CSSG. Reference [14] holds that it relates to the fact that there are not enough people with the skills required to meet the cyber security needs of businesses and organisations seeking such skills. Reference [15] argues that the CSSG is to do with the fact that cyber security skills are high in demand, yet short in supply. In this regard, the CSSG is the struggle to recruit and retain skilled security personnel to proactively defend against a rapidly evolving and often transnational cyber threat landscape. It is related to increased global competition for scarce specialist cyber security skills. Reference [16] states that the CSSG extends beyond just finding enough skilled personnel to meet current cyber security business demands. It includes the challenges faced by education and training institutions to keep pace with the growing demand for cyber talent with required employability skills.

The CSSG, also known as the cyber workforce shortage, is the 'headache' of the cyber security industry. Reference [17] describes it as 'troubling', arguing that the need for cyber security skills is exceedingly high and urgent. Irrespective of that, there are not enough skilled cyber security professionals to deal with an increasing number of attacks. Study [18] upholds that though cyber security personnel like penetration testers and ethical hackers are vital in protecting a business from attacks like a data breach, organisations find that employees with these skills are scarce to find, let alone to retain. He adds that the cyber security market is suffering a severe workforce shortage worldwide, with approximately two million jobs that are currently vacant. This workforce shortage is leaving businesses exposed to attacks of their sensitive data [18]. A study by [19] found that the current ratio of existing cyber security workers to cyber security job openings in the US is 2.3, compared to the national average of 5.8 for all jobs.

4   Features of the CSSG

Several academic studies, policy documents and company whitepapers are available about the CSSG, and they discuss various features of the dilemma. While [14] and [15] have attempted to define and contextualise the problem, [16, 20], and [21] have articulated some of the main challenges posed by CSSG. This section provides a summary of the CSSG under 5 distinct categories, which include the global workforce shortage, outdated or inadequate skills training, skills mismatch, diversity disproportion and financial limitations.

4.1   Global Workforce Shortage

The first and most prominent feature of the CSSG is the global shortage of skilled cyber security personnel. Reference [20] maintains that the worldwide shortage of cyber security professionals is close to 3 million. Due to this worldwide shortfall, cyber security hiring companies are looking for a wide range of skills and aptitudes. The abilities in demand include relevant work experience and cyber security certifications for cyber incident response (CIR) personnel, but many businesses are unable to fill existing vacancies. According to [15] more than 1.5 million cyber security jobs were left unfilled in 2019. In the US alone, more than 40,000 jobs for information security analysts go unfilled every year while a further 200,000 other cyber security-related roles are also left vacant [22]. Reference [23] reports that many businesses are unable to attract applicants to fill advertised positions, while [24] states that this is because technically proficient cyber security professionals are difficult to find. Moreover, it is not easy to retain qualified cyber security specialists, even in cases where there is an enticement of employer-paid training and certifications [24]. Reference [25] elaborates that fewer than 7 jobseekers clicked on every 10 cyber security jobs advertised on their international jobs' website and less than this number got to the stage of applying for the advertised role. Many cyber security experts report that due to the CSSG they have contact from recruiters seeking candidates for new positions daily [20].

The cyber security workforce scarcity remains a critical challenge for businesses and nation-states across the globe. In a survey of eight countries, Australia, France, Germany, Israel, Japan, Mexico, the United Kingdom (UK), and the United States (US), 71% of respondents attested that the CSSG had direct and measurable damage to business [26]. Besides that, one in three respondents confirmed that a shortage of CIR skills made their organisations more susceptible to cyber-attacks by criminal gangs. Others stated that the lack of cyber security staff with the right skills and expertise to defend against cyber threats has damaged their business's reputation and, in some cases, resulted to the loss of customer and other proprietary data [26].

4.2 Outdated or Inadequate Education

Reference [27] states that another characteristic of the CSSG is the issue of inadequate training. He maintains that current cyber security training is too traditional, boring, out of context and way too long. References [5] and [4] insist that cyber security training must evolve; otherwise, it will not be effective in helping businesses to fight against cyber threats which they experience. Studies [27] and [5] clarify that the main reason why many trainees often get distracted a few minutes into the training sessions is that it is not captivating. According to [21] and [22], the way new entrants into the profession are taught, both at university and during certification training, does not match to the evolving cyber threat landscape. They hold that training must offer opportunities for users to interact and practice what they have learnt from the theory, or else it would not adequately prepare them for the challenges of the industry [27]. Reference [4] attests that practice-based training helps trainees to put theory and concepts learnt in the classroom or from books to use, and by so doing, they develop the right skills for the job. Reference [28] agrees with this observation. They expound that training which offers practical, interactive learning experiences allows learners to blend theory and practice. Moreover, it reinforces students' understanding of what they already know and helps them develop critical thinking skills.

The current cyber threat landscape requires a blend of training and education approaches which allow trainees to learn in practical, real-world environments, rather than purely in a classroom. Such training should be innovative, proactive, and hands-on. It should offer trainees opportunities to learn at their own pace, which is something that is not usually possible in a classroom setting [5]. Besides that, the training must be agile, occurring often, and continuously being adapted because cyber threats are always evolving. Such approaches are beyond what the current methods used for certification and periodic training are offering. Most of the current programs are classroom intensive, using static measurements of skills and cannot keep pace with new cyber threats and technologies which are continually changing [5]. The new type of training should be fit for purpose and offer opportunities to practice and harness adaptive problem-solving skills which some recruiters argue are lacking for new graduates.

4.3 Skills Misalliance or Miscues

The issue of skills mismatch, especially the tendency for candidates to focus mainly on technical skills while ignoring critical nontechnical skills, is another feature of the CSSG. Reference [22] notes that this tendency is especially noticeable in many new graduates who appear to concentrate on technical skills while overlooking soft business sustaining aptitudes. Many graduates and aspiring professionals aiming to pursue a career in cyber security concentrate mainly on the "hacking" domain because they want to pursue a career as an Ethical Hacker. However, they fail to realise that the ethical hacking field is not the one in the highest demand [22]. The concentration on purely technical skills presents a dilemma for recruiters, businesses, and candidates. When this happens, recruiters judge candidates as not having the rights skills for the job. Equally, candidates end up without an appointment while vacancies continue to increase. In a survey of 461 cyber security managers and practitioners, 75% of participants indicated that the primary skills gap identified during cyber security candidates' interviews was a lack of fundamental soft skills. They observed that many applicants were not able to describe simple business processes. Besides that, a good number failed to explain why an understanding of business processes is a crucial skill required for cyber security professionals [24]. References [22] and [24] claimed that by failing to link security and business, many candidates failed to realise that the job of security is to protect the business, ensuring its profitability and continuity. Reference [22] reiterates the importance of having the right skills mix by asserting that in the cyber security domain, those who can talk the 'business lingo' and translate security into real benefit for the business can see their career and their compensation progress fast and high.

Reference [29] insists that organisations looking to build an efficient CSIRT, with successful incident handling capabilities requires people with a diverse set of skills. Such abilities must encompass technical and soft skills as both are necessary, and neither is enough [30]. CSIRT members should have skills that enable them to respond to incidents, including those required to perform incident analysis, document, and communicate the results with colleagues and stakeholders. Besides that, they must also be skilled problem solvers, who understand business processes. Reference [6] argues that technical ability alone, while a fundamental requirement for many security professions, is not enough if not complemented by the ability to align security with business requirements and to communicate security issues to decision-makers. The authors uphold that, to a certain extent, technical skill can be more easily taught and developed in isolation, whereas business sustaining soft skills come from practical experience and interaction within the industry. Reference [24] elaborates that although the cyber security field has a great need for technical competence and qualifications, it also suffers from a lack of business comprehension. Both [6] and [24] agree that it is not enough for cyber security staff to only be technically proficient. They must also be able to understand business processes so that they can align security to these business goals.

4.4 Lack of Diversity in the Workforce

Another feature of the CSSG is the lack of diversity of age, gender, and race within the workforce. Reference [20] argues that the broader cyber security workforce appears to be younger and more diverse than previously reported. Despite that, [31] contends that the diversity challenge is a huge problem. It includes the underrepresentation of women, the younger generation, and ethnic minorities. Due to the diversity disparity 'Baby Boomers', people born between 1944 and 1964 and 'Gen X', those born between 1965 and 1979 make up 49%, almost half of the cyber security workforce. Unlike, 'Gen Y' or 'Millennials', those born between 1980 and 1994 who comprise 35% of the field [20]. Women, who represent close to 50% of the overall population and global workforce, constitute only 11% or less of the cyber security workforce [32]. The figures for ethnic minorities are almost non-existent, which is an indication that representation among this group is insignificant, or there is no research in this area.

Reference [5] observed that the vast age gap is a clue that too few young people are making it through the doors into the cyber security sector. The problem of low numbers of women the authors argue is due to women choosing to leave a male-dominated profession [31]. They insist that women encounter gender biases which are especially widespread where the women were ethnic minorities such as being women of colour. This revelation is unfortunate in an industry which is becoming increasingly diverse and requires a suitably diverse workforce to meet increasing demand. It explains why [33] contends that the cyber security industry, must consider candidates from a variety of demographic groups, irrespective of age, social background, gender, ethnicity, disability, or sexual orientation. Without such diversification, the CSSG will continue to grow while an already struggling workforce may find it hard to serve the needs of communities underrepresented within the industry.

4.5 Financial Conundrum

The last of the 5 features of the CSSG is the financial puzzle. While it presents an opportunity for some, it is also a severe challenge for many businesses. This dilemma is noticeable, especially in the areas of recruitment, remuneration, retention, and training of cyber security personnel. References [34] and [35] argue that due to the CSSG, there is a very high demand for cyber security professionals than for other IT disciplines. As a result, businesses with substantial financial capacity, who can afford to pay top salaries have an advantage as they can afford to hire and retain highly skilled staff.

Meanwhile, those with limited financial resources struggle to hire and retain qualified cyber security personnel. Study [35] attested that businesses in the private sector that could afford to pay top salaries were able to hire highly skilled cyber security staff. On the other hand, many enterprises within the public sector known historically for paying lower wages struggled to employ suitably qualified staff.

The financial challenge is not limited to hiring; it extends to staff retention, ongoing training, and professional development issues. The high demand for skilled cyber personnel meant that those in less paying roles are targets to be headhunted. Study [35] confirmed that private sector businesses with a capacity to offer attractive pay, excellent allowances and expensive training packages commanded an advantage over those less financially viable in the search for skilled cyber security staff. Reference [26] agreed with this observation by stating that companies which hired cyber security staff without investing the time and money to develop those employees' skills to meet the changing cyber security challenges had a high staff turnover. The high turnover was a common factor in organisations which were small and not well resourced. Cyber security staff in these companies were much less qualified than those in businesses which are larger and better resourced [26]. Big and medium-sized companies had much less trouble hiring security operations staff, with just 38% reporting problems compared to 75% of respondents from small companies. This mixed fortune is a clear indication that the CSSG is a financial double-edged sword which can work in favour of businesses with sound financial resources and a severe challenge for those with limited monetary power.

5   TTXs or TTSGs

While the facts and figures about the CSSG are a huge concern, there are solutions which can be applied to remedy the situation. One such solution is practical training 'from within' or on the job training, which [19] asserts, is more beneficial. They suggest that 'on the job' training in cyber security is advantageous as it adds more human resources into an industry in need of staff without sacrificing speed or compromising on the security and compliance of businesses. Study [19] indicates that SGs elements like TTXs provide perfect training tools for new graduates and those already on the job and can help in addressing the CSSG.

TTXs or TTSGs are staged events where management and staff meet in an open forum to discuss actions for a response to a specific emergency scenario [36]. The informal format of TTXs eases participation and is structured to explore emergency procedures, recovery plan details, standard operating procedures and personnel resources required to recover critical functions in the event of a disaster [36]. Reference [37] clarified that the name 'tabletop exercise' came into existence because those involved with the exercises sit down at the table or gather around a table to execute them. TTXs provide opportunities for professionals, especially in CIR roles, to test their processes and procedures to identify what works well and what needs improvement. Reference [38] states that a TTX is a low-stress meeting environment where pre-defined incidents are discussed openly. They are a forum where participants deliberate and identify who will make decisions, review the impact of those decisions, and outline how each team will react to different real-world scenarios. Reference [39] maintained that TTXs are facilitated group discussions that simulate an emergency scenario in an informal, stress-free environment. TTXs sometimes make use of board game systems to strengthen the readiness to manage emergency incidents. They enable organisations to evaluate their incident response preparedness and help participants to practice and hone the skills which they need to perform their roles in an emergency response situation [39]. In the context of this study, TTXs are exercises and learning events used by cyber security and other incident response or emergency personnel to discuss, practice and refine procedures for dealing with an emergency. These may include but are not limited to practical hands-on exercises which use games and simulations, both in digital and non-digital forms [10].

TTXs are a category of SGs, when compared to other SGs they are often discussion-based, with participants and key personnel undertaking a role-play or discussing simulated scenarios in an informal setting [40]. TTXs can be used to assess plans, policies, and procedures to see what works well and what needs improving. On the other hand, most SGs currently developed for cyber security include a simulation of operations that often involves two or more teams. Moreover, such SGs usually take the form of a competition with scenarios involving threat actors and defenders, bound by rules, data, and procedures designed to depict an actual or assumed real-life situation [40]. Furthermore, such SGs incorporate game dynamics, which [41] argues include activities such as rankings, the collection of rewards such as badges or points systems. As opposed to TTXs which are mainly geared towards the validation of plans, policies, procedures, the clarification of roles and responsibilities, and identifying resource gaps, most of SGs tend to animate and motivate the players especially when participants have to collect as many coins as possible, obtain as many lives as possible or pass through to the highest level [41]. Despite that, TTXs are a category of SGs and share many common characteristics. They are designed in both digital and non-digital forms, with applications and activities used for purposes other than entertainment. SGs, including TTXs, offer educational content to users in an enjoyable way, using various approaches such as role-play, discussions and simulating scenarios which promote learning [42].

Table 1 below gives an outline of some of the features of TTXs or TTSGs and brief descriptions of the skills which they nurture.

Table 1. TTXs and their features

Features & Activities	Technical	Nontechnical	Reference
Planning, discussion, reviews and, improvement of resilience and readiness plans and procedures	Sometimes	Yes	[29, 30, 32, 33]
Review and improvement of skills and abilities of CSIRTs	Yes	Yes	[32, 34, 35]
Practicing and improving crisis management coordination, alert prioritisation, escalation procedures, crisis communication and crisis reporting strategies	Yes	Yes	[30, 32, 33, 36]
Reviewing and practicing handling and operation of tools and application used for incident response	Yes	Yes	[34, 37]
Practicing and familiarisation with different roles and responsibilities to be undertaken during an emergency incident	Sometimes	Yes	[14, 29, 34, 37]

Research into TTXs for cyber security education and training suggests that they could be useful in addressing the CSSG challenge. Study [43] argues that TTX programs provide tools and approaches which support a constructive learning environment. They contend that TTXs offer broad pedagogical benefits when designed and used as part of a comprehensive teaching method. Sections 5.1–5.4 explain why TTXs or TTSGs provide a viable solution to the CSSG.

5.1 TTX Encourage the Acquisition of Practical Experience

TTXs training programs are vital solutions to the CSSG because they have a track record of nurturing hands-on, experiential learning which is a useful tool in understanding how to defend information systems [44]. Reference [45] elaborates that TTSGs offer real-life cyber exercises which teach cyber security skills without putting businesses and their networks at significant risk. This element is essential because current cyber security training methods have been criticised for being too traditional. They have been condemned for being obsolete and too theory-oriented [43], and for not offering opportunities for experiential learning [5]. Practical hands-on experiences like those provided by TTXs are significant. Study [46] upholds that TTXs give students opportunities to extend learning beyond traditional lecture-based methods. References [37, 46], and [47] contend that TTXs enable participants to improve their skills in protecting and defending information systems in the context of a practical, real-life scenarios. They empower trainees with hands-on experience which they can demonstrate at interview to secure employment, thereby reducing the cyber workforce gap.

Studies [5, 15, 20] and [22] argued that TTXs are what is needed in the struggle to close the cyber workforce demand and supply gap. They contend that by enabling acquisition of practical experience, TTXs help trainees to blend practical, academic, and theoretical knowledge. Obtaining such knowledge and testing them by certifications is an urgent step towards addressing the CSSG. They provide an effective way of increasing the headcount in the cyber workforce which is in dire need of qualified professionals [48].

5.2 TTXs Nurture Both Technical and Soft Skills

A feature of TTXs which indicates they can help in reducing the CSSG is their ability to nurture diverse skills. TTXs assist with the acquisition of technical and non-technical skills which are necessary for a career in cyber security. TTSGs, especially those with full live scenarios dealing with technical issues such as network attacks allow participating businesses to evaluate both their technical abilities and their security postures [37]. They also provide opportunities to enhance a business' technical prowess, helping trainees to nurture the skills to defend critical assets, like data, and to respond more effectively to real-world cyber security incidents when they occur. Reference [49] admits that TTXs play a crucial role in testing the technical cyber capacity of many businesses, nation-states and non-profit organisations. TTXs for CIR have the capability of teaching technical proficiencies such as analysis, tools and techniques used when dealing with incidents, including where and when to deploy them [50].

TTX training programs teach soft skills like business process understanding [22]. They nurture interpersonal skills such as incident reporting to stakeholders and inter-action with related departments [51]. This characteristic of TTXs supports its case as a solution to the CSSG. Study [22] established that graduates and young professionals focused more time on the mastery of technical expertise while ignoring business-critical soft skills like communication and interaction which [51] insisted is what most hiring managers desired. According to [52], cyber security staff need to develop both technical and soft skills as technical knowledge alone is insufficient for today's cyber industry. Reference [30] noted that efficient cyber security teams are those with a blend of technical and business sustaining soft skills like communication. This observation confirms that TTXs have a pivotal role in the race to reduce the CSSG. They can help in the development of both technical and soft skills. Besides that, TTXs support astute technical personnel to master skills in protecting the confidentiality, availability, and integrity of data [51]. They also encourage the development of communication skills, enabling participants to discuss cyber threats to less technologically savvy decision-makers, those in administration, human resource management and other departments in a language that they understand [52].

5.3 TTXs Provide Opportunities for Reflective Practice

TTXs provide challenge and opportunities for reflection, enabling participants to self-review and improve as they train. Study [53] found that a significant factor in TTXs is that they can be made more challenging by adding multiple events or injects to force participants to think out of the box. By doing this, the participants are encouraged to find alternative ways of dealing with the scenarios they are addressing. TTX facilitators often introduce event variations into the exercise process. Reference [10] maintain that these enable training facilitators to test specific objectives set in the exercise and encourage participants to reflect about possible solutions to the problems at hand, including the steps taken to arrive at these as well as any alternative solutions [53]. Facilitators can choose to limit available time to complete tasks or add unforeseen complications to scenarios to encourage reflective practice and calculated risk-oriented responses.

TTX training also provides opportunities to test resources available to drill responders to ensure that they are in good working order. They help participants to identify areas for improvements in incident or disaster preparedness plans, including practicing and understanding or clarifying communication channels [54]. Study [37] upholds that TTX related training encourages continuous reviews as well as process improvement practices because they open avenues for CSIRTs to assess their processes and procedures to ascertain what works well and what needs improvement. This finding is an excellent reason to implement TTX training approaches as part of the solution to the CSSG because cyber threats are continually evolving, making it possible for criminals to improve their malicious exploits and charge ahead of security professionals [21]. As TTX training offers opportunities for reviews and improvement, including adapting incident response processes and skills, it sounds plausible to consider them as solutions to the fast-changing cyber threat landscape. Such a move is beneficial because one of the criticisms advanced by [5] and [27] is that classroom training is not readily adaptable, making it difficult for security staff to adjust to the always-changing tactics employed by cyber gangs.

5.4 TTXs Are Cost-Effective and Affordable

TTXs are cost-effective; they can be planned, resourced, and executed without incurring the same expenses associated with deploying resources in a functional drill or undertaking classroom-based or other training [55]. The low cost enables small businesses and charitable organisations that are not able to afford expensive staff training to tailor instruction to their needs [35]. [56] remarks that a significant advantage of TTXs is that they are inexpensive and have very few practical limitations as almost any scenario can form part of the training exercise. This view has been endorsed by [57] who claimed that a TTX is a useful training tool because they are a reasonably cost-efficient way to prepare personnel to respond to emergencies.

[50] holds that TTSGs are relatively straightforward, they can be planned faster and in a shorter time than other types of SGs. This observation is fitting as another criticism of current cyber security education and training at college or university is that the methods are often out of date. That they are not flexible or easily adaptable and, therefore, always playing catchup to the continually changing cyber threat landscape [5]. Some have advocated for a change, insisting that teaching and training methods must be agile and adaptable, and affordable, so that they can keep pace with new and developing cyber threats that even experienced and well-established security professionals are unfamiliar with [5]. Due to their flexible ability, TTXs can be structured to exercise sections of a business' emergency plan or the entire plan. Study [55] expounds that the idea of flexibility and adaptability suggests that TTXs training encourages students to consider different creative approaches to an IT security incident. They assert that this is very significant as there may be multiple correct solutions when dealing with a real-life cyber incident and several uncertainties and interdependencies need to be considered [55].

6 Conclusion

This paper reviewed the CSSG dilemma. It noted that cyber threats continue to grow in number and complexity. At the same time, companies experienced a persistent challenge in recruiting skilled cyber security professionals capable of protecting their systems against cyber threats [16]. It advanced that the CSSG can be classified into five key areas including global cyber security workforce shortage, outdated training, skills misalignment, lack of workforce diversity, especially in the areas of age, gender, and ethnicity as well as financial issues. The study maintained that cyber security scholars and security professionals within the industry agree that there is a need for an innovative training approach which can help to bridge the CSSG. It observed that there are some attempts in both academia and within the cyber security industry to plug the cyber workforce gap through education and training. Despite that, it remarks that some of the currently pursued training approaches have not been adequate and, therefore, not concretely addressing the CSSG.

It maintained that based on evidence from existing research the best way to meet the needs of the industry and reduce the CSSG is to pursue a practical hands-on training approach facilitated by SGs, especially a TTX game-based learning approach. TTXSG elements can contribute solutions to some of the gaps and challenges posed by the CSSG dilemma. They can provide opportunities for participants to harness both technical and business sustaining skills, like cyber threat analysis and incident response communication across departments. TTXs can give an understanding of cyber threat detection tools, including their usage, business process understanding, collaboration and communications skills amongst others, which are issues that worsen the CSSG crisis. They are cost-effective and can be easily adapted to different training environments and scenarios which lessens the financial burden experienced by many small businesses and those in the public sector where budgets are tight.

References

1. Buvat, J., Turner, M., Puttur, R.K., Slatter, M.: Cybersecurity talent: the big gap in cyber protection. Capgemini Digital Transformation Institute (2018)
2. Deloitte, The Changing Faces of Cybersecurity. Closing the Cyber Risk Gap. Deloitte LLP, Ontario (2018)
3. Patriciu, V.V., Furtuna, A.C.: Guide for designing cyber security exercises. In: Proceedings of the 8th WSEAS International Conference on E-Activities and Information Security and Privacy, pp. 172–177. World Scientific and Engineering Academy and Society (WSEAS) (2009)
4. Beyer, M., et al.: Awareness is only the first step: a framework for progressive engagement of staff in cyber security. Hewlett Packard Enterprise (2015)
5. Hadley, J.: Why the cyber security skills gap won't be solved in the classroom. Forbes Magazine, 12th September (2019). https://www.forbes.com/sites/jameshadley/2019/09/12/why-the-cybersecurity-skills-gap-wont-be-solved-in-the-classroom/
6. Pedley, D., McHenry, D., Motha, H., Shah, J.N.: Understanding the U.K. Cyber security Skills Labour Market – Research report for the Department for Digital, Culture, Media and Sport, Department for Digital, Culture, Media & Sport, London, UK (2018)
7. Fisher, T., Stevens, M.R.: Serious Games Humanitarian User Research. Imaginetec (2020)
8. Chen, S., Michael, D.: Serious Games: Games that Educate, Train, and Inform. Thomson Course Technology, Boston (2005)
9. Ulisack, M., Wright, M.: Games in Education: Serious Games. Futurelab (2010). www.futurelab.org.uk/projects/games-in-education
10. Angafor, G.N., Yevseyeva, I., He, Y.: Game-based learning: a review of tabletop exercises for cybersecurity incident response training. Secur. Priv. (2020). https://doi.org/10.1002/spy2.126
11. Klabber, J.H.G.: The emerging field of simulation & gaming: meanings of a retrospect. Simul. Gaming 32(4), 471–480 (2001). Sage Publications
12. Anderson, E., McLoughlin, L., Liarokapis, F., Peters, C., Petridis, P., Freitas, S.: Serious Games in Cultural Heritage, pp. 29–48 (2009)
13. Almeida, F., Simoes, J.: The role of serious games, gamification, and industry 4.0 tools in the education 4.0 paradigm. Contemp. Educ. Technol. 10(2), 120–136 (2019). https://doi.org/10.30935/cet.554469
14. Cobb, S.: Mind the Gap: Criminal Hacking and the Global Cyber security Kills Shortage, A Critical Analysis, Virus Bulletin Conference 2016, ESET, USA (2016)
15. Cisco, Mitigating the Cyber security Skills Shortage. Top Insights and Actions from Cisco Advisory Services (2015)
16. Crumpler, W., Lewis, J.A.: The Cybersecurity Workforce Gap, Center for Strategic and International Studies (CSIS) (2019)
17. Cobb, M.J.: Plugging the skills gap: the vital role that women should play in cybersecurity. Comput. Fraud Secur. (1) (2018)

18. Semafone, B.R.: Dangerous skills gap leaves organisations vulnerable. Network Secur. **2016**(8) (2016)
19. ZeroNorth, Why the Cybersecurity Skills Shortage is a Real Nightmare (2019). https://securityboulevard.com/2019/10/why-the-cybersecurity-skills-shortage-is-a-real-nightmare/. Accessed 21 May 2020
20. (ISC)²: Cybersecurity Professionals Focus on Developing New Skills as Workforce Gap Widens, 2018. (ISC)² Cybersecurity Workforce Study (2018). https://www.isc2.org/-/media/7CC1598DE430469195F81017658B15D0.ashx. Accessed 21 May 2020
21. FitzGerald, N.: What the Cybersecurity Skills Gap Really Means. https://www.csoonline.com/article/3331983/What-the-cybersecurity-skills-gap-really-means.html. Accessed 19 May 2020
22. Selensec: Addressing the Cyber security Skills Gap – A Reading for Policy Makers, Employers and Young Professionals, Selensec Academy, Sheffiel (2019)
23. ISACA, State of Cybersecurity 2017, February 2017, ISACA, IL (2017)
24. ISACA: State of Cybersecurity 2019 – Part 1: Current Trends in the Workforce Development, ISACA, IL (2019)
25. Indeed, Indeed Spotlight: The Global Cybersecurity Skills Gap. http://blog.indeed.com/2017/01/17/cybersecurity-skills-gap-report/. Accessed 19 May 2020
26. McAfee: Cybersecurity Talent Study. A deep dive into Australia's cybersecurity skills gap, McAfee, LLC. September 2018
27. Ferrara, J.: Why Most Cybersecurity Training Doesn't Work, (2012). https://www.wombatsecurity.com/news/why-most-cyber-security-training-doesnt-work. Accessed 19 May 2020
28. Sitnikova, E., Foo, E., Vaughn, R.B.: The power of hands-on exercises in SCADA cyber security education. In: Dodge, R.C., Futcher, L. (eds.) WISE 2009/2011/2013. IAICT, vol. 406, pp. 83–94. Springer, Heidelberg (2013). https://doi.org/10.1007/978-3-642-39377-8_9
29. Carnegie Mellon University: What Skills are Needed When Staffing Your CSIRT?. Software Engineering Institute, Pittsburgh (2017)
30. Pfleeger, S.L., Improving Cybersecurity Incident Response Team (CSIRT) Skills, Dynamics and Effectiveness, Air Force Research Laboratory, Dartmouth College, Hanover, NH (2017)
31. Peacock, D., Irons, A.: Gender inequality in cyber security: exploring the gender gap in opportunities and progression Int. J. Gender Sci. Technol. **9**(1). ISSN 20400748 (2017)
32. Fortinet, Exploring the Benefits of Gender Diversity in Cybersecurity (2019). https://www.fortinet.com/blog/business-and-technology/exploring-benefits-gender-diversity-cybersecurity.html. Accessed 19 May 2020
33. Wakefield, A.: Diversity, and Inclusion: What should this mean in the security sector, Security Institute, Warwickshire, UK, December 2018
34. KPMG: Hire a hacker to solve a cyber skills crisis' say UK companies (2014). http://www.kpmg.com/uk/en/issuesandinsights/articlespublications/newsreleases/pages/hire-a-hacker-to-solve-cyber-skills-crisis-say-ukcompanies.aspx. Accessed 17 May 2020
35. Vogel, R.: Closing the Cyber security Skills Gap. Salus J. **4**(2) (2016)
36. California Association of Health Facilities: Emergency Preparedness Training Exercise Guide for Nursing Homes, California: California Association of Health Facilities (2008)
37. Kick, J.: Cyber Exercise Playbook, Mitre Corporation (2014)
38. Everett, M.: Tabletop Exercise for Cybersecurity: Maintaining a Healthy Incident Response. Essextec, New York (2016)
39. Frégeau A., et al.: Use of tabletop exercises for healthcare education: a scoping review protocol, BMJ Open **10**, e032662 (2020). https://doi.org/10.1136/bmjopen-2019-032662, (2019)

40. California Hospital Association: What is the difference between a tabletop exercise, a drill, a functional exercise, and a full-scale exercise? (2017). https://www.calhospitalprepare.org/post/what-difference-between-tabletop-exercise-drill-functional-exercise-and-full-scale-exercise. Accessed 13 Aug 2020

41. Gamelearn: Eight examples that explain all you need to know about serious games and game-based learning (2020). https://www.game-learn.com/all-you-need-to-know-serious-games-game-based-learning-examples/. Accessed 13th Aug 2020

42. Abdellatif, A.J., McCollum, B., McMullan, P.: Serious games: quality characteristics evaluation framework and case study. In: 2018 IEEE Integrated STEM Education Conference (ISEC): Proceedings, pp. 112–119. IEEE (2018). https://doi.org/10.1109/ISECon.2018.8340460

43. Hobbs, C., Lentini, L., Moran, M.: The utility of table-top exercises in teaching nuclear security. Int. J. Nucl. Secur. **2**(1) (2016)

44. Hoffman, L.J., Rosenberg, T., Dodge, R., Ragsdale, D.: Exploring a national cyber security exercise for universities. IEEE Secur. Priv. Mag. **3**(5), 27–33 (2019)

45. Dodge, R.C., Ragsdale, D.J., Reynolds, C.: Organization and training of a cybersecurity team. IEEE Conf. Syst. Man Cybern. **5**, 4311–4316 (2003)

46. Thompson, S.: Apprenticeships as the answer to closing the cyber skills gap. Network Security **2019**(12), 9–11 (2019)

47. Marquardson, J., Gomillion, D.L.: Cyber security curriculum development: protecting students and institutions while providing hands-on experience. Inf. Syst. Educ. J. (ISEDJ) (2018)

48. Jewer, J., Evermann, J.: Enhancing learning outcomes through experiential learning: using open-source systems to teach enterprise systems and business process management. J. Inf. Syst. Educ. **26**(3), 187–201 (2015)

49. Sauls, J., Gudigantala, N.: Preparing Information Systems (IS) graduates to meet the challenges of global IT security: some suggestions. J. Inf. Syst. Educ. **24**(1), 71–73 (2013)

50. Seker, E., Ozbenli, H.: The Concept of Cyber Defence Exercises (CDX): Planning, Execution, Evaluation, 1–9 (2018). https://doi.org/10.1109/cybersecpods.2018.8560673

51. Yukiko, Y., Atsushi, F., Takeo, F., Kazuyo, S.: Enhancement of incident handling capabilities by cyber exercise. NEC Tech. J. **12**(2), Special Issue on Cybersecurity (2018)

52. Dawson, J., Thomson, R.: The future cyber security workforce: going beyond technical skills for successful cyber performance. Front. Psychol. **9**, 744 (2018). https://doi.org/10.3389/fpsyg.2018.00744

53. Adinoyi, J.A.: Games and Simulations, Drills and Exercises: In-Basket Exercise, Tabletop Exercise, Monodrama, Role Playing and Role (2014). Reversal. Accessed from https://www.researchgate.net/publication/327861197

54. Dewar, R.S.: Cyber Defense Report: Cyber Security and Cyber Defense Exercises. In: Center for Security Studies (CSS), ETH Zürich (2018)

55. Crimando, S.: The 10 Steps Model for Designing Tabletop Exercises. Everbridge, Inc., London, UK (2017)

56. Vandendriessche, T. (ed.): Exercitium: European Handbook of Maritime Security Exercises and Drills. Antwerp Port Authority (2015)

57. Bartnes, M., Moe, B.N.: Challenges in IT security preparedness exercises: a case study. Comput. Secur. 67 (2016)

Games for Learning

Theoretical Foundations and Evaluations of Serious Games for Learning Data Structures and Recursion: A Review

Alberto Rojas-Salazar[(✉)] and Mads Haahr

Trinity College Dublin, Dublin, Ireland
{rojassaa,mads.haahr}@tcd.ie

Abstract. Data structures and recursive algorithms are challenging concepts to learn because they are abstract and difficult to relate to familiar knowledge. Many researchers suggest that digital serious games may be a good tool to facilitate the learning process of these topics. This article presents a review of currently available digital serious games for learning that focus on teaching data structures and recursive algorithms. The review identifies and classifies the specific data structures and recursive algorithms covered by those games, analyzes the learning theoretical foundations for the games, and assesses the studies performed to evaluate the effectiveness of the games.

Keywords: Data structures · Literature review · Recursion · Serious games

1 Introduction

Data structures and recursive algorithms are fundamental topics in Computer Science [37]. Their proper usage ensures the good performance of a computational system. For this reason, the Association for Computing Machinery (ACM) recommends their study at an early stage of the undergraduate program [2]. However, advanced data structures and recursive algorithms are difficult topics because they are abstract and difficult to relate to familiar knowledge [3, 45]. Therefore, visualization tools have been created to facilitate the learning process. However, studies show that visualization tools do not increase learning gains due to the fact that students engage passively with such instruments [21]. For this reason, many researchers suggest that digital serious games may be useful for facilitating learning of data structures and recursive algorithms, because serious games allow students to visualize the data structure in an active way.

The aim of this article is to review the state of the art of digital serious games for learning that teach data structures and recursive algorithms. Specifically, this review aims to: (1) identify which serious games for learning focus on data structures and recursive algorithms, (2) identify and classify the specific data structures and recursive algorithms covered by those games, (3) analyze the learning theoretical foundations for the games, and (4) assess the studies performed to evaluate the effectiveness of each game.

© Springer Nature Switzerland AG 2020
M. Ma et al. (Eds.): JCSG 2020, LNCS 12434, pp. 135–149, 2020.
https://doi.org/10.1007/978-3-030-61814-8_11

2   Methodology

This review follows the guidelines suggested by Kitchenham and Charters [26] for carrying out systemic literature reviews in computer science, which were later adapted by Calderón and Ruiz [6] and Petri and von Wangenheim [33] for reviewing serious games. The following sections describe the review objectives and protocol.

2.1   Research Questions

The research questions (RQ) covered by this review are:

- Topic

  - RQ1. What are the data structures or recursive algorithms covered by the reviewed digital serious games?

- Theoretical foundations

  - RQ2. What are the learning theories or approaches used by the digital serious games to ensure learning?
  - RQ3. Which types of cognitive processes are required to achieve the digital serious games learning objectives?
  - RQ4. Which dimensions of knowledge are supported by the digital serious games?

- Evaluation aspects

  - RQ5. Which factors are evaluated during the experiments?
  - RQ6. Which experimental design is used to evaluate the digital serious games?
  - RQ7. Which data collection tools are used in the study?
  - RQ8. Which data analysis methods are used to analyze the data?

2.2   Inclusion and Exclusion Criteria

For this review, we included articles that reported on one or more digital serious games that cover data structures and recursion topics. Specifically, we focused on articles written in English, available via digital libraries and published between 1999 and 2019. We did not include articles that report on gamification or non-digital serious games. However, articles lacking information to answer all the research questions were included as long as they could answer some of the questions. Additionally, we assessed the quality of the reviewed articles; we only considered articles published in peer-reviewed journals and conference proceedings. Finally, articles not clearly written or possessing serious methodological problems were excluded.

2.3 Extracted Data and Classification Criteria

To answer the RQs, we developed guidelines to extract and classify the articles' data as enumerated in the following list.

1. **Covered topic**. The covered topic consisted of the name of the data structure or recursive algorithm covered by the game. Data structures were presented without classification in order to be as comprehensive as possible. Finally, recursive algorithms were aggregated and presented under a category named "recursive algorithm."
2. **Learning theory or principle**. For each article, the learning theory or principle that the digital serious games used to facilitate learning was extracted. Learning theories were defined as theories that explain how humans learn (e.g., Situated Learning [28] or Kolb's Experiential Learning Theory [27]). Learning principles were defined as constructs, concepts, methodologies, or processes that facilitate learning (e.g., scaffolding [49], or learning by analogies and metaphors [15]). We only extracted the learning theory/principle if it was reported in the article.
3. **Cognitive process and knowledge dimension**. To classify the cognitive processes that a player must apply to achieve the learning objective and dimension of knowledge delivered by the game, Bloom's revised taxonomy framework [1] was used. According to [1], there are six cognitive process: *remember*, *understand*, *apply*, *analyze*, *evaluate*, and *create*. Additionally, there are four dimensions of knowledge: *factual*, *conceptual*, *procedural*, and *metacognitive* [1]. Usually, the cognitive processes and knowledge dimensions of a learning tool should be reported in the learning objectives section [4]. However, if an article did not mention them explicitly, we deduced these aspects from the game description, paying attention to the actions (verbs) that the player must perform while playing the game (the learning activities).
4. **Evaluated factors**. Evaluated factors commonly assess the users' behaviors or opinions about the game. To classify these factors, we used the factor classification framework suggested by Petri and von Wangenheim [33]. The framework has ten categories: learning, motivation, user experience (UX), usefulness, usability, instructional aspects, correctness, completeness, quality, and 7S-model features. Some articles do not explicitly report the evaluated factor. In those cases, we deduced the factors from the article's description of the data collection instruments.
5. **Research design**. Research designs were classified using the classification framework suggested by [33]. This framework divides experimental designs into four categories: *ad-hoc*, *non-experimental*, *quasi-experimental*, and *experimental*. The ad-hoc category includes designs that analyze "learner's informal comments after they played the game or describing some observations of pilot studies" [33]. The *non-experimental* category consists of systematically defined evaluations that do not follow a strict experimental design. Experimental designs use random assignment to allocate the participants in either the treatment or the control group. In contrast, quasi-experimental designs do not employ the random assignment approach.
6. **Instrument**. Data collection tools used in the game evaluations, such as qualitative surveys, tests/questionnaires, interviews, and observations were extracted from the selected articles.

7. **Data analysis methods**. The name of the analysis methods and type of method (quantitative or qualitative) were extracted from each article. Quantitative methods used were classified as either descriptive or inferential statistics.

2.4 Search Strategy

Digital libraries reviewed included ACM Digital Library, IEEE Xplore, SpringerLink, SAGE Journals, ScienceDirect, and Scopus. We selected these data sources because they have great influence in the Computer Science domain. Furthermore, we searched for additional related articles using Google Scholar to consider studies indexed on different journals outside of the mentioned databases.

For each data source, we defined a search string using core concepts and their synonyms. The following key words were used for the construction of each string: *educational games*, *serious games*, *game-based learning*, *data structures*, *recursion*, and *sorting*.

2.5 Execution of the Review

We performed the systematic literature review between December 2019 and June 2020. The review was executed in three stages. Table 1 shows the results (number of articles) of each stage. In the first stage, the initial search, queries were executed in all selected digital libraries and Google Scholar. After executing the queries, 9795 articles were retrieved.

Table 1. Number of articles reviewed and analyzed during the literature review.

	ACM	IEEE Xplore	Springer-Link	SAGE	Elsevier	Scopus	Google Scholar	Total
Stage 1. Initial Search	23	32	1053	65	594	78	7950	9795
Stage 2. Brief analysis	23	32	1053	65	594	78	350	2195
Stage 3. Complete analysis	5	15	1	0	0	3	7	31
Final selection	4	11	1	0	0	1	2	19

In the second stage, the title of each article retrieved from the digital journals (including the 350 most relevant articles pulled from Google Scholar) were read. In total, this led to us reviewing 2195 articles in the second stage. When the title did not provide enough information to exclude or include the article, we proceeded to read the article's abstract.

All repeated articles were excluded. At the end of the second stage, 31 promising articles were identified.

In the third stage, we proceeded to read the whole article and to extract the data. During this stage, some articles were excluded due to the following reasons: some were not digital games, others were not legibly written, and others were about gamifications or visualization tools. At the end of this stage, we found nineteen articles reporting data on fifteen serious games and two bundles of mini games designed to teach data structures and recursion.

3 Results and Analysis

3.1 Topic

With regard to RQ1, we identified nine data structures (array, 2D array, stack, queue, linked list, dictionary, tree, binary tree and the Adelson-Velsky and Landis tree) and six recursive algorithms (Hanoi Tower recursive algorithm, tree traversal, binary search, deep-first search, Fibonacci and Factorial). Eight digital serious games were found to focus on a single data structure or algorithm while seven games were found to cover more than one topic. Regarding the bundles, each mini game was found to focus on a single data structure or algorithm. Table 2 summarizes information extracted from the articles regarding data structures and recursive algorithms covered in each digital serious game or bundle. In the table, the name, associated reference, and data structures or algorithms for each game are presented. As mentioned above, all recursion algorithms were aggregated in a single column. A grey box with an "X" indicates the primary topic covered, while a white box with an "X" indicates a secondary topic by a game.

3.2 Theoretical Foundations

In relation to the learning theories and principles (RQ2), eleven games/bundles (65% of the reviewed games) reported one or more learning theories or principles that support learning while playing the game. In total, we found eleven theories/principles: immediate feedback [19], Pink's Motivation Theory [34], gamification [11], intrinsic motivation [41], motivation [41], analogies and metaphors [15], productive failure [25], learning by doing [5], the Flow [10], scaffolding [49] and constructionism [20]. Constructionism theories and principles were the most widely used (nine of seventeen). The second column in Table 4 lists the learning theories/principles used by each game.

Concerning cognitive processes (RQ3), only *Stack Game* was found to explicitly report this aspect. Consequently, we deduced the cognitive processes of the rest of the games based on the descriptions in the articles. It was found that in fourteen of the seventeen games, players must employ the *apply* cognitive process. Additionally, we found that in four of the five minigames of the *DSLEP Bundle* as well as *Star Chef*, *Stacks and Queues*, and *Ramle's Stack Game*, players must employ the *remember* cognitive process. These games are simpler and therefore only require players to remember facts about the relevant data structure or algorithm (e.g., the stack follows the last-in-first-out principle) in order to solve game challenges. In contrast, *Stack Game*, *Space Traveler* and *Elemental* include coding challenges which require players to write well-known algorithms

Table 2. Data structures covered by the games.

Game	Array	2D Array	Stack	Queue	Linked List	Dictionary	Tree	Binary Tree	AVL Tree	Recursion***
Wu's Castle [16, 17]	X	X								
Star Chef [30]			X							
Stacks and Queues [32]			X	X						
Stack Em Up [22]			X							
Stack Game [13, 14]			X							
Ramle's Stack Game [36]			X							
Space Traveller [47]					X					
La Petite Fee Cosmo [24]					X					
Mario [43]								X	X	
AVL Tree Game [40]									X	
Elemental [7]								X		X
HTML5 Hanoi Tower [42]			X							X
Recursive Runner [48]										X
Critical Mass [29]		X					X			X
Resource Craft [23]	X					X				
Prototypes Bundle* [38]					X			X		X
DSLEP Bundle** [9]	X		X	X	X					

* The prototype bundle includes the following games: Binary Search Game, Singly Linked List Game, and Binary Search Tree Game.

** This bundle includes the following games: Piperray, Hanoi Tower, Asterostacks, Queue Race, and Snake Linked List.

*** The recursive algorithms are Hanoi Tower recursive algorithm, tree traversal, binary search, deep-first search, Fibonacci, and Factorial.

(e.g., depth-first-search or the linked list insert and remove algorithms). Therefore, to achieve the objectives for this set of games, players must employ the *understand*, *apply*, and *analyze* cognitive processes. Finally, *Critical Mass* and *Resource Craft* were found to involve the widest range of cognitive processes. In these advanced coding games, players are required to code a program capable of playing the game. This involves creating an original program which the player must then evaluate and optimize, taking into account the results given by the game system. Consequently, the player must use all the cognitive processes listed in Bloom's revised taxonomy.

Concerning the knowledge dimension (RQ4), results showed that fourteen games deliver procedural knowledge with only three games and four mini games of the *DSLEP Bundle* delivering factual knowledge. The challenges of these games require that the player only remember certain facts or principles of the data structure. However, some games were found to deliver both factual and conceptual knowledge. For example, in certain serious games, the game story or in-game messages provided players with conceptual and factual information that they could use to solve challenges of the game. Finally, three games were found to deliver factual, conceptual, and procedural knowledge.

Table 3 summaries the learning theories/principles, dimensions of knowledge and cognitive processes associated with each game. The term NI (not included) is used to note cases where articles did not report a learning theory or principle.

Table 3. Theorical foundations delivered by the games.

Game	Learning theory or Learning approach	Dimension of knowledge[a]	Remember	Understand	Apply	Analyze	Evaluate	Create
Wu's Castle [16, 17]	Feedback Scaffolding	P		X	X			
Star Chef [30]	NI	F	X					
Stacks and Queues [32]	Constructionism	F	X					
Stack Em Up [22]	Constructionism The Flow	F/C/P			X			
Stack Game [13, 14]	Constructionism Learning-by-doing	F/C/P		X	X	X		
Ramle's Stack Game [36]	Scaffolding	F	X					
Space Traveler [47]	NI	P		X	X	X		
La Petite Fee Cosmo [24]	Productive failure	P			X			
Mario [43]	NI	P			X			
AVL Tree Game [40]	Constructivism Scaffolding	P			X			
Elemental [7]	Scaffolding Analogies & Metaphors	F/C/P		X	X	X		
HTML5 Hanoi Tower [42]	NI	P			X			
Recursive Runner [48]	NI	P			X			
Critical Mass [29]	Motivation	P	X	X	X	X	X	X
Resource Craft [23]	NI	P	X	X	X	X	X	X
Prototypes Bundle [38]	Constructionism Intrinsic motivation	P			X			
DSLEP Bundle [9]	Gamification Pink's motivation theory The Flow	F/P	X		X			

NI means "not included".
[a]The types of knowledge are Factual (F), Conceptual (C), and Procedural (P).

3.3 Evaluation Aspects

Twelve of the seventeen articles reviewed included a game evaluation. All evaluations involved users and intended to measure users' abilities or opinions about the game.

Concerning the evaluated factors (RQ5), we identified fifteen factors which are listed in the second column of Table 4. It was found that most studies (eleven of thirteen) evaluated more than one factor. The factor classification framework suggested by [33] was used to classify the factors into seven categories. The factors identified most commonly fell under the learning, UX, and usefulness categories. Studies that evaluated perceived learning were classified under the usability category. Figure 1 shows the number of studies which were found to evaluate factors for each category.

Regarding the research design (RQ6), seven studies were classified as quasi-experiments, three studies as ad-hoc, three as non-experimental, and only one as experimental. The third column of Table 4 lists the research design used by each game.

Table 4. Evaluation aspects: Evaluated element, evaluation design, number of participants, instrument, and analysis methods.

Game	Evaluated elements	Evaluation Design (N° participants)	Instruments	Analysis methods
Wu's Castle [16, 17]	Learning, enjoyability, preference, perceived learning, motivation, usability.	Quasi-experiment (27) Experiment (55)	Test Qualitative survey	DS: percentages, averages. IS: t-test
Star Chef [30]	Technology acceptance (usefulness, easiness, and attitude towards the tool)	Quasi-experiment (110)	Qualitative survey Interview Observation	DS: mean, standard deviation, and standard error IS: ANOVA Informal analysis
Stacks and Queues [32]	Usability, perceived learning, preference.	Non-experimental (32)	Qualitative survey	DS: histograms, percentages
Stack Em Up [22]	Suitability.	Non-experimental (15)	Qualitative survey	DS: histograms, percentages
Stack Game [13, 14]	Learning, motivation, usefulness, perceived learning, preference, clarity, provided support, enjoyability.	Quasi-experiment (29)	Test Qualitative survey	DS: mean, standard deviation, and percentages IS: t-test, Cohen's d
Ramle's Stack Game [36]	Learning, usability, user interface, interactivity.	Quasi-experiment (29)	Test Qualitative survey	DS: percentages.

(continued)

Table 4. (*continued*)

Game	Evaluated elements	Evaluation Design (N° participants)	Instruments	Analysis methods
Space Traveler [47]	Learning, motivation, perceived learning, enjoyability, and usefulness.	Quasi-experiment (13)	Test Qualitative survey	DS: mean, median, standard deviation, variance, histograms, percentages.
AVL Tree Game [40]	Enjoyability and engagement	Ad-hoc (5)	Observation Qualitative survey	Informal analysis
Elemental [7]	Learning, enjoyability, perceived learning, and preference.	Quasi-experiment (42)	Test Qualitative survey	DS: percentages, means, standard deviation, histograms. IS: t-test, Cohen's d
HTML5 Hanoi Tower [42]	Learning	Non-experimental (17)	Test Qualitative survey	DS: mean, standard deviation, and histograms
Recursive Runner [48]	Leaning, enjoyability, perceived learning, motivation, preference.	Quasi-experiment (31)	Test Qualitative survey	DS: average, medians, standard deviation, histograms
Critical Mass [29]	Learning, Preference, and perceived learning	Ad-hoc (42)	Assignment Qualitative survey	DS: percentages
Resource Craft [23]	Learning and self-motivation	Ad-hoc (102)	Qualitative survey	DS: percentages

DS means "descriptive statistics". **IS** means "inferential statistics".

Concerning data collection tools (RQ7), thirteen evaluations were found to use a qualitative survey, seven a test or questionnaire, two an observation method, one an assignment, and one an interview. It is important to note that with the exception of the evaluation of *Star Chef* (which used the TAM scale [12]), all studies analyzed utilized an informal instrument (an instrument that was not validated or calibrated) to evaluate game factors. The fourth column of Table 4 lists the instruments used by each game.

In terms of data analysis methods (RQ8), twelve evaluations were found to use descriptive statistics (means, variance, standard deviations, histograms, and percentages), while only four were found to use inferential statistics (t-test and ANOVA). Finally, two studies were found to employ informal methods to analyze the qualitative

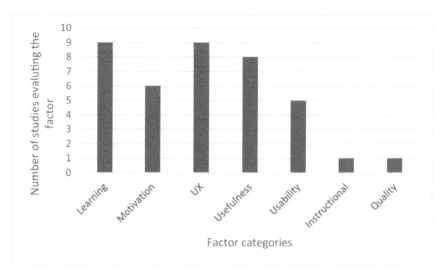

Fig. 1. Frequencies of the evaluated factors.

data collected from interviews and observations. The fifth column of Table 4 presents the methods used in each evaluation.

4 Discussion

Our results show that the most common data structure covered in the serious games reviewed was the stack; the stack appeared in seven of seventeen games reviewed. A reason for this finding may be that the stack is a simple but fundamental data structure, which makes it ideal for fast prototyping and testing of potential uses of learning games in the field. Additionally, stacks may appear more due to the fact that the Association for Computing Machinery (ACM) recommends that the stack be included as an essential topic in undergraduate programs [2]. However, we noticed that apart from the *Stack Game*, all the digital serious games that focus on stacks are trivial. For instance, three games used the Hanoi Tower puzzle as the main game challenge, while in the other three games, the only game mechanics available were the queue and dequeue operations. As a result, these games may fail to engage the player due to their lack of sophistication. In contrast, *Stack Game* uses the Hanoi Tower puzzle in a clever way. In this game, the player must arrange blocks of different colors in a certain order following the last-in-first-out principle to unlock doors. Additionally, *Stack Game* offers different challenges, such as puzzles, which require that players evaluate arithmetic infix and postfix expressions as well as execute coding puzzles. We suggest that following *Stack Game*'s example, serious games that teach data structures employ data structure properties in a clever and creative way to create more engaging game challenges and game mechanics. The more engaged a player is, the more motivated he or she will be, which helps to facilitate the learning process.

Furthermore, we noticed that most of the reviewed games focus on teaching simple data structures (e.g., array, 2D array, stack, queue, linked list, and dictionary) and recursive algorithms (e.g., Hanoi Tower algorithm, Fibonacci, Factorial, and Binary Search). Only a few games were found to focus on teaching medium-complexity data structures (e.g., binary trees and AVL trees) and algorithms (e.g., tree traversal and depth-first search). This finding suggests that more research on digital serious games that teach advanced data structures and recursive algorithms, such as complex trees (e.g., red-black trees or B-trees), graphs, and their associated algorithms is needed.

Concerning theoretical foundations, 65% (eleven of seventeen) of the studies reviewed reported a learning theory or principle. The most common theory observed was Constructionism (five of eleven) followed by scaffolding (four of eleven), a concept based on Vygotsky's Proximal Developmental Zone [35]. This finding is consistent with the results obtained in other literature reviews. For example, Wu et al. [46] performed a literature review of serious games for learning and likewise found that most of games reviewed reported a constructivist theory. In another literature review focusing on serious games for learning science, Cheng et al. [8] found that most of the reported learning theories were either constructivist or based on Vygotsky's theories. Similarly, our findings suggest that most of the reviewed works (eight of eleven) explain learning through games as an active process that requires the construction and socialization of knowledge (Vygotsky's theories).

In our review, only one study was found to explicitly report learning objectives. In general, learning objectives facilitate the extraction of cognitive processes and the type of knowledge delivered by a game. Consequently, it was necessary to deduce these aspects from the game description of the rest of the games.

We found that in almost all games reviewed (fifteen of seventeen), it was necessary for the learner to employ the *apply* cognitive process to achieve the learning activities. Additionally, the most common type of knowledge delivered by the games reviewed was found to be *procedural* (fourteen of seventeen). This finding was not surprising due to the interactive nature of video games. However, games with complex tasks that required higher cognitive processes were identified. For example, in order to succeed in the coding games reviewed, *Critical Mass* and *Resource Craft*, players had to employ the *create* and *evaluate* cognitive processes, the highest cognitive processes of Bloom's taxonomy. This finding confirms previous observations made by game scholars (e.g., [19, 39]) who suggest that video games support the acquisition of skills and knowledge that require higher cognitive states. Finally, concerning type of knowledge, it was found that some games used narrative elements to deliver factual and conceptual knowledge (e.g., *Elemental* and *Stack Game*). This indicates that game elements can be used to deliver different types of knowledge.

It is a concern that sixteen of seventeen games reviewed did not explicitly report the learning objectives of the games. Learning objectives are important because they define the level of mastery of a topic that a learner should have at the end of a learning experience [4]. Furthermore, learning objectives specify the scope of the learning material, tool, or program. It is desirable to define learning objectives using frameworks that systematically describe the complexity of tasks that learners are expected to master [4]. Normally, these frameworks are hierarchical, with their classification categories possessing an ordinal nature (e.g., SOLO taxonomy [4], Bloom's taxonomy [1], etc.). It is also desirable that learning tools, such as serious games for learning, state their learning objectives [31] during their design stage. By doing this, the designer is able to align the learning activities to fulfil the objectives and develop accurate assessment tools of the learner and the game itself. The latter aspect is quite important in terms of research which require proper assessment tools; without a proper assessment, it is not possible to develop good theory about serious games.

Concerning evaluation aspects, we found that in general, researchers were interested in evaluating games' (1) efficacy to teach data structures and recursion; and (2) affective outcomes. Most of the evaluations conducted were quasi-experiments; in total, thirteen games were evaluated using a quasi-experimental design. In contrast, only one study was evaluated using a full experiment. A reason for this finding may be that quasi-experiments are easier to carry out; researchers may not need to divide the sample into random groups, and they may not need a control activity. Therefore, this type of experiment is easier to design, execute and analyze than a full experiment. However, such results are not as conclusive as those obtained through a full experiment [26].

In terms of data collection tools, we found that with the exception of one instrument, all tools were informal. By informal, we mean instruments that were not validated nor calibrated to behave as a scale. Consequently, data collected using such instruments cannot be evaluated using parametric statistical methods such as t-tests or ANOVA. Excluding one evaluation, all collected data was analyzed using descriptive statistics. Of these, three studies employed parametric methods to analyze ordinal data (scores of tests) which is unfortunate as doing so departs from best practice [18]. Additionally, studies that used qualitative instruments (three of thirteen; e.g., interviews and observations) did not report any protocol describing how the data was collected and analyzed. Consequently, results obtained by these methods are not conclusive. Therefore, like other scholars (e.g., [44]), we suggest that more qualitative or mixed experiments be carried out to properly analyze the nature of learning through digital serious games.

5 Conclusion

This article has reviewed the state of the art of serious games that teach data structures and recursive algorithms reported between 1999 and 2019. In total, seventeen digital serious games were identified which together covered a total of nine data structures and six recursive algorithms with the stack appearing the most frequently. None of the data structures or algorithms covered were found to be advanced. Consequently, there is great potential for further research involving serious games that teach advance data structures. Additionally, our results showed that several serious games were able to provide players with tasks that required them to use the highest cognitive processes of Bloom's taxonomy. This finding suggests that serious games have the potential to provide users with learning activities that facilitate the acquisition of complex learning objectives. However, our results showed that improvements in the methodology used to evaluate serious games for learning in this field are sorely needed. For example, most games reviewed did not report the learning objectives necessary for posterior evaluation. Likewise, it was found that improvements in the selection or development of data collection instruments as well as the selection of analysis methods appropriated for collected data are needed. Finally, we noticed a lack of evaluations of games following experimental designs or qualitative methodologies. Improving evaluation methods will allow researchers to develop accurate theories regarding serious games and learning.

References

1. Anderson, L.W., Krathwohl, D.R.: A Taxonomy for Learning, Teaching, and Assessing: A Revision of Bloom's Taxonomy of Educational Objectives. Longman, New York (2001)
2. Association for Computing Machinery (ACM) Joint Task Force on Computing Curricula, IEEE Computer Society: Computer Science Curricula 2013: Curriculum Guidelines for Undergraduate Degree Programs in Computer Science, New York, NY, USA. ACM (2013)
3. Becker, K., Beacham, M.: A tool for teaching advanced data structures to computer science students: an overview of the BDP system. In: Proceedings of the Second Annual CCSC on Computing in Small Colleges Northwestern Conference, pp. 65–71 Consortium for Computing Sciences in Colleges, USA (2000)
4. Biggs, J., Tang, C.: Teaching for Quality Learning at University. Open University Press, New York (2007)
5. Bruce, B.C., Bloch, N.: Learning by doing. In: Seel, N.M. (ed.) Encyclopedia of the Sciences of Learning, pp. 1821–1824. Springer, Boston (2012). https://doi.org/10.1007/978-1-4419-1428-6_544
6. Calderón, A., Ruiz, M.: A systematic literature review on serious games evaluation: an application to software project management. Comput. Educ. **87**, 396–422 (2015). https://doi.org/10.1016/j.compedu.2015.07.011
7. Chaffin, A., et al.: Experimental evaluation of teaching recursion in a video game. In: Proceedings of the 2009 ACM SIGGRAPH Symposium on Video Games, New York, NY, USA, pp. 79–86. ACM (2009). https://doi.org/10.1145/1581073.1581086
8. Cheng, M.-T., Chen, J.-H., Chu, S.-J., Chen, S.-Y.: The use of serious games in science education: a review of selected empirical research from 2002 to 2013. J. Comput.in Educ. **2**(3), 353–375 (2015). https://doi.org/10.1007/s40692-015-0039-9
9. Costa, E.B., Toda, A.M., Mesquita, M.A.A., Matsunaga, F.T., Brancher, J.D.: Interactive data structure learning platform. In: Murgante, B., et al. (eds.) ICCSA 2014. LNCS, vol. 8584, pp. 186–196. Springer, Cham (2014). https://doi.org/10.1007/978-3-319-09153-2_14
10. Csikszentmihalyi, M.: Flow: The Psychology of Optimal Experience. Harper & Row (1990)
11. Dicheva, D., et al.: Gamification in education: a systematic mapping study. J. Educ. Technol. Soc. **18**(3), 75–88 (2015)
12. Davis, F.D., et al.: User acceptance of computer technology: a comparison of two theoretical models. Manage. Sci. **35**(8), 982–1003 (1989)
13. Dicheva, D., et al.: On the design of an educational game for a data structures course. In: 2016 IEEE International Conference on Teaching, Assessment, and Learning for Engineering (TALE), pp. 14–17 (2016). https://doi.org/10.1109/TALE.2016.7851763
14. Dicheva, D., Hodge, A.: Active learning through game play in a data structures course. In: Proceedings of the 49th ACM Technical Symposium on Computer Science Education, pp. 834–839, New York, NY, USA. ACM (2018). https://doi.org/10.1145/3159450.3159605
15. Duit, R.: On the role of analogies and metaphors in learning science. Sci. Educ. **75**(6), 649–672 (1991)
16. Eagle, M., Barnes, T.: Experimental evaluation of an educational game for improved learning in introductory computing. In: Proceedings of the 40th ACM Technical Symposium on Computer Science Education, pp. 321–325, New York, NY, USA. ACM (2009). https://doi.org/10.1145/1508865.1508980

17. Eagle, M., Barnes, T.: Wu's castle: teaching arrays and loops in a game. In: Proceedings of the 13th Annual Conference on Innovation and Technology in Computer Science Education, pp. 245–249, New York, NY, USA. ACM (2008). https://doi.org/10.1145/1384271.1384337

18. Field, A.: Discovering Statistics Using IBM SPSS Statistics. Sage Publications Ltd. (2013)

19. Gee, J.P.: What Video Games Have to Teach Us about Learning and Literacy. Palgrave Macmillan, New York (2007)

20. Gogus, A.: Constructivist learning. In: Seel, N.M. (ed.) Encyclopedia of the Sciences of Learning, pp. 783–786. Springer, Boston (2012). https://doi.org/10.1007/978-1-4419-1428-6_4049

21. Hundhausen, C.D., et al.: A meta-study of algorithm visualization effectiveness. J. Visual Lang. Comput. 13(3), 259–290 (2002). https://doi.org/10.1006/jvlc.2002.0237

22. Ismail, M. et al.: Realization of conceptual knowledge through educational game. Presented at the CGAT 2013, the 6th annual international conference on computer games, multimedia and allied technologies (2013). https://doi.org/10.5176/2251-1679_CGAT13.06

23. Jiau, H.C., et al.: Enhancing self-motivation in learning programming using game-based simulation and metrics. IEEE Trans. Educ. 52(4), 555–562 (2009). https://doi.org/10.1109/TE.2008.2010983

24. Kannappan, V.T., et al.: La petite fee cosmo: learning data structures through game-based learning. In: 2019 International Conference on Cyberworlds (CW), pp. 207–210 (2019). https://doi.org/10.1109/CW.2019.00041

25. Kapur, M.: Productive failure in learning math. Cognit. Sci. 38(5), 1008–1022 (2014). https://doi.org/10.1111/cogs.12107

26. Kitchenham, B.: Procedures for Performing Systematic Reviews. Technical Report TR/SE-0401. Keele University and NICTA, United Kingdom (2004)

27. Kolb, D.A.: Experiential Learning: Experience as the Source of Learning and Development. Pearson, New Jersey (2014)

28. Lave, J.: Situated Learning: Legitimate Peripheral Participation. Cambridge University Press, Cambridge (1991)

29. Lawrence, R.: Teaching data structures using competitive games. IEEE Trans. Educ. 47(4), 459–466 (2004). https://doi.org/10.1109/TE.2004.825053

30. Liu, T., et al.: Using computer games in a computer course to improve learning. In: Proceedings of IEEE International Conference on Teaching, Assessment, and Learning for Engineering (TALE) 2012, pp. W2C-16–W2C-19 (2012). https://doi.org/10.1109/TALE.2012.6360301

31. Mayes, T., de Freitas, S.: Review of E-Learning Theories, Frameworks and Models. Joint Information Systems Committee, London (2004)

32. Park, B., Ahmed, D.T.: Abstracting learning methods for stack and queue data structures in video games. In: 2017 International Conference on Computational Science and Computational Intelligence (CSCI), pp. 1051–1054 (2017). https://doi.org/10.1109/CSCI.2017.183

33. Petri, G., Gresse von Wangenheim, C.: How Games for Computing Education Are Evaluated? A Systematic Literature Review. Comput. Educ. 107, C, 68–90 (2017). https://doi.org/10.1016/j.compedu.2017.01.004

34. Pink, D.H.: Drive: the surprising truth about what motivates us (2009)

35. Podolskiy, A.I.: Zone of proximal development. In: Seel, N.M. (ed.) Encyclopedia of the Sciences of Learning, pp. 3485–3487. Springer, Boston, (2012). https://doi.org/10.1007/978-1-4419-1428-6_316

36. Ramle, R., et al.: Digital game based learning of stack data structure using question prompts. Int. J. Inter. Mob. Technol. 13(7), 90–102 (2019)

37. Sedgewick, R., Wayne, K.: Algorithms. Addison-Wesley (2014)

38. Shabanah, S.S., et al.: Designing computer games to teach algorithms. In: 2010 Seventh International Conference on Information Technology: New Generations, pp. 1119–1126 (2010). https://doi.org/10.1109/ITNG.2010.78

39. Squire, K.: Video Games and Learning: Teaching and Participatory Culture in the Digital Age. Teachers College Press, New York (2011)

40. Šuníková, D., et al.: A mobile game to teach AVL trees. In: 2018 16th International Conference on Emerging eLearning Technologies and Applications (ICETA). pp. 541–544 (2018). https://doi.org/10.1109/ICETA.2018.8572263

41. Touré-Tillery, M., Fishbach, A.: How to measure motivation: a guide for the experimental social psychologist. Soc. Person. Psychol. Compass. 8 (2014). https://doi.org/10.1111/spc3.12110

42. Vasić, D. et al.: Experimental evaluation of teaching recursion with HTML5 game. Presented at the 6th international conference on e-education, ICeE 2014, At Mostar, Bosnia and Herzegovina, vol. 1 (2014). https://doi.org/10.13140/2.1.1669.2481

43. Wassila, D., Tahar, B.: Using serious game to simplify algorithm learning. In: International Conference on Education and e-Learning Innovations, pp. 1–5 (2012). https://doi.org/10.1109/ICEELI.2012.6360569

44. Whitton, N.: Digital Games and Learning: Research and Theory. Routledge, New York (2014)

45. Wu, C.-C., et al.: Conceptual models and cognitive learning styles in teaching recursion. SIGCSE Bull. **30**(1), 292–296 (1998). https://doi.org/10.1145/274790.274315

46. Wu, W.-H., et al.: Re-exploring game-assisted learning research: the perspective of learning theoretical bases. Comput. Educ. **59**(4), 1153–1161 (2012). https://doi.org/10.1016/j.compedu.2012.05.003

47. Zhang, J. et al.: Reinforcing student understanding of linked list operations in a game. In: 2015 IEEE Frontiers in Education Conference (FIE). pp. 1–7 (2015). https://doi.org/10.1109/FIE.2015.7344132

48. Zhang, J. et al.: Using a game-like module to reinforce student understanding of recursion. In: 2014 IEEE Frontiers in Education Conference (FIE) Proceedings, pp. 1–7 (2014). https://doi.org/10.1109/FIE.2014.7044093

49. Zydney, J.M.: Scaffolding. In: Seel, N.M. (ed.) Encyclopedia of the Sciences of Learning, pp. 2913–2916 Springer, Boston (2012). https://doi.org/10.1007/978-1-4419-1428-6_1103

Improving Learning Outcome by Re-using and Modifying Gamified Lessons Paths

Jannicke Baalsrud Hauge[1,2(✉)] and Ioana Stefan[3]

[1] BIBA – Bremer Institut für Produktion und Logistik GmbH, 28359 Bremen, Germany
baa@biba.uni-bremen.de
[2] KTH-Royal Institute of Technology, 15181 Södertälje, Sweden
jmbh@kth.se
[3] ATS, Targoviste, Romania
ioana.stefan@ats.com.ro

Abstract. A main challenge for teachers is to provide good educational offers that appear both appealing as well as motivating to students to learn about the content according to the curriculum. Educational games are thought to be a good complementary way of provide this learning environment, but, so far, the adaption of educational games to a specific context is not only costly but also requiring a lot of knowledge related to game design. This article provides some examples on how gamified lessons paths can be changed in a simple way and how different components can be re-used, in order to save costs and time and to improve the overall quality of the learning experience.

Keywords: Minigame · Metagame · Reuse · Adaption of lessons paths

1 Introduction

For teachers it is important to create a positive, rich and motivating learning environment, to try to spark interest amongst the classroom, but also to ensure a streamlined and successful learning process. Using games for learning is a great way to make learning motivating and engaging [1].

In the last decade, more and more tools have been developed to support teachers in their efforts to create more engaging and immersive learning experiences. Digital Educational Games (DEG) and gamified educational applications have emerged as a mean to balance the ludic approach, and the didactical goals. [2] has highlighted the difficulty to leverage DEG outcomes, stating that their success depends on the context, the content, the topic, and the pedagogical competences of the teachers. These factors coupled with the diversity of game genres, the multitude of age groups targeted by serious games [3], the advanced skills required to perform adaptation of games to new learning contexts and also the difficulty to transfer the DEG learning outcomes to the real world [4] make DEG design challenging. Research has also explored the use of learning versions of existing games [5], highlighting a new dimension of complexity to the learning design.

© Springer Nature Switzerland AG 2020
M. Ma et al. (Eds.): JCSG 2020, LNCS 12434, pp. 150–163, 2020.
https://doi.org/10.1007/978-3-030-61814-8_12

Research efforts made to support a better DEG design have been diverse, stressing upon the importance of the learning design phase. The iLearnTest Framework [6], for example, has focused on providing game templates that could facilitate game construction. The Activity Theory-based Model of Serious Games (ATMSG) discussed by [7] provided a representation of how the game elements are interconnected, and how these elements contribute to the achievement of the desired pedagogical goals. [8] have presented the evaluation of the design of Collaborative-Competitive SG (CCSG), and identified a set of guidelines for future educational CCSG.

In this context, the key aim of the BEACONING project was to provide an ecosystem that reunite tools that enable teachers to easily construct, adapt and reuse playful pervasive learning experiences. The Gamified Lesson Path (GLP) is the core concept around which the experience is build. Such GLPs can be created and customized using two main authoring tools: the Authoring Tool for Gamified Lesson Paths and the Authoring Tool for Context-Aware Challenges. These authoring tools enable different levels of the customization of metagames, which are narratives that drive the game play on the student side, and of minigames that are used as the main assessment tools of the learning outcome. With the support of these tools, teachers can personalize the learning units to the specific student's needs [9]. In order to ensure the reuse of the different learning paths, a set of templates, as well as a taxonomy have been developed [10], however, past experiments have shown that the application is not that intuitive as intended, and thus there is a need for practical examples on how either re-purpose or re-design GLPs.

This paper therefore presents an easy-to-use authoring tool can support reuse and adaption of GLPs. The main objective is to show how such a tool can reduce the teachers' workload while enabling the personalisation and adaption of learning material to specific subjects. The approach is based upon principles presented in [11–13] and is based on the experience collected in the small- and large- scale piloting [14].

The overall BEACONING piloting focused on STEM with a large age distribution. The four pilots related to logistics had a narrower age – 18–24. This is obvious related to the fact that logistics is not a part of a standard curriculum for the younger age groups. The section below describe the different pilots and the experiments with around 400 participant.

The next section will first outline the requirements for reusability, then describe the adapting process. Sections 3, 4 and 5 describe the two case studies, while chapter four derives some guidelines. Section 6 concludes and give an outlook to next steps.

2   Requirement for Re-use

Previous works have defined a set of components that are suitable for reuse [15], as well as resources that nurture personalization of gamified learning experiences to specific settings. The main purpose of adapting existing applications is not only to reduce costs, improve quality and reduce the time to market for games, but also provide support for teachers that embark on the adaptation of game-based learning experiences. However, most serious games are one of a kind development and even small changes require a mix of specific knowledge making it difficult for teachers to carry out this process without additional support.

A framework that support the reuse have been developed in [16–18]. It defines specific components and how these needs to be described for easy reuse. A main challenge is to connect the instructional design and with the overall game design. According to [18] the usage of narrative serious games mechanics can support this process and a tool that specifically support this is ATMSG [7] in the analysis of the original gamified lessons path in order to ensure that the learning mechanics and the game mechanics are well aligned (Fig. 1).

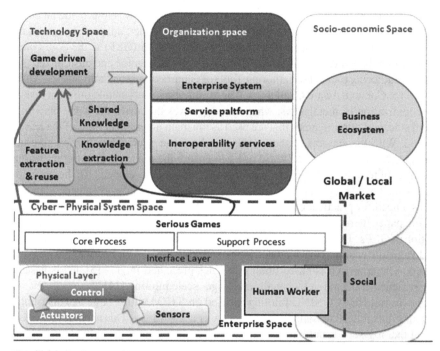

Fig. 1. Game embedded in ecosystem [17]

However, the application of such analysis methods are not so trivial, so in this article we show how an authoring tool can be used instead [17]. By cloning we can keep the passive components (i.g. narrative structure) and graphical assets, and the teacher can focus on repurposing the active components (i.e. components that evolves and changes such as the learning content that is adapted for a specific subject or the tests carried out via the minigames). The reason for choosing this approach is that teachers are very familiar with developing lessons plans, in which they align the class content with the intended learning outcomes and decide upon the tools to use for mediating this content to the individual students. The BEACONING project intended to provide 'anytime anywhere' learning by exploiting pervasive, context-aware and gamified techniques and technologies, framed under the Problem-Based Learning approach [10]. The backbone of the solution is a platform that offers teachers the possibility to create just one gamified lesson and reuse it in different ways by using an authoring tool. The main goal of this is to lower the barrier for Science, Technology, Engineering, and Mathematics

(STEM) teachers to introduce and use personalised and pervasive learning as a part of their classes. One of the innovative aspects of the Beaconing platform is the possibility to reuse a GLP [18]. A main aspect so far was the overall usability and the relation to the learning experience for those used to experiential learning, as well as the usage of the authoring tool, and the supporting material in the form of different types of guidelines for the GLP construction and adaption at project level. In addition, a user guideline for this specific GLP making the ILOs clearer to the students was developed for this specific GLP.

3 Experiences in Using GLPs on Logistics

Experimental Set Up of the 3 Studies
This section is based on the analysis of a small scale pilot (with 22, 18, 16 participants) carried out at university level and 2 large scale pilot studies for VET ((200 participants, and 100 students+30 teachers) within the field of logistics [14]). 2 of the pilots were location based, while one large scale pilot was PC based. The course topics on the university courses where on technology support in logistics, while the topics for the VET were on cohesion and technical knowledge.

The university students were very familiar with game based learning as teaching method, but this does not hold for the VET. Age range were 20–24 and 15–21.

The GLPs
University Level: A location based GLP with 6 quests was used for this purpose. The lesson path is an introduction to logistics and technology usage in a warehouse and production environment. The main focus is on the technologies and how they work. It is designed to be used before the students are familiar with the logistics operations (processes). The player has to physically walk through the hall and to observe how the implemented technologies work in different operations.

Large Scale 1 VET. As a part of the large-scale piloting, ORT, a global education network that coordinated the piloting activities in the BEACONING project, developed two different GLPs on logistics topics: one location based and one designed for PC usage. The pilot was carried out in collaboration with PROMOTRANS (Beaconing, 2019b).

This pilot used a geolocation based GLP (ESCAPE game). This was created by the teachers (11) and played by 200 students age 18–20, BTS, 1. & 2. Year. The GLP aimed at building cohesion between the teams, as well as to check the technical knowledge (through the mini-games) and was used during the first school day. It also offered the students the possibility to explore the surroundings. The teachers who constructed the GLP got support from the ORT team, which was very experienced in developing GLPs and using the BEACONING authoring tools.

The second large-scale pilot was also organised by the same organisations. The setting was based on this experience and therefore a PC based GLP was developed. This time 30 teachers, and 100 students were involved. The age group was 15–21 years, coming from Bac Pro, 1st and 2nd year and 10th Grade. The game play took around 30 min [14].

Results

University Pilot. The experiment showed that the pedagogical approach- PBL, experimental was considered as motivating and realistic. The pedagogical approach was well known to students and teachers and they were therefore comfortable with the way the GLP was implemented. The large majority of the students achieved the intended learning outcomes. However, the GLP contained six different quests, some of these mini-games were perceived as knowledge tests and not well related to the topic. Regarding the devices that players used for the location based game, they all stated that it is not playable on a smart ´phone, but they had good experience with using tablets. Furthermore, none of the participants had special needs, so this part could not be tested.

VET Pilot 1. The feedback from the participants showed that the tool is very suitable for fostering team cohesion, as well as several management topics. It was highly appreciated that the teachers could integrate their own questions. Even though it was perceived as a good learning experience, there is room for improvements- this is specifically related to the knowledge retention of the geolocation based. This could be solved by using a flipped-class room approach with a PC GLP. Secondly, regarding the usage- the teachers suggest to re-use it every quarter- both for team cohesion as well as for giving the students an opportunity to test their progress. Regarding the technical equipment, this pilot used smart phones and concluded that 3 smartphones are needed per group.

VET Pilot 2. The perception of the ability of the game to foster discussion and interaction between the younger and the older students as well as for discovering new fields was good. Furthermore, it was also perceived as positive that the game play could be prepared 1 day in advance. Weaknesses were also discovered - it is noted that it is very important that the students can reach the mini-games even if they did not manage within the time frame. This was only possible using the teacher interface, furthermore- from a technical point of view, approaches like bring your own device is a challenge and also the risk of connectivity issues. The different pilots indicates that there is still a challenge in the usage of the authoring tool, which was perceived as too complex and time consuming, the usage of quests in the location based GLP and the subjective perception of learning with new methodologies. A new set of guidelines for adapting GLPs was developed and used for the re-design of the logistics described below.

Reuse of an Existing GLP on Logistics in a Different Context

Based on the experiences in the previous pilots and the challenges in reported by the university teachers in doing the adaptions, we redesigned that one using the cloning function of the VET 1 and then adapting this to fit the needs of the students and the target group- reusing the some of the minigames from the university pilot.

The new game play consists of two GLPs with 5 and 4 quests that the players need to complete. The quests are designed using 5 minigames namely Generic Quiz, Checkers Game, Drag IT, Match IT and Planet Ninja. As reinforcement and repetition is crucial while learning, Generic Quiz and Planet Ninja is repeated in the GLPs. It makes it easier for the player to focus more into the lesson content rather to explore the mechanics of it. This GLP is based upon elements from the existing GLPs. It has been re-purposed to target different aspects of logistics compared with what covered so far. The narrative concerns logistics for off shore wind-power plant segment placements. Important for this type of logistics processes is the often-low access to infrastructure, the weather related restrictions both in constructions phase as well as in operating and maintaining phase. The narrative is constructed in such a way that it can easily be adapted to on-shore and off-shore wind power parks, but the one tested so far is related to off-shore logistics (Fig. 2).

Fig. 2. Starting screen for repurposed logistics GLP

The GLPs covers the topics of safety and security regulations in harbour area, risks both within the harbour area and off shore as well as regulations on heavy goods on vessels. For the monitoring the development of the GLP as well as the technical testing of the GLP, the same testing protocols as described in [14]. The testing was carried out by a test engineer. The first experiments with the new GLPs were carried out in the last week of June 2019 with around 15 students from the University of Bremen. The preliminary results of the tests shows that the students improved their skills on harbour logistics. The results of PoI 1 – which were related to generation of energy shows that the students could not relate this to the overall learning objective of the course and that the relevant questions were perceived as a knowledge test (similar to the previous test). The results of PoI2 and 4 which comprises topics on loading, unload, safety and risks show that the students achieved the intended learning outcome for the safety regulation and fairly well for risks. PoI 3 was related to tools for management of the complex logistics handling. First results shows that most students failed this ILO. In the future, we therefore intend to integrate a video showing the operations and the interactions. Furthermore, we also intend to investigate the integration of a haptic game in the GLP for this issue, but for that more tests with a larger user group will be carried out.

Regarding the challenges in developing and adapting new GLPs, the feedback from the responsible teacher indicates that it was much easier than in previous versions, also because she could look at different GLPs and clone parts and that the guidelines have reduced the time needed to implement, but that a support from technical team and more experienced GLP developers. In order to compare, we also set-up a second case study for a different topic and a different age group.

4   Re-purposing a GLP on Chemistry

The starting point was a simple GLP designed to be used in Romanian Secondary schools. The target group of this particularly GLPs was high school students. The intended learning outcome was set according to the curriculum in chemistry related to the Periodic Table and element construction and characteristics. The whole GLP was constructed as a narrative, explorative geo-located treasure hunting game, using the Authoring Tool for Context-aware Challenges (AT-CC) [20]. The students had to play the role of a detective and the game mission was to discover who stole an important re-search paper. They had to find the intruder and the documents stolen by visiting different locations in the city of Targoviste in Romania (Figs. 3 and 4).

Fig. 3. Location based game template

During the game play, the students were further evaluated through three minigames, integrated into the narrative flow that is directly related to the intended learning outcome:

- The *It's elemental game* was created using the minigame "Drag IT", where students must discover the missing elements from the periodic table. The expected duration was 120 min, and upon arrival on specific pre-defined points of interests, additional information was provided.
- The *Atomix* game was created using the minigame "Generic Quiz", where students must give correct answers to five questions about the characteristics and atomic structure of five periodic elements. No time limit had been customized for this minigame and some of the questions provided hints for the answer.
- The *Molecularium* game was created using the minigame "Match IT", where students must match the name of a chemical product with its graphical representation. As a hint, students could use the chemical formula provided, in order to identify the molecule.

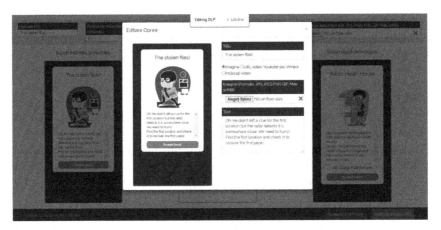

Fig. 4. Location based game - narrative flow

Re-purposing

The initial GLP on chemistry and environmental sustainability was constructed as a geo-located experience that let the student explore the environment of the city they live in and it comprised a set of minigames on chemistry. Both of these components can be reused as such or can be customized. The example below reuses the geo-located part of the GLP and replaces the minigames with other minigames. This is the simplest form of re-purposing a GLP, since it does not require the teacher to re-align the instructional design, nor the higher order learning-mechanics with the game mechanics [15]. It is sufficient to replace the different minigames.

One of the two examples discussed here aims to teach students about the history of Targoviste targeting the same age group. The students can explore various époque specific architectural styles and such constructions characteristics can be used to identify in which period the building has been built (Figs. 5 and 6).

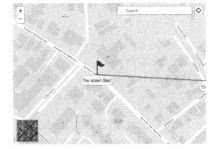

Fig. 5. First clue   **Fig. 6.** Location: Public Health House

The structure of the GLP can be repurposed as follows:
Starting point: The Students' Club
Title: Looking for the thief!

Text: After searching through the room, you discovered that the intruder left a note with five locations where he will hide the documents. In order to find out where he is hiding and to recover the papers, you need to go to all the locations, following the clues. Hurry up! Time is limited.

Clue for the first POI: This institution protects public health and well-being

POI 1

Screen before the challenge

Title: The stolen files!

Text: Strange! In this note, three chemical elements are specified: 10 Neon, 24 Chromium and 80 Mercury. What does it mean? Find the first location and solve this riddle in to recover the first paper.

Screen after the challenge

Title: Public Health House

Text: Yes! you found the first paper. It was hidden in the Public Health House. Did you know that the Public Health House from Targoviste has a recent history? It was founded in 1999.

Clue for the next POI: Bears the name of the one who built the Royal church from Targoviste (Fig. 7).

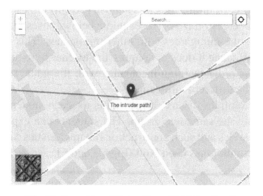

Fig. 7. Location: "Petru Cercel" high school

Screen before the challenge

Title: The intruder path!

Text: Did you read the clue? We need to hurry! If the paper gets on dubious hands, it is bad!

Screen after the challenge

Title: Petru Cercel, ruler of Valachia

Text: Yey! You recovered the second document. It was hidden in the School "Petru Cercel". Despite the fact that Petru Cercel ruled only 3 years, he built one of the most important churches in the city but also he created the first zoo in the country.

Clue for the next POI: There is a pharmacy, but also a private clinic.

POI 3

Screen before the challenge

Title: Neon, Chomium, Mercury

Text: Another note with some strange text. In this one it is specified 118 Gold and "Light and colourless". Who knows what that means, but I think this information will be useful.

Screen of the challenge

Minigame: Generic quiz

Screen after challenge

Title: Hyperici pharmacy

Text: Congratulation! You discovered the third location. Hyperici derives from the word "Hypericum", which means "Above the heath" and it is also a genus of flowering plants. From this type of genus, it can be created two anthraquinone derivative: Hypericin, which acts as an antibiotic and Hyperforin which is a reuptake inhibitor.

*Clue for the next PO*I: University building in whose name is included the symbol of Potassium.

POI 4

Screen before the challenge

Title: Atom 3D model

Text: Hurry up and find the next location!

Screen of challenge

Check In

Screen after the challenge

Title: International Conference Center of University Valahia

Text: Yes, you found it! Did you know that here will take place between 14-16 September 2018, the National Conference of Chemistry - Pre-university Education, 10th edition.

Clue for the next POI: In 1930, a plate was placed here with the text "In memoriam Dr. Dimitrie Oprescu, primary care physician".

POI 5

Screen before the challenge

Title: Molecule challenge

Text: What is this all about? Another note with ambiguous content! Three red, one blue, one white - Nitric acid and "A lot of molecules - Lemon salt"

Screen of the challenge

Minigame: Matchit

Screen after the challenge

Title: Dambovita County Hospital

Text: Hurray! You found the last document which was hidden in the County Hospital. Did you know that the first county hospital was built in 1822 and contained 4 rooms, a house for the doctor and another one for the pharmacy?

Finish

Title: Did you catch the thief?!

Text: Well, we found all the documents but where is the thief? Oh! He left a note where he specified that he will go back to the lab to take the rest of the research paper. We need to hurry back to the lab!

The second example presents the repurposing of the GLP for a different age group, in our case bachelor students entry year as an idea of how playful repeat basic knowledge. As explained above, there is a set of minigames that support the course specific learning objectives. The story as such is quite general. Since we have decided to keep the geo-located part of the GLP, it is important that we ensure that the minigames we replace are replaced so that the player feel immersed in the game play- the simplest form of doing this is to keep the context-awareness. This can simply be done by adjusting the difficulties in the tasks. As an example: instead of searching for the missing elements, the students could look for isotopes and other more detailed information and then use a minigame of type Match It to configure molecules. In this case, it is however important to keep the narrative in mind. In principle, one would assume that the second adaption is easier than the first, since we keep most of the initial structure.

This is currently designed for high school students, and thus it needs to be re-assessed that such a story is relevant and engaging for the new age group. This will require some more alignment works, but the steps will in both cases be similar. The generic approach is described in the next sub section for all three cases

5   Stepwise Approach for Reusing and Adapting

The Authoring Tools developed within the Beaconing project combined with the open-source approach enable various interventions that facilitate reuse and adaptation. Even if the H2020 project has ended, the Beaconing Platform remains functional and the authoring tools are available for users that authenticate.

The GLPs presented in this paper can be subject to different levels of adaptation:

a. *Cloning a GLP.* Such a GLP has exactly the same structure, the same narratives but not the same learning content as the original.
b. *Removing or replacing a minigame with a new one.* To increase the flexibility of the adaptation process, the structure of a GLP can be altered and the minigames used in the initial GLP can be removed or replaced. In our example, we reuse a GLP designed for high school for undergrad students. In this case, it is not so suitable to use the Drag it minigame (which was used for the missing elements of the periodic system), so it was replaced with a different type of game - the Swipe and seek minigame.

Even if the opportunity for reuse significantly reduces the time and resources required to create gamified learning experiences, perpetual reuse can impact the player experience in a negative way, leading to demotivation and lack of engagement, as the user is exposed to the same narratives and images. Therefore, changing the learning content does not suffice. Since most of the Beaconing code has been made available as open source, further levels of adaptation are possible by applying changes directly in the code.

c. *Changing the narratives.* Narratives represent a key mechanic of engagement. The structure of a GLP can be reused (POIs, minigames), and the narratives can be changed to create a new experience for the players. This reduces the time required to create a new GLP from scratch and provides more flexibility in adapting a GLP for a specific subject of topic.

d. *Changing the images in a GLP*. Seeing the same images over and over again can have a negative impact on player motivation. Changing the narratives might not suffice. Therefore, exposing players to a new set of images can increase their motivation to play the GLP.

6 Discussion and Conclusions

Employing gamified lessons paths provide engaging alternatives to traditional learning environments. However, to empower teachers to fully harvest the benefits that GLPs can bring, it is necessary to address the barriers that prevent successful GLPs redesign and adaptation. These steps can be used for re-purposing every existing GLP and is a straight forward approach. But, even though the teachers adapting the GLPs reported that the new guidelines and the authoring tool supported the process quite well, they also highlighted the following:

- The current version of the AT-GLP does not provide an overview of the minigames; therefore, teachers find it difficult to follow the content that is associated to a minigame, e.g. if a quiz has several questions, it is difficult to navigate between them.
- It remains difficult for teachers to identify quickly how a particular game is relevant to a certain component of the curriculum, as well as assess the accuracy and appropriateness of the content within the game with the subject that is being taught, which shows that we are still dealing with the same challenges in alignments [15, 16, 18, 21].
- Even if a GLP provides an engaging setting, using the same narrative structure and the same images over and over again makes students loose interest. Personalizing a GLP requires access to digital resources such as images and especially sets of images that can be used across a narrative path to redesign a GLP. In addition, as pointed out in example 2, where we changed the target group- the narrative has a very important function in the current GLPs, and therefore this needs to be very well aligned to the target group [18, 19].
- Moreover, the current versions of the authoring tool enable limited access to such changes. For example, to change the images within a GLP, the teacher has to make changes in the GLP code. Therefore, the skills required for substantial changes across a GLP are still high. Even if the source code is available, advanced ITC skills are required to perform more in-depth changes and adapt a GLP to meet specific requirements of a certain subject or of specific learning objectives.

The paper presents the reuse settings of a GLP, using tools developed in the Beaconing project and presents approaches to reuse and customization. Future work includes testing of the customization capabilities, in order to further improve the experience both on the teacher side, as learning designers, and on the student side, as players.

References

1. Iten, N., Petko, D.: Learning with serious games: is fun playing the game a predictor of learning success? Br. J. Educ. Technol. **47**(1), 151–163 (2016)

2. Giessen, H.W.: Serious games effects: an overview. Procedia - Soc. Behav. Sci. **174**, 2240–2244 (2015). https://doi.org/10.1016/j.sbspro.2015.01.881. ISSN 1877-0428
3. Mouaheb, H., Fahli, A., Moussetad, M., Eljamali, S.: The serious game: what educational benefits? Procedia - Soc. Behav. Sci. **46**, 5502–5508 (2012). https://doi.org/10.1016/j.sbspro.2012.06.465. ISSN 1877-0428
4. Mayer, I.: Towards a comprehensive methodology for the research and evaluation of serious games. Procedia Comput. Sci. **15**, 233–247 (2012). https://doi.org/10.1016/j.procs.2012.10.075. ISSN 1877-0509
5. Khenissi, M.A., Essalmi, F., Jemni, M.: Comparison between serious games and learning version of existing games. Procedia - Soc. Behav. Sci. **191**, 487–494 (2015). https://doi.org/10.1016/j.sbspro.2015.04.380. ISSN 1877-0428
6. Paiva, A.C.R., Flores, N.H., Barbosa, A.G., Ribeiro, T.P.B.: iLearnTest – framework for educational games. Procedia - Soc. Behav. Sci. **228**, 443–448 (2016). https://doi.org/10.1016/j.sbspro.2016.07.068. ISSN 1877-0428
7. Carvalho, M.B., et al.: An activity theory-based model for serious games analysis and conceptual design. Comput. Educ. **87**, 166–181 (2015). https://doi.org/10.1016/j.compedu.2015.03.023. ISSN 0360-1315
8. Buchinger, D., da Silva Hounsell, M.: Guidelines for designing and using collaborative-competitive serious games. Comput. Educ. **118**, 133–149 (2018). https://doi.org/10.1016/j.compedu.2017.11.007. ISSN 0360-1315
9. Baalsrud Hauge, J.M., Stefan, I.A., Stefan, A.: Exploring pervasive entertainment games to construct learning paths. In: Munekata, N., Kunita, I., Hoshino, J. (eds.) ICEC 2017. LNCS, vol. 10507, pp. 196–201. Springer, Cham (2017). https://doi.org/10.1007/978-3-319-66715-7_21
10. BEACONING Project: D3.3 learning environment system specification (2017)
11. Bell, B.: Investigate and decide learning environments: specializing task models for authoring tool design. J. Learn. Sci. **7**(1), 65–105 (1998). https://doi.org/10.1207/s15327809jls0701_3
12. Wiley, D.A.: Connecting learning objects to instructional design theory: a definition, a metaphor, and a taxonomy. Instr. Use Learn. Objects **2830**(435), 1–35 (2000)
13. Martinez, M.: Designing learning objects to personalize learning margaret martinez. Instr. Use Learn. Objects **2830**(435), 151–172 (2000). in Wiley, D.A.
14. Stănescu, I.A., et al.: Strategies and tools to enable reuse in serious games ecosystems and beyond. In: Proceedings of the 10th International Scientific Conference, eLearning and Software for Education (2014)
15. Stanescu, I.A., Baalsrud Hauge, J., Stefan, A., Lim, T.: Towards modding and reengineering digital games for education. In: de De Gloria, A., Veltkamp, R. (eds.) GALA 2015. LNCS, vol. 9599, pp. 550–559. Springer, Cham (2016). https://doi.org/10.1007/978-3-319-40216-1_59
16. Baalsrud Hauge, J., et al.: Serious game mechanics and opportunities for reuse. In: Roceanu, I. (ed.) Rethink Education by Leveraging the eLearning Pillar of the Digital Agenda for Europe, Proceedings of the 11th International Conference on eLearning and Software for Education (eLSE), Bucharest/Romania, vol. 2, pp. 19–27. Carol I NDU Publishing House, Bucharest (2015)
17. Stanescu, I.A., Stanescu, A.M., Moisescu, M., Sacala, I.S., Stefan, A.: Enabling interoperability between serious game and virtual engineering ecosystems. In: Proceedings of the ASME 2014 International Design and Engineering Technical Conferences & Computers and Information in Engineering Conference (IDETC/CIE2014), Buffalo, New York, USA (2014)
18. BEACONING Project: D6.3 validation and usability report (2019)
19. Lim, T., et al.: The LM-GM framework for serious games analysis (2013). https://pdfs.semanticscholar.org/7df0/20237a6d3995860e7345c77dab28e4d0a001.pdf?_ga=2.140232560.2103361417.1593945229-977332475.1569848762. Accessed 04 July 2020

20. Baalsrud Hauge, J., et al.: Exploring context-aware activities to enhance the learning experience. In: Dias, J., Santos, P.A., Veltkamp, R.C. (eds.) GALA 2017. LNCS, vol. 10653, pp. 238–247. Springer, Cham (2017). https://doi.org/10.1007/978-3-319-71940-5_22
21. Lim, T., et al.: Narrative serious game mechanics (NSGM) – insights into the narrative-pedagogical mechanism. In: Göbel, S., Wiemeyer, J. (eds.) GameDays 2014. LNCS, vol. 8395, pp. 23–34. Springer, Cham (2014). https://doi.org/10.1007/978-3-319-05972-3_4

Serious Games for Learning: A Quantitative Review of Literature

Manuel J. Ibarra[1]([✉]) [ID], Vladimiro Ibañez[2] [ID], Ismar Frango Silveira[3] [ID], Cesar A. Collazos[4] [ID], Günter Wallner[5] [ID], and Matthias Rauterberg[5] [ID]

[1] Micaela Bastidas National University of Apurímac, Abancay, Peru
manuelibarra@gmail.com
[2] National University of Altiplano Puno, Puno, Peru
vibanez@unap.edu.pe
[3] Mackenzie Presbyterian University, São Paulo, Brazil
ismar.silveira@mackenzie.br
[4] University of Cauca, Popayán, Colombia
ccollazo@unicauca.edu.co
[5] Eindhoven University of Technology, Eindhoven, The Netherlands
{g.wallner,g.w.m.rauterberg}@tue.nl

Abstract. There exists a considerable amount of digital games that are described and published in the scientific literature. Among them, there are those considered as "serious games", whose foremost goal differs from pure entertainment, being conceived mainly for training, capacity building, and education among other ends. Serious digital games for learning represent an important part of this whole set, and it is relevant to observe the actual state-of-the-art about the research in this field. In this sense, this paper presents a quantitative literature review on previous papers published in peer-reviewed conference proceedings or journals related to digital games for learning.

Keywords: Serious games · Game-Based learning · Digital games · Learning · Educational games

1 Introduction

The incorporation of Information and Communication Technologies (ICTs) in the processes of teaching and learning is increasing quickly. Nowadays, the meaning of "education through ICT", is not simply to give people computers; rather, it implies that teachers are ready for the adoption of this paradigm, improving students' skills, using the appropriate software tools, combining adequately artistic elements like sound, animation and design in educational contexts, and using playful elements to facilitate students' learning [1].

Serious games (SG) have been originally defined by Abt [2] as having *an explicit and carefully thought-out educational purpose and are not intended to be played primarily for amusement. This does not mean that serious games are not, or should not be, entertaining.* This classical definition may be seen to contrast with another foundational definition of

© Springer Nature Switzerland AG 2020
M. Ma et al. (Eds.): JCSG 2020, LNCS 12434, pp. 164–174, 2020.
https://doi.org/10.1007/978-3-030-61814-8_13

games themselves, given by Huizinga [3], as *a free activity standing quite consciously outside "ordinary" life as being "not serious", but at the same time absorbing the player intensely and utterly*, although Huizinga remained vague on the notion of 'not serious' (see [4] on this matter).

Among the wide array of SGs, the focus point of this paper are those SGs intended to promote learning (of something) and have the intrinsic intention of improving the learning and/or teaching processes, unlike "pure" entertainment games. In a broad sense, educational games, or SGs for learning, represent a subset of SGs, even though educational – or at least training – aspects are always involved in the conception of a SG if viewed under the lens of its traditional definition. However, many definitions of SGs blur the differences among SGs and SGs for learning, such as the one from Michael and Chen [5]: *a serious game is a game in which educating (in its various forms) is the main objective, instead of entertainment.* This range of definitions of SGs and related genres such as game-based learning further complicate the discussion surrounding these terms (see also [6]). Sometimes, for example, citizen science games, where players collaboratively produce data on scientific tasks are considered serious games as well (e.g., [7, 8]). In an effort to overcome this 'genrefication', others have thus attempted to offer more holistic definitions and proposed terms such as 'applied games' [6]. However, despite this long-lasting discussions and efforts, the term SG continues to be widely used within academia and industry.

Serious Games cannot be simply defined as digital games made with educational and entertainment value added as decorators: the educational aspects must be present in the whole conception of the game. Serious games have being gaining importance in the educational field [9], offering positive learning experiences [10]. They were found to be effective, in many cases, for learning, skills development, and information retention and some results show that they facilitate knowledge acquisition [11]. More than this, they bring an important factor to the learning process, that is, motivation [12, 13]. However, as mentioned by Vandercruysse et al. [14], the positive results are dependent on many variables that range from the students' background to game design aspects and the subject being learned.

In this sense, this work presents an additional contribution to previous works [10, 11, 14], among others, indicating the continuous growth of SG research. This contributes to the current state-of-the-art of investigations related to serious games that support learning.

1.1 On the Various Definitions Around Serious Games

Despite having broad definitions, as above mentioned, SGs are games that are designed in a way such that the player is meant to learn something, to train some ability, or to acquire some skill [15]. Undoubtedly, since they often present a considerable potential in the teaching-learning process [16, 17], they frequently are confused with the subset of educational games.

The effective use of SGs allows to address challenges in the learning process, especially if: they are adaptive; they propose clear goals and sub-goals; they allow or even induce collaboration between players/students, even though this collaboration is achieved through competition; and people are satisfied when they play them – a real immersion is desirable.

SGs are also related to Game-Based Learning (GBL). According to some authors (e.g., [18, 19]), GBL refers to any learning process that is motivated, induced, or conducted by one (digital or physical) game – or a suite of them. Many authors, like Deguirmendjian et al. [1] and Miljanovic and Bradbury [20], for instance, have recently conducted studies that are related to SGs and GBLs.

The overall aspect in GBL is to use games as triggers to involve (and hopefully improve) students in their own learning processes, as well as to serve as aiding tools for teaching processes, too. In GBL, through the use of games, the main role of the teacher becomes to motivate and empower students' knowledge to develop a deep and meaningful learning [21]. However, to properly achieve this purpose with digital games, teachers must have a solid knowledge of how to integrate ICTs into curricula and syllabi, and how to integrate GBL activities into the classroom [22].

The player experience of a serious game will be guided by a problem, while entertainment games will generally be full of action and have lots of possibilities. Also, according to [23] it is advised *to develop the story in a serious game based on the user's action, while in an entertainment game random effects are often applied.*

2   Literature Review

This paper deals with a quantitative assessment of literature related to papers about SGs designed to improves students' learning. The articles were selected in May 2019 and are indexed in the international conference and journal databases Scopus[1], DBLP[2], ACM Digital Library[3], IEEExplore[4], Google Scholar[5], and Science Direct[6].

2.1   Search String

At first, papers were searched using only the word "game". However, as this search is extremely broad and the results, as expected, included all kinds of entertainment games as well as other unrelated papers (like those related to enterprise games, physical games, sports in general and game theory, or the field of artificial intelligence). As such, the search term was replaced by the term "serious game". Some search engines did not consider the word "games" in the plural, so the search had to be refined using wildcards "serio*" and the logical connector AND "game*" so that both words are considered within the search. The wildcard "*" in "game*" means that the engine can search words like: "games", "gamer", "gamers" and other words that start with "game".

During this process, it has been observed that there is a considerable amount of papers that are related to SGs, but their metadata considered the word "Educate" instead.

---

[1] https://www.scopus.com (Accessed: August, 2020).

[2] https://dblp.uni-trier.de/ (Accessed: August, 2020).

[3] https://dl.acm.org/ (Accessed: August, 2020).

[4] https://ieeexplore.ieee.org/Xplore/home.jsp (Accessed: August, 2020).

[5] https://scholar.google.com/ (Accessed: August, 2020).

[6] https://www.sciencedirect.com/ (Accessed: August, 2020).

However, "Educate" (root word) has several derivative words, as well, for example: education, educational, educative, educated, educates, educating. Therefore, it was decided to use a wildcard for this word as well, that is "educa*".

Finally, to further refine the search string for SGs focused on education and also incorporate papers related explicitly to educational games, it was needed to use some logical connectors:

(((educa*) OR (serious*)) AND (game*))

where the "*" represents any character or set of characters.

2.2   Filtering Criteria

Metadata searching criterion. The search string is compared to the following metadata: the "title", "abstract" or "keywords" in each of the scientific repositories and indexes. Two additional criteria were as well: date and language.

Chronological criterion. When reviewing the literature, it has been verified that there are published papers related to SG going back to the 1990s. However, in our case, only the last 8 years have been considered to focus on recent activity in the field. That is, the first filter criterion was to consider only papers published between 2011 to 2018.

Language criterion. The second filter criterion was to consider only articles that were written in English, since the databases that are part of this study generally consider articles written in that language.

2.3   Flowchart for Research Papers Collection

Given the selection, filter, and optimization criteria discussed above, the process of collecting scientific articles can be summarized in the flowchart depicted in Fig. 1. Each database considered for this study was analysed individually and sequentially; that is, one was processed after the other. For each database, the search string described in Sect. 2.1 was applied, containing the derivable terms "educa*" or "serious*" joint with the derivable term "game*". These terms were searched for within the metadata (i.e., *title, keywords,* or *abstract*) of the published article. Then the articles are filtered based on the criteria outlined in Sect. 2.2 (only English articles published between 2011 to 2018).

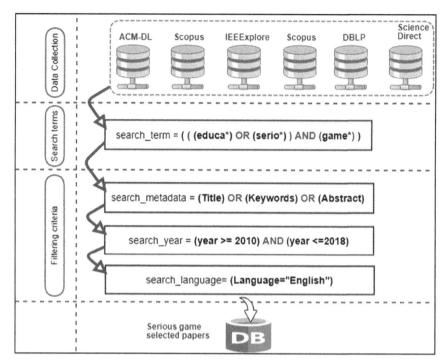

Fig. 1. Flowchart for research papers collection

3   Results and Discussion

Having defined the process of collecting the scientific articles from the aforementioned databases, results were obtained from each of the databases.

In the following we will contrast the results when only considering the field *"title"* – because, most of the search engines index the title of the research articles – with results obtained by searching within all three fields, that is, *"title"*, *"abstract"* and *"keyword"*, in this way there are more possibilities to find research articles.

3.1   Results

Table 1 shows the results obtained when searching within the *"title"* only. The column *"source"* indicates the database from which the information has been extracted; the *"total"* column gives the total number of scientific articles that the query has returned; the *"query"* column shows the query that has been used to obtain the results; and finally the *"target field"* column indicates the field on which the query was applied. In this first case, for all databases, the search was performed within the *"title"* field.

In each of the databases, the language used to make the queries differs from each other with respect to the use of logical connectors. For example, in the ACM Digital Library (DL) the query is `"acmdlTitle:(+game* serious* educa*)"`, which means that looking in the field `"Title"`, `"+game*"` requires the presence of the "game*" term

Table 1. Searching by title only

Source	Total	Search String	Target Field
ACM-DL	4,994	`acmdlTitle:(+game* serio* educa*)`	Title
IEEExplore	1,189	`((("Document Title":educa*) OR "Document Title":serio*) AND "Document Title":game*)`	Title
Scopus	4,599	`TITLE (((education OR serious OR educational OR educative) AND (game OR games)))`	Title
DBLP	2,996	`(educa* || serio*) && (game*)`	Title
ScienceDirect	453	`Title: (education OR serious OR educational OR educative) AND (game OR games)`	Title
Google Scholar	4,100	`allintitle:(game OR games) and (education OR serious OR educational OR educative)`	Title
Total	**18,331**		

(and its derivatives) and must additionally find the term *serious** (and its derivatives) or the term *educa** (and its derivatives). In contrast, ScienceDirect does not accept the use of wildcards, so all the derived words must be put together by the logical OR connector.

Table 2. Searching by 3 or more fields

Source	Total	Search String	Target Field
ACM-DL	11,042	`(+game* serio* educa*)`	Any field
IEEExplore	6,807	`((("Document Title":educa*) OR "Document Title":serio*) AND "Document Title":game*)`	Title, abstract, keywords
Scopus	21,340	`TITLE-ABS-KEY (((education OR serious OR educational OR educative) AND (game OR games)))`	Title, abstract, keywords
DBLP	2,996	`(educa* || serio*) && (game*)`	Title
ScienceDirect	1,287	`Title, abstract, keywords: (education OR serious OR educational OR educative) AND (game OR games)`	Title, abstract, keywords
Google Scholar	19,000	`serious game education educational educative`	Any field
Total	**62,472**		

Table 2 shows the results obtained from the second search. In this case, the "*target field*" includes in some cases the search for "*title*", "*abstract*" and "*keyword*". In the case of the ACM-DL and Google Scholar, the search does so in all fields, including within the same document or the name of the conference or journal.

Table 3 shows the evolution of SG publications in conferences or journals from 2011 to 2018. The last column labelled with "%" shows the growth from 2011 to 2018 in percentages. For example, the "ACM-DL" database (digital library contains 1,235 publications published in 2011, and 1,648 publications published in 2018, resulting in a growth of 33.44%.

Table 3. Evolution of SG publications from 2011 to 2018

	2011	2012	2013	2014	2015	2016	2017	2018	Total	%
ACM-DL	1,235	1,271	1,233	1,338	1,347	1,459	1,511	1,648	11,042	33.44%
IEEExplore	872	806	895	946	764	756	823	945	6,807	8.37%
Scopus	1,913	2,028	2,242	2,525	2,827	3,116	3,297	3,392	21,340	77.31%
DBLP	291	263	365	414	442	405	440	376	2,996	29.21%
Science Direct	90	116	95	150	192	170	216	258	1,287	186.67%
Google Scholar	1,690	2,130	2,200	2,440	2,560	2,690	2,620	2,670	19,000	57.99%
								Total	**62,472**	

In summary, the number of publications on serious games for learning purposes has increased in recent years. Google Scholar and Scopus have more papers indexed in their databases than the other ones.

3.2 Discussion

Comparisons were made between searching just in *title* field versus searching in several fields: *title*, *abstract* and *keywords*. As expected, results are five times more numerous in almost all databases, except for DBLP, as seen in Fig. 2.

The ACM-DL is a library that specializes in computer science and is focused on gathering research in that area. It indexes articles of conferences, specialized magazines, technical reports, books, et cetera. For this reason, it has a considerable amount of documents related to Serious Games. Around 5,000 papers were found when searching within the title of publications and more than 11,000 when including other target fields.

IEEExplore is a database that indexes the title, the abstract, author, citations, references, DOI, published in (conference or journal name), and the content of research papers related to science, computing, electronics, electrical, and related branches, therefore, the coincidences of the term sought can be better in some cases. Numbers are lower if compared to the ACM-DL: 1,000 papers found by title only and almost 7,000 when expanding the search to other fields.

Scopus is a database with a greater volume of information because it covers all areas of knowledge. Besides storing journals, it has information on monographies, conference

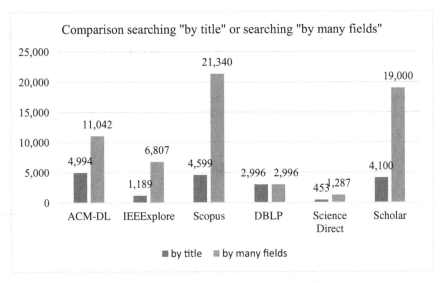

Fig. 2. Comparison of two types of searching

proceedings, book chapters and others, and its coverage reaches back to 1970. That is one of the reasons that we found more articles indexed and related to serious games: just a few papers less than the ACM-DL when searching for title, but an impressive number of papers retrieved when the expanded search was performed – more than 20,000 papers related to the topic in some manner.

DBLP only looks for matches of the search string in the title and the search includes the author metadata automatically. For example, it also includes results if the term game* is part of the author name. DBLP does not have a way to exclude terms that match the name, as such the exclusion has to be done manually, which sometimes could not be an addressable issue. On the other hand, the main feature of DBLP is that it is a database specialized in Computer Science. DBLP also only indexes the titles of the articles, so there is no option to add search fields for the abstract and keywords. Therefore, the search for "title" and "multiple fields" returned around 3,000 papers for both cases, as shown in Fig. 2.

ScienceDirect was the database with the lowest number of articles related to the search terms, when compared with the other databases (both in the search by title and in the search by several fields): around 500 papers in the first case, and 1,500 in the second. This is mainly because it only indexes scientific articles from conferences, magazines, and book chapters; in addition, an article listed in ScienceDirect always implies that it comes from a peer-reviewed source, which is a more demanding requirement than posed by other databases.

In the case of Google Scholar, it has the characteristic that it is not necessary to use wildcards to include the derived words, since the search engine does it automatically. For example, if "game" is placed as a term, it automatically considers the derivative words such as game, games, gaming, gamer. Google Scholar is a search engine that searches several databases; therefore, it is like a metasearch engine for scientific articles and, consequently, it is expected that the amount of retrieved papers is large in comparison – in the reported search, around 4,000 papers were retrieved by "title" and more than 19,000 were retrieved in the extended search.

Each database analysed was growing in number of publications from 2011 to 2018. Figure 3, shows that publications covering SGs are growing continuously.

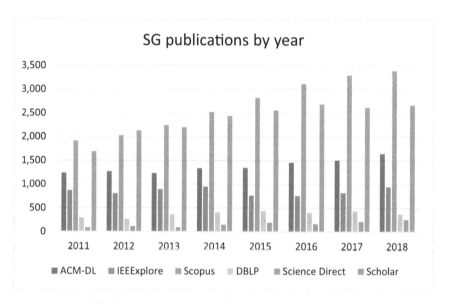

Fig. 3. Evolution of SGs publications in the last 8 years

4   Conclusion and Future Work

This work presented a quantitative overview of literature related to the publication of scientific articles on serious games for learning in the last 8 years (2011-2018) in the most relevant scientific databases in computer science related fields: ACM-DL, IEE-Explore, Scopus, DBLP, ScienceDirect, and Google Scholar. A flowchart for searching and extraction process of the articles was presented and a search string including terms related to serious games and game-based learning was defined.

Searches were performed in two ways: first, the search was only performed in the "title" section of the article, returning a total of 18,331 papers. The second search considered a broader search, accepting the search string appearing in the "title", "abstract", or "keywords" of each article, resulting in 62,472 papers. The large amount of publications is growing every year, showing the increased interest of researchers in SGs.

Future work aims to perform a systematic literature review, following a strict protocol to exclude those articles that are not really related to SGs for learning, but were wrongly included for some reason, such as a mismatch with any other academic field.

On the other hand, as a further work, it is proposed to automate this search by creating a search engine that could extract the data automatically, then processing the filters, then excluding articles that seem to have been wrongly selected, and finally showing the results through appropriate tables or charts. In such an approach, it would be enough to insert the search string and the system would automatically determine the derived words. Clearly some text mining and artificial intelligence techniques will need to be applied to achieve this.

Acknowledgment. This project was financed by the Micaela Bastidas National University of Apurimac.

References

1. Deguirmendjian, S.C., de Miranda, F.M., Zem-Mascarenhas, S.H.: Serious game developed in health: Integrative literature review. J. Health Inform. **8**, 110–116 (2016)
2. Abt, C.C.: Serious games (1970). https://books.google.com.pe/books?id=axUs9HA-hF8C&printsec=frontcover&hl=es#v=onepage&q&f=false
3. Huizinga, J.: Homo Ludens: Essay on the Social Function of the Game. Serisia. Gallimard, Paris (1951)
4. Rodriguez, H.: The playful and the serious: An approximation to Huizinga's Homo Ludens. Game Stud. **6**, 1604–7982 (2006)
5. Michael, D.R., Chen, S.L.: Serious Games: Games that Educate, Train, and Inform. Muska & Lipman/Premier-Trade (2005)
6. Schmidt, R., Emmerich, K., Schmidt, B.: Applied games–in search of a new definition. In: International Conference on Entertainment Computing, pp. pp. 100–111 (2015)
7. Baaden, M., Delalande, O., Ferey, N., Pasquali, S., Waldispühl, J., Taly, A.: Ten simple rules to create a serious game, illustrated with examples from structural biology (2018)
8. Dippel, A., Fizek, S.: Laborious Playgrounds: Citizen science games as new modes of work/play in the digital age. In: The playful citizen: civic engagement in a mediatized culture. Amsterdam University Press (2018)
9. Carvalho, M.B., et al.: An activity theory-based model for serious games analysis and conceptual design. Comput. Educ. **87**, 166–181 (2015)
10. De Freitas, S.: Are games effective learning tools? a review of educational games. J. Educ. Technol. Society. **21**, 74–84 (2018)
11. Backlund, P., Hendrix, M.: Educational games-are they worth the effort? a literature survey of the effectiveness of serious games. In: 2013 5th international conference on games and virtual worlds for serious applications (VS-GAMES), pp. 1–8 (2013)
12. Wouters, P., Van Nimwegen, C., Van Oostendorp, H., Van Der Spek, E.D.: A meta-analysis of the cognitive and motivational effects of serious games. J. Educ. Psychol. **105**, 249 (2013)
13. Connolly, T.M., Boyle, E.A., MacArthur, E., Hainey, T., Boyle, J.M.: A systematic literature review of empirical evidence on computer games and serious games. Comput. Educ. **59**, 661–686 (2012)
14. Vandercruysse, S., Vandewaetere, M., Clarebout, G.: Game-based learning: A review on the effectiveness of educational games. In: Handbook of research on serious games as educational, business and research tools, pp. 628–647. IGI Global (2012)
15. Marsh, T.: Slow serious games, interactions and play: Designing for positive and serious experience and reflection. Entertainment Comput. **14**, 45–53 (2016)

16. Guillén-Nieto, V., Aleson-Carbonell, M.: Serious games and learning effectiveness: the case of It'sa Deal! Comput. Educ. **58**, 435–448 (2012)
17. Baalsrud Hauge, J., Judd, N., Stefan, I.A., Stefan, A.: Perspectives on accessibility in digital games. In: Clua, E., Roque, L., Lugmayr, A., Tuomi, P. (eds.) ICEC 2018. LNCS, vol. 11112, pp. 402–406. Springer, Cham (2018). https://doi.org/10.1007/978-3-319-99426-0_51
18. Ruiz-Molina, M.-E., Gil-Saura, I., Berenguer-Contri, G.: Information and communication technology as a differentiation tool in restaurants. J. Foodservice Bus. Res. **17**, 410–428 (2014)
19. Qian, M., Clark, K.R.: Game-based Learning and 21st century skills: a review of recent research. Comput. Hum. Behav. **63**, 50–58 (2016)
20. Miljanovic, M.A., Bradbury, J.S.: A review of serious games for programming. In: Göbel, S., Garcia-Agundez, A., Tregel, T., Ma, M., Baalsrud Hauge, J., Oliveira, M., Marsh, T., Caserman, P. (eds.) JCSG 2018. LNCS, vol. 11243, pp. 204–216. Springer, Cham (2018). https://doi.org/10.1007/978-3-030-02762-9_21
21. Cerinšek, G., et al.: Recommendations to leverage game-based learning to attract young talent to manufacturing education. In: Alcañiz, M., Göbel, S., Ma, M., Fradinho Oliveira, M., Baalsrud Hauge, J., Marsh, T. (eds.) JCSG 2017. LNCS, vol. 10622, pp. 187–202. Springer, Cham (2017). https://doi.org/10.1007/978-3-319-70111-0_18
22. Shah, M., Foster, A.: Developing and assessing teachers' knowledge of game-based learning. J. Technol. Teach. Educ. **23**, 241–267 (2015)
23. De Bock, R.: Serious Games: games for Learning. (2018)

Game Design and Study

Costs to Compete - Analyzing Pay to Win Aspects in Current Games

Thomas Tregel[✉][iD], Miriam Claudia Schwab, Thanh Tung Linh Nguyen, Philipp Niklas Müller, and Stefan Göbel

Technical University of Darmstadt, Multimedia Communications Lab - KOM, Darmstadt, Germany
thomas.tregel@kom.tu-darmstadt.de

Abstract. Microtransactions, in the form of loot boxes, are items in a digital game, bought with real money that contains semi-randomized content. They are a commonly used concept for monetarization in current games that are also often free to play. When purchasable items give players a decisive advantage in a game, people often call it pay-to-win: competitive advantages through real-money in-game purchases.

In this study, we analyze and identify different aspects of current video games, to assess, whether a game has partial, or strong pay-to-win elements. Within a user study of 96 participants, these aspects are then rated individually and compared to the users' subjective opinion whether a presented game has strong pay-to-win elements, differentiating between players that actively play a respective game and those who do not.

We then analyze two popular games, regarding their expected costs, to stay in a highly competitive environment. Due to the virtual power gained by investing money into those games, players can feel obliged to invest to stay competitive and increase their chances of winning. Our results indicate that selected aspects are clear indicators to predict whether a game is perceived as being pay-to-win. Additionally, our main conclusion shows the threat of new players having to invest heavily in a loot box system already compared to gambling in multiple countries.

Keywords: Competitive games · Loot box · Pay-to-win

1 Introduction

Loot boxes, in general, are purchasable items in video games that contain a randomized selection of virtual items. These items range from simple customization options for a player's avatar or character to game-changing equipment such as weapons and armor, or even powerful temporary items of limited use. Similar to real-world trading of collecting card games, players do not know the boxes' content before opening it. Zendle et al. [9] identifies seven different aspects in which loot boxes differ from each other. This includes the aspect of "paying to win":

© Springer Nature Switzerland AG 2020
M. Ma et al. (Eds.): JCSG 2020, LNCS 12434, pp. 177–192, 2020.
https://doi.org/10.1007/978-3-030-61814-8_14

boxes containing items that give "players a distinct advantage when playing the game itself" [9]. In many cases, the available items cannot be directly purchased with real money. This means that to acquire such items by spending money, the only option players have is buying loot boxes [8].

In many games, these loot boxes contain purely cosmetic content, giving no competitive advantage to the player. No matter how much money a player invests in the given game, they do not increase the likelihood of winning due to their expenses.

In competitive games, players compete against each other for different reasons, like glory or price money. With eSports becoming more popular and competing for participants and viewers with traditional sports [4], communities aim to find the best performing players among them. Especially in these highly competitive areas, an equal playing field is important to find the better player [6].

However, when individual game elements that can be influenced by real money purchases have a direct impact on a game, the game's outcome can become skewed. Especially newer players are not only required to overcome the gap in experience, game knowledge, and skill, but also need to compensate for, or catch up with the spending of their more successful opponents.

Our goal in this work is divided into two research goals:

- RG 1: Identify and compare different aspects of popular games, contributing to the public opinion of calling a game "pay-to-win".
- RG 2: For selected identified games: Analyze the expected required costs to be able to compete in a competitive environment with equal chances.

2   Related Work and Research Goal

Due to many recent discussions on the tie between loot boxes and gambling, most of the scientific work focuses on the gambling severity aspect. It analyzes the human and behavioral aspects for loot boxes in general, with no specific focus on the competitiveness of a game: For gambling assessment, the Problem Gambling Severity Index is used [2]. Studies found a close similarity between gambling and loot boxes in the motivation [5,9], reward structure [3,10], and visual representation [7]. In individual countries like Belgium, loot boxes are therefore entirely banned [13]. In other countries, game developers are required to specify the exact chances for each individual item, including all possible contents [12].

To the best of our knowledge, there is no scientific research on individual games and their associated costs to successfully compete. Due to their different game mechanics, competitive environment, and loot box integration, each game has to be treated individually. Because of this, most data and discussion can be found within the individual game communities: forums, community websites, or blogs of experienced players. This includes analysis platforms for online auctioning systems [17,21], breakdowns and analysis of successful setups [16,19], or simulators to predict the chances of obtaining a specific item or achieving a specific goal within the set amount of loot box openings [15,17,20]. The latter is especially important in the context of awareness and education, as loot boxes try to take advantage of many psychological aspects of human behavior [1].

3   Pay-to-win Aspects

3.1   Methodology

The first consideration for a self-determined pay-to-win factor is to investigate the connection between money spent by players and success in the game. A core problem here is to obtain reliable and robust data. However, the significance of the correlation is also problematic: The fact of having spent a lot of money in a game has no bearing on whether a player has won because of his financial resources or his outstanding skills. However, there is a likely correlation between time (and thus experience) spent playing the game and money spent on it. The mere possession of expensive weapons or playing cards does not make a player better or worse in pure gameplay. Free alternatives might be equally powerful, or a player might lack the skill to make use of his expensive items.

Table 1. Criteria with the highest relative frequency of being voted "Definitely pay-to-win" out of 28 surveyed criteria.

Nr	Criterion	Agreement	Score
1	At some point in the game it is impossible or inconvenient to further succeed/win/level up without paying money	96%	12
2	At some point in the game it is impossible or inconvenient to continue playing at all without paying money	91%	11
3	You can buy advantageous game items that cannot be obtained other than with real money	88%	11
4	You can obtain items that give you advantage in the Player versus Player (PVP) area	73%	9
5	You can obtain game items that give you permanent advantage	72%	9
6	You can obtain game items that have an influence on the game balance	58%	7
7	You can buy loot boxes with guaranteed success	52%	6
8	You can pay money to make a faster game progress	51%	6
9	You can buy game items that you would otherwise have to grind a lot to obtain them	51%	6
10	You can spend at least $10.000 on game items	51%	6
11	Game includes pay walls you can either skip by paying money or by waiting a certain period	48%	6
12	You can obtain items that give you advantage in the Player versus Environment (PVE) area	47%	6
13	Main game is fairly small and only gets interesting with DLCs/paid content	43%	5

Our approach involves the evaluation of games based on clearly defined criteria. For this purpose, criteria must be defined that describe pay-to-win aspects and investigate their application to games. Public opinions are widely scattered and not objectively ascertainable. In order not to undermine the subjective perception of a person for the evaluation, a collective opinion of the player community is required. To this end, potential criteria, frequently debated in discussion forums, are collected and integrated into a survey in an unbiased manner. Participants rate the aspects on a three points scale between "Not pay-to-win at all", "Can be pay-to-win", and "Definitely pay-to-win".

In a second step, 18 selected games, which have an in-game monetarization system employed, are to be rated on a four-point scale from "Not pay-to-win at all" over "Some (...)", and "moderate (...)", to "A lot (...)", with the option opt-out if the respective game is unknown to the participant. The games were selected, based on whether they are frequently discussed controversially concerning pay-to-win aspects, as well as currently popular multiplayer games not in the focus of discussion for comparison.

3.2   Identified Pay-to-win Aspects

Each factor is assigned a score according to how important it was deemed by the survey's participants. The scores were introduced to abstract from the agreement ratios, utilizing a better communicable score system, similar to game ratings in local and online press, allowing for an easier comparison.

Table 2. Sorted in descending order according to the determined criteria in Table 1. No opinion was collected for the beta version of Star Wars: BF II in the survey. Games annotated with an asterisk(*) have been rated down by local game press due to their controversial in-game monetarization concept.

Game	1	2	3	4	5	6	7	8	9	10	11	12	13	Score	User
World of Tanks*	✓	-	✓	✓	✓	✓	✓	✓	✓	✓	-	-	-	72	79
Hearthstone*	-	-	-	✓	✓	✓	✓	-	✓	✓	✓	✓	-	55	67
Star Wars: BF II (Beta)	✓	-	-	✓	✓	✓	-	✓	✓	✓	-	-	-	55	-
NBA 2K20*	-	-	-	✓	✓	✓	-	✓	✓	✓	-	✓	-	49	81
FIFA 20*	-	-	-	✓	✓	✓	-	-	✓	✓	-	-	-	37	91
FIFA 19*	-	-	-	✓	✓	✓	-	-	✓	✓	-	-	-	37	91
The Elder Scrolls Online	-	-	✓	-	✓	-	-	✓	-	✓	-	-	-	32	39
Eve Online	✓	-	-	-	-	-	-	✓	-	-	-	-	-	18	67
PUBG	-	-	-	-	-	-	-	-	✓	✓	-	-	-	12	14
Star Wars: BF II	-	-	-	-	-	-	-	-	-	✓	-	-	-	6	75
CS: GO	-	-	-	-	-	-	-	-	-	✓	-	-	-	6	11

Based on the 13 criteria in Table 1, we selected ten of the 18 games, which we examined and evaluated in more detail. Star Wars: Battlefront II was evaluated for both its current version and its beta version, which was criticized heavily before its release [14], to be able to compare both versions. If a criterion applies to the examined game, the scores are added up to the total score. Table 2 shows the evaluation based on the criteria, including the calculated score and the user scores from the second part of the survey.

All games have been assessed based on their current version between 23 Dec 2019 and 23 Jan 2020, during the time the online survey took place. The survey was distributed over the online platform Reddit in the respective gaming categories, and had a total of 96 participant with a dropout rate of 11.4%. In Fig. 1, we compare the scores assigned by active players of the respective game and players knowing about the game. In all but three cases active players rate the game as being less pay-to-win. The exceptions here are Hearthstone, Star Citizen, and Guild Wars 2. We measure the average deviation to be at 9.95 points with the highest deviations for League of Legends, World of Tanks, and Fortnite, which get rated substantially more pay-to-win by non-players.

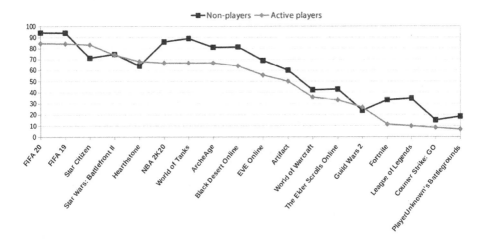

Fig. 1. Reported pay-to-win scores comparing active players and non-players.

3.3 Discussion

While some scores only vary slightly, there are scores with high variances. It is noticeable that the trade press (GameStar and GamePro) devaluated exactly those five titles that have the highest score out of the ten analyzed games. For some games, a high difference between calculated score and user score can be observed, which we look into further.

For EVE Online, although only a few criteria were met, those have a large influence on the specific game experience. Due to the game's freemium business model, players can double their training speed by using paid currency, thereby having a strong trade-off between time and money investment.

We have included two subsequent versions of the FIFA series to analyze whether the subjective opinion changes for each title, which could not be confirmed. Participants rated both games identical. For the NBA 2K20 game a similar assessment was received. For both series, the usage of loot boxes as a core game mechanics is discussed frequently, which seems to strongly impact the participants' opinion.

The difference of the impact score between the Beta- and the current version of Star Wars Battlefront II was particularly high. The reason for this is a drastic change in their monetarization concept after a heavy outbreak of negative feedback [14] during the game's beta version, leading the publisher to remove all microtransactions for the game's release. Later on, purchasable loot boxes were integrated again, however, limited to purely cosmetic items, without any options to buy virtual player power. Nevertheless, the survey participants still rated the game as being definitely pay-to-win.

In Fig. 2, we compare two factors of the same game area with each other. Aspects including, a guarantee of success, an advantage over another human player, and its permanence, were strongly related to pay-to-win aspects by the participants.

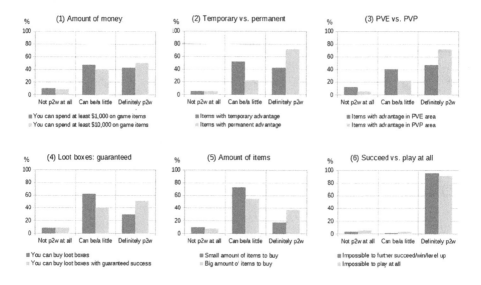

Fig. 2. Direct comparison of individual factors.

4   Game Analysis

To answer the question of what the costs to compete are on an individual basis, we choose to analyze two strongly competitive games. We select the two games based on their high data availability, game popularity, large competitive scene, and high assigned score in Sect. 3.2: FIFA20 and Hearthstone.

5 Hearthstone as Collectible Card Game

Hearthstone is a free-to-play digital collecting card game. just like most traditional card games (e.g.. Magic the Gathering, Yu-Gi-OH, Pokémon, etc.), its core gameplay revolves around two players battling against each other with a deck of cards. In Hearthstone, a deck consists of 30 cards from one of ten classes, out of a large card pool that increases after each expansion. Expansions are released about once every four months [18]. In addition to more than 300 cards at the initial launch of the game, each expansion added about 130 to 145 new cards. As of the "Savior of Uldum" expansion, released on 6th August 2019, there are 3,177 [18] cards in the game, which differ by rarity: common, rare, epic, and legendary.

5.1 Obtaining Cards in a Competitive Game Format

Cards are obtainable in two different ways: either by opening purchasable card packs (a form of loot box) or by directly crafting them [18]. Each expansion features a new card pack, containing only the newly introduced cards. With new expansions being released, older expansions are being excluded after, on average, two years from the available pool in the "Standard" game mode, which is the core competitive game mode for ranked play and tournaments. Trading systems are not available, and there is no way to directly buy a single card other than crafting it. Every card can be crafted using material (arcane dust, short: dust), which can be gained by destroying ("dusting") unwanted or duplicate cards. Each card rarity has a fixed crafting and dusting cost, with no differences between expansions[1]. As shown in Table 3, a player needs to dust four cards (for high rarities) up to eight cards (for lower rarities) to craft a select card of similar rarity. On average, by opening one pack, one can expect to gain from 100 to 110 dust by dusting every card[2]. A casual player who plays six games per day (each lasting about ten minutes) can, on average, obtain 70 to 75 gold with a 50% win-rate, including quests rewarding gold, with which they can buy about 20 packs (100 gold per pack) per month.

As of the 7th April 2020[3], there is a new card pack mechanism in place, modifying its content to always yield cards not currently or previously in the player's possession, while still following rarity chances. This reduces the number of card packs required when approaching a full collection based on rarity. As long as a substantial amount of cards in an observed rarity category is missing, this only resolves the chance for unpleasant duplicates.

---

[1] https://hearthstone.fandom.com/wiki/Crafting.

[2] http://hearthstone.blizzpro.com/2018/12/03/rastakhans-rumble-buyers-guide-how-many-packs-should-i-buy/.

[3] https://playhearthstone.com/en-us/news/23319441/welcome-to-the-year-of-the-phoenix.

Table 3. Dust crafting costs and rarity for different Hearthstone cards.

Rarity	Crafting cost	Dust gain	Chances to obtain
Common	40	5	Every other card
Rare	100	20	At least 1 or rarer per pack
Epic	400	100	Average of 1 per 5 packs
Legendary	1,600	400	Average of 1 per 20 packs

5.2   Assessing the Costs of Popular Decks

Due to the randomness introduced by the game's card packs, a probabilistic model is required to assess the estimated cost for a specific card deck or a full card collection. The resulting costs to create a single competitive deck thereby depend on multiple factors: luck to receive cards of the same class that also are relevant for the respective deck, and the players' flexibility to use a deck they obtained the most expansive cards for, by chance.

By using a simulation-based approach[4], a card opening process can be emulated showing a high completion rate for lower rarities, with small amount of card packs. Because the rarity appearance ratios of cards do not match the rarity chances of opening card packs, players only possess a fraction of available epic and legendary cards when completing their common and rare collection[5].

Building a good and competitive deck requires good preparations, a good understanding of the "metagame" (how the game is currently played by the successful players), and more importantly, having the right cards at hand. It is hard to quantify the effort needed to construct competitive decks, given how many factors are in place: acquiring the right cards by simply unpacking or having enough dust to craft them; or how one card can be underwhelming at first glance but turns out to be really good.

Since it is theoretically possible to craft all the cards needed to construct a new deck using the dust gained from opening and dusting card packs; a deck's value can be quantified by the amount of dust needed to craft it from the ground up as an upper bound. A more dust-expensive deck might not be better than ones that cost less, but it definitely requires more work to put together. In a competitive environment, having more options to choose from is always more preferable, especially in card games where the balance between decks could play out like a game of rock-paper-scissors. Additionally, due to the oftentimes higher power and attractiveness of rarer cards, the total costs of a competitive deck mostly contains rarer and thereby more expensive cards.

Throughout the year, there are many professional tournaments being held in the Hearthstone professional scene, with high prize money involved. Here, only the best players with the most well-thought-out decks take part. We now analyze decks from four different tournaments, divided into two pairs of the same rule sets.

---

[4] https://speedodevo.github.io/packr/.
[5] https://www.reddit.com/r/hearthstone/comments/79ykoa/the_real_cost_of_hearthstone/.

Competitive Tournaments. All data of the following tournaments has been extracted from hearthstonetopdecks[6]. The first two tournaments we look at are Masters Tour Las Vegas 2019 (14–16 Jun 2019) and Masters Tour Seoul 2019 (16–18 Aug 2019). Both tournaments were played under the Specialist format, which includes all the cards available in Standard. Each player can only select one class and build three decks for that class: with one primary deck and two variations of it. It is noteworthy that the grand finals of Masters Tour Seoul 2019 had players with perfectly identical decks, down to every single card. Additionally, they were also the most expensive ones by a margin of over 4,000 dust, as shown in Table 5. For Table 4, a slightly lower average deck cost can be observed. For most of the played decks, a high amount of legendary cards (L) can be observed, which contribute most to the total costs, followed by epic cards (E) and rare cards (R). The rest of each deck consists of common and basic (free) cards.

Table 4. Masters Tour Las Vegas 2019

Placement	Class	L	E	R	Dust costs
1	Mage	6	7	4	13,040
2	Warrior	6	8	8	13,840
3	Mage	3	7	4	8,400
4	Mage	4	8	4	10,320
5	Warrior	6	10	6	14,400
6	Mage	5	6	6	11,280
7	Rogue	5	2	8	10,000
8	Mage	4	6	5	9,620
Average cost: 11,362.5				Per card: 378.8	

Table 5. Masters Tour Seoul 2019

Placement	Class	L	E	R	Dust costs
1	Mage	10	8	5	19,740
2	Mage	10	8	5	19,740
3	Hunter	8	3	4	14,880
4	Warrior	4	10	6	11,280
5	Warrior	5	9	7	12,580
6	Priest	1	2	10	3,840
7	Hunter	8	3	6	15,000
8	Rogue	4	4	4	8,880
Average cost: 13,242.5				Per card: 441.4	

After gaining an impression of the costs of a singular successful competitive deck, two questions arise: What are the costs in a format when multiple decks can be brought, and what are the costs for decks in Standard ranked play? Similar to the previous evaluation, we assessed two tournaments with a format where players had to bring four decks of different classes. The dust costs are as follows:

 – Masters Tour Bucharest 2019 - Average cost: 35,283; Sample SD: 10,726; per card cost: 294.0
 – Hearthstone Global Finals 2019 - Average cost: 36,653; Sample SD 5,205; per card cost: 305.4

While the played decks have similar proportions of different rarities to the previous tournaments, and thereby different singular deck costs, the average card costs are significantly lower. The reason for this is the aspect of neutral cards: cards that are not limited to a specific class but can be used by all of them.

---

[6] https://www.hearthstonetopdecks.com/.

Since the sample size of tournaments is quite small (n = 4) and eight finalists each, we do not compare the different cost of popular decks and their tournament placement. However, the average dust costs remain a metric for the overall costs of a deck, which we will now compare to the openly available ranked play.

Ranked Play. For Standard ranked play, the official competitive environment for everybody to participate, there is a more diverse selection of decks that can perform well at any given time. In Table 6, we investigate the top five performing decks, with each sample three weeks apart from each other to signify a possible shift in the metagame[7]. We here focus on a deck's average win rate across all player skill levels, its dust cost, and how many cards from the latest expansion (DoD), at the time of the sample, were included. The latter aspect states how many new cards need to be acquired during the expansion, with the remaining cards introduced in the basic game or previous expansions. This serves as an indicator of new definite costs at the start of an expansion.

Table 6. Disposition of three different meta snapshots with the top five competing decks. Decks with same name can have slight card variations, leading to different costs.

Date	Deck name	Win rate(%)	% of DoD cards	Dust costs
29 Dec 2019	Pirate Warrior	54.35	33.33	7,580
	Galakrond Zoo Warlock	53.74	52.94	6,160
	Galakrond Warrior	53.52	40.00	14,240
	Secret Highlander Hunter	53.32	20.00	15,040
	Token Druid	53.17	25.00	4,840
	Average		34.25	9,572
20 Jan 2020	Galakrond Shaman	55.63	77.78	9,600
	Pirate Warrior	54.15	31.25	7,580
	Secret Highlander Hunter	54.05	13.04	15,040
	Face Hunter	53.45	27.27	3,840
	Galakrond Zoo Warlock	53.45	46.67	14,240
	Average		39.20	10,600
10 Feb 2020	Mech Paladin	55.45	14.29	5,680
	Highlander Dragon Hunter	55.22	39.13	16,440
	Secret Highlander Hunter	54.02	13.04	15,040
	Token Druid	53.88	20.00	4,840
	Dragon Hunter	53.65	64.29	4,480
	Average		30.15	9,296

We can conclude that the new expansion has an immediate impact on the game, with a lot of the strongest decks requiring a considerable amount of cards from it. The average dust cost of above 9,000 for these decks, is only slightly lower than those of professional players in tournaments. This cost is comparable with

---

[7] https://hsreplay.net/meta/.

four months of saving as calculated above. Given how expansions are normally three to four months apart, it is possible for players to craft one strong deck to play with right at the beginning of each expansion cycle. However, this only applies, when they play the aforementioned time, to gain the on average daily 70 to 75 gold, meaning to never miss a daily quest, and do not use any excessive gold or dust obtained during the expansion to purchase or craft additional decks. For a deck with a cost of 9,000 dust and the assumed 100 to 110 dust per card pack, the expected costs range between 100$ and 128$ based on different bundle purchase prices, which also vary on a currency-basis[8].

Due to shifts in the metagame, the stability of a deck cannot be predicted as only one deck in Table 6 was present during all three snapshots. All these decks had a win rate above 53%, which is significant given the sample size being over 100,000 played matches across all player ranks. However, whenever a chosen deck performs poorly during an expansion, players are required to either purchase card packs or invest a considerably larger amount of time. The same holds true for players aiming to play different decks for reasons of variety, fun, or because they are required to due to tournament formats. To make matters worse, you cannot predict every deck's performance immediately after an expansion release.

6 FIFA20 Ultimate Team

The FIFA game series is an annually released soccer sport simulation game. In the online competitive play mode, called FIFA Ultimate Team (FUT), players are expected to build their own teams and play them, simulating real-life soccer. A team thereby consists of cards, each representing a real soccer player, with different statistics (short: stats), strengths, and weaknesses. How the soccer player performs correlates with its card's stats, which numerically represent a player's attributes like shooting, passing, dribbling, or defending, up to a score of 100 each. In general, the higher and more specialized a card's stats are, the better it performs, and thus, the more valuable it becomes.

6.1 Obtaining Cards in a Competitive Game Format

Generally, most cards are acquired by buying and opening card packs (loot boxes) or trading. At the point of the analysis, there are more than 16,000 cards available in the latest edition of the series, with more added every week. The virtual representation of a soccer player is thereby affected by his real-life counterpart. In addition to regular cards, FIFA also offers special edition ones, which feature the same player but with better and upgraded stats. One of the most common special card, is the "Team of The Week" (TOTW) edition[9]. Every week the developer selects from 18 to 23 players based on their good real

---

[8] https://hearthstone.gamepedia.com/Card_pack#Purchasing.

[9] https://www.fifauteam.com/fifa-20-players-cards-guide/.

performances, across all licensed leagues, and presents them in a single TOTW squad. In the respective week, these special cards can be found in regular or special card packs, replacing the original card. After the week, the card can only be acquired by trading with other players.

Other special cards are created based on national, international, and intercontinental matches, awards, or holiday specials. The "Team of The Year" (TOTY) thereby resembles a squad of cards with highly elevated stats, offered once per year, with an added score from five to twelve, making them the most sought after cards in the game.

There are different ways to earn new cards in FIFA. The first way is to complete in-game challenges or to place high in the time-limited ladder. Since this depends a lot on the player's skill and time spent, it's hard to quantify and will not be attributed in this paper. The second way is to purchase card packs with real money using FIFA Points, which can be purchased from the game's official Origin Store or FIFA Coins, an in-game currency obtained by trading or discarding unwanted items. A selection of available purchasable card packs is shown in Table 7, including their reported chance of a player card having at least a specific score. Only the chances for the highest available scores are specified, as chances for player cards of higher scores increase.

Table 7. Overview over selected available packs, their prices and expected minimum discard or sell values. Packs annotated with an asterisk(*) are promotional and/or time limited. All cards from "Gold" packs up always contain scores of 75 and above (75+).

Name	Price		Min players	Min discard (coins)	Min sell (coins)	Score chance	
	Points	Coins				82+	Higher
Bronze	0	400	3	78	465	-	-
Silver	50	2,500	3	433	709	-	-
Gold	100	5,000	3	1,193	2,283	7.7%	82+: 3.4%
Premium Gold	150	7,500	3	1,239	2,329	19%	83+: 4.7%
Jumbo P. Gold*	300	15,000	6	2,409	4,928	40%	85+: 4.6%
Rare Gold*	500	25,000	3	2,292	3,157	55%	86+: 3.9%
Mega*	700	35,000	9	3,780	7,302	77%	87+: 5.6%
Rare Players*	1,000	50,000	12	7,200	7,980	78%	88+: 6.5%
Ultimate Pack*	2,500	125,000	30	18,000	19,950	99%	90+: 2.4%

Due to the high number of available cards, the chances to receive a singular sought after card are minimal. However, since it is possible to use the trading functionality, a set of cards can be obtained using the respective currency. To assess the overall costs, we will assume the following restricted worst-case scenario for a player wanting to use a highly competitive deck:

- The player does not have any of the desired cards at the beginning and has to purchase them on the market using coins.
- Between two cards, the one with the higher average stats is considered better.
- A team consists of one goalkeeper, four defenders, four midfielders and two strikers (4–4–2).

Data is taken by using the online trade market available at futbin.com, taken on 13 Jan 2020, using PS4, as it has the highest amount of auctions and thereby data[10]. The player aims to build the best team available, and therefore regularly updates their team when new packs are released. We choose to analyze the teams after every five newly released TOTW packs (so the best team available would consist of the absolute best cards after the TOTW5, TOTW10, and TOTW15 updates) and after the TOTY pack is released. By trading replaced cards away, players can make up for the cost of buying new cards. A card's market value thereby depends on the community, where older cards can drastically change when better substitution cards are available. In Table 8, we show the total team costs and their substitutions for the described approach. It is important to note that a card's price can be highly unstable in the first days or weeks after their release, due to their popularity.

Table 8. Coin prices of selected FUT teams according to futbin [17] on 13.01.2020.

Time	Card costs	Team costs	Substitutions
Basic	$\bar{x}$:403,622 SD:603,050	4,439,837	Whole new squad
TOTW5	$\bar{x}$:462,549 SD:600,016	5,088,035	Lewandowski (TOTW5), De Bruyne (TOTW2)
TOTW10	$\bar{x}$:742,111 SD:1,037,000	8,163,226	Ronaldo (TOTW10), Lewandowski (TOTW9), Messi (TOTW9), Hazard (TOTW10), Walker (TOTW8)
TOTW15	$\bar{x}$:1,095,000 SD:1,041,000	12,048,160	Salah (TOTW14), Neymar Jr (TOTW15), van Dijk (TOTW12), Vertonghen (TOTW14)
TOTY	$\bar{x}$:3,683,000 SD:2,387,000	40,511,705	Whole new squad

We can conclude that the addition of special cards has a high impact on the total costs of a team. Due to their higher score, they can perform better than their counterparts. Thereby, players optimizing their teams to increase their chances in competitive gameplay are tempted to change their team accordingly.

A survey conducted in 2019 [11] has shown that a large percentage of the participants (n = 1352) has spent money on FIFA Ultimate Team across versions, on top of the game's retail price. Individual participants reportedly spent tens

---

[10] https://www.futbin.com/market/auctions.

of thousands of dollars on opening packs. Since a new game is launched annualy, it is not uncommon to purchase everything again from zero in a following year.

One particularly outspoken player is Ivan 'BorasLegend' Lapanje, a professional eSport player with two championships under his belt. Lapanje spoke out against new qualification rules of FIFA's eSport tournament, the Global Series Qualifiers for FIFA20. According to him, this requires teams worth around 20,000,000 coins, which equates to 6000\$[11]. Lapanje is also quite open about his spending in the game to stay competitive at the highest level, citing an investment of 1700\$ to gain a head-start at the beginning of FIFA20[12]. Other pro players also supported his statements, criticizing the publisher's methods and standards. Another source also calculated the cost of competing in such an eSport tournaments, citing an average cost of 32,000,000 coins (27,000\$) in the playoff of the tournament[13].

7   Conclusion

Gaming is one of the most popular hobbies nowadays, where most games include elements allowing to use real money to purchase in-game elements. In an online study, we identified different criteria to assess whether a game has partial or strong pay-to-win elements, according to our first research goal. We observed that the players' opinions can differ greatly based on the presented elements or the respective game. For the case of Star Wars: Battlefront II, we observed one of the overall strictest user scores for a game that has close to no identified pivotal elements in place, for their enquired version. One reason for this could be the previously high media resonance, leading to a reversal of their monetarization concept.

In the next step, according to our second research goal, we analyzed two popular games regarding their expected costs for highly competitive play. Both games discussed have in common that they lock the acquisition of items behind loot boxes, which can be purchased as microtransactions. In the case of Hearthstone and FIFA Ultimate Team, by spending real money, players can, at the very least, significantly speed up their progress of acquiring game elements. By analyzing these elements, we identify an influence on the gameplay components and the games' respective competitive environment, be it on the ranking ladder available to all players or the most prestigious tournaments for professional players. When these pay-to-win elements are in place, there will always be a non-zero chance of someone successfully achieving a victory by outspending their opponents rather than outplaying them. The competitive integrity of the game could then be compromised, as it is hard for players to attribute their loss to player skill difference or team strength.

---

[11] https://twitter.com/ivanlapanje/status/1189484779445587968.

[12] https://twitter.com/ivanlapanje/status/1174386291217174530.

[13] https://twitter.com/fut_economist/status/1088928000907853826.

References

1. Drummond, A., Sauer, J.D.: Video game loot boxes are psychologically akin to gambling. Nature Hum. Behav. **2**(8), 530–532 (2018). https://doi.org/10.1038/s41562-018-0360-1
2. Ferris, J.A., Wynne, H.J.: The Canadian Problem Gambling Index. Canadian Centre on Substance Abuse Ottawa, ON, Canada (2001)
3. Griffiths, M.D.: Is the buying of loot boxes in video games a form of gambling or gaming? Gaming Law Rev. **22**(1), 52–54 (2018). https://doi.org/10.1089/glr2.2018.2216
4. Hamari, J., Sjöblom, M.: What is eSports and why do people watch it? Internet Res. **27**(2), 211–232 (2017). https://doi.org/10.1108/IntR-04-2016-0085
5. King, D.L., Delfabbro, P.H.: Video game monetization (eg,'loot boxes'): a blueprint for practical social responsibility measures. Int. J. Mental. Health Addict. **17**(1), 166–179 (2019). https://doi.org/10.1007/s11469-018-0009-3
6. Macey, J., Hamari, J.: ESports, skins and loot boxes: participants, practices and problematic behaviour associated with emergent forms of gambling. New Media Soc. **21**(1), 20–41 (2019). https://doi.org/10.1177/1461444818786216
7. Moshirnia, A.V.: Precious and worthless: a comparative perspective on loot boxes and gambling. Minnesota J. Law Sci. Technol. **20**(1), 77–114 (2018)
8. Tomić, N.Z.: Economic model of microtransactions in video games. J. Econ. Sci. Res. **1**(01), (2018). https://doi.org/10.30564/jesr.v1i1.439
9. Zendle, D., Cairns, P., Barnett, H., McCall, C.: Paying for loot boxes is linked to problem gambling, regardless of specific features like cash-out and pay-to-win. Comput. Hum. Behav. **102**, 181–191 (2020). https://doi.org/10.1016/j.chb.2019.07.003
10. Zendle, D., Meyer, R., Cairns, P., Waters, S., Ballou, N.: The prevalence of loot boxes in mobile and desktop games. In: Addiction, Wiley Online Library (2020). https://doi.org/10.1111/add.14973
11. Akerman, N.: Is it too expensive to be good at fifa? (2019). https://bleacherreport.com/articles/2836528-is-it-too-expensive-to-be-good-at-fifa. Accessed 2 Jun 2020
12. McAloon, A.: Online games will be required to disclose random loot box odds in China (2016). Gamasutra.com. https://www.gamasutra.com/view/news/287258/Online_games_will_be_required_to_disclose_random_loot_box_odds_in_China. Accessed 2 Jun 2020
13. Taylor, H.: Belgian Gaming Commission recommends criminal prosecution over illegal loot boxes (2018). GamesIndustry.biz. https://www.gamesindustry.biz/articles/2018-05-10-belgian-gambling-commission-lays-out-recommendations-over-illegal-loot-boxes. Accessed 2 Jun 2020
14. Williams, M.: Star Wars: Battlefront 2 Fans Angry At Hero Unlock System And EA's Response (2017). usgamer.net. https://www.usgamer.net/articles/star-wars-battlefront-2-fans-angry-at-hero-unlock-system-and-eas-response. Accessed 2 Jun 2020
15. Convars CS:GO Case Simulator Homepage. https://convars.com/case. Accessed 2 Jun 2020
16. FIFA Analytics Homepage. https://fifa-analytics.com. Accessed 2 Jun 2020
17. FUTBIN Homepage. https://www.futbin.com. Accessed 2 Jun 2020

18. Hearthstone Gamepedia. https://hearthstone.gamepedia.com/. Accessed 2 Jun 2020
19. HSReplay Homepage. https://hsreplay.net. Accessed 2 Jun 2020
20. Packr: a Hearthstone mass pack opening simulator Homepage. https://speedodevo.github.io/packr/. Accessed 2 Jun 2020
21. Steam-Community Market. https://steamcommunity.com/market/. Accessed 2 Jun 2020

Leaderboards – A Motivational Tool in the Process of Business Education

Małgorzata Ćwil$^{(\boxtimes)}$ (iD)

Kozminski University, Jagiellońska 57/59, 03-301 Warsaw, Poland
mcwil@kozminski.edu.pl

Abstract. The main aim of this article is to examine the possibility of using leaderboards as a motivational tool in the process of business education. Rankings represent one of the main elements of gamified systems and appear to be an ever-increasing part of many educational tools. With the rising popularity of game-like systems, there is a growing need to conduct research concerning the particular elements and the mechanics that create them. The objective of the study is to compare individuals' reactions and attitudes to scores presented using traditional tables versus a group absolute ranking system.

The quantitative study in question has been conducted in order to examine the utilization of leaderboards in the process of education. In the questionnaire featured in the study, respondents were asked to compare two different methods of score presentation – a traditional one (table-based) and one in the form of a ranking. The study has been conducted among 150 students at one of the Polish business universities.

The results show that the majority of business school students in the sample prefer it when their results are presented to them in a leaderboard rather than in a traditional table. Students find it more motivating when they can see how many peers from their group get better and worse scores than they do. The matter of the influence of gender and students' score on their perception of rankings is also explored.

Keywords: Leaderboards · Motivation · Rankings · Gamification · Business education

1 Introduction

Nowadays, people around the world are surrounded by all sorts of games and gamified systems. They have become a part of their everyday lives. The gaming market is booming, with a visible significant growth of demand and revenues year by year. More systems and services are being gamified as well. People use them at work or in their free time, often not even aware of being 'exposed' to game-based mechanics. The main purpose of introducing such game-based frameworks is to internalize motivation [1]. The potential positive impact of incorporating gamification into education has been noticed as well. It is manifested in the growing number of gamified educational applications, as well as in the rapidly increasing number of studies conducted in this area.

© Springer Nature Switzerland AG 2020
M. Ma et al. (Eds.): JCSG 2020, LNCS 12434, pp. 193–203, 2020.
https://doi.org/10.1007/978-3-030-61814-8_15

This paper describes the potential for one of the gamified elements - leaderboards - as a motivational tool in business higher education. The study compares also the usage of leaderboards with more traditional tools as tables presenting scores.

2 Gamification and Game Elements in Education

The idea of using game elements and design in education is based on the observed surprisingly high and passionate level of engagement people appear to demonstrate whilst taking part in seemingly unimportant or 'just-for-fun' recreational routines like board or computer games. Games are especially known for their ability to engage and excite, and when playing games, people commonly experience a whole range of different feelings, e.g. mastery, competence, enjoyment, immersion, or flow, all of which are characteristic of intrinsically motivated human behaviour [2–5].

The term *gamification* was first used in 2008 in a blog post by Brett Terrill. According to Huotari and Hamari [2], gamification refers to a process of enhancing a service with affordances for a gameful experience in order to support the overall user value creation. A different definition offered by Detering [6] refers to the use of game design elements in non-game contexts. Meanwhile, Werbach [7] defines gamification as "the process of making activities more game-like" – adopting a designer's point of view.

The existing reviews on gamification literature have indicated that education and learning are the most common contexts for empirical research of gamification [5, 8, 9]. The adoption of game-like elements in the process of education is really widespread – gamification can be introduced into the framework of many different subjects (from foreign languages through science to physical education), for learners on any level of education – from primary school through high schools and universities to corporate training [10, 11]. Sometimes the whole process of education is gamified, with the storyline starting during the first class and developing till the last one. In other situations, only some extracurricular applications and systems feature game-based elements.

Introducing gamification in the process of education usually is described to have positive effects on students short-term and long-term cognitive outcomes – it makes them more motivated to study, students spend more time studying and have better results [12–14]. However, introducing gamified elements does not influence all students the same, it does not boost the level of motivation of all of the students, some of them can even get more frustrated when using gamification [15–17]. Other studies indicate that students performance during the classes (their scores) or such characteristics as gender influence the way gamification is perceived by them [18–20]. Boys and girls prefer different types of games [21] and as a result, they also differ in gamification elements that do influence them [2, 22]. However, as effects of gamification were studied broadly, the usage of single game-based elements in education still needs to be researched.

In order to create a gamified system, it is necessary to design and introduce mechanics derived from games, such as: points, badges, levels, storytelling, achievements, leaderboards, virtual goods, progress bars, feedback or avatars. The most popular mechanisms found in gamified education systems are points, badges, levels, and leaderboards [23, 24]. In this research, the usage of rankings will be studied and their influence on the level of students' motivation.

3 Leaderboards

A game mechanism that is really frequently used in gamified education systems is a leaderboard [25]. It is a list of game users or participants and the scores achieved by each of them. The most common way of showing the results in a leaderboard is to order the scores from highest to lowest – taking into consideration the number of points gained, badges collected, or tasks completed. It is important to compare the performance of participants of a gamified system based on their behaviour and the progress that they make towards the desired outcome.

There are a few types and typologies of leaderboards [26] and they are presented in Table 1. Taking into account the number of users whose scores are presented in a leaderboard, three types of rankings can be distinguished: global, group, and relative. Global leaderboards present the scores of all participants, while group (filtered) ones show scores of only a certain subgroup of users. In gamified education systems, it can be a particular class, subject, or school. It is also possible to show the results of users with similar scores – for example, 10 people ranked below and 10 people ranked above a certain score. This is the aforementioned relative ranking.

Table 1. Types of leaderboards.

Types of leaderboards		
Global ranking	**Group ranking**	**Relative ranking**
All users	A group of users	Users with similar scores
Absolute ranking		**Incremental ranking**
Number of points		Growth rate of the number of points

Taking into consideration the way of presenting scores, two major types of rankings can be distinguished – absolute and incremental. The first one presents the number of points (or badges collected, tasks completed, etc.) gained by users in a certain time range. An incremental ranking shows the rate of growth of one's score – expressed in the number of points (badges collected, tasks completed, etc.) or percentagewise. In this type of ranking, the leader does not have to have the highest number of points; they rarely do, in fact.

The main aim of a leaderboard in a gamified system is to present the results of participants of a given activity in a manner that makes them more intrinsically motivated to achieve better scores [25, 26]. The most involved students can be rewarded accordingly. The type of ranking should be adjusted to the group, the kind of students, the subject, and the aim of its introduction.

However, there are situations in which a wrongly designed leaderboard can diminish the motivation to learn among the participants of an activity [27]. It is especially common in the case of global rankings and people with a low position in a given hierarchy [28]. If there are many students in one leaderboard, it may seem impossible for those outside the first hundred to reach the top. Participants need to know that it is possible to advance and reach a better position. What is also important is to instil a belief that the learning outcomes are the most important part of gamified education systems, regardless of the rank achieved.

4 Research Methodology

Following a literature review, the following research question has been defined:

RQ: Is using leaderboards perceived as motivating by its participants?

In order to conduct a quantitative study a set hypotheses has been conceptualized additionally, each of them will be statistically tested:

H1: People prefer when the results of their education are presented in the form of a leaderboard rather than in a traditional table.

H2: People perceive leaderboards more motivating than traditional tables with scores.

H3: People perceive leaderboards fairer than traditional tables with scores.

H4: There are no differences between men and women in leaderboard preferences.

H5: People with positive scores prefer leaderboards more in comparison to people with negative scores.

The research has been conducted using a questionnaire designed solely for the purpose of this study. It was carried out at one of the business universities in Poland between 2017 and 2019. The sample consisted of 150 participants, the majority of whom were females (55%). These were students of three different subjects:

- operations management - 17 MSc students,
- statistics - 48 BSc and 50 MSc students,
- simulation games - 35 BSc students.

The majority of the sample consisted of people who passed the subjects they studied (81% of respondents).

In the questionnaire, the scores that the students achieved in the course of study were presented to them in two different ways – using a traditional table and a leaderboard. It was a group absolute ranking featuring the sum of the points that each student got in a particular subject during the whole semester. The main differences between the two methods of presenting the results – the table and the leaderboard – were:

- the order of participants – ordered according to student ID number or to the number of points,
- colours – in the leaderboard, the best scores were highlighted in green, the lowest – in red,
- ranks – in the leaderboard, people were assigned ranks.

The data presented in the tables or leaderboards was real – it was the scores that students achieved when studying a certain subject. Examples of the table and the leaderboard shown to the students are provided in Fig. 1. Student ID numbers were anonymized in the figure.

	Student ID number	SUM	GRADE		Student ID number	SUM	GRADE
1.	RRR	97	5		AAA	92	5
2.	NNN	95	5		BBB	78	4
3.	III	94	5		CCC	31	2
3.	MMM	94	5		DDD	87	4,5
5.	AAA	92	5		EEE	82	4
6.	SSS	88	4,5		FFF	77	4
7.	DDD	87	4,5		GGG	75	3,5
8.	HHH	86	4,5		HHH	86	4,5
8.	KKK	86	4,5		III	94	5
10.	TTT	84	4		JJJ	41	2
11.	EEE	82	4		KKK	86	4,5
12.	BBB	78	4		LLL	76	4
13.	FFF	77	4		MMM	94	5
14.	LLL	76	4		NNN	95	5
15.	GGG	75	3,5		OOO	60	3
16.	PPP	70	3,5		PPP	70	3,5
17.	OOO	60	3		RRR	97	5
18.	JJJ	41	2		SSS	88	4,5
19.	CCC	31	2		TTT	84	4

Fig. 1. Example of the leaderboard (on the left) and the table (on the right) showing the final scores of students.

In the questionnaire, the respondents were asked to answer questions concerning their preferences towards both styles of presentation of their final results. They also expressed their opinions on how fair and motivating they considered both of the systems to be.

5 Results

To test the first hypothesis, i.e. that people prefer the results of their education to be presented in the form of a leaderboard rather than as a traditional table, a binomial test has been conducted. In this test, only people who chose leaderboards or tables were included – excluding students who did not see any difference between those two ways of presenting the scores. H1 was fully supported as the percentage of people choosing rankings over traditional tables was significantly higher than 50% (p < 0.001). In our sample, almost 70% of students prefer leaderboards, whereas only 17% prefer traditional

Table 2. Frequency table – preferred form of result presentation.

		Frequency	Percent	Valid Percent
Valid	Non-leaderboard	25	16.7	17.1
	Leaderboard	104	69.3	71.2
	No difference	17	11.3	11.6
	Total	146	97.3	100.0
Missing	System	4	2.7	
Total		150	100.0	

Table 3. Results of a binomial test – preferred form of result presentation.

Category	N	Observed Prop.	Test Prop.	Exact Sig. (2-tailed)
Non-leaderboard	25	.19	.50	.000
Leaderboard	104	.81		
Total	129	1.00		

tables with scores (Table 2 and 3). 11% of people are neutral and do not see the difference, while 3% of students did not answer the question.

The second hypothesis, stating that people perceive leaderboards more motivating than a traditional table with scores, was also tested by means of a binomial statistical test. The binomial test indicated that the proportion of people stating that leaderboards was more motivating than traditional tables with scores was higher than 50%.

($p < 0.001$). In the sample, 75% of students chose rankings as more motivating, 7% chose tables, and 15% of people did not see a difference – they found both ways of presenting scores equally motivating (Table 4 and 5). Only 4 out of 150 students did not share their opinion.

Table 4. Frequency table – which form of result presentation is more motivating.

		Frequency	Percent	Valid Percent
Valid	Non-leaderboard	10	6.7	6.8
	Leaderboard	113	75.3	77.4
	No difference	23	15.3	15.8
	Total	146	97.3	100.0
Missing	System	4	2.7	
Total		150	100.0	

Table 5. Results of a binomial test – which form of result presentation is more motivating.

Category	N	Observed Prop.	Test Prop.	Exact Sig.(2-tailed)
Non-leaderboard	10	.08	.50	.000
Leaderboard	113	.92		
Total	123	1.00		

According to the third hypothesis, people perceive leaderboards fairer than traditional tables with scores. The conducted binominal test did not support this hypothesis (p = 0.052). In our sample, 33% do not see a difference in the level of fairness between the two ways of result presentation, 39% find leaderboards fairer, and 25% choose tables as a fairer way to show students' results (Table 6 and 7).

Table 6. Frequency table – which form of result presentation is more motivating.

		Frequency	Percent	Valid Percent
Valid	Non-leaderboard	38	25.3	26.0
	Leaderboard	58	38.7	39.7
	No difference	50	33.3	34.2
	Total	146	97.3	100.0
Missing	System	4	2.7	
Total		150	100.0	

Table 7. Results of a binomial test – which form of result presentation is more motivating.

Category	N	Observed Prop.	Test Prop.	Exact Sig. (2-tailed)
Non-leaderboard	38	.40	.50	.052
Leaderboard	58	.60		
Total	96	1.00		

In the following hypotheses, the researcher wanted to check if there were differences between man and women and between people with positive and negative scores in terms of leaderboard preferences. To verify those hypotheses, a Chi-square test was performed. It turns out that there are no statistically significant differences between men and women in terms of their preferences regarding leaderboards versus tables (p = 0.423), the level of motivation (p = 0.612), or justice (p = 0.588) ensured by both these forms of result presentation (Table 8).

There are no statistically significant differences in terms of the overall preferences regarding leaderboards and tables (p = 0.420) and the level of the perceived justice

Table 8. Results of chi-square tests.

	Preference	Motivation	Justice
Gender	0.423	0.612	0.588
Positive/negative score	0.420	**0.013***	0.519

(p = 0.519) for both those with positive scores and those with negative scores achieved in a particular subject. However, the test revealed significant differences between people with positive and negative scores in the level of motivation provided by each of the considered forms (p < 0.05). What is interesting is the fact that among the people with negative scores (i.e. who gained less than 60% of achievable points) no one named a traditional table with points as a more motivating form of result presentation (Table 9). All of the people with poor results said that seeing oneself at the end of the ranking makes them motivated to work more in the future.

Table 9. Cross-tabulation – score and which form is more motivating.

		Positive score	Negative score	Total
Which form is more motivating?	Non-leaderboard	9	0	9
	Leaderboard	92	**18**	110
	No difference	14	9	23
Total		115	27	142

6 Discussion and Conclusions

Game elements are more and more widely adopted in the process of education and this is the reason why the use of game mechanics is important to understand. Leaderboards are among the most often used gamified elements. The aim of the research was to find out the perceived differences between two forms of result presentation – using a traditional table and a group absolute ranking system. The main outcomes are presented in Table 10.

It turns out that the majority of business school students in the surveyed sample prefer their results to be presented in the form of a leaderboard rather than as a traditional table (H1). Students find it more motivating when they can see how many peers from their group got better and worse scores than they did (H2). However, there are no significant differences in the level of the perceived justice as offered by rankings and tables with scores (H3). Furthermore, there are no differences between genders in the perception of rankings – both men and women chose leaderboards over tables as the preferred means to present results, and both find them more motivating for future work (H4). Nevertheless, there is a significant difference among business school students with high and low scores in their perception of motivation that leaderboards provide. In the opinion of people

Table 10. Conclusions concerning stated hypotheses.

Hypothesis	Supported?
H1: People prefer when the results of their education are presented in the form of a leaderboard rather than in a traditional table.	Yes
H2: People perceive leaderboards more motivating than traditional tables with scores.	Yes
H3: People perceive leaderboards fairer than traditional tables with scores.	No
H4: There are no differences between men and women in leaderboard:	
a) Preference b) Motivation c) Justice	Yes Yes Yes
H5: People with positive scores .... leaderboards in comparison to people with negative scores:	
a) prefer b) find more motivating c) find fairer	No Yes No

with low scores and/or negative results, rankings are more motivating in comparison to traditional tables presenting non-ordered results (H5). At the same time, there are no statistically significant differences between students with good and bad results as far as fairness of leaderboards and traditional tables are concerned.

To conclude, most of the students surveyed in the research found leaderboards more encouraging and motivating compared with the scores presented in tables. This motivation aspect is especially important for student with low scores. They do not want to be at the bottom of the leaderboard, which makes them more motivated to work harder in the future. At the same time, both of the forms of result presentation – rankings and tables – are perceived as equally fair by everyone – regardless of their gender or the number of points achieved.

7 Limitations and Further Research

The conducted study is not without limitations. One of the main drawbacks come from the nature of the sample, which consisted of business school students and is therefore not representative for the whole society – and not even for students of all majors studied at the business school where the study has been conducted. As a result, most of the participants were in their early twenties, which made it impossible to compare people belonging to different age cohorts.

In the future study it would seem to be reasonable to include a wider group of people and – even more importantly – other types of game-based mechanics in the research. Similar studies can be also conducted for different elements incorporated from games, such as badges, levels, or storytelling. It would also be interesting to see how individuals from other countries perceive the use of leaderboards in the process of education.

References

1. Hamari, J.: Do badges increase user activity? a field experiment on the effects of gamification. Comput. Hum. Behav. **71**, 469–478 (2017)
2. Huotari, K., Hamari, J.: A definition for gamification: anchoring gamification in the service marketing literature. Electron. Markets **27**(1), 21–31 (2016). https://doi.org/10.1007/s12525-015-0212-z
3. Deci, E.L., Ryan, R.M.: The "what" and "why" of goal pursuits: Human needs and the self-determination of behavior. Psychol. Inquiry **11**(4), 227–268 (2000)
4. Nakamura, J., Csikszentmihalyi, M.: The concept of flow. Flow and the Foundations of Positive Psychology, pp. 239–263. Springer, Dordrecht (2014). https://doi.org/10.1007/978-94-017-9088-8_16
5. Koivisto, J., Hamari, J.: The rise of motivational information systems: a review of gamification research. Int. J. Inf. Manage. **45**, 191–210 (2019)
6. Deterding, S., Dixon, D., Khaled, R., Nacke, L.: From game design elements to gamefulness: defining "gamification". In: Proceedings of the 15th International Academic MindTrek Conference: Envisioning Future Media Environments, pp. 9–15, September 2011
7. Werbach, K.: (Re) defining gamification: a process approach. In: International Conference on Persuasive Technology, pp. 266–272. Springer, Cham, May 2014. https://doi.org/10.1007/978-3-319-07127-5_23
8. Majuri, J., Koivisto, J., Hamari, J.: Gamification of education and learning: a review of empirical literature. In: Proceedings of the 2nd International GamiFIN Conference, GamiFIN 2018. CEUR-WS (2018)
9. Seaborn, K., Fels, D.I.: Gamification in theory and action: a survey. Int. J. Hum.-Comput. Stud. **74**, 14–31 (2015)
10. Huang, W.H.Y., Soman, D.: Gamification of education. Research Report Series: Behavioural Economics in Action, Rotman School of Management, University of Toronto (2013)
11. Legaki, N.Z., Xi, N., Hamari, J., Assimakopoulos, V.: Gamification of the future: an experiment on gamifying education of forecasting. In: Proceedings of the 52nd Hawaii International Conference on System Sciences, January 2019
12. Connolly, T.M., Boyle, E.A., MacArthur, E., Hainey, T., Boyle, J.M.: A systematic literature review of empirical evidence on computer games and serious games. Comput. Educ. **59**(2), 661–686 (2012)
13. Wouters, P., van Nimwegen, C., van Oostendorp, H., van der Spek, E.D.: A meta-analysis of the cognitive and motivational effects of serious games. J. Educ. Psychol. **105**(2), 249–265 (2013)
14. Martí-Parreño, J., Méndez-Ibáñez, E., Alonso-Arroyo, A.: The use of gamification in education: a bibliometric and text mining analysis. J. Comput. Assisted Learn. **32**(6), 663–676 (2016)
15. Hanus, M.D., Fox, J.: Assessing the effects of gamification in the classroom: a longitudinal study on intrinsic motivation, social comparison, satisfaction, effort, and academic performance. Comput. Educ. **80**, 152–161 (2015)
16. Mohamad, S., Salam, S., Bakar, N.: An analysis of gamification elements in online learning to enhance learning engagement. In: Zulikha, J., Zakaria, N.H. (eds.) Proceedings of the 6th International Conference on Computing & Informatics, pp. 452–460. School of Computing, Sintok (2017)
17. Domínguez, A., Saenz-de-Navarrete, J., de Marcos, L., Fernández-Sanz, L., Pagés, C., Martínez-Herráiz, J.-J.: Gamifying learning experiences: practical implications and outcomes. Comput. Educ. **63**, 380–392 (2013). https://doi.org/10.1016/j.compedu.2012.12.020

18. Arnup, J.L., Murrihy, C., Roodenburg, J., McLean, L.A.: Cognitive style and gender differences in Children's mathematics achievement. Educ. Stud. **39**(3), 355–368 (2013)
19. Admiraal, W., Huizenga, J., Heemskerk, I., Kuiper, E., Volman, M., Ten Dam, G.: Gender-inclusive game-based learning in secondary education. Int. J. Inclusive Educ. **18**(11), 1208–1218 (2014). https://doi.org/10.1080/13603116.2014.885592
20. Khan, A., Ahmad, F.H., Malik, M.M.: Use of digital game based learning and gamification in secondary school science: The effect on student engagement, learning and gender difference. Educ. Inf. Technol. **22**(6), 2767–2804 (2017). https://doi.org/10.1007/s10639-017-9622-1
21. Ćwil, M., Howe, W.T.: Who identifies as a gamer? a cross-cultural comparison of the United States and Poland. In: 70th Annual International Communication Association Conference (2020)
22. Toda, A.M., Oliveira, W., Shi, L., Bittencourt, I. I., Isotani, S., Cristea, A.: Planning Gamification strategies based on user characteristics and DM: A gender-based case study (2019). arXiv:1905.09146v2
23. Dicheva, D., Dichev, C., Agre, G., Angelova, G.: Gamification in education: a systematic mapping study. J. Educ. Technol. Soc. **18**(3), 75–88 (2015)
24. Nah, F.F.H., Zeng, Q., Telaprolu, V.R., Ayyappa, A.P., Eschenbrenner, B.: Gamification of education: a review of literature. In: International Conference on HCI in Business, pp. 401–409. Springer, Cham (2014). https://doi.org/10.1007/978-3-319-07293-7_39
25. Ortiz-Rojas, M., Chiluiza, K., Valcke, M.: Gamification through leaderboards: an empirical study in engineering education. Comput. Appl. Eng. Educ. **27**(4), 777–788 (2019)
26. Marczewski, A.: Even Ninja Monkeys Like to Play: Gamification. Game Thinking and Motivational Design, Blurb (2015)
27. Chou, Y.K.: Actionable gamification: Beyond points, badges, and leaderboards. Packt Publishing Ltd (2019)
28. Jia, Y., Liu, Y., Yu, X., Voida, S.: Designing leaderboards for gamification: perceived differences based on user ranking, application domain, and personality traits. In: Proceedings of the 2017 CHI Conference on Human Factors in Computing Systems, pp. 1949–1960. May 2017

Using a Participatory Design Approach for Adapting an Existing Game Scenario – Challenges and Opportunities

Jannicke Baalsrud Hauge[1,4(✉)] 🆔, Heiko Duin[1] 🆔, Valentin Kammerlohr[2] 🆔, and Barbara Göbl[3] 🆔

[1] BIBA – Bremer Institut Für Produktion Und Logistik GmbH, 28359 Bremen, Germany
{baa,du}@biba.uni-bremen.de
[2] Faculty of Surveying Informatics and Mathematics, Hochschule Für Technik Stuttgart, 70174 Stuttgart, Germany
valentin.kammerlohr@hft-stuttgart.de
[3] Faculty of Computer Science, University of Vienna, 1010 Vienna, Austria
barbara.goebl@univie.ac.at
[4] KTH-Royal Institute of Technology, 15181 Södertälje, Sweden
jmbh@kth.se

Abstract. Designing Serious Games (SGs) is a complex process, often putting game play in a central role during the design process. Therefore, the game mechanics can create unwanted tangential outcomes. Further challenges emerge from the time constraints to deliver a purposeful product that meets the requirements of the target group, while maintaining a low budget. The re-use of game components and a participatory design may contribute to overcome these challenges. This paper presents and reports on a case study integrating reuse and re-purposing of a game-engine while involving the future users in the early phase of the design process.

Keywords: Participatory design · Agile development · Modding · Serious game design

1 Introduction

Serious Game (SG) design is often a pedagogical, design-driven top-down approach [32]. Insofar, SG designers, mindful of the game objectives, try to work along a scale of fun to simulation, while keeping the game's requirements in mind. This then determines the pedagogical approach implemented, implying a top-down approach to the game's design. This often leads to a disconnection of low-level game implementation aspects and high-level instructional design aspects of SGs, i.e. it is a challenge to manage the relation between the instructional design and actual game design implementation in an appropriate manner. Therefore, previous work identifies a lack of suitable methodologies [1], resulting in the development of new methodologies like Learning Mechanics-Game Mechanics (LM-GM) [2], focusing on the construct of SG mechanics as the mechanics

© Springer Nature Switzerland AG 2020
M. Ma et al. (Eds.): JCSG 2020, LNCS 12434, pp. 204–218, 2020.
https://doi.org/10.1007/978-3-030-61814-8_16

supporting the required transition [3, 4]. This is also addressed by the Activity Theory-based Model for Serious (ATMSG) method [5] that considers several involved viewpoints and supports a systematic way of connecting learning objectives with game play objectives, as well as instructional aspects.

Developing SGs is not only challenging, but also costly and time consuming [1] and thus the idea of reusing components, assets and knowledge in design, development and implementation processes [6] is based upon the believe that this will not only lead to lower costs, but also higher quality, in terms of more efficient resources usage, enhanced error handling, higher usage of standards and less time consumption in the game design process [1, 6–9]. The idea of reusing software components is nothing new [7]: considering SGs, component such as design patterns, application frameworks, program libraries, program generators and so on, are suitable for re-use [10]. However, the challenge to connect instructional design and game design remains, and is often addressed by SG mechanics. In a previous project, some re-use principles were established [1]:

- Passive components and assets that are reused as such, like the narrative. Yet, to enable successful reuse, such items should be accompanied by sufficient and easily accessible documentation that provides guidance based on previous experiences.
- Active components and assets that evolve and are repurposed, like an activity to carry out using a specific game mechanics or something else that evolves or changes in the play. In this context version control issues should be given special attention.

As mentioned above most games are specifically designed to fit both a specific target group and a specific objective (often a learning objective [1]). However, while reusing components might be a good consideration from a quality and cost perspectives, this has consequences regarding newly introduced requirements and needs and their influence on the actual game design. Flexibility and adaptability of the re-used game (or game component) play a major role. In order to investigate this more, we have defined two research questions and used a case study to investigate this:

1. How does the reuse of game component influence the implementation of a target group's needs?
2. How to include participants in the redesign process of a game scenario?

In order to address the research question, a single, empirical case study was conducted. The case study method facilitated an in-depth understanding of potential benefits and challenges of participatory design of serious games in the context of reuse [11]. According to Meredith [12], a case study is an suitable method in situations with a significant amount of unknown elements. Thus, considering the limited number of empirical studies regarding participatory design on reuse of SGs, this method was considered appropriate.

2 Sota

There are several frameworks that can be used to design new games, but few are useful as a design and analysis tool – an important characteristic for reuse [13–16]. As described in previous work [13, 14], and above, the reuse of existing games is often difficult: they are designed for a very specific purpose and the possibility of modding games is limited [14, 16], since they are often linked to different domains and thus, experiences [16]. Previous work shows, that it is necessary to use a manual process to investigate to what extent components can be changed and how this can be done: by using an authoring tool, changing the source code, adding plug & play components, etc. [13] and then create a "new game" scenario, thus going beyond mere content change. Furthermore, SGs are often developed using agile development methods [17], with regular testing and incremental improvements, in order to adjust the different game components to the game's purpose. This is a tedious and costly process. While there are several suitable models for designing new games, few consider re-design. As mentioned above, models considering both analysis and design can address this issue. Two SG frameworks integrating these aspects are the LM-GM model [2–4] and the ATMSG model [5, 19].

The LM-GM model allows users to describe games on the basis of different pedagogical approaches. Learning mechanics (LM), including various pedagogical aspects, can be mapped to different game mechanics (GM). A list of learning and game mechanics can be found in [4]. Application in game analysis is quite straight forward: for each game situation the user identifies the GM and LMs and connects it to a certain level of Blooms revised taxonomy [4]. After that, in order to re-use a set of LM-GM, it is required to understand their relationship and the implementation, as well as, and that is the only tricky part, the dynamics in the game flow.

The ATMSG is a conceptual model that supports a systematic and detailed representation of educational SGs, depicting the ways that game elements are connected to each other throughout the game, and how these elements contribute to the achievement of the game's desired pedagogical goals. It was designed by Carvalho [18] to fill the gap as presented in the introduction. It supports the user both in analysis of existing games, applicable for evaluating re-use potential (or to implement internal improvements), as well as in the design of new games. To achieve this, the ATMSG provides a structured way to connect several levels of the game, reaching from high-level game requirements, both educational and entertainment-related, down to the game mechanics. In re-use, it helps to decompose a game in order to understand the interaction, as well as the connection, of the game's pedagogic and 'fun' elements on several levels. A very detailed description of the method can be found in [18].

Furthermore, in addition to the software patterns, there are also specific patterns that are related specifically to games. In their work Björk, Lundgren and Holopainen [33] investigates patterns of different games, and defined a set of core elements that needs to be included. Their intention was to create a tool that support creative work, which is essential in the game design process as well as useful for problem-solving. However, a main challenge in designing games by re-using existing games is, as addressed by our research questions, the balance between the realism of what the potential users need and the limitation of the existing software. A way of overcoming this challenge is to involve the users in the design process, so that his/her needs can be captured and matched against the limitation.

There are several different kinds of participatory methods, but all are characterized by the involvement of participants for solving a problem [20]. The level of involvement and engagement as well as the required knowledge of the participants may vary. But the main intention remains to involve stakeholders (i.e. the invited participants) and give them an opportunity to influence the decision-making process [21]. The type of methods may vary, but include methods such as brainstorming, surveys and questionnaires, tours, focus groups, participatory planning, and expert panels. This approach brings additional challenges, such as selecting the right level of participation in the design process, which has been discussed in several studies [22–24]. Additionally, [25, 26] list a poor connection between game and players, a poor representation of the real system by a game, a poor reach of the intended goals of the game and more as typical challenges for participatory design in serious games. According to [27], the required elements and the game play/game scenario need to be sufficiently realistic, and mirror the processes, the structure and the outcome of the corresponding real world problem adequately, but there is still a difficulty to transfer the real life experience to a game [28]. As [29] confirms, this may lead to low acceptance and validity of the game.

3 Experimental Set up (Case Study)

3.1 Existing Requirements

In the cross-institutional research project DigiLab4U[1], real laboratories are digitized to offer a hybrid IoT learning and research environment. The project consists of two German and one Italian Universities as well as a research institute and intends to expand even further to increase the laboratory variety. The goal of the case study is to establish a digital laboratory offering that can be used by any kind of students from bachelor to doctoral students. In order to realize the resource sharing of the different laboratory providers, the underlying trust relationship, that is required to share laboratory resources within the cooperation, has been examined. The laboratory providers need to know and trust on: "(1) states (conditions) of shareable assets in regard to capacity, presence and/or (idle time), capability; (2) previous experience in the sharing of same resource; (3) restrictions and compensation; (4) level of behavioral congruence of actors participating in the sharing; (5) regulatory issues and dispute resolution" [30]. Successful cooperation between different parties or organizations always depend on several aspects, e.g. personal characteristics, previous experience or behavior. These cooperative projects bring many advantages such as reduced cost or additional knowledge and resources. Nevertheless, involved parties might be driven not only by common but also individual goals, leading to opportunistic or unexpected behavior. The aim of the serious game is to simulate several scenarios and to let the player learn and raise awareness about various roles' motives, actions and their consequences. Sharing resources might be beneficial but also stressful or arouse unrealistic expectations. Eventually, a player should be aware of interdependencies, gains and common pitfalls in cooperative projects. Additionally, this game is should be used to analyze player interactions and behavior to further investigate the trust model.

---

[1] https://digilab4u.com/.

3.2   Description Existing Game Engine

The be.mog (BIBA Engine for Multi-player Online Games) engine, which has been chosen for reuse as discussed below, supports process-oriented scenarios. A process is divided into process steps, which are executed successively. The be.mog engine supports the following entities:

- **Games and Scenarios**: A be.mog game is spread over one or more scenarios, which are played in a sequential order. These scenarios are equivalent to game levels. Associated to each scenario is a topic, which is essentially a description of the subject under consideration. In this example, there is only one scenario with the topic given above.
- **Players, Groups, Sub-Groups and Roles**: In each scenario the players could be organized in groups and sub-groups, which might represent companies and their departments in real life. Groups and sub-groups have their own descriptions. Each player can have a different role in each sub-group, e.g. an employee or a group leader. Beside name, user identifier, password, and other relevant information, a characteristic role description is provided to the player. The case study features two groups (universities), where each has one sub-group (department).
- **Process and Process Steps**: A specific process is associated to each group which needs to be followed by the players to play the game. The process is further divided into process steps which need to be completed in a sequential order. Each of these steps needs to be completed to conclude the overall process. A process step can be either completed by performing some action or by completing a set of documents.
- **Actions**: Some process steps may be completed by applying an action, chosen out of a set of actions. Actions are always assigned to a specific player. The application of an action reveals further information for the player. Actions can only be applied by players.
- **Events**: Events can only be set by a facilitator. The facilitator may choose an event from a predefined list of events and apply it to a specific group of players. The players are informed about the occurrence of the event and get further information about it. Events can be set in any of the process steps and may rewind to the process to one of the preceding steps.
- **Documents**: Documents are associated to process steps and players. A document is a collection of document entries (fields), which can be edited by the player who owns the document. Each document entry has a type (e.g. text or numeric) and may have a predefined value and a target value. Documents might be visible from the beginning or they are created when specific process steps are completed. Players can work on documents while they are visible and until document completion. The associated process step is completed when all documents associated to this process step are completed. The owner of a document can manage the access rights of the document by providing view and edit rights to other players.

During the game, three performance indicators (related to a virtual time, costs, and quality) are updated upon the completion of each process step. Also, the occurrence of events can influence the values of these performance indicators. These indicators are used when playing against a given goal like reaching the fastest time, least cost, or highest quality. During game play, a facilitator is watching and supervising the players. The facilitator can observe the results of the players (the content of documents and actions applied by players so far) and intervene by setting some disruptive events, which may influence the direction of some of the players.

3.3 Approach

The approach employed in this case study consisted of five steps. First, exploratory work-shops have been organized to initiate the development of different game scenarios and to identify game requirements. Second, requirements have been analyzed and mapped on existing be.mog entities. Third, one of the scenarios served as basis for game design, which was subsequently implemented with the be.mog engine. Fourth, the scenario has been tested with a small group of potential users (N = 4). And, fifth, an evaluation workshop has been carried out.

The exploratory workshops led to two main scenarios called "Remote Lab Lecture" and "New IOT Remote Lab". Within the first scenario, Klaus is a lecturer from Koblenz who wants to use the Position Lab at the HFT Stuttgart to demonstrate a practical example during his lecture. He is already a user of the virtual labs network. He uses his account to book a slot suitable for his lecture. Lukas is the lab admin at the HFT Stuttgart and receives that request. He must prove whether the lab is available and whether Felix, a lab technician, can provide support for Klaus before and during that time slot. Eventually, Klaus can rate his experience with booking and using the HFT lab remotely on a scale of 0 to 5 stars.

Within the second scenario, Eric belongs to the academic staff at the University of Paris. Maja, his superior wants to integrate their IoT sensor lab into the Virtual labs network platform, to improve utilization. Eric contacts the support team. Paula receives his request and provides a form that she and Eric fill in together to sum up all necessary data for the University of Paris to join the project. The filled form is sent to Tom, a platform manager, who reviews the form. Tom and Maja discuss all critical points and prepare a contract. Eventually, Paula and Eric are organizing all further steps, while Magalie handles the technical set up of the integration.

The roles and steps of interactions have been identified together with their require-ments. The identified game requirements were mapped to common game elements to create a list of elements that should be supported by a game that serves as a potential basis for reuse. The conclusion from this step was that the entities provided by be.mog are sufficient to allow the implementation of the scenarios as be.mog game scenarios. The scenario called "Remote Lab Lecture" has been refined and detailed information has been collected to implement it as a be.mog game scenario. This work included the detailed specification of the necessary entities (roles, organizations, groups, pro-cess steps, actions, documents, etc.). With this level of detail, the necessary data was provided for the be.mog engine and the scenario became executable (playable) as first prototype. Figure 1 provides an overview on the main entities of the first scenario. The solid lines represent the process flow, while the dotted lines represent dependencies between individual process steps.

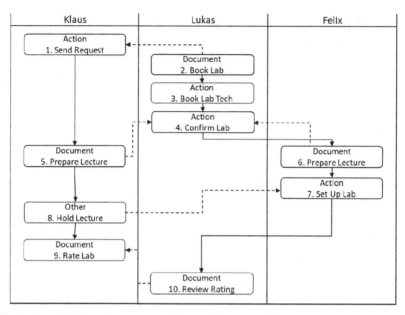

Fig. 1. Organizations, departments, roles, and the process flow of "Remote Lab Lecture"

The playable scenario has been tested with various users. This was organized within a workshop setting where the participants first played the game scenario, and second, provided open and unstructured feedback. These testing sessions were used to adapt and enhance some of the present entities for the second prototype.

Finally, a bigger workshop has been organized with 18 participants playing the game scenario and providing structured feedback through questionnaires concerning the game evaluation. In total, 18 questionnaires have been collected.

4   Results

In general, players considered the implemented game mechanics suitable. Remarks show that the use of roles as game mechanics was well understood, but the remarks also show that there is a need for elaborating these role descriptions in more detail in order to create a more realistic scenario. Conclusions about individual roles are difficult to draw. A further observation was, that early user involvement was appreciated, however, it was a challenge, that the team was changed and extended during the design process. Nevertheless, this is rather common in such research project, so that even if organizations are involved at an early stage, their members vary over time.

The answers of two open questions and their impact on the game mechanics of the be.mog engine and the content of the scenario (or story or its presentation) is analysed in detail below. The answers of the question "If you feel like the kind of game or the reused games are not an appropriate choice, please tell us why" and the resulting consequences are shown in Table 1.

Table 1. Answers and consequences of question "If you feel like the kind of game or the reused games are not an appropriate choice, please tell us why"

Comments	Impact on game mechanics	Impact on scenario/story/ presentation
"I think that a real tutorial is missing. And for me, it would be helpful to get the flow chart you showed before. I really like to use storyboards and flow charts and would use it in reality as well - and if not provided and this is an activity I only need to perform once at a time, I would have created something like a chart myself. It would be clearer to me, why I am waiting and what my next steps are."	None	Include a tutorial; Include a flowchart (avoid waiting times)
"The game has potential, but at present it is fairly hard to understand one's impact on the results, due to the limited number of options available per each choice, and therefore the fact that those options are relatively "necessary". The only choice for Klaus was to plan either a standard lecture, or an add-ons one, but there seemed to be no reason to select the second option (higher cost, lower quality, no apparent benefits). In this way, it is hard to feel the impact of one's actions on the game."	None	Increase the number of options in choices; Better presentations of pros and cons of options (e.g. option of Klaus to prepare an adds-on lecture which needs more time and costs)
"The goal is fine, and the game may have some potentialities. Yet playing is quite cumbersome. Interacting with other players is not that easy and waiting times are boring. Also, decisions are too constrained and not very realistic."	Better interaction possibilities between players	Make decisions more realistic; Reduce waiting time (by restructuring the scenario)
"The mechanics are fine but there is too much waiting without consequences involved. A more fast-paced game might be better suitable."	None	Reduce waiting time (by restructuring the scenario)

Some players had difficulties to use the game engine at first. Even after presenting the user interface in detail, a demand for a tutorial remained. Some players claimed to have a better overview if they had insight into the processes of both participating organizations, but this was intentionally not provided to create a realistic setting, in which people would not know the processes of other cooperation partners. The options presented to players seemed to be too simplistic and not well explained. Therefore, an increase in options and better explanations will help to create a more realistic implementation of that game scenario. A further discussed feature is be.mog's integrated chat function that supports communication between players. Some participants reported that this technique felt a bit outdated and asked for more modern communication means within the game. Other participants lamented the pace of the game (again, a feature closely aligned with similar real scenarios) and asked for reduced waiting times, which could be achieved by restructuring the processes of the scenario. Altogether, there is no need to change the game mechanics except the communications means, but there is potential in refining the story structure and its presentation.

The questionnaire provided a possibility for further comments, which are shown below in Table 2, including the resulting consequences.

Some participants criticized the responsiveness of the be.mog engine, which could be improved by an enhanced notification system and additional pop-up messages. Gender balance must be improved by introducing female roles, and again the "realism" of the game scenario has been criticized. Additionally, a reflection phase (on the pros and cons of cooperation) should be included and the introduction of push-events has been suggested. One participant provided a list of potential improvements. Amongst others, there was a demand for directly influencing the performance indicators (costs, time,

Table 2. Answers and consequences of question "If you have any further comments, please let us know"

Comments	Impact on game mechanics	Impact on scenario/story/presentation
"The communication can be a little difficult due to the fact that players didn't receive notification when a message is arriving from the other players."	Enhance notification system	None
"Popup Messages in Chat for a faster view."	Popup message when new message in chat	None
"I am used to gender discussions… we should use female roles in some scenarios as well, if not already planned."	None	Include female roles in scenarios
"I think a reflection phase on: what has happened? What could have been happened better? What did the events change concerning the cooperation? could be helpful for the game and in a further step to talk about expectations of the different roles/Players."	None	Integration of a reflection phase
"The kind of game and the game engine are ok, the problem is the low level of interactions at every level, that does not make the game look like real (e.g. a computer virus happened, but it is not clear what it caused)."	None	Increase "realism" (more realistic descriptions of causes, e.g. in events)

(continued)

Table 2. (*continued*)

Comments	Impact on game mechanics	Impact on scenario/story/presentation
"The within-game communication was a bit challenging because one had to actively check whether new messages have appeared or not. There was a small confusion whose step is the next (within the inter-operation among the different players) and it was unclear for a bit who needs to do what and what effects this actions/activities have overall on the gameplay and the flow. So… there was an interlock among the players and it took a bit of time to figure out who should do the next step. And combined with the message board checking for new chats/messages it took a bit more time than usual to sort out this interlock."	Popup message when new message in chat	Better explanation of the game flow; Better explanations of actions' outcomes
"I think a game-design with more push-events (e.g. time driven or driven by real-time interactions of players) would increase the charm and authenticity of the game scenario and by this the involvement of the players."	Introduction of push-events	Define content for push-events
"I think the game has potential. A few ideas: - different personas to choose from for the same job (different skills/personalities) - character should have an impact on the costs/values of actions - maybe introduce real time delay? let for example take one action 1 min in real time and others 5 min or so. I think this might increase the pressure to hurry up as the colleagues are waiting - It should be clearer (visually) what everyone has to do next"	Introduce another layer of personas (linked to the characters/roles) Impact on costs/values (maybe through measures?) Introduce real time delays	Better visualization of next steps

and quality). This can be achieved by implementing another game engine entity called measures. Measures can be compared with events with the main difference that measures are under the control of the players, not the facilitator. Additionally, the concept of visualizing the next steps in the game can be enhanced. Altogether, there were three serious proposals for game mechanics enhancements: 1) Enhanced notification and pop-up messages, 2) push-events, and 3) measures, and some suggestions for story and presentation enhancements concerning better visualization and explanation, a reflection phase, gender balance, and increased "realism".

5 Discussion

As described in Sect. 4, we started the involvement of the users at an early stage, before the question of whether to re-use existing an existing game or develop a new one had been decided. The starting point was a set of scenarios that had been developed based on an analysis of the project objectives and the consortium construction. The groups were asked to provide further input on two (out of four) of these scenarios. The matching process between user requirements and existing game scenario limitation was a manually process, as expected according to [13, 14]. For this step we used the ATMSG and, based on the results, took the decision that re-use of the be.mog structure would fit the purpose, though limiting the outcome. According to the re-design [15, 16] recommendations, this will allow a re-use of corresponding game mechanics, and this assumption was to a large extent confirmed by the case study participants. Of specific interest in the improvement is that 16 out of 18 find the use of interdependent steps and 13 out of 18 scenario and role description as mechanic suitable. These mechanics have the advantage that they can be easily changed or extended, so that the flexibility of the game scenario is high, and a customization is possible. A result that requires some more thoughts and investigation in order to improve is connected to resource management (3 of 18 did not find this suitable at all). This is an essential game mechanic for the scenario outcome, and thus it is vital for the game experience that it is perceived as at least neutral. A reflection on why we got these results, is connected to the focus in the underlying re-used scenario. In the design of those scenarios we so far have implemented using the be.mog engine for different purposes, we put much attention on these mechanics on role and scenario descriptions (i.e. the narrative setting) and the interconnection between the different work processes. Resource management has also been a part in these scenarios, but more as a help function (i.e. passive component) for the decision-making, it was never an active component nor did we ever do an alignment of this specific LM-GM relation in the existing game plays. It was required for being able to address the risk assessment, the ideation of new ideas and served as a boundary to make the scenario more realistic.

Furthermore, comparing two other results, appropriateness of re-using this game and the game experience (Fig. 2) shows a different picture: The figure below shows that the participants had a strong feeling of learning about risks and uncertainties, while not so much on benefits. This clearly indicates that we in the re-construction did not manage to decouple the LM-GM connection on risks and the uncertainty (a main objective of one of the game scenarios originally design [31] and re-connect that mechanic in such a way, that the emphasis on risks and benefits would be similar experience in the game play. Since this was actually given in the narrative, it is to assume that we need to analyze the constructive alignment in the first game in more detail, in order to achieve a proper decomposition and then make a new alignment of the LM-GM connection. A second observation which is also connected to the instructional design and the balancing of the game play is the realism, as mentioned by [20, 25, 27, 28]. Some of the participants reported, that they did find their first input sufficiently well covered, but still the realism was not assessed as sufficient. Based on the remarks, one reason for this was in the values of key performance indicators we used (time, costs, quality). For development reasons, and due to lack of real values from the processes (i.e. the time it takes for a certain process, the cost model behind each decision and each process etc.), the values of indicators were arbitrary and not realistic. From a game design perspective, i.e. for a software engineer to check and test whether it is functional or not, it is normally sufficient to implement the mechanic to see how it work, but for the game experience, this case study showed how big the influence of using the right values actually have on this user group (i.e. non-game designer or developers). For designing new games, we would still have used software engineers, developers and game designer for this phase of the development process. However, since we re-used a game engine, the game was playable (and bug-free) to a much larger extent than normally, and we assumed that it would be sufficient to just tell this user group (i.e. participant taking part in the project but having no competencies in game design) that the key performance indicator values would not reflect reality. This shows how important the alignment of abstraction level and which user groups we involve when, of high relevance is when using participatory approaches are.

Fig. 2. Game experience results

Summarized, we can therefore state that the results of the case study indicate that the influence of the re-used components is high. Of specific attention for a successful re-usage is not the re-use of game mechanics but the relation of GM and LM and the dynamics. This further confirms the observation made in [4, 14–16] that it is essential to know how the first game designer thought when constructing the LM-GM relationship as well as the dynamic in the game play was constructed, while designing a new scenario. This can, to some extent, also answer why there is so little re-usage, even if analysis tools like LM-GM and ATMSG models provide good support, this study shows that it is necessary to know the reasoning behind the starting scenarios in order to understand specific results in the assessment of the new scenario. This either requires that the same designers are involved or that the documentation of the considerations behind a scenario needs to be very detailed. Therefore, it is expected that the re-use of a specific game mechanic is much higher than the reuse of the construct game mechanics-learning mechanic.

Based on the remarks related to the usage of participatory design methods, it can be concluded that in line with [27, 28], it is essential for a game scenario to involve the users early in the process in order to ensure the realism. However, as the usage of arbitrary values of specific key performance indicators show, that attention needs to be paid to when a stakeholder group is involved in the process, since the level of abstraction depends much upon their knowledge. It would probably therefore have been beneficial to ask the users for suitable values and implementing something similar also in the prototype, instead of only asking for the function (the key performance indicators). Consequently, the answer to research question 2 based on our case study results is that the stakeholders should be involved at an early stage, and then probably first when the scenario is sufficiently realistic. This will however need more verification, since we only had one scenario and 18 participants.

6   Conclusion and Next Steps

This paper uses a case study for investigating if participatory design approaches and agile software development methods are appropriate in terms of re-usage of game components or game scenarios.

Since this is just one case study, more studies will need to be carried out for making a clear statement, but in general, this study confirms the relevance of user involvement already at the conceptual level, before any decision on game design has been made. Regarding the re-usage, the study indicates that a thorough alignment of the input of future users (here the game scenarios they developed) with existing re-usable game components at an early stage has a very positive influence. However, when it comes to testing, the study indicates that the timing and the group selection needs to be better aligned to the real competencies of the user groups, since we see a clear discrepancy between what we wanted to test (function of the KPI as GM and design element) and what the participants focused on (realism), since this is imperative for the game experience.

In the next steps, we have therefore asked the participants to further elaborate on the scenarios and improve those as well as elaborate more on the indicators. This feedback will be integrated in an updated scenario and we will carry out a new set of experiments.

Acknowledgement. This work has been funded by the German Federal Ministry of Education and Research (BMBF) through the project DigiLab4U (No. 16DHB2112/3). The authors wish to acknowledge the BMBF for their support. We also wish to acknowledge our gratitude to all DigiLab4U project partners for their contribution.

Barbara Göbl is supported by a DOC-team fellowship of the Austrian Academy of Sciences.

References

1. Baalsrud Hauge, J., et al.: Study design and data gathering guide for serious games' evaluation. In: Psychology, Pedagogy, and Assessment in Serious Games. IGI Global, 2014. 394–419. Web. 3 Nov. 2013. (2014) https://doi.org/10.4018/978-1-4666-4773-2.ch018

2. Lim, T., et al.: Serious game mechanics, workshop on the ludo-pedagogical mechanism. In: De Gloria, A. (ed.) GALA 2014. LNCS, vol. 9221, pp. 174–183. Springer, Cham (2015). https://doi.org/10.1007/978-3-319-22960-7_17

3. Lim, Theodore., et al.: Narrative serious game mechanics (NSGM) – insights into the narrative-pedagogical mechanism. In: Göbel, Stefan, Wiemeyer, Josef (eds.) GameDays 2014. LNCS, vol. 8395, pp. 23–34. Springer, Cham (2014). https://doi.org/10.1007/978-3-319-059 72-3_4

4. Lim, T. et al.: The LM-GM Framework for Serious Games Analysis (2013). https://pdfs.sem anticscholar.org/7df0/20237a6d3995860e7345c77dab28e4d0a001.pdf?_ga=2.140232560. 2103361417.1593945229-977332475.1569848762. Accessed 04 Jul 2020

5. Carvalho, M.B., et al.: An activity theory-based model for serious games analysis and conceptual design. Comput. Edu. **87**, 166–181 (2015). https://doi.org/10.1016/j.compedu.2015. 03.023

6. Stănescu, I.A., et al.: Strategies and tools to enable reuse in serious games ecosystems and beyond. In: Proceedings of the 10th International Scientific Conference eLearning and software for Education (2014)

7. Leach, R.J.: Software Reuse: Methods, Models, Costs. McGraw-Hill, New York (1997)

8. Adams, E., Dormans, J.: Game Mechanics: Advanced Game Design. New Riders Games, Thousand Oaks (2012)

9. Mellarkod, V., et al.: A multi-level analysis of factors affecting software developers' intention to reuse software assets: an empirical investigation. Inf. Manag. **44**(7), 613–625 (2007)

10. Shalloway, A., Trott, J.R.: Design Patterns Explained: A New Perspective on Object-Oriented Design. Pearson Education, (2004)

11. Yin, R.K.: Case Study Research: Design and Methods, 5th edn. SAGE, London (2014)

12. Meredith, J.: Building operations management theory through case and field research. J. Oper. Manag. **16**(4), 441–454 (1998)

13. Baalsrud Hauge, J., et al.: Serious game mechanics and opportunities for reuse. In: Roceanu, I., (eds.): Rethink education by leveraging the eLearning pillar of the Digital Agenda for Europe, Proceedings of the 11th International Conference on eLearning and Software for Education (eLSE), vol 2, pp. 19–27 (2015)

14. Stanescu, Ioana Andreea., Baalsrud Hauge, Jannicke., Stefan, Antoniu, Lim, Theodore: Towards modding and reengineering digital games for education. In: de De Gloria, Alessandro, Veltkamp, Remco (eds.) GALA 2015. LNCS, vol. 9599, pp. 550–559. Springer, Cham (2016). https://doi.org/10.1007/978-3-319-40216-1_59

15. Baalsrud Hauge, J., et al.: Integrating gamification in mechanical engineering systems to support knowledge processes. In: American Society of Mechanical Engineers (eds.): International Design Engineering Technical Conferences and Computers and Information in Engineering Conference, Proceedings of the 35th International Conference on Computers and Information in Engineering Conference (ASME), Boston, USA, pp. 4–16, ASME Digital Library, New York (2015). ISBN 978-0-7918-5705-2

16. Stanescu, I.A., et al.: Accessibility, reusability and interoperability in the European serious game community. In: Proceedings of the 9th International Scientific Conference eLearning and software for Education (2015)

17. Kortmann, R., Harteveld, C.: Agile game development. In: Lessons learned from software engineering, ISAGA (2009)

18. Carvalho, M.B.: Serious games for learning: a model and a reference architecture for efficient game development. Eindhoven: Technische Universiteit Eindhoven, Thesis, (2017)

19. Carvalho, M.B., et al.: Towards a service-oriented architecture framework for educational serious games. In: Sampson, D.G., Huang, R., Hwang, G.-J., Liu, T.-S., Chen, N.-S., Kinshuk, Tsai, C.-C., (eds.) Advanced Technologies for Supporting Open Access to Formal and Informal Learning, Proceedings of the International Conference on Advanced Learning Technologies (ICALT), Hualien, Taiwan, pp. 147–151, IEEE Computer Society, Piscataway (2015). ISBN 978-1-4673-7333-3

20. Elliott, J., et al.: Participatory methods toolkit. a practitioner's manual. 2nd ed. King Baudouin Foundation. In: The Flemish Institute for Science and Technology Assessment (viWTA) (2006). http://cris.unu.edu/participatory-methods-toolkit-practitioners-manual-second-edition

21. Kornevs, Maksims., Baalsrud Hauge, Jannicke, Meijer, Sebastiaan: Gaming simulation validation: matching participants' worldviews with their decisions. In: Hamada, Ryoju (ed.) Neo-Simulation and Gaming Toward Active Learning. TSS, vol. 18, pp. 537–552. Springer, Singapore (2019). https://doi.org/10.1007/978-981-13-8039-6_50

22. Reason, P., Bradbury, H.: Handbook of action research- participatory inquiry and practice; SAGE (2001). https://www.embracingcomplexity.com/wp-content/uploads/2020/02/handbook_of_action_research.pdf. Accessed 15 Jun 2020

23. DeSmet, A., et al.: Is participatory design associated with the effectiveness of serious digital games for healthy lifestyle promotion? Meta-Analysis J. Med. Internet Res. **18**(4), e94 (2016)

24. Ampatzidou, C., Gugerell, K.: Participatory game prototyping – balancing domain content and playability in a serious game design for the energy transition. CoDesign **15**(4), 345–360 (2019). https://doi.org/10.1080/15710882.2018.1504084

25. Royle, K.: Game-Based learning: a different perspective. Innovate J. Online Edu. **4**(4), (2008). https://core.ac.uk/reader/51073530

26. Fernández-Manjón, B.et al.: Challenges of serious games. EAI Endorsed Trans. Serious Games **2**(6), (2015). https://eudl.eu/doi/10.4108/eai.5-11-2015.150611

27. Raser, J.R.: Simulation and Society: An Exploration of Scientific Gaming. Allyn and Bacon (1969). https://books.google.se/books/about/Simulation_and_Society.html?id=rqfrAAAAMAAJ&redir_esc=y. https://doi.org/10.1177/1046878109353570

28. Theodosiou, S., Karasavvidis, I.: Serious games design: a mapping of the problems novice game designers experience in designing games. J. E-Learning Knowl. Soc. **11**(3),.(2015) https://www.learntechlib.org/p/151929/

29. Kornevs, M.: Assessment of Application of Participatory Methods for Complex Adaptive Systems in the Public Sector; Thesis (2019)

30. Baalsrud Hauge, J., Kammerlohr, V., Göbl, B., Duin, H.: Influence of trust factors on shared laboratory resources in a distributed environment. In: Camarinha-Matos, L.M., Afsarmanesh, H., Antonelli, D. (eds.) PRO-VE 2019. IAICT, vol. 568, pp. 624–634. Springer, Cham (2019). https://doi.org/10.1007/978-3-030-28464-0_55

31. Baalsrud Hauge, J.: Mediating skills on risk management for improving the resilience of Supply Networks by developing and using a serious game, Universität Bremen, (2014)

32. Fullerton, T.: Game Design Workshop: A Playcentric Approach to Creating Innovative Games, Third Edition (2014)

33. Björk, S., et al. Game Design Patterns Digital Games Research Conference 2003, 4–6 November 2003, University of Utrecht, The Netherlands (2003)

The Effects of Esports School Tournaments on Positive Behavioural Change

Bobbie Fletcher[1]($\boxtimes$), Rachel Gowers[2], and Shahneila Saeed[3]

[1] Department of Games and Visual Effects, Staffordshire University, Stoke-on-Trent, UK
`b.d.fletcher@staffs.ac.uk`
[2] Staffordshire University London, Digital Institute, London, UK
`Rachel.Gowers@staffs.ac.uk`
[3] Digital Schoolhouse the Association of UK Interactive Entertainment (Ukie), London, UK
`shahneila@ukie.org.uk`

Abstract. Over the last decade there has been growing concern over the effect of playing computer games on the wellbeing of young people. With the rise of esports, a cooperative style of team orientated competitive gaming. This study seeks to identify the positive behavioural changes that competing in an esports school tournament can bring. By utilising two dimensions, the friendship dimension and the personal growth dimension this study developed and used an adapted Bales' Interaction Process Analysis (IPA) to identify how these school-based tournaments are a vehicle for positive behavioural change in the participating students. This study took place within the UK High School educational system with a student age range on 12–19.

Keywords: Education · Esports · Positive impact

1 Introduction

This research is a collaboration between the Digital Schoolhouse of The Association for UK Interactive Entertainment (UKie) and Staffordshire University.

Ukie's Digital Schoolhouse powered by PlayStation, delivers its annual esports tournament for schools. The esports tournament is the innovative vehicle by which The Digital Schoolhouse offer careers education and is in addition to the core provision of recruiting schools and running workshops. The 2018 project saw 15,000 students engage with the computing curriculum and over 2,500 teachers.

The Digital Schoolhouse was launched in order to engage students and teachers in the next generation of the computer curriculum. Besides competitive game play, it offers workshops on careers, algorithms, hardware and data and connects the schools with industry professionals to give them an insight into real-life roles in the industry.

This paper focuses on the research question "Does participating in esports create positive behavioural change in young players that will translate into behaviour modification in other aspects of their lives?" The methodology is based around the work by Sanders et al. [1] which identifies the research philosophy as interpretivism, the approach

© Springer Nature Switzerland AG 2020
M. Ma et al. (Eds.): JCSG 2020, LNCS 12434, pp. 219–229, 2020.
https://doi.org/10.1007/978-3-030-61814-8_17

as inductive, the strategy as grounded theory and the time horizon as cross-sectional. Positive behavioural change is measured by: the reinforcement of friendship bonds and the development of transferable skills.

2 Methodology

An autoethnographic approach was taken to study the types of communication which took place between the players during the three versus three Overwatch tournament. Overwatch is a team based multiplayer first-person shooter, that can be played in Assault, Control, Escort or Hybrid modes which are map dependent. A limitation of this study is that only one game was used, and experiences may differ depending on the game used.

There are a variety of possible frameworks for observation; single category systems such as Chapple [2], Multiple category systems such as Bales [3], Multidimensional systems such as Leary [4] and Couch [5] and Multilevel systems such as SYMLOG [6].

Because of the ease of adaptability for this specific situation, the framework used to capture this data was grounded in Interaction Process Analysis (IPA) developed by Bales [3]. IPA was adapted by using relatable phrases that the players could see in themselves and in their teammates for the player age range 11–19. These phrases represent the 12 IPA categories shown in Table 1.

Table 1. Adapted IPA Framework

1	Says "Well done good job"	5	Says "I've looked at the situation and I think we should….."	9	Asks "What should I do?
2	When something goes wrongs laughs and jokes about it	6	Say "You should be…." Then repeats, clarifies and confirms	10	Disagrees, but doesn't suggests a way to help
3	Say "I agree, we should do that"	7	Ask "Where are…?" Then repeats the request and asks for confirmation	11	Doesn't ask for help, just does their own thing
4	Suggests "Perhaps you could …"	8	Asks "What do people think about………?"	12	Criticises other players and brings them down

Each player was also asked to complete a sociogram, Moreno [7] of their team to indicate how strong the existing friendships bonds were within the team both prior to the tournament and at the end to ascertain how this had changed. This was measured on a scale of 1–10, 0 for those who don't know each other to 10 for those who are best friends as demonstrated in Fig. 1.

The rationale for this was to explore how friendship bonds were increased or decreased by the act of playing within a team and to examine if there was a correlation between improved behaviours and strength of friendships.

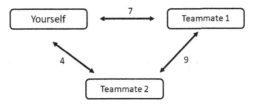

Fig. 1. Sociogram of Team Friendship Bonds

As well as the autoethnographic study, a questionnaire was completed by the players which asked how participation in the tournament had affected their perception of their own soft skills. This was then followed up by case studies based on anecdotal evidence.

The sample size for the questionnaire was 47 and the autoethnographic study looked at 10 teams of 3 player, which were picked at random from the 20 schools involved in the tournament, from 4 geographical regions. These regions were North West, Midlands, South West and South East. This selection did not take into account how successful the teams were in the tournament.

3 Results and Analysis

3.1 The Friendship Dimension: Paired Process Analysis

According to Feld and Carter [8] 'Friendship is the most voluntary type of personal relationship'. In most instances friendships are formed as part of regular social interactions, e.g. neighbours who see each other every day, work colleagues who collaborate on projects, and have shared interests and commonality. It is likely that a sense of shared values, beliefs and norms are embedded in the relationship as a result of their shared foci and therefore the relationship is based on a large number of interconnecting spheres. Those interconnecting spheres are partly how we make the choice over whom we make relationships with and the ongoing strength of those relationships. However according to the same research, those relationships which are born of shared activity do not continue after the commonality has passed, they found that in order for friendships to be maintained there must be a continued sharing of interests or close physical proximity.

In other studies on friendship the motivating factors were explored to ascertain why young people like to belong to teams in sport. In their study of friendship quality in youth sport Weiss and Smith [9] identified six major dimensions: companionship, emotional support, loyalty and intimacy, similarity, conflict resolution, and experiences of conflict, reflecting the main aspects by which youth sport friendship quality tends to be experienced. Their study examined the experiences of tennis players aged 10–18 and found that the most impactful motivator was loyalty and intimacy for the older participants whilst companionship was more important for the younger of the sample.

Parsons and Bales [10] examined interpersonal interactions in small groups or teams and identified two functions of groups which they defined as socio-emotional and task orientated. They identified six problems faced by groups, which are reintegration, tension reduction, decision, control, evaluation and communication as seen in Table 2. These

Table 2. Six Problems faced by groups

	Category	Function		Problem relating toPaired Processes
		Socio-emotional	Task Oriented	
1.	Shows solidarity	Positive		Reintegration
2.	Shows tension release	Positive		Tension reduction
3.	Agrees	Positive		Decision
4.	Gives suggestion		Answer	Control
5.	Gives opinion		Answer	Evaluation
6.	Gives orientation		Answer	Communication
7.	Asks for orientation		Question	Communication
8.	Asks for opinion		Question	Evaluation
9.	Asks for suggestion		Question	Control
10.	Disagrees	Negative		Decision
11.	Shows tension	Negative		Tension reduction
12.	Shows antagonism	Negative		Reintegration

problems were then explored in relation to either the socio-emotional function or the task oriented function and whether there was a positive or negative impact on team dynamics.

The adapted Interpretative phenomenological analysis (IPA) framework was applied to the intensive study of ten teams in the Digital Schoolhouse project. The results were displayed in a radial diagram format in order to look for a pattern within the results.

Teams were considered Positive Teams if their friendships increased during the tournament and conversely Negative Teams were ones whose friendships decreased during that time period. Neutral Teams were those where friendships did not change. A total of 10 teams were analysed in depth. The limitation of this study is that it was taken over a short period of time.

Shows Solidarity - Reintegration. Lindenberg et al. [11] states, 'Any group or society heavily depends on the willingness of its members to help other in need, to contribute to a common good, to show themselves worthy of trust and to be fair and considerate'. He examines what makes some people behave in solidarity in one situation and not in others. Findings included the fact that usually there are two main goals, one is to get the job done and the other is to maintain smooth social relationships. All teams showed solidarity during the tournament. The positive and neural teams showed no antagonism, whereas the negative teams did.

In the negative teams, where friendships deteriorated during the tournament the maintenance of relationships was perhaps not seen as a priority for the group and resulted in a heightened degree of antagonism. In the team which saw the friendships decreased the most negative comments were captured 'choosing a team member from a different team to replace one of ours' 'not choosing a terrible team and to go in a better team' and when asked what worked well they said 'nothing'. Comments were very personal and heightened antagonism rather than resolving the conflict that occurred.

Shows Tension Release - Tension Reduction. Research of Bormann and Borman [12] states there are primary and secondary tensions that take place in groups. Secondary tension emerges after groups have passed the forming stage of group development and begin to have conflict over member roles, differing ideas, and personality conflicts. A certain amount of secondary tension is to be expected, but were it reaches above an acceptable threshold indirect means of dissipation is needed such as diplomacy or appropriate humour. Teams that do not have the ability to do these will end in conflict.

All the three different types of teams showed tension was present, but the Negative teams performed badly at tension reduction, whereas both the Positive Teams and Neutral Teams had that mechanism present within the team structure. In the comments section the positive teams used phrases like 'what makes you do best in competitions is good communication' and 'teamwork, skill coordination and callouts'. Even their negative comments were supportive 'less emotional decisions' 'my team needed better communication'.

Agrees - Decision. According to Janis [13] groups tend to agree on decisions when there is a high degree of cohesiveness in the team and the need to fit in with the group overrides the motivation to evaluate the information that the decision is being make upon effectively.

The Positive and Neutral Teams tended to agree on decisions more often that disagree, whereas in the Negative Teams this mechanism broke down and there was as much agreement as disagreement during play. The notion of groupthink has been well explored and whilst we don't know if the decision made by the teams in the Digital Schoolhouse turned out to be the best decisions it would certainly explain why there was less conflict in the positive and neutral groups. A notable comment from one of the neutral teams was that 'if we lost we tried the same tactic again' showing there was a lack of wanting to break away from the group decisions that were made.

Gives Suggestion - Control. McGrath [14] in his examination of group interaction and performance, examined Bales work and noted that 'there is a focal thrust to solve the task; that so-called attempted answers (to suggestions) are efforts toward that goal'. 'These reactions serve as feedback, reinforcement, courtesy, flow regulators, tactics to get the floor, and the like'. Across the positive, negative and neutral teams little differences were noted in the results, with all teams showing similar levels of giving suggestions and asking for suggestions, but the negative team asked for more suggestions but did not respond by offering more suggestions in return. in the free comments box the neutral teams left little feedback and only one word answers like 'teamwork' 'communication' but little depth of answers were demonstrated.

Gives Opinion - Evaluation. In Seeking Opinions in Groups, Frey et al. [15] discusses the factors within groups that influence their propensity to seek out the opinion of others in the team. Leadership, group size, confidence in self and the team and whether the group is homogeneous in its opinion are all contributing factors. The likelihood of the information being evaluated in order make the decision was also affected by group dynamics. Groups that were considered homogenous tended to be less critical of the opinions and were more likely to agree than in heterogeneous groups 'homogenous groups are consistently more self-confident and ignorant to risky aspects of their decision'.

In both the positive and negative teams they don't score highly on asking opinions from other team members whereas the neutral teams, who were largely friends prior to the tournament displayed more ability to ask opinion from other players. One of the neutral teams commented that 'our teamwork and communication were very strong which helped us excel in the competition'.

Gives Orientation - Communication. Oyserman, Coon, and Kemmelmeier [16] studies of communication suggest individualism predicts an emphasis on direct, clear communication, where collectivism is associated with indirect communication that takes into account the other person's feelings. This is somewhat demonstrated in the results of this study as the Neutral Teams were the best at this aspect, possibly because Neutral Teams were largely made up of team players which had close friendship bonds already in place prior to the tournament. Examples of direct comments included 'to think of tactics', 'strategies between each other'. both showing support and direct feedback to their other team members.

The Balance of Positive and Negative Socio-emotional Functions in Teams. Of the teams who felt their friendships had increased (Group Type Positive in Fig. 2) and the ones where it had remained the same (Group Type Neutral in Fig. 2) there was increased solidarity, higher tension relief and more agreement generally than in the teams where friendship had decreased (Group Type Negative in Fig. 2). Indications would suggest that the maintenance of social relationships was more important to these teams than the task and that the lack of need to conform in the negative teams leads to more friction.

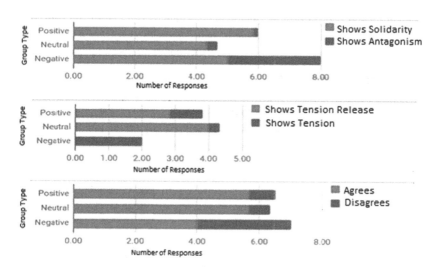

Fig. 2. Positive and Negative Socio-Emotional Functions in Teams

3.2   The Personal Growth Dimension

According to Allender et al. [17] the motivation to participate in sporting activity changes according to life stage. In the early years the main motivators are experimentation, unusual activities, parental support and safe environment. This change during later teenage years to be about weight management and body shape. 'Participation for young children was found to be more enjoyable when children were not being forced to compete and win but encouraged to experiment with different activities'. MacPhail et al. [18] found providing children with many different types of physical activity and sport, encouraged participation. Mulvihill [19] cited that 'Enjoyment and support from parents were also crucial. Parents play a large role in enabling young children opportunities to be physically active' and Bostock [20] found that mothers with young children discouraged their children from playing in an environment perceived as unsafe. Porter [21] showed that parents are more supportive of activity with easy access, a safe play environment, good 'drop-off' arrangements and activities available for other members of the family.

It therefore seems logical to suggest that any form of team activity, in a safe environment (closed on-line community) and removed from their day to day activity would be favoured by young people and their parents, and that taking part would not only benefit them immediately but build their attitude to a healthy, well balanced lifestyle for the future. In '10 Psychological and Social Benefits of Sport for Kids' Cox [22] the benefits of team sports are cited as; 'creating a sense of belonging, learning to lose, building self-esteem, patience, controlling emotions, respecting authority, dedication, working together, less selfish and resilience. During the study when asked if they would be more likely or less likely to participate in other team sports as a result of taking part in the Digital Schoolhouse challenge 81.8% of students said they were more likely to.

In the results in Fig. 3 there is evidence that the positive teams reacted favourably to taking part in other team sports, possibly based on their recent positive experiences, the same group also saw the most positive responses to taking part in further computing based

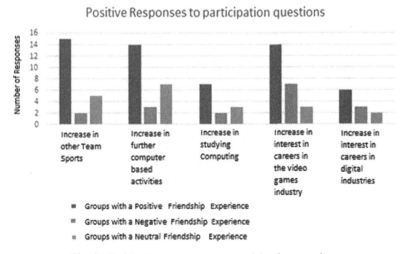

Fig. 3. Positive team responses to participation questions

activities. However, the positive teams were less enthusiastic about studying computing or working in the video games industry or digital industries. The neutral and negative teams were proportionality more inclined to want to follow careers in gaming and the digital industries which might indicate they took the experiment seriously as they see it developing into a career for them.

Transferable Skills. In the second part of the study the students were asked about their transferable skills and if they felt they had improved as part of the Tournament. They were asked about their Communication, Team working, Perseverance, Problem solving and Social Skills as well as being asked if they were more or less likely to take part in other team sports as a result of the tournament.

Results in Table 3 show the highest gains were in communication and team working but all showed significant increases.

Table 3. Results of Soft skills Questionnaire

	Communication	Team working	Perseverance	Resilience	Problem Solving	Social Skills
Yes %	73%	79%	58%	67%	67%	58%
No %	26%	20%	41%	32%	32%	41%

In Fig. 4 the negative teams stood out as having the lowest score in skills development, one team member scored 6 negative responses out of six, whilst another scored five out of six. In the positive teams whilst overall they scored highly on the skills development, there were two team members who felt they had not developed at all. However the neutral teams tended to be more mixed in their positive and negative responses with balanced answers over the six skills and no one team member scoring less than 3 out of six yes answers.

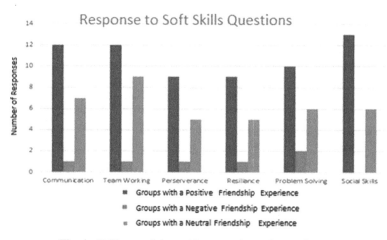

Fig. 4. Skills growth in positive, negative and neutral teams

Case Studies. Teachers, Students and Parents were asked if the esports tournament had benefited them and if yes how. All of the case studies are centred around confidence.

Case Study: Bullying and Isolation
"The tournament has had an impact on one student in particular. This student was a victim of some quite severe bullying at school which led to them to contemplating taking their own life.

They were invited to the Gfinity grand final and spent the day working with professionals, the effects of which have been literally life changing.

Working with professionals and being treated as an equal throughout the event gave them self-belief and confidence moving forward.

Back at school, the bullying has stopped. Those responsible can see that their actions are no longer having the same impact, they know - and has seen first-hand - they are better than the bullies would have them believe."
Case Study: Overcoming Shyness
"I never knew what a shout-caster was before the event and my mates kinda got me into it.

Doing it really pushed my confidence now I'm looking at courses in college where they might help me pursue this further and my mum thinks it's great because I'm not as shy as I was."
Case Study: Anxiety and Communication
"When one of our students who participated in the esports competition first started, they were very anxious, really nervous about coming into the classroom, afraid to talk to new students.

Over the year we told them about the esports tournament with Overwatch - one of their favourite games. They had a lightbulb moment and were really determined to get into the final three.

They worked really hard, they started communicating more with students and also staff. Their attendance improved. They went to the event, participated and loved it.

Unfortunately they got knocked out, but they've come back, they've been a better person for it. They're just a different person.

Talking more, better communication, problem solving. They sit there and try to work out problems with their assignment, whereas before they would put their head in their hands. It's been a game changer."

With roughly one in four students reporting being bullied at school, joining a sports team could be a much-needed source of social support. In fact our study showed that as a result of this tournament 82% of participants said that it had increased their interest in other team sports (Fig. 4).

4   Conclusion

In conclusion this study has found that involvement in esports team activities has a positive impact on interpersonal relationships and as a result builds confidence in young people to tackle other challenges. The perceived increase in their communication, team working skills and resilience has opened up the possibility of new activities and challenges which may not have been considered before thus allowing the positive impact of the tournament to penetrate other areas of their lives.

One distinct area that warrants further study is the increase in interest in participation in other team sports, as this is counterintuitive to the perceptions of avid gamers.

Autoethnographic studies are limited in their success as they rely on the participants being able to accurately observe their own behaviours and that of the group. Research by Luft, and Ingham, [23] explored the idea of interpersonal awareness in the form of a graphical model known as the Johari Window. This is a study of how well the behaviours of others (Peers) and the self (Subject) are observed within the group and form four quadrants. The upper right quadrant is termed as "Open" where Peers and the Subject both agree on the behaviour. The lower left quadrant is "Hidden" were the Subject believes they have behaviours the Peers have not observed. The Upper Left quadrant is

"Blind Spot". This is where the Subject believes they display behaviours that their Peers do not believe they possess. The final Lower Right quadrant " Unknown" is where neither observe that behaviour. When the Johari Window is applied to this study an average of 68% of the authoethenographical observed behaviours lie in the Upper Left and Lower Right quadrants, showing that within the teams that behaviour are verified by one or both of the team members in over two thirds of the observed behaviours (Fig. 5).

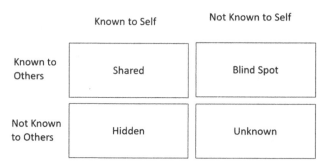

Fig. 5. Johari Window

The next natural progression is to extend this autoethnographic study and improve the accuracy by introducing the observation of the interactions by an external agent.

References

1. Saunders, M., Lewis, P., Thornhill, A.: Research Methods for Business Students, 6th edn. Pearson, London (2007)

2. Chapple, E.D.: Measuring human relations: an introduction to the study of the interaction of individuals. Genetic Psychol. Monographs **27**, 3–147 (1940)
3. Bales, R.F.: Interaction Process Analysis. University of Chicago Press, Chicago (1950)
4. Leary, T.: Interpersonal Diagnosis of Personality. Ronald, New York (1957)
5. Couch, A.S.: Personality determinants of interpersonal behavior. Ph.D. diss, Harvard University (1960)
6. Symlog: A System for the Multiple Level Observation of Groups. Free Press, New York (1979)
7. Moreno, J.L.: Who Shall Survive?. Beacon House, New York (1934)
8. Feld, S., Carter, W.: Foci of activity as changing contexts for friendships, Cambridge Press, Vol: Structural analysis in Social Sciences (1998)
9. Weiss, M.R., Smith, A.L.: Quality of youth sport friendships: measurement development and validation. J. Sport Exercise Psychol. **21**, 145–166 (1999)
10. Parsons, T., Bales, R.F. (eds.): Family, Socialization and Interaction Process. Free Press, New York (1955)
11. Lindenberg, S., Fetchenhauer, D., Flache, A., Buunk, B.: Solidarity and Prosocial Behaviour. An Integration of Sociological and Psychological Perspectives. Springer, Boston (2006). https://doi.org/10.1007/0-387-28032-4
12. Bormann & Borman: Effective Small Group Communication, 4th edn. Burgess Publishing, Santa Rosa (1988)
13. Janis, I.: Victims of Groupthink, p. 9. Houghton Mifflin, Boston (1972)
14. Frey, V. et al.: cited In: Witte, E, Davis, J. (eds.) Understanding Group Behaviour, vol. 2, Psychology Press (2009)
15. McGrath, J.E.: Group Interaction and Performance. Prentice-Hall (1984)
16. Oyserman, C., Kemmelmeier, R.: Individualism and Collectivism (2002)
17. Evaluation of Theoretical Assumptions and Meta-Analyses. American Psychological Association, vol. 128, no. 1, pp. 3–72
18. Allender, S., Cowburn, G., Foster, C.: Understanding participation in sport and physical activity among children and adults: a review of qualitative studies. Health Educ. Res. **21**(6), 826–835 (2006)
19. MacPhail, A., Gorley, T., Kirk, D.: Young people's socialisation into sport: a case study of an athletics club. Sport Educ. Soc. **8**, 251–267 (2003)
20. Mulvihill, C., Rivers, K., Aggleton, P.: Physical Activity 'At Our Time': Qualitative Research among Young People Aged 5 to 15 Years and Parents, 2000, London Health Education Authority
21. Bostock, L.: Pathways of disadvantage? Walking as a mode of transport among low income mothers. Health Soc. Care Community, **9**, 11–18 (2001)
22. Porter, S.: Physical Activity: An Exploration of the Issues and Attitudes of Parents of pre Fives, London Scott Porter Research and Marketing (2002)
23. Cox, A.: 10 Psychological and Social Benefits of Sport for Kids, Sport Play your Way (2015)
24. Luft, J., Ingham, H.: The Johari window, a graphic model of interpersonal awareness. In: Proceedings of the Western Training Laboratory in Group Development. University of California, Los Angeles (1955)

Flex Your Muscles: EMG-Based Serious Game Controls

Philipp Niklas Müller$^{(\boxtimes)}$ ⓘ, Philipp Achenbach ⓘ, André Mihca Kleebe,
Jan Ulrich Schmitt, Ute Lehmann, Thomas Tregel, and Stefan Göbel

Multimedia Communications Lab (KOM),
Technical University of Darmstadt, 64283 Darmstadt, Germany
{philipp.mueller,philipp.achenbach,thomas.tregel,
stefan.goebel}@kom.tu-darmstadt.de

Abstract. In recent years, non-traditional input devices for digital
games and applications such as wearable sensors have become increasingly available and affordable. Electromyography (EMG) promises some
unique advantages over traditional input devices such as keyboards or
gamepads by collecting input data directly at a person's muscle. As long
as the corresponding muscle is intact, EMG can be used even when physical movement is not possible, for example when a person is injured or
has an amputated limb. It also allows for unique wearable positioning on
the body, potentially allowing for a larger freedom of movement.

In this paper, we examine whether an EMG-based input device is
feasible to control an in-game character in a digital game. In order to
do so, we first assess different EMG-related technologies and available
EMG devices. Based on this assessment, we develop an EMG-based
input device that can be connected to a computer. We develop a side
scrolling game which can be connected to the EMG-based input device
and allows for the player to switch between keyboard- and EMG-based
controls. Lastly, we evaluate our developed system empirically and discuss the feasibility of EMG-based game controllers based on observed
practical and theoretical limitations of the technology.

Keywords: Human-computer interaction · Health games ·
Electromyography

1 Introduction

Typical input devices for games and other digital applications rely on directly
capturing a person's movements, be it through a keyboard's buttons, a mouse's
optical sensor or a game pad's joystick. In some cases, however, these methods
can be impractical or even unusable, e.g. when the person's hand is in a cast
because of an injury. Muscle-based controllers in general and Electromyography (EMG) in particular promise to be utilizable as an input device in these
scenarios. Since EMG measures the resulting difference in current occurring

© Springer Nature Switzerland AG 2020
M. Ma et al. (Eds.): JCSG 2020, LNCS 12434, pp. 230–242, 2020.
https://doi.org/10.1007/978-3-030-61814-8_18

whenever a muscle is activated, it can be utilized even when the intended movement cannot be carried out or measured. In addition to allowing people with physical limitations to interact with a game or an application, an EMG-based input device could also collect relevant medical data in a health game. This data could be used to adapt the game's difficulty in real time, or later be analyzed by a patient's physician in order to get more detailed information on the patient's health. Furthermore, an EMG-based input device can be utilized without obstructing a person's hands or other limbs, letting them interact with other objects instead.

In this paper, we examine the feasibility of using EMG as an input device for digital games, focusing on the usability of such a system at the player's home, i.e. without requiring a stationary setup or the oversight of a specialist. We first assess different technologies and hardware devices that can potentially be used in such a scenario. We present a prototypical EMG input device and a corresponding game which can be entirely controlled through the EMG input device. Lastly, we present and discuss our findings with respect to the usability of such an EMG input device in a practical scenario.

2   Background and Related Work

In this chapter we look at the background and the functioning of EMG and the new field of Mechanomyography (MMG) as an alternative to EMG. We also show related work where EMG devices are used to control applications and serious games. Finally, we introduce and compare a selection of applicable EMG devices.

2.1   Electromyography

EMG is used for measuring myoelectric signals. These are electrical signals that are generated during muscular activity of the skeletal muscles, which are responsible for voluntary, active body movements [17]. The signals can be measured by two different kinds of electrodes: Non-invasive/surface EMG-electrodes (sEMG), which can be placed on the skin, or invasive/intramuscular EMG-electrodes, which can be placed directly in the muscle. These sensors can be used to check whether a muscle is active, whether a muscle is tiring, how active a muscle is, in which movements a muscle is active and also the force exerted by a muscle [8].

Muscle activity causes potential changes at the muscle membrane. With surface EMG this signal is not measured directly on the muscle but is transmitted from the surrounding tissue to the skin and measured there. Thus the measurement depends on the conductivity of the tissue, which varies due to body fat and the condition of the skin. Signals from other muscles, including the heart, can also influence the measurement [17]. Accurate placement of the sensors is therefore essential, ideally near the muscle to be measured on shaved and disinfected skin. The use of an electrolyte gel to increase conductivity is not uncommon, so is the use of a reference electrode on a non-active limb [8,18].

The surface EMG can be used with different types of electrodes [17]:

Monopolar electrodes When measuring with only one electrode, the direct process of the potential change of the observed muscle is measured. Interferences therefore have a direct effect on the signal, which is the reason why this method is rarely used [17].

Bipolar electrodes When measuring with two electrodes, both electrodes measure the same muscle. Since the potential change of the muscle is wavelike, it reaches the two electrodes at different times. A difference can now be calculated from the measured signals. This difference is less susceptible to interference than in a monopolar measurement, because the interference affects the electrodes in equal parts and is eliminated by the difference calculation [17].

Electrode Array An electrode array is used when larger areas of the skin are to be covered and thus several different muscles are to be measured simultaneously. It consists of several electrodes in series or as a matrix. The latter allows to bypass an exact positioning of individual electrodes. The measurements of the electrodes can be used separately or in sum - as in the bipolar measurement [15].

EMG is mainly used in the field of medicine and diagnostics, but also in the field of sports science [8]. Another area of application which is becoming more and more important is the field of Human-Computer-Interface (HCI) [18].

2.2 Mechanomyography

MMG is an alternative method of measuring muscle activity. Compared to EMG it measures the physical changes of the muscles and not the electrical signals which are emitted during muscle contraction [16]. Physical changes of skeletal muscles can lead to measurable acceleration, vibration and acoustics. MMG can therefor subdivided into three different approaches: Acceleromyography, vibromyography and phonomyography [6].

Talib et al. [16] analyzed various studies on MMG and were able to divide the used sensors into five categories: Accelerometers, microphones, piezoelectric sensors, displacement sensors and composite sensors.

MMG offers the advantage of a high signal-to-noise ratio combined with low sensitivity in sensor placement. It also has easy handling of setup up with the reliability of data [3].

A major disadvantage of MMG is that the technology is still in its beginnings and relatively unresearched. Therefore, there are no ready-to-use sensors to purchase at the moment [16].

2.3 Muscle Controlled Application

As mentioned in the introduction, EMG offers two major advantages when used as an input device:

Firstly, EMG can be used to detect muscle activity without the need of movement. This may happen when the corresponding limb is restricted in movement, but also when it is completely absent, for example during an amputation. EMG can then be used to offer the patient an opportunity for interaction and is therefore also used in prostheses [4,14]. Prahm et al. [14] describe a concept of using (serious) games to permanently motivate patients with prostheses to train their muscle coordination on a playful way and thus to better accept the prosthesis. The authors used three different kinds of games for their study: a racing game, a rhythm-based game and a dexterity game. The games were controlled by two EMG-electrodes, which allowed movement by one Degree of Freedom (DoF).

There are also other play-oriented approaches for people with prostheses, such as an adaptation of the commercial video game Guitar Hero© III, which is controlled by six or more EMG electrodes and does not require the use of any keys [4]. Oppenheim et al. [11] developed WiiEMG, a EMG-based Wii™ controller, to promote the rehabilitation of the patients' motor skills.

The second advantage of EMG is, that muscle activity of limbs can be measured without restricting the limbs themselves. For example, the movement of a hand can be measured while interacting with objects or gesticulating freely. Wu et al. [19] use four EMG-electrodes in combination with one Inertial Measurement Unit (IMU) to recognize signs. Their approach recognizes 80 commonly used ASL signs with an accuracy of up to 96.16%.

The EMG wristband *Myo* from the company *Thalmic Labs* for example also supports the control of drones and robots via gestures captured with the wristband [1].

Another example is described by Pai et al. [12], who present a system that uses eye tracking for cursor movement and EMG on a user's forearm to make selections in Virtual Reality (VR).

2.4 EMG-Devices

The design of a muscle-based gesture controller should be preceeded by a comprehensive literally hardware analysis. Since a muscle-controlled game is to be developed, the following aspects should be considered:

- Ease of use (weight, size, wired/wireless, etc.)
- Real-time capability
- Usability for the scenario of a muscle-controlled game
- Sufficient number of channels to track muscle activity of up to five fingers and arm
- Technical key figures like Sampling Rate, Bandwidth/filter and gain
- Problems and ambiguities that could arise when using the setup

The following is an overview of EMG sensors available on the market.

Grove-EMG-Detector:[1] The *Grove-EMG detector* is a basic EMG-sensor which allows 3 disposable skin surface electrodes to be connected simultaneously via wire. The EMG signal is amplified and filtered, but further details

---

[1] https://wiki.seeedstudio.com/Grove-EMG_Detector/ - Last visited on 03.07.2020.

are not known. The sensor is compatible with the *Grove* system - a plug-in system to make cable connections between different components easier. For *Arduino Uno* there is a *Grove* extension, the *Grove Shield*. However, it has only 4 analog connectors and can therefore only be equipped with up to 4 EMG-sensors. For the *Arduino Mega* there is also a larger version, the *Grove Mega-Shield*, with 8 analog connectors.

The producer explicitly states that the sensor is not suitable for medical purposes.

The system is for example used by Krivosheev et al. [9] for recognizing gestures and by Borisov et al. [5] for controlling a prosthetic hand.

MyoWare Muscle Sensor: [2] The *MyoWare* muscle sensor is a simple EMG sensor like the *Grove - EMG detector*. In contrast to this one, it can not only be used with external skin surface electrodes, but can also be attached directly to the body. The output signal can be either a rectified and integrated analog signal or the analog RAW data. The gain is adjustable.

Medical devices are mentioned as an application example, but a corresponding certificate is missing.

The system is for example used by Krivosheev et al. [10] for designing a muscle and flex sensor controlled robotic hand for disabled persons and by Borisov et al. [2] for building a EMG-driven nobility assistance robot for disabled persons.

Thalmic Myo: [3] The *Thalmic Myo* is a All-in-one solution in the form of a EMG wristband. In addition to medical stainless steel EMG sensors, it consists of a 9-DoF-IMU and an integrated ARM Cortex M4 processor. It can transmit data wirelessly via integrated Bluetooth. The possibility of haptic feedback and an integrated lithium-ion battery complement the system. It has a sampling rate 200 Hz (sEMG) at 8 bit and a notch filter 50 Hz.

Pizzolato et al. [13] compare the *Talmic Myo* in their paper with 5 other EMG systems (including the *Cometa Waves + Dormo* and *Delsys Trigno* presented here) and used the approach of using two wristbands simultaneously, among other things. These were placed slightly shifted to each other on the same arm.

Using two wristbands could increase the accuracy by about 25% compared to one wristband and is comparable to the *Delsys Trigno*, which gave the most accurate results but also cost 30 times more than two *Thalmic Myos*.

Cometa miniWave: [4] The *Cometa miniWave* is a small, compact, lightweight and wireless All-in-one solution. It has a resolution of 76 nV/bit at a sampling rate of 2 kHz at 16 bit and a bandwidth with HPF 10 Hz and LPF at 1 kHz. The gain is 1,000.

---

[2] https://www.sparkfun.com/products/13723 - Last visited on 03.07.2020.

[3] https://www.vdc-fellbach.de/leistungen/technikbewertung-var/thalmic-labs-myo-gesture-control-armband/ - Last visited on 03.07.2020.

[4] https://www.cometasystems.com/products/mini-wave - Last visited on 03.07.2020.

One unit has two EMG electrodes and a 3-DoF accelerometer and can measure one muscle. The battery life is 10 h and can be recharged by inductive charging.

Delsys Trigno Wireless System:[5] The *Delsys Trigno Wireless System* consists of several sensors that measure acceleration and orientation in addition to EMG signals. Each sensor can be attached directly to the body and transmits the data wirelessly. The power supply is provided by a built-in rechargeable battery. The resolution is 168 nV/bit with a sampling rate of 2 kHz at 16 bit and a bandwidth of 20–450 Hz/10–850 Hz. The gain is 909 ± 5.

Pizzolato et al. [13] compare in their work 6 different EMG-systems where the *Delsys Trigno*) could provide the most accurate results.

Bagnoli EMG System:[6] This setup is a classic wired system with the emphasis on easy handling. It has 16 channels, where the amplification can be adjusted individually. It has a bandwidth of 20–45 Hz ± 10 at a gain of 100/1000/10000. The system manages and conditions the signals and provides feedback if signals are cut off due to excessive gain. The output is analog, but the system can be connected directly to a PC with a special card.

The system is approved as a medical device and is for example used by Khushaba et al. [7] for improving control of prosthetic fingers.

The advantages and disadvantages of these EMG systems can also be found in Table 1.

3   Approach

In the following, we will present the prototype we developed to assess the feasibility of an EMG input device for a digital game to be played at home. Our prototype consists of a wearable surface EMG system which records EMG signals of two different skeletal arm muscles as well as a game which processes the recorded data in real time in order to control the player's character.

3.1   EMG System

Whereas intramuscular EMG has significant advantages over surface EMG in many areas such as signal to noise ratio or number of applicable muscles, it is also highly invasive and cannot be safely used by an untrained person at home. With one of our requirements being the usability for a player at home, we therefore use a less invasive surface EMG system for our prototypical EMG controller.

Our EMG controller consists of a MyoWare muscle sensor to record muscle activity and an Arduino Uno which acts as an analog-to-digital converter before sending the converted data to the computer running the game using a

---

[5] https://www.delsys.com/trigno/research/ - Last visited on 03.07.2020.
[6] https://www.delsys.com/bagnoli/ - Last visited on 03.07.2020.

Table 1. Advantages and disadvantages of several examined EMG systems

System	Type	Advantages	Disadvantages
Grove-EMG-Detector	Sensor	– Easy data exchange and power supply through Grove system – Data easily accessible	– Wired – Only 4/8 channels – Not suitable for medical purposes
MyoWare Muscle Sensor	Sensor	– Easy to assemble – Raw and Integrated Data – Easy to scale up – Easily expandable for different purposes	– Wired – Only 4/8 channels – Not suitable for medical purposes
Thalmic Myo	All-in-one solution (wristband)	– Easy to wear bracelet – Does not require any preparation on the skin	– Fixed electrode spacing – No longer available
Cometa miniWave + Dormo	All-in-one solution	– Small, light and handy – Wireless	– Requires as many units as muscles to be measured – Preparation on the skin necessary for the electrodes
Delsys Trigno Wireless	All-in-one solution	– Wireless – Suitable for sports applications – Precise measurement results	– Expenditure for real-time applications must be clarified – Larger sensors, unsuitable for narrow places (hand) – Scalability must be clarified
Bagnoli EMG System	All-in-one solution	– Simple setup – Usable for gesture recognition – Direct access to (analog) data – Certified for medical purposes	– Cabled – Real-time data only with additional hardware – 16 channels, not scalable

USB connection. The USB connection doubles up as a power source for the system. Alternatively, a Bluetooth module and a battery holder can be added to enable wireless functionality at the cost of additional weight. Whereas our prototype utilizes a relatively large Arduino Uno as a microcontroller board, smaller boards such as the Arduino Nano or custom microcontroller boards can be used in practice to reduce the impact on player comfort. Compared to complete solutions such as the Thalmic Myo, our approach has the advantage of being easily adaptable and extensible to a given use case while also being more affordable in practice. For example, a more complex game might require additional EMG sensors or a disabled player might require sensors in different positions to be able to use the EMG controller.

Figure 1 shows our EMG controller when applied to the player's arm. For our system, we apply three electrodes in total; two electrodes to measure the activity of the Biceps brachii and one electrode as a reference electrode. The Biceps brachii is one of the primary muscles involved in the flexion of the forearm at the elbow. By measuring its muscle activity, we can therefore determine whether the player is currently attempting to flex their forearm. The reference electrode is placed at an arbitrary part of the forearm without muscle activity, e.g. a bony part of the elbow. The muscle activity for the Biceps brachii is then calculated

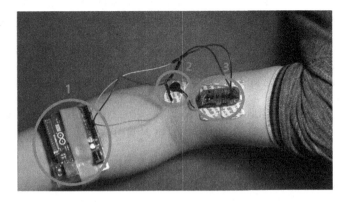

Fig. 1. Applied EMG system consisting of an Arduino Uno (1), a reference electrode (2) and a MyoWare muscle sensor applied to the Biceps brachii (3)

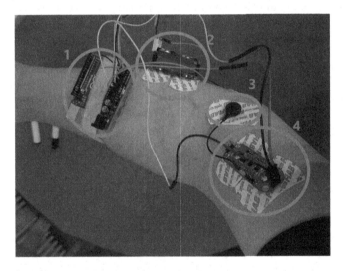

Fig. 2. Applied EMG system consisting of an Arduino Uno (1), a MyoWare muscle sensor applied to the Flexor carpi ulnaris (2), a reference electrode (3) and a MyoWare muscle sensor applied to the Biceps brachii (4)

as the difference between the electrical activity measured at the Biceps brachii and the electrical activity measured at the reference electrode.

Figure 2 shows how the EMG controller can be expanded by additional muscle sensors. The additional muscle sensor is applied to the Flexor carpi ulnaris at the player's forearm. The Flexor carpi ulnaris is one of the primary muscles involved in the flexion of the wrist. By measuring its muscle activity, we can therefore also determine whether the player is currently attempting to flex their wrist. Since each MyoWare muscle sensor uses their own reference electrode, an additional reference electrode is placed at the back of the elbow (not visible in Fig. 2).

The Biceps brachii and the Flexor carpi ulnaris were chosen as appropriate muscles to measure muscle activity based on their distinct function and high accessibility via surface EMG as a result of their respective size and position. A large number of muscles, particularly in the forearm, are either concealed by other muscles or too small for accurate surface EMG measurement and are therefore not suited for a surface EMG approach. Even though our setup can be easily expanded by additional muscle sensors, this puts a hard limit on the number of muscles that can be measured by this approach in a given area of the body.

3.2   Software

The microcontroller on the Arduino Uno converts the rectified and integrated EMG signal produced by the MyoWare muscle sensors into a digital signal and forwards it to the connected computer, appending a unique identifier for each source muscle sensor to each data package. On the computer, an API stores all received muscle sensor data for a fixed time span of one second before discarding it. A game can utilize this API to access the latest sensor data values, rescaled to a desired value range, at any given point in time.

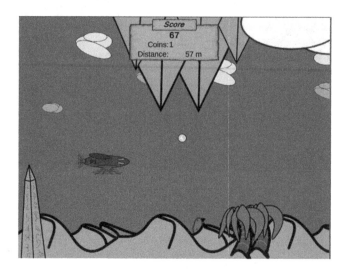

Fig. 3. The developed side scrolling game with a controllable space ship

In order to assess whether our system can be used as an effective input device for a game, we designed a simple side scrolling game in Unity[7] in which the player controls a space ship (see Fig. 3). The goal of the game is to avoid touching any obstacles for as long as possible while collecting as many coins

---

[7] https://unity.com/ - Last visited on 04.07.2020.

as possible on the way. Without the EMG-based input device, one key on the keyboard can be used to move the space ship upwards whereas another key can be used to shoot. The space ship continuously moves rightwards and slowly moves downwards if no upwards command is input. With the EMG-based input device, two different modes exist: If the basic setup with a single muscle sensor is used, that muscle is used to move the space ship upwards and the ship automatically shoots continuously. The space ship can therefore be moved upwards by tensing the Biceps brachii, e.g. by flexing the forearm, and moved downwards by releasing the tension. If the setup with two muscle sensors is used, the second muscle sensor is used to shoot. A player can thus shoot by tensing the Flexor carpi ulnaris, e.g. by flexing their wrist.

Fig. 4. EMG calibration process

Before starting the game, the player has to choose whether to use an EMG-based input device and, if so, whether a second muscle sensor is used to shoot. If an EMG-based input device is selected, all muscle sensors are then calibrated as shown in Fig. 4. For each input type (*thrust* or *shoot*), the player selects the according muscle sensor by its device ID. For each muscle sensor, the player is then asked to relax and then tense the respective muscle for five seconds each. The recorded values are then used to determine a minimum and a maximum muscle sensor value for the given muscle sensor in order to translate sensor values into game inputs. During gameplay, the game periodically polls the API for the latest sensor data value for each connected muscle sensor. The sensor value is then converted into an input value using the minimum and maximum values determined during calibration and used similar to how e.g. a joystick's angle would be used.

4   Discussion

We could not conduct an extensive user study for our developed system because of the aggravated regulations following the outbreak of COVID-19. Instead, we rely on the empirical data collected when developing and testing the system in order to assess whether our system in particular and EMG-based systems in general are applicable as input devices for digital games.

With correctly applied electrodes, we found the EMG-based input device to be a usable input device after a settling-in period of typically less than a minute, i.e. players were able to control the space ship to a comparable degree to the key-based input. An input delay was noticeable but not large enough to be disruptive for our game. We expect this to be a problem for faster and more reaction-based games though and thus would not recommend an EMG-based input device for such games.

Despite only using a maximum of two muscle sensors, we found the process of applying the single-use adhesive electrodes to be unpleasant and relatively time-consuming compared to traditional input devices, especially since they require very clean and hairless skin to achieve good contact. Furthermore, we found the system to be susceptible to artefacts when connecting additional wired electrodes to the muscle sensors, particularly when their respective cables moved. Whereas conductive fabric electrodes can be used to alleviate these issues, we expect them to provide significantly more noisy data in general since they do not ensure as good skin contact as adhesive electrodes.

Lastly, our approach comes with significant limitations, most of which apply to surface EMG in general. One such limitation is the noise related to surface EMG when compared to intramuscular EMG, preventing precise movements from being accurately captured. Furthermore, surface EMG can only be used for muscles close to the skin surface which are large enough to provide a significant electrical signal and not covered by other muscles. It can therefore not be used to capture all movements that traditional input devices can capture.

Overall, we consider a surface EMG-based controller to be a feasible input device for digital games, albeit only for very specific scenarios and types of games where their distinct advantages fully apply, such as when a player is physically impaired or EMG data is also used for medical purposes. We don't recommend using it in games where quick reactions or precise movements are mandatory.

5   Conclusion

EMG offers many interesting applications in the fields of medicine, sports and, as shown in this paper, also in the field of HCI. We developed an EMG-based input device as well as an accompanying side scrolling game which can be played entirely by muscle activation. The game supports two different arm movements for which muscle activity between tense and relaxed is translated into game input, allowing for the game to be fully controlled with just muscle activation.

Whereas the EMG-based input device works well for the simple side scrolling game we developed, we could identify a number of restrictions that apply when utilizing such an input device for other games and scenarios. An EMG-based input device is therefore not suited for games that require quick reflexes or precise movements and cannot be used for movements with inaccessible muscle regions.

In future work it is worth looking at whether additional muscle sensors can be utilized to detect finer movements such as finger movements. In order to achieve more precise results, an EMG-based approach could also be augmented by additional sensors such as IMUs. Furthermore, it is worth looking into the accuracy that can be achieved by EMG-based systems for different movements and how it compares to traditional input devices.

References

1. Ackerman, E.: Myo Armband Provides Effortless Gesture Control of Robots, Anything Else - IEEE Spectrum, June 2020. https://spectrum.ieee.org/automaton/robotics/robotics-hardware/thalmic-myo-armband-provides-effortless-gesture-control-of-robots. Library Catalog: spectrum.ieee.org
2. Ahmed, S.F., et al.: Mobility assistance robot for disabled persons using electromyography (EMG) sensor. In: 2018 IEEE International Conference on Innovative Research and Development (ICIRD), pp. 1–5. IEEE (2018)
3. Alves, N., Chau, T.: The design and testing of a novel mechanomyogram-driven switch controlled by small eyebrow movements. J. NeuroEng. Rehabil. **7**(1), 22 (2010). https://doi.org/10.1186/1743-0003-7-22. ISSN 1743–0003
4. Armiger, R.S., Vogelstein, R.J.: Air-Guitar Hero: a real-time video game interface for training and evaluation of dexterous upper-extremity neuroprosthetic control algorithms. In: 2008 IEEE Biomedical Circuits and Systems Conference, pp. 121–124 (2008)
5. Borisov, I.I., Borisova, O.V., Krivosheev, S.V., Oleynik, R.V., Reznikov, S.S.: Prototyping of EMG-controlled prosthetic hand with sensory system. IFAC-PapersOnLine **50**(1), 16027–16031 (2017)
6. Islam, A., Sundaraj, K., Ahmad, B., Ahamed, N.U., Ali, A.: Mechanomyography sensors for muscle assessment: a brief review. J. Phys. Ther. Sci. **24**(12), 1359–1365 (2012)
7. Khushaba, R.N., Kodagoda, S., Takruri, M., Dissanayake, G.: Toward improved control of prosthetic fingers using surface electromyogram (EMG) signals. Expert Syst. Appl. **39**(12), 10731–10738 (2012)
8. Konrad, P.: EMG-Fibel. - Eine praktische Einführung in die kinesiologische Elektromyographie, January 2011
9. Krivosheev, S., Borisov, I., Olejnik, R., Reznikov, S.: First Experiments and Results, Various Control Strategies for the Artificial Hand Using Surface EMG Sensors (2016)
10. Latif, S., Javed, J., Ghafoor, M., Moazzam, M., Khan, A.A.: Design and development of muscle and flex sensor controlled robotic hand for disabled persons. In: 2019 International Conference on Applied and Engineering Mathematics (ICAEM), pp. 1–6. IEEE (2019)
11. Oppenheim, H., Armiger, R.S., Vogelstein, R.J.: WiiEMG: a real-time environment for control of the Wii with surface electromyography. In: Proceedings of 2010 IEEE International Symposium on Circuits and Systems, pp. 957–960 (2010)
12. Pai, Y.S., Dingler, T., Kunze, K.: Assessing hands-free interactions for VR using eye gaze and electromyography. Virtual Real. **23**(2), 119–131 (2019). https://doi.org/10.1007/s10055-018-0371-2. ISSN 1434–9957

13. Pizzolato, S., Tagliapietra, L., Cognolato, M., Reggiani, M., Müller, H., Atzori, M.: Comparison of six electromyography acquisition setups on hand movement classification tasks. PLOS One **12**(10), e0186132 (2017). https://doi.org/10.1371/journal.pone.0186132. https://journals.plos.org/plosone/article?id=10.1371/journal.pone.0186132. ISSN 1932–6203

14. Prahm, C., Vujaklija, I., Kayali, F., Purgathofer, P., Aszmann, O.C.: Game-based rehabilitation for myoelectric prosthesis control. JMIR Serious Games **5**(1),e3 (2017). https://doi.org/10.2196/games.6026. http://www.ncbi.nlm.nih.gov/pubmed/28183689. ISSN 2291–9279

15. von Rosenberg, H.: Identifikation von Willkürsignalen zur Bewegungskontrolle einer Beinprothese (2012)

16. Talib, I., Sundaraj, K.,Lam, C.K.: Choice of mechanomyography sensors for diverse types of muscle activities. J. Telecommun. Electron. Comput. Eng. (2018, accepted for publication)

17. Weitz, M.: Messung und Analyse myoelektrischer Signale. Ph.D. thesis, Diplomarbeit. Universität Kassel, Kassel (2006)

18. Wheeler, K.R.: Device control using gestures sensed from EMG. In: Proceedings of the 2003 IEEE International Workshop on Soft Computing in Industrial Applications, SMCia/03, pp. 21–26. IEEE (2003)

19. Wu, J., Sun, L., Jafari, R.: A wearable system for recognizing American sign language in real-time using IMU and surface EMG sensors. IEEE J. Biomed. Health Inform. **20**(5), 1281–1290 (2016)

Rethinking Serious Games Design in the Age of COVID-19: Setting the Focus on Wicked Problems

Carlo Fabricatore[1]([✉]) [iD], Dimitar Gyaurov[2] [iD], and Ximena Lopez[2] [iD]

[1] E.H.E. Europa Hochschule EurAKA, Erlenstrasse 31, 4106 Therwil, Switzerland
carlo.fabricatore@gmail.com
[2] University of Huddersfield, Queensgate, Huddersfield HD1 3DH, UK

Abstract. We live in a complex world, in which our existence is defined by forces that we cannot fully comprehend, predict, nor control. This is the world of wicked problems, of which the situation triggered by the COVID-19 pandemic is a notable example. Wicked problems are complex scenarios defined by the interplay of multiple environmental, social and economic factors. They are everchanging, and largely unpredictable and uncontrollable. As a consequence, wicked problems cannot be definitively solved through traditional problem-solving approaches. Instead, they should be iteratively managed, recognizing and valuing our connectedness with each other and the environment, and engaging in joint thinking and action to identify and pursue the common good. Serious games can be key to foster wicked problem management abilities. To this end, they should engage players in collective activities set in contexts simulating real-world wicked problem scenarios. These should require the continuous interpretation of changing circumstances to identify and pursue shared goals, promoting the development of knowledge, attitudes and skill sets relevant to tackle real-world situations. In this paper we outline the nature, implications and challenges of wicked problems, highlighting why games should be leveraged to foster wicked problem management abilities. Then, we propose a theory-based framework to support the design of games for this purpose.

Keywords: Serious games · Wicked problems · Complexity · Game design

1 Introduction: The Wicked Age of COVID-19

We live in the age of COVID-19, an epoch in which a pandemic is forcing us to acknowledge that the world is not what we believed and perhaps wished it was. In this epoch we are realizing that a virus can trigger and catalyze processes that are changing our world in uncertain, concerning, and somewhat irreversible ways. In the age of COVID-19 we are reminded on a daily basis that our world is shaped by forces that generate extraordinary problematic situations, which affect our society, economy and environment, while overcoming our ability to comprehend and control circumstances. These are labelled "wicked problems", because they shape the future of our world and our future in it, and

© Springer Nature Switzerland AG 2020
M. Ma et al. (Eds.): JCSG 2020, LNCS 12434, pp. 243–259, 2020.
https://doi.org/10.1007/978-3-030-61814-8_19

because they defy and defeat ordinary approaches to "solving" problems [30]. Wicked problems situations are to a large extent unpredictable and uncontrollable, which makes them seemingly chaotic and intractable [21, 30]. However, wicked problems can be continuously managed to promote the adaptation of social systems to everchanging and threatening circumstances [11, 26]. If appropriately designed, serious games can represent an optimal platform to develop knowledge, attitudes and skills specifically required for wicked problem management.

In this paper, we present a framework to support the design of serious games to learn wicked problem management. First, we review the nature, relevance and challenges of wicked problems. We then explain why games should be leveraged to learn how to manage wicked problems. Finally, we propose a theory-based framework to support the design of wicked problem management serious games.

2   The Ordeal: Nature and Implications of Wicked Problems

2.1   The Heart of Wickedness: Complexity, Conflicting Actors, and Problem Systems

Wicked problems are extraordinary types of problems. Just like an ordinary problem, a wicked problem is determined by an undesirable state of affairs that needs to be changed. However, ordinary problems can be analyzed to define what conditions need to be changed (initial state), what new state of affairs should be attained in order to improve things (goal state), and what approach should be adopted to transition from the problematic to the desirable state of affairs (problem solution) [1]. It can then be definitively solved by implementing the planned approach. This is not the case for wicked problems, since they are ill-defined situations in which problematic conditions, possible goals and viable approaches are to some extent unclear and mutable, due to their complexity [21].

Wicked problems are defined by large numbers of factors that interact in multiple ways [30]. This makes them highly complicated. Their complexity, however, transcends sheer complicatedness. Interacting factors change over time, and so do the ways they interact, as factors evolve and reorganize to adapt to external changes [28]. Furthermore, interactions between factors generate emergent systemic effects that propagate across time and space, and cannot be fully understood nor predicted based on the examination of individual factors and their interactions [24, 28]. In this sense, wicked problems behave as wholes greater than the sum of their parts. Complicatedness, adaptive change and emergent effects ultimately determine the true complexity of wicked problem situations, and make them not fully knowable, uncertain, unpredictable, and therefore uncontrollable. To worsen things, wicked problems usually involve diverse actors, who have different and often conflicting interests and needs, and are therefore affected in different ways by the same circumstances [8, 25]. Finally, wicked problems never come alone, as one problematic situation usually indicates the existence of a whole system of interacting problem scenarios [30].

Altogether, complexity, multiplicity and heterogeneity of actors, and co-occurrence of interacting problem scenarios make it impossible to determine, for any given situation, what the "problem" is, and what a "solution" could be. This makes wicked problems intractable through classic problem-solving approaches [21, 25, 30].

2.2 How to Tackle Wicked Problems: Adaptive Problem Management

The ill-defined and seemingly chaotic nature of wicked problems should be continuously managed through iterative and adaptive processes [2, 26, 30]. These should rely on collaborative meaning-making, action and learning [3, 11, 25]. To this end, the management of a wicked problem should continuously integrate exploration and evaluation of circumstances, planning and action, and should be continuously informed by relevant environmental feedback (Fig. 1).

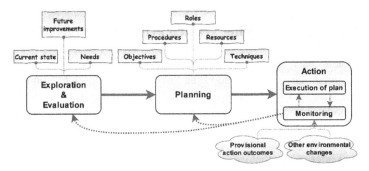

Fig. 1. Adaptive problem management process.

Exploration and evaluation are necessary to gain a systemic understanding of the current state of affairs, its implications for the involved actors, and possibilities for future improvements [2, 26]. These understandings should drive the planning of objectives to pursue and strategies to adopt. Objectives should reflect changes in the current state of affairs beneficial for all the involved actors, while strategies should define roles, procedures, techniques and resources required to achieve these changes [8, 11]. Planning should then drive action, acknowledging that in the arena of wicked problems there can be no "sticking to the plan". The execution of a plan should be underpinned by continuous monitoring and evaluation of provisional outcomes, and other environmental changes that might require adapting the problem management process, through a direct revision of ongoing plans, or a more substantial re-evaluation of the entire problem situation [3, 26].

Meaning-making is crucial in wicked problem management. Wicked problems require to continuously interpret things, relationships and events in order to infer how the world works, and define what should be done, why and how [17, 25]. Meaning-making ought to be collective and ensure the participation of all the actors affected by the problem situation. This is crucial to harmonize and integrate diverse and possibly conflicting worldviews and needs, identifying the common good and ensuring that objectives and plans reflect a shared vision of what should be done, why and how [11, 12, 25]. By extension, collective meaning-making should drive collaborative action. This is essential to enact plans requiring a diversity of competencies and resources that can only be provided through the joint effort of all actors [8, 11].

Finally, collective meaning-making entails collaborative learning. In order to identify mutually beneficial changes to pursue, formulate plans and adapt to changing circumstances, actors need to learn about one another and their environment [21]. The need to harmonize diverse and possibly conflicting interpretations of reality requires this learning to be an action-driven process of social construction of knowledge [11, 25]. This process benefits actors through enhancing their understanding of the world, developing their ability to devise and pursue better futures, and leading them to ponder and modify subjective beliefs and assumptions that might hamper the pursuit of the common good [3, 11].

3 The Challenge: Fostering Wicked Problem Management Abilities

Wicked problem management (WPM) requires knowledge representations suitable to identify and pursue the common good, and skill sets and attitudes required to form this knowledge and act accordingly [7, 21, 24]. Knowledge representations consist in conceptual models of problem scenarios, formed through meaning-making and suitable to drive decision-making and action. These models should be holistic, representing circumstances starting from global phenomena, and then modelling parts (human beings included) and interactions that might cause them, or be affected by them [11]. Models should also be pluralistic, acknowledging, reflecting and harmonizing diverse views and interpretations that actors involved in the problem situation might have [8, 25]. Attitudes consist in affective dispositions suitable to motivate purposeful engagement in wicked problem scenarios. Overall, these should promote a disposition to look after people, non-human beings and the broader environment, in the short and long term; and the confidence in the ability to act meaningfully to pursue the common good, even though this means constantly facing and adapting to circumstances that cannot be controlled [11, 21, 33]. Skill sets are cognitive and practical capabilities suitable to explore and transform problem scenarios, through engaging in purposeful interactions with relevant actors and environmental elements involved in them [7, 17, 34]. Altogether, the function of attitudes, skill sets and knowledge representations can be conceptualized as a form-inform-transform schema, whereby their interplay serves to (i) *form* new or revised knowledge representations, through continuous exploration of the problem situation and relevant environmental feedback; (ii) *inform* definition of goals and plans through these knowledge representations; and (iii) *transform* a problem situation based on set goals and plans.

Serious games represent optimal platforms to foster wicked problem management abilities, due to their potential to: (i) simulate complex dynamics and elicit problem management in conditions of complexity [16, 19, 22]; (ii) contextualize gameplay activities reproducing real-world settings and dynamics [35]; (iii) promote the integrative development of knowledge, attitudes and skill sets through engagement in meaningful activity [15, 20]; and (iv) function as collective learning environments exempt from spatiotemporal constraints that limit formal learning contexts [19, 35]. The nature of WPM suggests that these potentialities can be leveraged to foster WPM abilities by designing serious games based on the principles presented in Table 1.

Table 1. Principles to foster WPM abilities through serious games.

Gameplay contexts should mirror a wicked problem scenario of interest and promote iterative management abilities by reproducing:

1	**Complexity conditions.** Gameplay scenario involving (i) game space articulated as a system of interrelated systems; (ii) events engendering change, unknowability, unpredictability, uncontrollability and uncertainty; (iii) ill-defined situations requiring players to make evaluations and decisions with incomplete and uncertain information; and (iv) collective tasks, involving social construction of knowledge, and collaborative evaluation of circumstances, decision-making and action
2	**Contents.** Gameplay scenario (i) involving physical, social, economic and cultural settings characterizing a real-world scenario of interest; (ii) defined by multiple actors with conflicting needs and interests, emphasizing the significance of the scenario from different perspectives; (iii) promoting the development of knowledge representations, higher-order thinking and operational skill sets, and affective dispositions, relevant to tackle real-world scenarios
3	**Process.** Iterative gameplay tasks (i) driven by and promoting meaning-making; (ii) requiring progressive construction of solutions, with ongoing revisions of plans and objectives; and (iii) fostering activity-based learning

Addressing these principles requires rethinking: (i) what players should engage in and with; (ii) how learning processes involved in the gameplay experience unfold; and (iii) how these processes should be promoted "by design". To support the creation of wicked problem management serious games, we developed the WPM-SGD design framework. WPM-SGD comprises theory-based conceptual tools (models and guidelines) to facilitate the design of games suitable to promote wicked problem management abilities. The remainder of this article presents WPM-SGD components key to address the first of the three principles: complexity conditions. To this end, we outline the WPM-SGD tools relevant to incorporate key complexity conditions in WPM, discussing their theoretical underpinnings, and presenting related examples where appropriate.

4 Rising up to the Challenge: Designing Complexity in Serious Games to Foster WPM

WPM-SGD was developed adopting a human factors design approach. The discipline of human factors and ergonomics (HFE) investigates the interaction between subjects and systems, to design systems to enhance human activity, psychophysical wellbeing, and overall systemic efficiency [27]. In terms of game design, adopting an HFE approach requires modelling the game space from a player perspective [18], accounting for (i) how players perceive and make sense of the game space, (ii) why and how they interact with it, (iii) how learning stems from their interactions with the game space, and (iv) which game elements are key to enable or hinder desirable interactions and their effects.

4.1 Modeling Gameplay Contexts as Systems of Systems: Key Requirements

In order to foster WPM, serious games should engage players with the conditions of complexity that make wicked problems intractable through ordinary problem-solving approaches. Managing wicked problems requires embracing a "system of systems" perspective. A wicked problem scenario should be treated as a part of a larger whole which comprises many other interdependent systems, so that what happens within a problem scenario may alter external systems, and vice versa [10, 30, 36]. Events local to a given problem scenario may generate effects that propagate globally, across time and space, affecting other systems. These effects may be somewhat indiscernible, unpredictable and uncontrollable. By the same token, the state of a problem scenario may be altered by external events. These events, their consequences and origins may also be somewhat indiscernible, unpredictable and uncontrollable. The degree of discernibility of all this depends on the information flows available to interpret what is happening or has happened, when, where, why and how. By extension, information flows allow anticipating future events and their effects, as knowledge of the past allows inferring patterns to predict future happenings [6]. Altogether, dynamics of propagation of event effects and information flows across systems generate change, unknowability, uncontrollability, unpredictability and uncertainty that define the complexity of wicked problems and make them extremely difficult to address [2, 30, 36]. In terms of game design, this implies that key complexity conditions characterizing real-world wicked problems can be reproduced through designing suitable (i) networks of interacting game elements, (ii) event generation and propagation schemas and (iii) mechanics of generation and propagation of game state information flows.

4.2 Systemic Design of Game Contexts

To support the systemic modeling of the game context, we formulated a systemic model of game context expanding on our previous work [18]. Based on leading HFE perspectives, we conceptualized the gameplay context as a hierarchical system composed of *interaction clusters* (sub-systems) involving volitional agents, objects and environmental conditions [6, 10, 36]. Volitional agents can act purposefully to satisfy their needs, alone or in groups, whereas objects are purely reactive entities that change their states in response to external stimuli [18]. Environmental conditions are factors that affect the state of agents and objects, as well as their ability to interact with the rest of the environment [10, 36]. As they unfold, interactions between these elements change the state of the game space generating *events*. Some events involve state changes that can directly or indirectly affect the player's activity. We denominate these *defining events*, and their potential consequences for the player *gameplay effects*. Events can be directly or indirectly originated by player actions (*player-triggered events*), or by other game elements (*non-player-triggered events*). To exemplify all this, consider a hypothetical geopolitical simulation game, in which the player is a policy maker in the Republic of Muchocalor. Assume that the player has to deal with a situation in which a prolonged drought required extensive groundwater pumping, which caused severe groundwater depletion. In this case, groundwater depletion would represent a non-player-triggered defining event. The source of this event would be an interaction cluster comprising the landowners that recur to groundwater pumping (volitional agents), groundwater basins (objects), and the draught (environmental condition). Assuming that the player would have to regulate this problematic situation, a gameplay effect of groundwater depletion would be an increased gameplay challenge.

This conceptualization also supports the design of *propagation of events*. An event generated by an interaction cluster C1 could involve game state changes that interact with another cluster C2, generating a new propagating event. For example, in the above scenario, the groundwater depletion event would also involve depleted underground water basins turning into pits. These could then interact with another interaction cluster such as a road system, causing a cascading event: land subsidence due to loss of support below ground. This new event could then affect ground transportation, etc. Propagations could unfold as far as the designer decides, generating expanding networks of interdependent phenomena increasingly harder for players to interpret and predict.

Figure 2 presents a schema of interaction clusters, generation and propagation of events, and illustrates the examples discussed above. This model can be used to plan networks of interacting elements, and the related generation of events. Through planning amount and scope of interaction clusters, events, and interaction and propagation chains, designers can define the complexity that players should tackle.

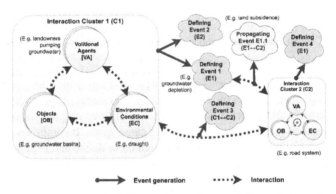

Fig. 2. CIEP model: prototypical **C**luster, **I**nteractions, and **E**vent **P**ropagation schema.

In real-world wicked problem scenarios not all events are equally discernible and influenceable by the involved actors [11, 26]. This is an important condition that should be reproduced in WPM serious games, as it is key to define unknowability, unpredictability, uncontrollability, and uncertainty of game situations. To support this, we propose a three-tiered hierarchical model of propagation of game events and information flows, based on our past research [18].

As subjects act, they perceive and interpret their surrounding environments acknowledging that there are dimensions that they cannot directly discern and/or influence with their actions [5]. Accordingly, we modelled the game context as a three-tiered system, to allow defining "by design" players' possibilities to perceive and interact with different elements of the game space. The three tiers consist in a *micro, meso* and *macro levels* (Fig. 3). The micro-context is players' primary focus of attention. It comprises:

(i) entities that players can directly perceive, interact with, and are in fact involved in an ongoing gameplay task (e.g. helpers, enemies and tools involved in a current action plan); and (ii) environmental conditions that players could alter, and which influence the state of elements directly involved in ongoing gameplay tasks (e.g. ambient lighting affecting the visibility of enemies). The meso-context comprises elements that players can directly perceive and could interact with, even though these are not involved in any ongoing gameplay task. Players might need to deal with these elements, should their plans change (e.g. alternative or complementary tools that could be used; optional objects that could be collected; distant enemies that might be tackled; etc.).

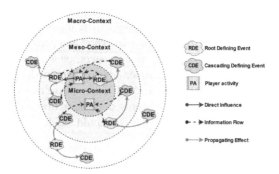

Fig. 3. 3T-Context: game context model to tierize clusters, events and information flows.

The meso-context thus represents a space of possibilities, which may allow or require players to modify their courses of actions by adapting current plans or formulating new ones. The macro-context reflects large-scale phenomena that originate from interplaying game events, and affect multiple aspects of the game space. It comprises elements that players cannot directly interact with, even though these define and explain many things and relationships in the game space (e.g. political systems; value systems; physical models; etc.). The macro-context reflects the history of past events leading to the present game state, and its understanding is crucial for players to forecast game states. Players can indirectly affect elements of the macro-context through cascading effects of gameplay tasks (e.g. a political system cannot be directly affected, and its existence can only be comprehended through manifestations such as trade regulations; however, actions boycotting trade can lead to a change in the political system). We propose in Fig. 4 key patterns of propagation of events and information flows, suitable to help designers plan the game context and anticipate possible effects on the player.

Altogether, the models presented in Fig. 3 and Fig. 4 can help designers plan the distribution of interaction clusters, and map propagation of events and game state information flows. This can be useful to control what players should be able to discern and interact with, and consequently generate conditions of ill definition and uncontrollability that they should tackle. To further support this work, we propose in Table 2 a procedure to guide the design of game contexts.

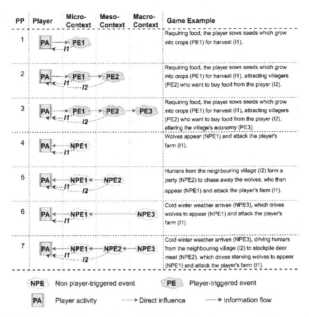

Fig. 4. ProPat model: key event and information flows propagation patterns.

Table 2. Core procedure for the systemic modeling of gameplay contexts.

1	**Hierarchical systems modeling.** Define the gameplay context as a network of key interaction clusters, establishing for each cluster:
1.1	Components (volitional agents, objects and environmental conditions interacting in the cluster)
1.2	How components can interact
1.3	Defining events generated by interactions within the cluster
2	**Events description and propagation.** For each defining event, establish:
2.1	Game state changes generated
2.2	Gameplay effects engendered by the game state changes
2.3	Propagating events that can be generated, identifying additional clusters that contribute to their generation
3	**Tierization of game elements and events in micro, meso and macro-context:**
3.1	Situate interaction clusters and events, in order to define possibilities/limitations for players to interact with them
3.2	Define information flows propagation across tiers, in order to define possibilities/limitations for players to discern relevant aspects of the game context

4.3 Detailed Planning of Information Flows

As they play, players engage in meaning-making to continuously interpret the state of agents and objects, their interactions, the resulting events and the corresponding effects [5, 18]. Providing players with information adequate to feed meaning-making is essential to promote gameplay motivation and progression [18], support desirable game-based learning [20], and elicit the development of desirable knowledge representations, skill sets and attitudes [17, 21]. Information should also be limited, to reproduce ill definition characterizing real-world wicked problem scenarios [8, 17]. Planning game information flows is therefore challenging, and requires accounting for how information can affect meaning-making, learning, motivation and decisions-making. Fabricatore and Lopez [20] proposed a human factors model of the gameplay activity suitable to address all this (Fig. 5). The authors conceptualized game-based learning as the outcome of continuous meaning-making processes unfolding through interaction with the gameplay context. Meaning-making is intended as a process of formation and update of mental representations of the game context [6]. Through this process, players perceive and interpret things, events and relationships as they interact with the game space, forming and updating mental representations based on their thoughts and feelings [6, 20]. Players then use mental representations to define further interactions with the game space, in a cyclical process that engenders the integrative development of knowledge representations (i.e. mental representations), affective dispositions, and skill sets required to think, feel and act meaningfully upon the game space [20, 23]. Learning can then be the product of social exchanges and negotiation [14], when players are required to interact with other game actors (both human and synthetic).

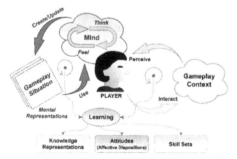

Fig. 5. InAcLE model: process integrating Interpretation, Action and Learning through meaning-making.

Based on these conceptualizations, we argue that in WPM serious games information flows should be planned accounting for:

1. What information fully describes a relevant interaction cluster, an event, its source, and its designed gameplay implications.
2. How players could interpret this information.
3. What knowledge representations they could form based on the provided information.
4. Which decisions they could take, based on their interpretations.

To support this, we created TFLD (Fig. 6), a tool for the design of information flows suitable to promote the formation of mental representations driving desirable player thinking, feeling, learning and decision-making. TFLD comprises a method for the analysis of gameplay situations, and the consequent planning of information flows suitable to:

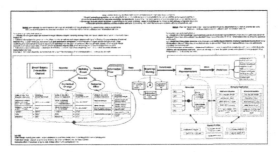

Fig. 6. TFLD tool: conceptual instrument to support the design of information flows to promote desirable Thinking, Feeling, Learning and Decision-making.

1. **Support gameplay progression**, by promoting the formation of mental representations suitable to motivate and define gameplay goals and tasks.
2. **Promote the development of desirable knowledge representations**, by providing information suitable to focus the player attention on relevant matters.
3. **Encourage desirable player decisions**, by promoting the formation of mental images that emphasize the relevance and adequacy of specific decisions.
4. **Stimulate desirable attitudes and interpretation skill sets**, by providing information that stimulates desirable affective dispositions, and elicit required skills.

The method is complemented by a model to support the analysis of gameplay situations in order to identify key information that defines the situation, possible interpretations that players could give to this information, and key decisions that they could make based on these interpretations. The TFLD tool is available online at: https:/bit.ly/2DD qN2P.

4.4 Collective Engagement

Player engagement in collective processes is a further condition that WPM games should reproduce. This is important for two reasons. Firstly, the complexity of wicked problem scenarios is largely due to the involvement of social communities and actors with diverse and often conflicting needs and worldviews [8, 26]. Hence, WPM usually requires engaging in shared and oftentimes conflictive evaluation, decision-making and action processes [11, 12]. Secondly, fostering learning in complexity scenarios requires engaging learners in collective processes of knowledge construction [14, 21].

Exploring how to promote collaboration in serious games is beyond the scope of this paper. A large body of literature has already investigated the benefits and implementation of collaborative learning in serious games [9, 29]. The field of computer-supported collaborative learning represents another valuable source of information concerning why and how to promote collaborative learning through simulations and games [13]. We will however highlight that, in order to promote WPM, collective gameplay activities should be designed accounting for three key principles:

1. Players/learners should engage in social construction of knowledge, and collaborative evaluation of circumstances, decision-making and action [8, 11, 14, 19, 21].
2. Players should interact and negotiate with other agents, who should have different and conflicting roles, needs, interests and worldviews [16, 19, 20].
3. Collective activity does not require engagement with other human players. Agents driven by artificial intelligence can also be leveraged to create single-player games suitable to promote collective activities in complex scenarios [4].

4.5 Target Skill Sets and Attitudes

The tool presented in Sect. 4.3 emphasizes the importance of designing situations and related information flows suitable to promote desirable skill sets and attitudes [20]. Fabricatore and Lopez [21] proposed an integrative framework of skill sets and attitudes relevant to engage in WPM (Table 3 and Table 4), extrapolated from an extensive review of the literature on wicked problems [e.g. 8, 17, 26, 30]. In order to support the design of WPM serious games, we expanded this framework by formulating transferable design approaches to promoting WPM skill sets and attitudes in new games based on the commercial games *Sky: Children of the Light* (thatskygame.com) (Table 3) and *Minecraft* (www.minecraft.net) (Table 4).

Table 3. Attitudes required to manage wicked problems

Attitude	Example from *Sky*	Design approach
Global belongingness. Sense of belonging to a global community which forms an organic whole with the environment. Fosters sense of responsibility for life and diversity, present and future	Always present shadows of other players who are striving towards restoring the light in the universe together with the player	Highlight to players real-time state of other players engaged in pursuit of shared goals and/or affected by shared circumstances
Emotional commitment to sustainable development. Sense of responsibility to safeguard the future of our global community and its environment	Player reliving the tragic memories of Ancestor Spirits and meeting other players who are struggling against the darkness	Highlight to players the emotional influence that game characters have on each other and the player
Compassionate altruism. Concern for the well-being of human and non-human others, and disposition to support others. Fosters sense of responsibility for life and diversity	Ability of players to gift each other hearts and candles as a form of communication towards building friendships to defeat the darkness	Highlight to players alternative ways of communicating with and helping each other by giving up personal resources for shared goals

(*continued*)

Table 3. (*continued*)

Attitude	Example from *Sky*	Design approach
Confidence action capacity. Reliance on individual and collective capacity to act. Fosters overcoming feelings of powerlessness originated by the scale, uncertainty and uncontrollability of wicked problem situations	Support and guidance that players receive from others who have walked the challenging path in front of them to reunite the stars in the sky	Highlight to players the guidance and success of others who have encountered similar challenges in the game
Hope in action effects. Confidence that individual and collective action can have meaningful impacts. Fosters overcoming powerlessness originated by wicked problem situations	Ability of players to leave light behind for others in the hope of helping them the same way they were helped with light left behind from past spirits	Highlight to players ways of guiding and supporting each other after overcoming challenging obstacles in the game
Adaptivity. Acceptance that change, uncertainty and uncontrollability drive our world, and that we can as well change, adapt and develop. Fosters resilience to external changes, and iterative processes of co-evolution with the environment	Need to re-explore the continuously updating realms of Heaven in order to achieve their aim of defeating darkness	Highlight to players the changing state of the game's world and the progression requirement for them to re-explore newly developed scenarios

Table 4. Skill sets required to manage wicked problems

Skill set	Example from *Minecraft*	Design approach
Creative thinking. Ability to purposefully generate novel ideas to model and act on a situation of concern, possibly dissociated from previously-acquired frames of reference. Fosters adaptation to environmental changes, devising feasible goals, and evaluating implications of action	Players explore new paths in the world, building new structures for survival and crafting new tools for progression through the interaction with the grid of blocks which makes up the game's world	Highlight to players the alternative states and functions of game objects and agents which players can interact with for unique purposes
Systems thinking. Ability to interpret real-world entities through conceptualizing them as systems, presenting emergent properties and behaviors that cannot be explained considering parts in isolation. Fosters managing mutability and unknowability of wicked problem situations	Complex relationships between the game's day and night cycle, biomes' features, block types, extracted resources and mobs' behaviors (animals and creatures)	Highlight to players their influence on game states after interacting with objects and agents, and the relationships between these game elements
Ill-defined problem solving. Ability to continuously manage problem situations through an iterative process of design and implementation of strategies, pivoting around emergent results of action. Fosters dealing with complex environments	Unpredictable and uncontrollable behaviors of passive and hostile mobs who players have to deal with	Highlight to players the unpredictable nature of game states, objects and agents that they have to interact with

(*continued*)

Table 4. (*continued*)

Skill set	Example from *Minecraft*	Design approach
Analogical reasoning. Ability to identify similarities between two situations, and use these to hypothesize other similarities. Fosters identifying systemic recurrences, establishing patterns and predicting future situations accordingly	Similar response to players interacting with or creating new and different types of blocks in the game such as wood, crops, ore, enemies, buildings, etc.	Highlight to players the similar response to interacting with different but related game objects and agents
Deductive reasoning. Ability to formulate logical conclusions based on generally accepted statements or facts. It allows to safely predict results, informing "justification"	Day and night cycle which affects enemy behavior and player's vital signs in the game	Provide information regarding simple causal relationships and then require players to use it to deduce new causal relationships
Inductive reasoning. Ability to form a generalized conclusion based on what is particularly known or observed. It allows to form hypothesis, informing "discovery"	Predictable generation of valuable ore blocks or lava blocks promoting meaningful decision-making	Highlight to players the probable state of game objects and agents based on previously revealed information
Abductive reasoning. Ability to form a probable conclusion based on the information that is known. It allows to create value, informing "design"	Players choosing locations for their shelter, mine, farmland and craft area based on real-world information and the grid of blocks	Highlight to players the functional similarities between states, objects and agents in the game and their respective real-world analogues
Social skill sets (pluralism, negotiation, dialogue, communication, sharing). Abilities that enable and drive social negotiation processes key to understand others' perspective, formulate shared worldviews and purposes, and plan joint action. Foster adequate involvement of all key stakeholders	In-game chat allowing players to communicate while sharing limited resources and tools and negotiating preferences and responsibilities for mining ore, gathering food or building shelter	Highlight to players the ways they can communicate with each other in order to manage shared resources and achieve common goals
Operational skill sets. Abilities required to interact with reality by operating objects which, depending on the context, may serve to achieve set purposes. They are essential to implement planned actions	Similarity and simplicity of operations such as collecting grass, mining ore and attacking enemies which allow for complex and meaningful actions	Highlight to players the similar ways in which they can interact with different objects in the game for unique purposes

5   Conclusions

The future of our world is shaped by forces that we cannot fully comprehend, predict nor control. These originate wicked problems that define our environments, challenge our ways of life, and even threaten our very existence. In this paper we explored what wicked problems are, and why they defeat ordinary problem-solving approaches. We emphasized that wicked problems cannot be definitively solved. However, they can be iteratively managed through collective processes aimed at identifying and pursuing the common good, in order to continuously adapt to changing circumstances.

Managing wicked problems requires specific attitudes, skill sets and knowledge representations that cannot be easily fostered through formal education. Serious games can be leveraged to overcome this limitation. To this end, they should be designed to engage players in gameplay contexts mirroring wicked problem scenarios. Unfortunately, the literature on serious games and wicked problems is scarce. To our knowledge, there are very few contributions aimed at supporting the design of serious games focused on wicked problems [e.g. 31, 32], and none of them focuses on what wicked problems are, how and why they should be tackled through iterative problem management processes, and how games should be designed to foster WPM abilities. We developed the WPM-SGD framework to address this gap.

In this paper we presented WPM-SGD conceptual tools aimed at supporting the replication of key complexity conditions that characterize wicked problem scenarios, and the design of information flows suitable to motivate and support gameplay progression, and foster the development of WPM skills sets and attitudes. These tools represent a portion of what is needed, as WPM-SGD is a work in progress. In line with the principles presented in Table 1, we plan to complete the WPM-SGD framework by developing conceptual tools focused on supporting the reproduction of key types of contents commonly found in wicked problem scenarios (e.g. sociocultural and physical settings), and the articulation of gameplay tasks to mimic the structure of WPM processes. Furthermore, we plan to develop instruments for the evaluation of serious games focused on wicked problems (e.g. sustainability games).

In conclusion, we believe that significant efforts should be made to advance research into the design and use of serious games to promote wicked problem management abilities. We consider WPM-SGD a contribution to this endeavor, and we hope that it can serve to support designers, and orient future research.

References

1. Ackoff, R.L.: The Art of Problem Solving. Wiley, New York (1978)
2. Ackoff, R.L.: Systemϖ Trist, E., Murray, H. (eds.) The Social Engagement of Social Science, pp. 417–438 (1997)
3. Argyris, C.: Double loop learning in organizations. Harv. Bus. Rev. **55**(5), 115–125 (1977)
4. Bae, H., Glazewski, K., Hmelo-Silver, C.E., Lester, J., Mott, B.W., Rowe, J.: Intelligent cognitive assistants to support orchestration in CSCL. In: Computer-Supported Collaborative Learning Conference, CSCL, vol. 2, pp. 947–948 (2019)
5. Bedny, G.Z., Karwowski, W., Jeng, O.J.: The situational reflection of reality in activity theory and the concept of situation awareness in cognitive psychology. Theor. Issues Ergon. Sci. **5**(4), 275–296 (2004). https://doi.org/10.1080/1463922031000075070
6. Bedny, G., Meister, D.: The Russian Theory of Activity: Current Applications to Design and Learning. Psychology Press, New York (2014)
7. Beinecke, R.H.: Introduction: leadership for wicked problems. Innov. J. **14**(1), 1–17 (2009)
8. Buchanan, R.: Wicked problems in design thinking. Des. Issues **8**(2), 5–21 (1992). https://doi.org/10.2307/1511637
9. Buchinger, D., da Silva Hounsell, M.: Guidelines for designing and using collaborative-competitive serious games. Comput. Educ. **118**, 133–149 (2018). https://doi.org/10.1016/j.compedu.2017.11.007

10. Carayon, P.: Human factors of complex sociotechnical systems. Appl. Ergon. **37**(4), 525–535 (2006). https://doi.org/10.1016/j.apergo.2006.04.011
11. Checkland, P., Poulter, J.: Soft systems methodology. In: Reynolds, M., Holwell, S. (eds.) Systems Approaches to Managing Change: A Practical Guide, pp. 191–242 (2010). https://doi.org/10.1007/978-1-84882-809-4_5
12. Conklin, J.: Dialogue Mapping: Building Shared Understanding of Wicked Problems. Wiley, New York (2005)
13. Cress, U., Rosé, C., Wise, A., Oshim, J. (eds.): International Handbook of Computer Supported Collaborative Learning. Springer, Heidelberg (2020)
14. Davis, B., Sumara, D., Luce-Kapler, R.: Engaging Minds: Changing Teaching in Complex Times, 2nd edn. Routledge, New York (2008)
15. Dieleman, H., Huisingh, D.: Games by which to learn and teach about sustainable development: exploring the relevance of games and experiential learning for sustainability. J. Clean. Prod. **14**(9–11), 837–847 (2006). https://doi.org/10.1016/j.jclepro.2005.11.031
16. Diniz dos Santos, A., Strada, F., Bottino, A.: Approaching sustainability learning via digital serious games. IEEE Trans. Learn. Technol. **12**(3), 303–320 (2019). https://doi.org/10.1109/TLT.2018.2858770
17. Dorst, K.: Design problems and design paradoxes. Des. Issues **22**(3), 4–17 (2006)
18. Fabricatore, C.: Underneath and beyond mechanics: an activity-theoretical perspective on meaning-making in gameplay. In: Suter, B., Kocher, M., Bauer, R. (eds.) Games and Rules: Game Mechanics for the "Magic Circle", pp. 87–112 (2019). https://doi.org/10.14361/978 3839443040-006
19. Fabricatore, C., López, X.: A model to identify affordances for game-based sustainability learning. In: Busch, C. (ed.) Proceedings of the 8th European Conference on Game Based Learning, pp. 99–109 (2014). https://doi.org/10.13140/2.1.5028.0967
20. Fabricatore, C., Lopez, X.: Game-based learning as a meaning making-driven activity process: a human factors perspective. In: Elbæk, L., Majgaard, G., Valente, A., Khalid, S. (eds.) Proceedings of the 13th International Conference on Game Based Learning, ECGBL 2019, pp. 218–226 (2019). https://doi.org/10.34190/GBL.19.177
21. Fabricatore, C., Lopez, X.: Education in a complex world: nurturing chaordic agency through game design. In: Visser, J., Visser, M. (eds.) Seeking Understanding: The Lifelong Pursuit to Build the Scientific Mind, pp. 325–353. Brill I Sense, Leiden (2020)
22. Gyaurov, D., Fabricatore, C., Lopez, X.: An analysis instrument for gameplay information flows supporting sustainability complex problem-solving. In: Elbæk, L., Majgaard, G., Valente, A., Khalid, S. (eds.) Proceedings of the 13th International Conference on Game Based Learning, ECGBL 2019, pp. 863–871 (2019). https://doi.org/10.34190/GBL.19.171
23. Gordon, G., Esbjörn-Hargens, S.: Integral play: an exploration of the playground and the evolution of the player. AQAL J. Integral Inst. **2**(3), 62–104 (2007)
24. Holland, J.H.: Emergence: From Chaos to Order. Addison-Wesley, Redwood City (1998)
25. Houghton, L., Tuffley, D.: Towards a methodology of wicked problem exploration through concept shifting and tension point analysis. Syst. Res. Behav. Sci. **32**(3), 283–297 (2015). https://doi.org/10.1002/sres.2223
26. Jones, P.H.: Systemic design principles for complex social systems. In: Metcalf, G.S. (ed.) Social Systems and Design. TSS, vol. 1, pp. 91–128. Springer, Tokyo (2014). https://doi.org/10.1007/978-4-431-54478-4_4
27. Karwowski, W.: The discipline of human factors and ergonomics. In: Salvendy, G. (ed.) Handbook of Human Factors and Ergonomics, 4th edn., pp. 3–37. Wiley, Hoboken (2012)
28. McDaniel Jr., R.R., Driebe, D.J.: 1 uncertainty and surprise: and introduction. In: McDaniel Jr., R.R., Driebe, D.J. (eds.) Uncertainty and Surprise in Complex Systems, pp. 3–11. Springer, Heidelberg (2005). https://doi.org/10.1007/10948637_1

29. Ravyse, W.S., Seugnet Blignaut, A., Leendertz, V., Woolner, A.: Success factors for serious games to enhance learning: a systematic review. Virtual Real. **21**(1), 31–58 (2017). https://doi.org/10.1007/s10055-016-0298-4
30. Rittel, H.W.J., Webber, M.M.: Dilemmas in a general theory of planning. Policy Sci. **4**(2), 155–169 (1973). https://doi.org/10.1007/BF01405730
31. Sicart, M.: Moral dilemmas in computer games. Des. Issues **29**(3), 28–37 (2013). https://doi.org/10.1162/desi_a_00219
32. Swain, C.: Designing games to effect social change. In: 3rd Digital Games Research Association International Conference: "Situated Play", DiGRA 2007, pp. 805–809 (2007)
33. Tilbury, D., Wortman, D.: Engaging People in Sustainability. IUCN, Gland (2004)
34. Van Eijnatten, F.M.: Chaordic systems thinking: some suggestions for a complexity framework to inform a learning organization. Learn. Organ. **11**(6), 430–449 (2004)
35. Whitton, N.: Digital Games and Learning: Research and Theory. Routledge, New York (2014)
36. Wilson, J.R.: Fundamentals of systems ergonomics/human factors. Appl. Ergon. **45**(1), 5–13 (2014). https://doi.org/10.1016/j.apergo.2013.03.021

Game Debriefing

Construction of Debriefing Designed for Applying Experiences of History Game to Contemporary Issues

Masahiro Ohyama[1]([envelope]) [iD], Hiroki Baba[2] [iD], and Jun Yoshinaga[1] [iD]

[1] Kobe University, 3-11 Nada-Ku, Kobe-City, Hyogo, Japan
masa_yama1001@yahoo.co.jp
[2] Chiba Keizai University, 3-59-5 Todoroki-Cho Inage-Ku, Chiba-City Chiba, Japan

Abstract. The aim of this study is to demonstrate the effectiveness of debriefing which applies experiences of a history game to contemporary issues, through an evaluation of its practice. Recently, the game has been expected to engage students in a problem-solving process as citizens in social studies lessons. But there are only a few studies of simulation & gaming about history learning, because the method is not clear for students to apply the outcomes of history learning to solutions of contemporary issues. Therefore, a lot of students cannot have the reasons why they need to learn history in school. To solve the above problems, this study designs the debriefing referring to the theory of Kriz, W.C. (2010) and verifies the effectiveness by an evaluation of an experiment. This study organizes the following process in lessons; "Historical Subject" (in the game) → "Transfer Subject" (in the debriefing) → "Contemporary Subject" (in the debriefing). In Contemporary Subject, students think about a contemporary issue by the experiences of the game. Transfer Subject is an exercise to make it easier for students to connect a contemporary issue with a history game. The results of the lessons indicate the following 2 points; 1) the students became able to establish their own opinions about Japanese politics by applying experiences of a history game to contemporary issues. 2) the students became to understand the importance of history learning.

Keywords: History learning · Debriefing · Experience of the game · Applying to contemporary issues

1 Introduction

The aim of this study is to demonstrate the effectiveness of debriefing which applies experiences of a history game to contemporary issues, through an evaluation of its practice.

Debriefing focuses on what participants may have learned from playing the game (Peters, V., Vissers, G. 2004: 73), and it can be said "The learning begins when game engagement stops and when debriefing engagement is under way" (Crockall, D. 2014: 426). Debriefing is widely defined as a learning process after each game in this study. Constructing the debriefing of history games is essential to history learning.

© Springer Nature Switzerland AG 2020
M. Ma et al. (Eds.): JCSG 2020, LNCS 12434, pp. 263–275, 2020.
https://doi.org/10.1007/978-3-030-61814-8_20

Recently, the national curriculum of subjects in school education has been revised in Japan. The revision requires the application of the outcomes of learning to students' life and organization of an active learning style. Especially, social studies in Japanese schools aim not only to foster the understanding of social phenomena, for example, geography, history, political systems, and so on, but also to cultivate citizenship in students. Therefore, it has been expected to introduce games which engage students in a problem-solving process as citizens in social studies lessons.

But the introduction of games in history learning has not been popular, because the method is not clear for students to apply the outcomes of history learning to the solution of contemporary issues. On the contrary, it is easy for students to apply the experiences of the game to contemporary issues in geography or politics, because the subjects are related directly to our present lives. For example, the game of immigration issues enables students to have and express their opinions on the immigration issues of the real world.

However, in history learning, understanding of the structure and causal relationship of historical facts is not immediately related to contemplate contemporary issues, because historical facts do not perfectly correspond to contemporary issues. Therefore, a lot of students cannot have reasons why they need to learn history in school. Actually, there are only a few studies of simulation & gaming about history learning (Corbeil, P. 2011; Corbeil, P., Laveault, D. 2011).

Solving the problems as the above, this study focuses on the design of debriefing for applying history to contemporary issues. According to Kriz, W.C. (2010), the design of debriefing is divided into six phases as follows; 1. How did you feel? Sharing participants' emotions, 2. What has happened? Collecting and analyzing information, 3. In what respects are the events in the gaming simulation and the reality connected? Examining the relationship between the experience and the reality, 4. What did you learn? Identifying participants' most important learning, 5. What would have happened if…? Exploring the essential principles and terms of the gaming simulation, 6. How do we go on now? Committing to clear, realistic, and measurable goals for future actions of all involved. Can Phase 6 be considered as the learning for applying experiences of a history game to contemporary issues?

In preceding studies, the design of debriefing in history game verified phases 1 to 5 and not 6 yet (Corbeil, P. 2011). So, this study designs the debriefing of Phase 6. Figure 1 shows the process in each lesson. In Contemporary Subject, students think "how do we go on now?". Transfer Subject is an exercise to make it easier for students to connect a contemporary issue with a history game.

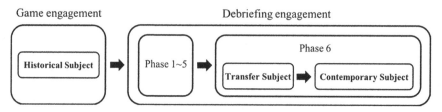

Fig. 1. A process in the lesson

Furthermore, the term "apply" in this study means that students can have their own opinions about contemporary issues based on experiences of a history game. The only way in which history learning can contribute to cultivating citizenship in a democratic society is not to cultivate the faculty of reproducing a solution in historical facts, but to make each student form opinions about contemporary issues. It is not clear whether the solution in historical facts is right or wrong. Therefore, students can never find the significance of history learning until they realize that history learning works effectively to have their own opinions about contemporary issues.

From the above, this study examines the following two hypotheses; 1) Students become able to establish their own opinions about Japanese politics by applying experiences of a history game to contemporary issues. 2) Students become to understand the importance of history learning. The construction of this study is as follows; 1) Concrete contents of the designed debriefing are presented, 2) Evaluation methods and results are described.

2   Method

This study is an improved debriefing of INDEPENDENCE DAY, which is diplomatic Negotiation Game and developed for history learning (Baba, H. et al. 2019). The hypotheses are tested through this game and debriefing.

2.1   Contents of INDEPENDENCE DAY and Conventional Debriefing

INDEPENDENCE DAY is a negotiation game to make students virtually experience diplomatic negotiations between Japan and the United States (the U.S.) after World War II (WWII). In this game, the situation and the name of the countries are abstracted, for example, Country A is the U.S., Country B is Japan and Country C is the Soviet Union. Because, the aim of this game is to make students freely think of the concept of national independence or diplomacy without any prior-knowledge about the historical event.

Students belong to either team A or B. One team represents one diplomatic corps and has about 3 people. A's mission is to negotiate with B over the conflict with C. B's mission is to negotiate with A for their country's independence. After the discussion with negotiation repeated twice, each group makes an agreement.

Conventional debriefing is as follows;

1)   Each group announces its own agreements and impressions.
2)   The facilitator makes a coordinate plane which is composed of "Large-Scale Japanese Army—Small-Scale Japanese Army" and "High Independence—Low Independence" (Fig. 2). Then the facilitator questions; Where do you place your agreement? The students place it in the coordinate plane.
3)   The facilitator hands out the agreement as historical facts and questions; Where do you place it?

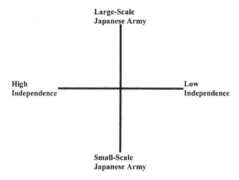

Fig. 2. Coordinate plane

The ultimate aim of the conventional debriefing is to make students not only realize possible negotiations but also compare the results of the game with historical facts. This debriefing is based on Phases 1 through 5 of Kriz's theory. It is necessary to think how we go on now (phase 6) making use of the experience of thinking what would have happened if (phase 5).

2.2 Contents of Designed Debriefing in This Study

Contemporary Subject, which students need to think how we go on now through this debriefing consists of the following question; "How does Japan deal with President Trump's statement that the U.S. has to reconsider the national security between Japan and the U.S.?" Because the issue of the U.S. forces in Japan has been argued since the conclusion of the U.S.-Japan Security Treaty, students can consider this contemporary issue by applying the experiences of the game.

When students consider this issue, the teacher presents the following newspaper article. On G20 Summit meeting in July 2019, President Trump said, "If Japan is attacked by foreign countries, we must fight for Japan. But if The U. S. is attacked by foreign countries, Japan doesn't have to fight for the U. S.. This is unfair." As in this statement, President Trump required that allied countries should increase the military expenditure for the U.S. forces.

Furthermore, the following three Transfer Subjects are organized to apply the experiences of INDEPENDENCE DAY to Contemporary Subject. As stated above, Transfer Subject is an exercise to make it easier for students to connect a contemporary issue with a history game.

1) The Vietnam War: Japan was required to dispatch Japanese military forces for the first time, because this war broke out in the vicinity of Japan.
2) The Gulf War: Japanese cooperation was regarded as problematic by some countries because Japan only provided money.
3) The issues of trade friction between Japan and the U.S.: the U.S. increased the import duties against Japanese imported goods to increase its domestic sales.

2.3 Hypotheses and Methods

Hypotheses in this study are as follows;

1) The students establish their own opinions about Japanese politics by applying experiences of the history game to contemporary issues.
2) The students understand the importance of history learning.

Participants: Participants consisted of 39 university students. 3 or 4 students made a diplomatic corps of A or B to form 6 groups.

Study date: A questionnaire before the fact and the game were conducted on October 23, 2019. The debriefing and a questionnaire after the fact were conducted on October 30, 2019.

Tasks and procedures: After the debriefing, the reactions from students through the lessons were examined using the questionnaire. To examine students' responses, a five-point scale and a free answer method were adopted in the questionnaire. In the five-point scale, "5" means "Agree very much," "4" means "Agree somewhat," "3" means "Cannot say either way," "2" means "Disagree somewhat," and "1" means Totally disagree."

To examine Hypothesis 1, the students' responses were examined by a free answer method with a question in the questionnaire after the fact: What do you think about the relation between Japan and the U.S. or the Japanese politics in the international relation by applying experiences of the game?

To examine Hypothesis 2, the students' responses were examined by the five-point scale with a question in the questionnaire before and after the fact: Do you think history learning is important for thinking about contemporary issues? Additionally, the reason why the students chose the point on the scale was analyzed by a free answer method.

3   Results

How students learn in Transfer Subject (The Vietnam War) and Contemporary Subject are introduced before examining the hypotheses.

3.1 Students' Discussion in Transfer Subject and Contemporary Subject

In Transfer Subject, the students discussed what level of cooperation was most appropriate to provide to Country A from Country B based on their agreements in the game when Country A made war on Vietnam. In Contemporary Subject, the students discussed what was the most appropriate response to the U.S. from Japan. The purpose of Transfer Subject was to make the students realize the correlation between one historical event with another, then the purpose of Contemporary Subject was to make students think about the real contemporary issue with something that they experienced in the game.

In the discussions of Transfer Subject and Contemporary Subject, the students tended to give their opinions from the perspective of diplomats they played in the game. For example, the students who played as diplomats in Country A tended to think about the issues from the perspective of Country A.

Not only in the discussion of Transfer Subject but also in that of Contemporary Subject, the students tended to have their opinions based on their role in the game. Discussions of one group that were particularly prominent are introduced as below.

Table 1 shows the discussion of group 1 in Transfer Subject. Their agreement made in the game described Country B had their own army and there was no description that they would cooperate with Country A when Country A makes war. In the discussion, in response to the student who played a diplomat of Country B saying, "We don't need to go to war in Vietnam.", the student who played a diplomat of Country A said, "No, you don't, as we agreed so" (see underlines 1 and 2). In addition, with regard to funding, Country A declared that it will procure it on its own (see underline 3). Thus, the discussion took place with an agreement on conditions favorable to Country B.

Table 1. Discussion of group 1 in Transfer Subject

B1: We don't need to go to war in Vietnam. (1)
A1: No, you don't, as we agreed so…(2)
B2: What about funding?
A2: What do you mean?
B3: The funding from country B to Country A.
A1: We have to give humanitarian assistance, so we need money, but...
B3: Because of the geographical proximity, Country A will need to send troops from a base in country B, which will increase our budget and other funds, what do you think?
A1: We will do it ourselves because it's our country's matter. (3)

Table 2 shows the discussion of group 1 in Contemporary Subject. The students discussed President Trump's statement referring to the actual agreement after WWII. The students were told to think from the perspective of Country B, but they tended to have their opinions based on their role they played in the game. The student who played a diplomat of Country B said, "I don't want to pay the money you required for the stationed army." (see underline 1). In response to Country B, the student who played a diplomat of Country A stated that the stationed army for alliance was necessary for both countries (see underline 2). When considering the actual historical agreement which was different from the one made in the game, the students of Country B asserted the national

Table 2. Discussion of group 1 in Contemporary Subject

B1: I don't want to pay the money you required for the stationed army. (1)
B2: I want you to pay money for your own issue.
B3: First of all, Why do stationed army exist?
A1: For alliance. (2)

interests of Country B, and the students of Country A asserted the validity of Country A's claim. Thus, the experience of negotiation in the game was reflected in considering Contemporary Subject.

As Group 1, other groups similarly discussed the issues as if they were diplomats which roles they played in the game. Not only in Transfer Subject but also in Contemporary Subject, the history game continued by the students.

Additionally, comments of the students after the lessons show that they could realize the correlation between one historical event with another. Some of the comments are as follows; "I realized that the content of the discussion in the game was related to the later events." "I realized the correlation of historical events by knowing that the end of WWII, the Cold War, and the situation in each country. I realized that each event in history was connected to one another."

3.2 Examination of Hypothesis 1

Hypothesis 1: The students establish their own opinions about Japanese politics by applying experiences of the history game to contemporary issues. As mentioned above, to examine Hypothesis 1, the students' responses were examined by a free answer method with a question in the questionnaire after the fact; What do you think about the relation between Japan and the U.S. or the Japanese politics in the international relation by applying experiences of the game?

As a reference, there is a data of answers to the question in the questionnaire before the fact as below. "How much are you interested in the international relations, such as the relationship between the U.S. and Japan?" The students' responses examined by a five-point scale were divided into two categories; responses of "5" and "4" were deemed positive; responses of "3," "2," and "1" were deemed neutral/negative.

6 students responded positively, and there were many other students who were not interested in international relations. The interesting things for the students who responded positively were the issues introduced in the news. For example, "the right of collective self-defense", "Environmental issues", and so on. These issues do not seem to be an actual problem for the students but seem to be mere objective facts.

But through the lessons, 38 out of 39 students could describe their own concrete opinions about Japanese politics by applying experiences of the game to contemporary issues. Table 3 shows representative descriptions of the students after the lessons. The description of one student was; "I have never been interested."

33 students described the current negotiations or relationship based on the historical facts as seen in Table 6. Thus, the negotiations experienced in the game were also used to think about the present or future of Japan. Another 5 students mentioned the need for peace (2 students), the need for personal interest (2 students), and the strengthening of Japanese military forces (1 student), recognizing the correlation of historical events. These descriptions are also made by experiencing the game. For example, the students, while mentioning the need for peace, struggled for an opinion in the discussion about military security, and as a result, they had an opinion that international peace is more important than anything else.

From the above, Hypothesis 1 can be backed up.

Table 3. Description of students after the lessons

- I do not think it is necessarily correct that Japan maintains the status quo about the relationship with the U.S.. The power of the U.S. may not always be strong today and in the future. Thus, I do not think that the relationship today will continue forever. It may be necessary for Japan to change its politics based on the transformation of its relationship with the U.S..
- When thinking about the relationship between Japan and the U.S., I think it is important to consider not only the current situation but also, at least, the history before and after the end of WWII. It is true that the U.S. protects us, but I think that we should not follow the U.S. by paying money, but we should act strongly. Japan should build a good relationship for Japanese interests, considering the interests of the U.S. as well.
- I think it is necessary to reconsider the post-war relationship between Japan and the U.S. and find a compromise that makes sense for each other. I think we should think not only about Japan, but also about related countries.

3.3 Examination of Hypothesis 2

Hypothesis 2; the students understand the importance of history learning. As mentioned above, to examine Hypothesis 2, students' responses were examined by a five-point scale with a question in a questionnaire before and after the fact; Do you think history learning is important for thinking about contemporary issues? The five-point scale was divided into two categories; responses of "5" and "4" were deemed positive; responses of "3," "2," and "1" were deemed neutral/negative. Additionally, the reason why the students chose the point on the scale was analyzed by a free answer method.

Table 4 shows the number of positive (P) and neutral/negative (N) answers in the questionnaire before and after the fact. The number of N decreased from 14 to 3 through the lessons. But this data only shows that the students thought of the importance of leaning history on their own judgement, and does not show that the students really understood the importance.

Table 4. The importance of history learning

	P	N
Before the fact	25	14
After the fact	36	3

To examine whether the students understood the importance of history learning, their descriptions were analyzed about the reason why the students chose the point. As a result, there was a qualitative difference between the descriptions before and after the fact. The number of concrete reasons increased after the fact. "Not concrete" refers to descriptions without any correlation between historical issues and contemporary issues. For example, "I think history learning is useful". "Study at school is meaningful".

Table 5 shows the number of descriptions with and without concrete reasons. The number of descriptions with concrete reasons increased from 8 to 30. Thus, the students became able to describe the importance of history learning with concrete reasons through the lessons.

Table 5. Description about the importance of history learning

	With concrete reason	No concrete reason
Before the fact	8	31
After the fact	30	9

The contents of the description with concrete reasons can be classified into three categories as follows. A: "Correlation with the present", B: "Isomorphism with the present", C: "Psychological closeness to contemporary issues".

Table 6. Description examples of each category

Category	Description examples
A: Correlation with the present	• It is clear that the agreement at the time of WWII is deeply related to contemporary issues, and the roots of contemporary issues cannot be understood without knowing historical issues. • We learned that we need to consider the past history to think about what is happening now as we thought about the current relationship between Japan and the U.S. in the lessons.
B: Isomorphism with the present	• The concept of politics can be understood through history learning. • I think we can learn a lot because the essentials are the same between historical and current issues. So, analyzing how senior members of society acted on certain issues is useful to solve contemporary issues.
C: Psychological closeness to contemporary issues	• The conversation between Prime Minister Abe and President Trump in Contemporary Subject seemed very familiar after playing the game. And I became to think more seriously about contemporary issues. • When I think about contemporary issues, it is useful to think how I would do if I were in a specific situation by considering the later results as I experienced in the game.

The description in Category A refers to the correlation between historical events and contemporary events. The description in Category B shows that the source of materials for thinking about contemporary issues can be learned in history learning, such as social science concepts of "politics", "National security", and historical facts similar to contemporary issues. The description in Category C was based on what the students thought as a player in the game and was only seen after the fact. Table 6 shows description examples of each category.

Table 7 shows the number of descriptions classified into each category before and after the fact. A single description that includes multiple elements was counted in multiple categories.

Table 7. Number of descriptions by category

	A Correlation with the present	B Iisomorphism with the present	C Psychological closeness to contemporary issues
Before the fact	6	2	0
After the fact	21	9	4

Category A has the largest number of descriptions before and after the fact, and the number has increased from 6 to 21. One reason is that the students were able to use their experience in the history game when dealing with Contemporary Subject.

The number in Category B is a little less than a quarter of the entire number after the fact, but has increased from 2 to 9. It proves the discussion on "diplomacy" and "national security" conducted in the history game has an effect. The students realized the essence of contemporary issues has not changed from the past.

Category C shows that experiences as a player in the history game connects historical issues and contemporary issues. Before the fact, there was no description in this category because the students had not experienced the game. It can be said that the students' interest in contemporary issues increased as a result of learning with the flow with a sense of being involved; history game → Transfer Subject → Contemporary Subject.

In summary, even before the lesson, the majority of the students thought that history learning was important for thinking about contemporary issues. However, most of them could not describe concrete reasons. Through the lessons, they were able to describe concrete reasons why they thought history learning was important. This is because they were able to apply their experiences in the history game for thinking about contemporary issues. Generally, people need concrete materials to think about certain issues, and the materials were in the experiences of a history game.

From the above, Hypothesis 2 can be backed up.

4 Discussion

4.1 Generalization

Through the lessons, the students became able to establish their own opinions about Japanese politics by applying experiences in a history game to contemporary issues and understand the importance of history learning. Then, can the debriefing presented in this study be used for all subjects of history learning?

The following description of a student after the lessons is related to the above question; "Because modern history is directly linked to contemporary issues, there is much value in learning. But I don't think learning ancient and medieval history is useful for thinking about contemporary issues". In the lessons, since there was a relatively short time span between the postwar period and the present time, it would be easy for the students to realize the correlation between the past issues and the contemporary issues.

The students' description in Category B in Table 6 suggests the concept of politics is the same in the ancient and the present times. We can use the concept learned in history lessons for thinking about contemporary issues. Thus, by learning concepts and social system models in the history game and applying the concepts to Transfer Subject and Contemporary Subject, it is possible to connect ancient and medieval times to the present.

4.2 Comparison with Other Studies

The authors once provided a concept of "perspective of a history as a problem-solving process" and demonstrated educational effects of INDEPENDENCE DAY in succeeding lessons in which the students learned about the Cold War (Baba, H. et al. 2018). As a result, the following two points became clear. 1) Students regarded the history of various countries during the Cold War as a problem-solving process for keeping independence, utilizing the perspective obtained from the experience of the game. 2) Students evaluated Japanese history after WWII by highly advanced standards through experiencing the game and was developed in the succeeding lessons.

The purpose of this study is to extend the author's previous research, which only utilized game experiences for learning about the Cold War period, and to link it to contemporary issues. In other words, in our previous study, there was no idea of connecting history lessons to the contemporary issues, and the lessons had a learning flow; history game → another history event. On the other hand, in this study, we developed a learning flow; games → another history events → the present event.

4.3 Possibilities of Further Verification

As the subjects of this research, lessons in only one class were experimented, and there can be insufficient points to generalize the results. Furthermore, the practice has not been performed in secondary education where history learning is conducted in Japan. In near future, it would be necessary to practice our study in secondary schools and analyze its effects.

Furthermore, there were only Japanese students who shared the same cultural back ground. So, it was easy for the students to understand the historical facts between Japan and the U.S. If foreign students are present, it may be better to explain the post WWII relationship after the game, not in the beginning of the lesson. Because the aim of this game is to make students freely think of the concept of national independence or diplomacy without any prior knowledge about the historical event as stated above.

It would also be necessary to verify that it is possible to apply the results of this study to history learning in general by developing history games of ancient and medieval times and debriefing of the games.

5 Conclusion

In this study, the authors developed debriefing of a history game to make students think about the contemporary issue, which is the final stage of the six stages of debriefing by Kriz. In order to connect the issue in the history game with the contemporary issue, Transfer Subject and Contemporary Subject were constructed to be regarded as an extension of the issue experienced by the students in the history game.

Hypotheses in this study are: 1) The students establish their own opinions about Japanese politics by applying experiences of the history game to contemporary issues, 2) The students understand the importance of history learning.

In the lessons, the students discussed a contemporary issue as if the game were still continuing. As a result, in the questionnaire after the fact, 38 out of 39 students became able to describe their opinions about the future of Japan by using experiences of the game. From the above, it can be said that Hypothesis 1 was backed up.

Furthermore, the number of the students who were able to describe the concrete reason of the importance of history learning increased from 8 to 30 through the lessons. The reason for the increase is that they understood the source of materials for thinking about contemporary issues were in historical events, and realized the correlation between historical issues and the contemporary issues. From the above, it can be said that Hypothesis 2 was backed up.

In the near future, in order to make the results of this study usable in history learning in general, it would be necessary to 1) practice the lessons in secondary education and mixed classes with foreign students 2) develop history games and debriefings for history learning of ancient and medieval times.

References

Baba, H., Ohyama, M., Takesada, T., Suga, K., Matsuyama, K., Yoshinaga, J.: Educational effects of active learning in succeeding lessons; a case study of game use in a history lesson curriculum. In: Proceedings the 49th Annual Conference of the International Simulation and Gaming Association, pp. 591–599 (2018)

Baba, H., Ohyama, M., Sato, M., Yoshinaga, J.: The effectiveness of negotiation games in citizenship education: an examination of diplomatic negotiation game Independence day in a Japanese high school. In: Naweed, A., Wardaszko, M., Leigh, E., Meijer, S. (eds.) ISAGA/SimTecT - 2016. LNCS, vol. 10711, pp. 360–370. Springer, Cham (2019). https://doi.org/10.1007/978-3-319-78795-4_25

Corbeil, P.: History and simulation/gaming: living with two solitudes. Simul. Gaming **42**(4), 418–422 (2011)

Corbeil, P., Laveault, D.: Validity of a simulation game as a method for history teaching. Simul. Gaming **42**(4), 462–475 (2011)

Crookall, D.: Engaging (in) gameplay and (in) debriefing. Simul. Gaming **45**(4–5), 416–427 (2014)

Greenblat, C.S.: Designing Games and Simulations, 1st edn. SAGE Publications, Newbury Park (1988)

Kriz, W.C.: A systemic-constructivist approach to the facilitation and debriefing of simulations and games. Simul. Gaming **41**(5), 663–680 (2010)

Peters, V.A., Vissers, G.A.: A simple classification model for debriefing simulation games. Simul. Gaming **35**(1), 70–84 (2004)

Petranek, C.F.: Written debriefing: the next vital step in learning with simulations. Simul. Gaming **31**(1), 108–118 (2000)

Petranek, C.F., Corey, S., Black, R.: Three levels of learning in simulations: participating, debriefing, and journal writing. Simul. Gaming **23**(2), 174–185 (1992)

Randel, J.M., Morris, B.A., Wetzel, C.D., Whitehill, W.B.: The effectiveness of games for educational purposes: a review of recent research. Simul. Gaming **23**(3), 261–276 (1992)

Towards the Management and Dissemination of Knowledge from Gaming Simulations

Bill Roungas[(✉)] and Sebastiaan Meijer

Department of Health Systems Engineering, KTH Royal Institute of Technology,
Hälsovägen 11, 14157 Huddinge, Sweden
vroungas@gmail.com, sebastiaan.meijer@sth.kth.se

Abstract. Nowadays, gaming simulations (games) are used for various different purposes and generate a wealth of knowledge. Yet, there is still lack of research on whether, and if so how, these games can be used by researchers and practitioners to build evidences on systems' behavior within a larger scheme and/or manage and exploit the knowledge produced by and in these games. This article proposes a knowledge management framework, which aims at enabling the development of a knowledge management system that can store, index, and disseminate the knowledge produced by and in games in an appropriate way. The proposed framework is built on the basis of several factors, like the type of knowledge and the prospective users, and is then validated with three case studies from the Dutch railway sector. Through the case studies, the proposed framework appears to be able to help the management and dissemination of knowledge derived from games. The framework is a proof of concept on the feasibility of developing a knowledge management system module for games.

Keywords: Knowledge management system · Game requirements · Tacit knowledge · Implicit knowledge · Explicit knowledge · Gaming simulations · Knowledge elicitation · Debriefing

1 Introduction

All knowledge is not created equally [9]. The same applies to the knowledge gained from gaming simulations (hereinafter referred to as games), in which research has dramatically increased over the last decade [30]. Despite this boost in popularity and research, and despite being a mature professional discipline, researchers have not as of today focused on how knowledge acquired through games can be retained and reused [30].

Games span in various different domains; the generated knowledge from games can be used for different purposes and they can be addressed to a diversified audience [34]. Hence, any analysis on games should first be based on a

© Springer Nature Switzerland AG 2020
M. Ma et al. (Eds.): JCSG 2020, LNCS 12434, pp. 276–288, 2020.
https://doi.org/10.1007/978-3-030-61814-8_21

comprehensive characterization. This article adopts the characterization proposed by Grogan & Meijer [11], and more specifically, it focuses on games for decision making, and particularly for engineering organisations.

1.1 Knowledge Management (of Games)

Knowledge management and reuse is not, and should not be, of academic interest only. The effectiveness of a corporation depends heavily on how it manages and reuses knowledge [16], or in layman terms, how in the first place it obtains and thereafter maintains the so-called "Know-how". As a corporation acquires and builds up on knowledge, it improves its know-how, and thus sustains or even increases its competitive advantage [9].

In order for the reader to be able to easily follow the rationale in this paper, certain terms need to be clarified in advance. Particularly terms including "knowledge management". Namely, these terms are:

Knowledge Management (KM), which is defined as a set of processes for storing, transforming, and transporting knowledge throughout an organisation [10].

Knowledge Management System (KMS), which is a class of information systems aiming at the creation, transfer, and application of knowledge in organisations [1].

Knowledge Management Framework (KMF), which is the reference for decisions about the implementation and application of a KM system within an organisation [18].

While theory on knowledge management can be used in games, it cannot be adopted without carefully considering the distinct characteristics of games. Moreover, KM of games should ideally not be seen as an independent artefact that an organisation needs to foster; it should rather be seen as a module that can greatly enhance the KM process of an organisation that utilises games extensively. In an organisation that has a poor, or even a complete lack of, KM culture, a KMF for games should have the capability to help those parts of the organisation that are involved with games even if that is only accomplished for a narrow small part of the organisation.

1.2 Motivation

Despite the fact that games have proven to be cost effective, in multiple occasions, they still involve a substantial financial cost [19], depending on several factors, like the degree of realism and the intended audience. In addition to development costs, there are costs associated with game sessions which, more often than not, are not trivial. Moreover, time is required to process the game outcomes and come with the best possible business decision. This additional time does not only increase the accrued costs but also delays decisions that sometimes are time-sensitive.

All of the above combined with the lack of a comprehensive methodology for managing and reusing knowledge acquired through games, lead companies, researchers, and game practitioners to "reinvent the wheel" by conducting consecutive and (almost) identical game sessions, accompanied by data analysis. The motivation for this study is hence triggered by our strong belief that the capturing, compilation, maintenance, and dissemination of knowledge requires a methodology that will maximise the game outcomes concurrently with the minimisation of the associated costs and risks [24]. Therefore, the paper's focus is on identifying and illustrating the components that constitute a KMF that can cover the totality of knowledge produced by and in games.

1.3   Overview

The purpose of this paper is to introduce and test the usability and applicability of a KMF for games relating to areas other than learning. In Sect. 2, the main components of a KMF are identified. In Sect. 3, the relations between the components of the KMF are defined. In Sect. 4, three case studies based on which the KMS is developed are presented and further analysed. Finally, in Sect. 5, the future steps of this research are identified and final remarks are made.

2   KMF Components

Due to gaming being a relatively young and immature field, characterised by a lack of literature in KM, existing literature in the general areas of knowledge capturing, compilation, maintenance, and dissemination is used, which creates a pathway towards KM of games. The main components of a KMF identified are the KM Strategy (Sect. 2.1), Purpose of KMS (Sect. 2.2), Users of the KMS (Sect. 2.3), and Type of Knowledge (Sect. 2.4). While the organisational is a vital building block of a KMS and to a considerable degree it influences its success or failure of a KMS, it is not taken into account in this instance. The reason is that a KMS for games is not a standalone artefact but a module that can only flourish in an organisation that has adopted KM, not just as a practice but deep in their culture.

2.1   KM Strategy

By looking into management consulting firms, Hansen et al. [12] distinguished two KM strategies, which in turn heavily influence the final implementation of the KMS. These strategies are called Codification and Personalization. Codification stores and makes available for reuse any acquired knowledge, which is in reality isolated from its source. On the other hand, Personalization is the exchange of knowledge that has been acquired in the past through one-to-one conversations and brainstorming sessions; it is a way to promote discussion and exchange of ideas and knowledge between people in a more personal manner.

Codification should be preferred when people want to learn from past projects and apply this knowledge in the future (secondary knowledge miners) [16], thus they would rather consult a documented and detailed record of these past projects. Personalization should be preferred when people inquire on experts' opinion but do not want to acquire their knowledge (expertise-seeking novices) [16], thus they would rather consult an expert in a one-to-one conversation.

2.2 Purpose of KMS

There are various reasons for which an organisation would want to build a KMS. Moreover, a single KMS might be built for more than one reason. Namely, these reasons are:

1. Own-project improvement, which refers to the utilisation of the knowledge acquired during the lifecycle of a game to improve the game itself and the project for which the game was built. With regards to the project for which the game was built, KM allows to capture, organise, maintain, and disseminate the knowledge from the game and through that build evidences that would steer stakeholders towards the solution of the problem under examination [30]. Moreover, KM can be used as a root cause analysis tool, which could help with the examination of problems or failures that might occur throughout the lifecycle of a game or due to decisions made based on a game [14].
2. Cross-project improvement and organisational learning, which refers to the utilisation of the knowledge acquired during the lifecycle of a game to improve other projects or create added value in an organisation [36]. The latter is considered to be a more long term investment, albeit one that significantly affects the competitive advantage of an organisation [35].
3. Network improvement, which refers to the use of a Personalization-type of KMS, in order to strengthen the relationships of individuals and teams within an organisation, especially in large organisations, by bringing awareness of the totality of knowledge possessed within.

2.3 Users of KMS

Regardless of its type and purpose, the primary function of a KMS is to manage and disseminate knowledge to people, i.e. users. Therefore, users are the epicentre of a KMS and any frameworks aiming at building a KMS should put users first.
Markus [16] identified three categories of users:

1. Knowledge producers, who are the people that contribute their knowledge into the KMS. They should be experts in their respective field, since the success of a KMS depends heavily on the credibility of the primary source of information. A person who aims at using knowledge previously acquired shall be confident of the expertise of the knowledge producers, and thus trust their respective findings [38].

2. Knowledge intermediaries are the people that manage the knowledge, by indexing, summarising, and to the extent that is possible and appropriate objectify it. One of the most important goals of a KMS should be the adaptation of methodologies for mitigating knowledge bias that derives from human subjectivity, which is an inseparable part of the contributed knowledge [20]. Knowledge producers need to feel confident that the time required to contribute to a KMS is not wasted time and that their input has high chances to be easily accessible and used.
3. Knowledge consumers are the end users of the KMS, thus the ones that benefit from it. Depending on the type and the purpose of the KMS, knowledge consumers can be the game designers, project managers, investigators, researchers, or even the participants of a game, to name a few.

2.4   Type of Knowledge

Knowledge can be defined in a number of ways. One of the most widely used definition is the distinction between explicit and implicit, the latter also known as tacit, knowledge [35]. According to this classification, explicit knowledge is considered to be data or information that is communicated in a formal language and/or digitally or printed information that can be shared, such as manuals. On the other hand, tacit knowledge focuses on the cognitive features of humans, such as mental models, beliefs, insights, and perceptions.

In cognitive sciences, explicit and implicit knowledge have conceptually different definitions. Explicit knowledge refers to conscious knowledge that resides in the working memory, whereas implicit knowledge refers to unconscious knowledge that is difficult to retrieve and verbalise [8]. This paper proposes a mixture of these two definitions, hence acknowledging the implicit knowledge that is consciously possessed by individuals or groups as opposed to the knowledge residing in the unconscious part of the human brain. In this paper, the former is referred to as implicit-explicit, or tacit, knowledge and along with explicit knowledge is analysed further below.

Explicit Knowledge
Explicit knowledge produced in and from games can be of quantitative or qualitative nature. In each phase of the game, explicit knowledge is produced that serves one or more of the purposes identified in Sect. 2.2.

There are five phases that intertwine in the lifecycle of a game [30]. Namely, these phases are:

1. Requirements elicitation, which is the first step towards developing a game. There are two sources from where requirements should be elicited, the client and the real system the game imitates [31]. Although requirements are usually considered to be relevant only for the game they are elicited for, according to Zave [40], requirements engineering is also concerned with the evolution of the relationships among the several factors of a system across software families. As such, requirements immediately become a tool for knowledge reuse, as

they provide common ground for comparing different systems and pointing similarities. These similarities can be used either to improve future game development, as domain specific knowledge [6], or in order to avoid building new games and reuse the outcome of previously created games to analyse a current issue.

2. Game design, which is the art and science of actually designing a game [25]. When it comes to game design, what is crucial in terms of knowledge management, is the proper structure and documentation. The primary advantage of documenting design-related information is that this could allow for a comparison between a previously created game and a potential new game, which, in turn, can determine whether the new game is actually required or not [30]. There have been several approaches towards the adaptation of game design documents from the entertaining industry to more "serious" games. Regardless of the approach one chooses to adopt, there are certain game elements that need to be taken into account [26].

3. Validation and Verification. Game validation deals with the assessment of the behavioural or representational accuracy of the game and addresses the question of whether we are creating the "right game" [3]. While, game verification deals with the assessment of the transformational accuracy of the game and addresses the question of whether we are creating the game in the right way [3]. The meticulous documentation of V&V processes has a twofold benefit for knowledge consumers [29,32]: i) they can ascertain, with rather minimal effort, whether the results of the game can be used for the intended purpose, and ii) they can, again with much less effort than without the V&V details, perform their own V&V study and hence, use the game for slightly or completely different purposes.

4. Game session, which is where the actual gameplay takes place and it includes the preparation for the gameplay (briefing), the actual gameplay, and the debriefing [27]. A game session can also be seen as a game instantiation. A game is usually designed once (involving several iterations) but can be played multiple times with a similar or a completely different setup. In other words, a game session is the application of a game with a specific scenario, stakeholders, and purpose. Therefore, this characterization helps to understand how an actual KMS can be built to support a game.

5. Data analysis, in which the data gathered during the game are analysed aiming at deriving meaningful insights [33]. While data analysis can be embedded in the game session through automated procedures, especially if the data are purely quantitative, in this article, it is treated separately. The reason for this distinction is that by using a KMS the aim is to be able in the future, whenever it is appropriate, to skip the game session, and use data gathered from a previous session to perform a new analysis.

Tacit Knowledge

Tacit knowledge is considered to be a tremendous resource for all activities within an organisation [15]. Particularly in games, tacit knowledge can correspond to pieces of knowledge or skills related to the game discipline (e.g. best game design practices, best game facilitation practices etc.), to the professional domain the game is applied in (e.g. experience, being mentored etc.), or the individual traits of people (e.g. talent in leadership or in creativity etc.). Yet, unlike explicit knowledge, tacit knowledge is not so straightforward to capture and manage. A database and a filesystem most probably would not be adequate to tackle the underline challenges. Therefore, different methodologies, which might also result in different approaches with regards to the implementation of the KMS, are needed. These methodologies should aim at converting the tacit knowledge to some sort of explicit knowledge [21], which can then be disseminated in a more unequivocal way. While literature is not exhaustive on how to capture and convert such knowledge, several approaches have been proposed, some examples of which are causal maps [2], the Q-methodology [37], the use of metaphors [17], or even social media [22]. In the case studies presented in Sect. 4, semi-structured interviews were used.

Semi-structured interviews are another tool that can help elicit tacit knowledge. While the purpose and structure of such an interview is predetermined, the essence of the "semi-structure" lies on the fact that interviewees are encouraged to answer questions by telling stories [2]. The story telling nature of these interviews allows people to manage the collective memory of an organisation [4], frame their experiences [39], and reflect on the complex social web of an organisation [5].

2.5   Conclusion of the Literature

In this section, the different components of a potential KMS were identified. The components span in four main areas: the KMS strategy, the purpose and the users of the KMS, and the type of knowledge. Next, in Sect. 3, the amalgamation of these components into a KMF is described.

3   The KM Framework for Games

In this section, the composition of the KMF, based on the components identified in the literature, is described. The primary aim of the framework is to provide the guidelines for implementing a KMS module for games in the form of a knowledge infrastructure [7]. An illustration of the KMF is shown in Fig. 1. Knowledge is the preeminent component of any KMS, hence it holds the lion's share when analysing games; yet, the centre of the KMF is the KMS strategy. The KMS strategy an organisation adopts determines how the acquired knowledge is disseminated and it is a decision that should be made even before eliciting any knowledge. Choosing between a Codification, a Personalization, or a hybrid strategy depends on:

– The organisational culture, which gives a strong indication on the quality of the contributed knowledge from the knowledge producers and its utilisation from the knowledge consumers.

- Its current technical infrastructure, in which case for an organisation that has a strong technical background and infrastructure, the implementation and maintenance of a codified KMS would be efficient and affordable. Whereas, for an organisation with a strong social factor among its employees, a KMS based on a Personalization strategy could be a more prudent solution.
- The type of knowledge, in which case the more explicit a piece of knowledge is the easier it is to store it in a database-based system (Codification), as opposed to a more tacit piece of knowledge that is more easily disseminated through conversation (Personalization).
- The purpose for which the organisation wants to build a KMS, which is directly shown in Fig. 1.

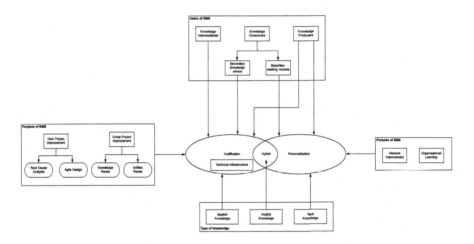

Fig. 1. An illustration of the knowledge management framework.

4   Application of the KMF

In order to validate and substantiate the structure and the components of the framework, three games conducted by the Dutch railway infrastructure manager (ProRail) are used as case studies, based on the type of questions asked by the principle stakeholders and the technological characteristics of the game (analog/digital). Namely, these games are:

1. OV-SAAL [28], which aim is to examine a potential increase in the capacity of the current infrastructure in the financial centre of the Netherlands. The project team for OV-SAAL requested a game session to support their decision-making on which infrastructure investment to make. The conclusions that were summarised and discussed in the game session were used to inform the project team about the outcomes.

2. A2 Chain Simulation, similarly to OV-SAAL, is a large-scale participatory simulation, in which disruptions were simulated on the main corridor Amsterdam with Eindhoven, in combination with the new high-frequency timetable for 2018. The aim of the simulation was to 1) test the feasibility of the implementation and management of the new timetable, 2) measure the bottlenecks and learn how to mitigate them in case of disruptions, and 3) get the operational and management personnel familiar with the new high-frequency timetable.
3. ERTMS, which stands for European Railway Traffic Management System, is a major industrial project that aims at replacing the different national train control and command safety systems in Europe. The game currently aims at testing a selection of 10 out of 66 newly developed user processes for ERTMS. Two game sessions were conducted, which had a combined focus of testing the technical development of the simulator and a number of new user processes.

4.1   KM Strategy and Purpose of KMS

Each game has its own unique characteristics, yet some components are common between them. Currently, ProRail is interested in building a system that would accommodate the knowledge produced from games as opposed to strengthening its culture and internal network; thus, the KM strategy governing all games is that of Codification. With regards to the purpose of the KMS, Cross project improvement is the "usual suspect" for which a KMS is built, and in this case there is no exception. The knowledge from all games examined in this paper is meant to improve future projects, yet the knowledge from some games is also meant for more than that. However, in the case of both OV-SAAL and the A2 chain simulation games, there has been no follow-up or request to retrospectively provide additional investigation, except for academic research on games. For the ERTMS game there is a potential use of Root-Cause Analysis, specifically in the case of investigations related to safety issues.

4.2   Type of Knowledge & Users of KMS

The type of knowledge as a component of the KMF can also be seen as the actual output of a KMS, in which the KMS obtains its physical structure. Due to size restrictions, more details on the type of knowledge of the games analysed in this paper cannot be provided; instead they could be found in [23].

With regards to the users of the KMS, in the three games examined in this paper, knowledge producers are mostly similar as the games are designed by a pool of experienced game designers and the games always include the knowledge of railway operators. Table 1 summarises the potential KMS users.

4.3   Final Remarks on the Application of the Framework

The analysis of the games reveals that the proposed KMF is able to help the management and dissemination of knowledge derived from games, and the KMF

Table 1. Potential KMS users for each game

Users	OV-SAAL	A2	ERTMS
Knowledge producers	Operators	Operators	Operators
	Game Designers	Game Designers	Game Designers
		Observers	
Knowledge intermediaries	Not defined yet	Not defined yet	Not defined yet
Knowledge consumers	Researchers	Project team	Researchers

itself is a proof of concept on the feasibility of developing a KMS module for games. Therefore, compared to other frameworks, the proposed framework does not claim that it can contribute towards a standalone KMS but rather towards enriching an existing KMS that could then also target games. Moreover, particularly for the games examined in this paper, which are designed for testing changes in the railway infrastructure, the strong focus is on the debriefing. In turn, debriefing becomes the primary source of knowledge, especially for tacit knowledge. Hence, capturing knowledge from games gives new opportunities for validity assessments at a higher level of detail, which both compliments and puts pressure to the current sense-making approaches [13].

5   Conclusion

This paper was concerned with games for decision making and particularly with games imitating engineering systems. Therefore, the theoretical contribution of this article is on how to approach the different levels of the engineering process, in order to improve the management and dissemination of the knowledge produced by and in these games, and particularly this type of knowledge that could be described as transferable tacit knowledge. As a result, this article proposed a knowledge management framework and used three design and/or research games from the Dutch railways in order to ascertain that the framework can capture and disseminate the knowledge in and around games and to contribute towards its integration within a knowledge management system. Moreover, the games provided additional insights on how such a framework can both enhance the validation process as well as help the organisation to grow. All in all, the framework provides general guidelines on the components to consider for the development of a module that would accommodate the particularities of games, in order to integrate the knowledge acquired through games in a knowledge management system. Specific details on how to develop the knowledge management system in general and the game module in particular are dependent on the organisation culture itself and the users that support and use the knowledge management system.

References

1. Alavi, M., Leidner, D.E.: Knowledge management and knowledge management systems: conceptual foundations and research issues. MIS Quarterly **25**(1), 107–136 (2001)
2. Ambrosini, V., Bowman, C.: Tacit knowledge: some suggestions for operationalization. J. Manage. Stud. **38**(6), 811–829 (2001). https://doi.org/10.1111/1467-6486.00260
3. Balci, O.: Verification, validation, and certification of modeling and simulation applications. In: Proceedings of the 35th Conference on Winter Simulation, pp. 150–158 (2003)
4. Boje, D.M.: Consulting and change in the storytelling organisation. J. Organizational Change Manage. **4**(1), 7–17 (1991). https://doi.org/10.1108/EUM0000000001193
5. Brown, J.S., Duguid, P.: Organizational learning and communities-of-practice: toward a unified view of working, learning, and innovation. Organ. Sci. **2**(1), 40–57 (1991). https://doi.org/10.1016/B978-0-7506-7293-1.50010-X
6. Callele, D., Neufeld, E., Schneider, K.: Requirements engineering and the creative process in the video game industry. In: RE 2005 Proceedings of the 13th IEEE International Conference on Requirements Engineering, pp. 240–252. IEEE (2005). https://doi.org/10.1109/RE.2005.58
7. Davenport, T.H., Prusak, L.: Working Knowledge: How Organizations Manage What They Know. Harvard Business School Press, Boston (1998)
8. Dienes, Z., Perner, J.: Implicit knowledge in people and connectionist networks. In: Underwood, G.D.M. (ed.) Implicit Cognition, pp. 227–255. Oxford University Press, New York (1996)
9. Dixon, N.M.: Common Knowledge: How Companies Thrive by Sharing What They Know. Harvard Business School Press (2000)
10. Gold, A.H., Malhotra, A., Segars, A.H.: Knowledge management: an organizational capabilities perspective. J. Manage. Inf. Syst. **18**(1), 185 (2001)
11. Grogan, P.T., Meijer, S.A.: Gaming methods in engineering systems research. Syst. Eng. **20**(6), 542–552 (2017). https://doi.org/10.1002/sys.21409
12. Hansen, M.T., Nohria, N., Tierney, T.: What's your strategy for managing knowledge? In: Woods, J.A., James, C. (eds.) The Knowledge Management Yearbook 2000–2001, pp. 1–10. Butterworth-Heinemann (1999)
13. van den Hoogen, J., Lo, J.C., Meijer, S.: Debriefing in gaming simulation for research: opening the black box of the non-trivial machine to assess validity and reliability. In: Tolk, A., Diallo, S.Y., Ryzhov, I.O., Yilmaz, L., Buckley, S., Miller, J.A. (eds.) Proceedings of the 2014 Winter Simulation Conference, pp. 3505–3516. IEEE Press, Savannah, Georgia, USA (2014)
14. Latino, R.J., Latino, K.C., Latino, M.A.: Root Cause Analysis: Improving Performance for Bottom-Line Results, Fourth edn., Taylor & Francis Group (2016)
15. Leonard, D., Sensiper, S.: The role of tacit knowledge in group innovation. California Manage. Rev. **40**(3), 112–132 (1998). https://doi.org/10.2307/41165946
16. Markus, L.M.: Toward a theory of knowledge reuse: types of knowledge reuse situations and factors in reuse success. J. Manage. Inf. Syst. **18**(1), 57–93 (2001). https://doi.org/10.1080/07421222.2001.11045671
17. Martin, J.: Stories and scripts in organizational settings. In: Hastorf, A.H., Isen, A.M. (eds.) Cognitive Social Psychology, pp. 255–305. Elsevier, New York (1982)

18. Metaxiotis, K., Ergazakis, K., Psarras, J.: Exploring the world of knowledge management: agreements and disagreements in the academic/practitioner community. J. Knowl. Manage. **9**(2), 6–18 (2005). https://doi.org/10.1108/13673270510590182
19. Michael, D.R., Chen, S.L.: Serious games: games that educate, train, and inform. Thomson Course Technology PTR (2005)
20. Musen, M.A.: Dimensions of knowledge sharing and reuse. Comput. Biomed. Res. **25**(5), 435–467 (1992). https://doi.org/10.1016/0010-4809(92)90003-S
21. Nonaka, I., von Krogh, G.: Perspective - Tacit knowledge and knowledge conversion: controversy and advancement in organizational knowledge creation theory. Organ. Sci. **20**(3), 635–652 (2009). https://doi.org/10.1287/orsc.1080.0412
22. Panahi, S., Watson, J., Partridge, H.: Social media and tacit knowledge sharing: developing a conceptual model. World Academy of Science. Engineering and Technology (WASET), pp. 1095–1102. France, Paris (2012)
23. Roungas, B.: An inquiry into gaming simulations for decision making. Ph.D. thesis, Delft University of Technology (2019). https://doi.org/10.4233/uuid:4fcec9c1-a165-4429-ae43-1f75c0feb1a5
24. Roungas, B., Bekius, F., Meijer, S., Verbraeck, A.: Improving the decision-making qualities of gaming simulations. J. Simulation (2019). https://doi.org/10.1080/17477778.2020.1726218
25. Roungas, B., Bekius, F.A., Meijer, S.: The game between game theory and gaming simulations: design choices. Simulation Gam. **50**(2) (2019). https://doi.org/10.1177/1046878119827625
26. Roungas, B., Dalpiaz, F.: A model-driven framework for educational game design. In: De Gloria, A., Veltkamp, R. (eds.) 4th International Conference, GALA 2015, Revised Selected Papers, vol. 9599, pp. 1–11. Springer, Rome (2016). https://doi.org/10.1007/978-3-319-40216-1_1
27. Roungas, B., De Wijse, M., Meijer, S., Verbraeck, A.: Pitfalls for debriefing games and simulation: theory and practice. In: Naweed, A., Wardaszko, M., Leigh, E., Meijer, S. (eds.) Intersections in Simulation and Gaming, pp. 101–115. Springer, Cham (2018). https://doi.org/10.1007/978-3-319-78795-4_8
28. Roungas, B., Lo, J.C., Angeletti, R., Meijer, S.A., Verbraeck, A.: Eliciting requirements of a knowledge management system for gaming in an organization: the role of tacit knowledge. In: Hamada, R. (ed.) Neo-Simulation and Gaming Toward Active Learning, pp. 347–354. Springer, Singapore, Bangkok, Thailand (2018). https://doi.org/10.1007/978-981-13-8039-6_32
29. Roungas, B., Meijer, S., Verbraeck, A.: A framework for simulation validation & verification method selection. In: SIMUL 2017: The Ninth International Conference on Advances in System Simulation, pp. 35–40. Athens, Greece (2017)
30. Roungas, B., Meijer, S., Verbraeck, A.: Knowledge management of games for decision making. In: Lukosch, H., Bekebrede, G., Kortmann, R. (eds.) Simulation Gaming. Applications for Sustainable Cities and Smart Infrastructures. ISAGA 2017. Lecture Notes in Computer Science, vol 10825. Springer, Cham, Switzerland (2018). https://doi.org/10.1007/978-3-319-91902-7_3
31. Roungas, B., Meijer, S., Verbraeck, A.: The tacit knowledge in games: from validation to debriefing. In: 50th International Conference of International Simulation and Gaming Association. Warsaw, Poland (2019)
32. Roungas, B., Meijer, S.A., Verbraeck, A.: A framework for optimizing simulation model validation & verification. Int. J. Adv. Syst. Measure. **11**(1 & 2), 137–152 (2018)

33. Roungas, B., Meijer, S.A., Verbraeck, A.: Harnessing Web 3.0 and R to mitigate simulation validation restrictions. In: Proceedings of 8th International Conference on Simulation and Modeling Methodologies, Technologies and Applications, pp. 44–54. Porto, Portugal (2018). https://doi.org/10.5220/0006861200440054

34. Roungas, B., Meijer, S.A., Verbraeck, A.: The future of contextual knowledge in gaming simulations: a research agenda. In: Rabe, M., Juan, A.A., Mustafee, N., Skoogh, A., Jain, S., Johansson, B. (eds.) Proceedings of the 2018 Winter Simulation Conference. IEEE, Gothenburg, Sweden (2018). https://doi.org/10.1109/WSC.2018.8632377

35. Smith, E.A.: The role of tacit and explicit knowledge in the workplace. J. Knowl. Manage. **5**(4), 311–321 (2001). https://doi.org/10.1108/13673270110411733

36. Spender, J.C.: Organizational learning and knowledge management: whence and whither? Manage. Learn. **39**(2), 159–176 (2008). https://doi.org/10.1177/1350507607087582

37. Stephenson, W.: The Study of Behavior: Q-Technique and its Methodology. The University of Chicago Press, Chicago (1953)

38. Watson, S., Hewett, K.: A multi-theoretical model of knowledge transfer in organizations: determinants of knowledge contribution and knowledge reuse*. J. Manage. Stud. **43**(2), 141–173 (2006). https://doi.org/10.1111/j.1467-6486.2006.00586.x

39. Wilkins, A.L., Thompson, M.P.: On getting the story crooked (and straight). J. Organ. Change Manage. **4**(3), 18–26 (1991). https://doi.org/10.1108/EUM0000000001194

40. Zave, P.: Classification of research efforts in requirements engineering. ACM Comput. Surv. (CSUR) **29**(4), 315–321 (1997). https://doi.org/10.1145/267580.267581

How to Utilize Unshared Knowledge in a Group Discussion?

Mieko Nakamura[✉]

Ryutsu Keizai University, Ryugasaki, Ibaraki 3018555, Japan
mnakamura@rku.ac.jp

Abstract. Through group discussion, we hope to reach a reasonably appropriate decision. However, if only a few members in a group have a certain point of view, they may not be listened to as there are few of them. Nonetheless, these members may have a much better understanding of the situation, and therefore, have more appropriate ideas. Can group discussion elicit ideas from the minority in a group? This study focuses on what happens when certain members understand a situation better than the rest of the group. I examined individual levels of understanding and outcome prediction before simulation and gaming of production management, and analyzed what contributes to a good or bad result. Based on this research, I intend to narrow down factors that are essential to designing a game aimed at teaching people how to utilize unshared knowledge in a group discussion.

Keywords: Appropriate decision · Group discussion · Production management · Simulation and gaming · Minority in a group · Unshared knowledge

1 Introduction

1.1 General Review

In the setting of simulation and gaming, participants often work as a team for planning, acting, and debriefing. When we hold group discussions, the goal is to reach better decisions. Buehler, Messervey, and Griffin [1] say "predictions generated through group discussion were more optimistic than those generated individually" (p. 47). They say that this may be because group discussion accentuates or heightens individual participants' tendencies. If so, individuals with less common opinions' contributions may mitigate group accentuation.

When we have enough information and understand the situation well, it is highly possible to reach a reasonably appropriate decision. Suppose that several group members have a good understanding of the situation; this would allow the group to find an appropriate solution. During the decision-making process, the group's majority opinion will generally mirror that of the largest group of voices. Minority opinions, however, may not be reflected in the same way. What happens if that smaller group has a better understanding and more appropriate ideas? Can group discussion elicit appropriate ideas from the minority in a group? How can a group utilize unshared knowledge in a group discussion?

© Springer Nature Switzerland AG 2020
M. Ma et al. (Eds.): JCSG 2020, LNCS 12434, pp. 289–302, 2020.
https://doi.org/10.1007/978-3-030-61814-8_22

This study focuses on the voices of those who understand a situation well in simulation and gaming. If the majority of group members understand a particular situation well, they will lead the group to a good outcome. However, if only a minority of group members appropriately understand a situation, they may face difficulty in being heard by the group. In the next sections, I describe planning fallacy in individual predictions and group accentuation in group discussions to further examine the problem. In the subsequent sections, I examine individual levels of understanding and outcome predictions before simulation and gaming, and analyze the differences between teams to see what contributes to a good or bad result. In future, based on this research, I intend to design a game aimed at teaching how to be open to hearing the voices of members who hold a minority opinion in a group discussion, but have more experience or a deeper understanding of the situation. The goal of the present research is to obtain data and extract the factors useful in designing an appropriate game.

1.2 Planning Fallacy

Planning fallacy (Kahneman and Tversky [2], Buehler, Griffin, and Ross [3], Kruger and Evans [4]) is a phenomenon shown in individual predictions regarding time and "the tendency to underestimate the duration that is needed to complete a task" (Moss [5]). Kahneman and Tversky [2] explain that planning fallacy occurs as people make plans by focusing on a project's specific aspect. If people consider their own faults or others' in past situations, this information should be used to be more careful and cautious when plans are made. People usually fail to consider the situation from outside perspectives and become narrow-minded. Buehler, Griffin, and Ross [3] say, "People tend to generate their predictions by considering the unique features of the task at hand and constructing a scenario of their future progress on that task" and "the act of scenario construction may lead people to exaggerate the likelihood of the scenario taking place" (p. 8).

Kruger and Evans [4] report several experimental results on how unpacking a task improves the quality of judgment. Here, unpacking a task is considering "each of the subcomponents of the task" (Kruger and Evans [4], p. 588). One example is holiday gift shopping plans. When participants were asked to predict the number of days required for holiday gift shopping, the answer was 5.2 days on average. The answer increased 1.4 times after the participants asked to make a list of what gifts would be given to whom. Similar results were obtained when editing a draft, cooking a meal, and dressing for a date; unpacking was effective in reducing underestimation (Kruger and Evans [4]).

In gaming and simulation settings, Nakamura [6] prepared informative questions to unpack the process of achieving the game's goal. Those who did not receive informative questions prior to the game were more optimistic when estimating net profits than those who received the questions beforehand. Nakamura [6] showed that unpacking improved the quality of estimation, while accuracy of estimation did not automatically lead to a positive result in the actual game. Here, I would like to point out that the estimated value was net profit gain, not time duration. However, estimating net profit gain requires an estimation of time duration. Therefore, Nakamura's [6] work is regarded as an example of how unpacking reduces planning fallacy in simulation and gaming settings.

1.3 Group Accentuation

Both individuals and groups tend to be optimistically biased when they predict a task's duration. Buehler, Messervey, and Griffin [1] examined three studies on collaborative prediction and obtained three findings: 1) a consistent optimistic bias in time predictions for collaborative group projects; 2) more optimistic predictions based on group discussion than on individual predictions; and 3) mediation of group discussion by individual group members' thought focus. They reasoned that group discussion heightened participants' tendency to focus primarily on factors that promoted successful task completion. They mentioned that, in their studies, group discussion was free and unstructured and posited that process interventions might improve time predictions for collaborative group projects.

Stasser and Titus [7] confirmed that unshared information tends to be omitted from discussion and has little effect on members' preferences during group discussion. They suggested that "unique or unshared information had little impact on groups' decisions." (p. 1477) Their experiments used judgmental tasks, such as choosing one candidate among three to be the student body president. Four-person groups exchanged information and decided which candidate was best suited for the position. The information given to each member before discussion was carefully prepared to be consistent in shared conditions and biased in unshared conditions. Participants were alerted that the information was incomplete and their fellow members might have information of which they were unaware. As a result, only 7%, four out of 56 groups, selected a candidate who was supported by less than two members. Thus, the group tended to choose a candidate with a plurality of initial support.

Stasser and Stewart [8] assumed that if there was a way to make participants pay attention to the unshared unique information, they would do so. They prepared a murder mystery and asked people to discuss the homicide investigation and identify the guilty individual among three potential suspects. Participants individually received unshared clues in each condition. In the solve conditions, groups were told to decide which of the three suspects was guilty. In the judge conditions, groups were instructed to decide on a ranking of the suspects from most to least likely to have committed the crime. When critical clues were unshared, 67% of the groups in the solve conditions identified the guilty suspect, while 31% of the individual members did. Groups were therefore more likely than individuals to identify the guilty person. However, no such difference was found between groups and individuals in the judge conditions; 35% and 28%, respectively, successfully identified the guilty person. Moreover, Stasser and Stewart [8] described that the "focus of discussion on critical information may be more important than the sheer number of times that critical information is mentioned." (p. 431) They found that "groups that discussed more were not necessarily more successful unless they were able to shift the focus on critical clues and away from other features of the case." (p. 431) In sum, intensive discussion on crucial factors rather than relaxed conversation affects the quality of decision-making.

1.4 Purpose of This Research

This research aimed to identify the relationship between individual levels of understanding and group performances in the context of simulation and gaming. If the majority has a good understanding of the situation, the group can produce an outcome by following the majority's plan. If the majority does not have an appropriate understanding of the situation, the group has difficulty in producing an outcome. A group must listen to the voices of members who have a good understanding of the situation. A pre-game questionnaire was prepared to examine individual levels of understanding and estimations. A post-game questionnaire was used to assess individual participants' attitudes regarding their understanding of the process, result predicting, etc. The purpose of this research is to clarify the factors that contribute to producing an outcome when the majority does not have a good understanding of the situation.

2   Method

2.1   An OPT Scheduling Game

In this study, I used the OPT scheduling game designed by Legg [9] and based on a concept outlined in *The Goal* by Goldratt and Fox [10]. It was designed to simulate a mechanism of optimized production technology that Legg named the OPT SCHEDULING GAME. This study used a Japanese version of this game [11].

In an OPT scheduling game, participants work in teams of approximately ten people. The goal of the game is to make as high of a profit as possible by producing airplanes with plain A4 paper. Individual members have eight tasks, as shown in Table 1.

Table 1. Eight tasks and contents

Task	Content
Draw lines	Draw two straight lines with a pencil and scale ruler on a sheet of A4 paper to trisect the long side of the paper
Cut	Cut a sheet of paper with a pair of scissors into three pieces along the two straight lines
Fold wings	Fold a strip and make a pair of wings
Write on the wings	Write "OPT" on each wing
Fold fuselages	Fold a strip and make a fuselage
Write on the fuselages	Write the name of a company such as "RYUTSU KEIZAI UNIVERSITY" and three words, "TRY," "OUT," and "OPT," on each side of the fuselage
Combine wings with fuselages	Combine a pair of wings with a fuselage into the shape of an airplane by stapling the two parts
Transport materials	Transport materials between members who are allocated different tasks at different places. The materials include A4 plain paper, strips of paper, and the work-in-progress

This game's total running time is 900 s. The process' bottleneck is found in the "write on the fuselages" step, which takes about 30 s to finish. Initial cost is ¥200,000 and the cost of a sheet of A4 plain paper is ¥3,000. In terms of profit, one airplane creates ¥20,000 in profit, one pair of wings creates ¥5,000, and one fuselage creates ¥10,000. To recoup the initial cost, at least 10 airplanes need to be produced. Making a profit is numerically possible since producing 10 airplanes takes a little over 300 s by simple arithmetic, which is much less than the 900-s running time. To solve the bottleneck, assigning the task of "writing on the fuselages" to another person would be a possible alternative. But this alternative should be denied, considering the cost of ¥500,000.

2.2 Participants and Procedures

Participants were those who registered in a project management course for the first grade's first semester. The course consisted of a class held once a week for 15 weeks. Two groups of students registered for the course, and the class size was around 50 for Group 1 and 55 for Group 2. The participants' ages ranged from 18 to 21. The percentage of male students was about 85%. During the semester, students experienced several types of simulation and gaming on subjects, including communication, information sharing, leadership, social dilemmas, and team building before participating in the OPT SCHEDULING GAME. The game was run for two class meetings in a row, with session 1 occurring at the end of June and session 2 in the beginning of July in 2019. The number of attendees for the two consecutive weeks are shown in Table 2.

Table 2. The number of participants in two consecutive sessions

	Session 1	Session 2	Common members
Group 1 (5 teams)	49 participants	49 participants	47 participants
Group 2 (6 teams)	56 participants	54 participants	52 participants

Session 1 was dedicated to preparation: understanding the game's rules and procedures, organizing teams, making plans, allocating tasks to each member, and rehearsing the process with the whole group. The participants primarily organized their own teams. They were instructed to form teams of 10 in Group 1 and 9 in Group 2. When the team size was too big or small, I mediated a transfer between groups. Five teams were organized for Group 1 and six teams were organized for Group 2.

Session 2 was dedicated to the game itself: checking the plans and executing them. Some students were absent for the first session but attended the second session. Others attended session 1 but were absent from session 2. At the beginning of session 2, I asked each team to check whether all members were present and rearranged the teams so that they were approximately the same size. As a result, Team A, B, D, E consisted of ten members, Team C and F through K consisted of nine members. Most teams had a few new members with little knowledge of the game or its procedures. The first topic for all teams in session 2 was to review what was discussed and agreed on in session 1 and to confirm or reconsider their previous plans within the team. This helped new members understand the team's plan and refreshed old members' memory.

2.3 Questionnaires

Before and after the game run, participants were asked to answer questionnaires. The details of the questionnaires are as follows.

Questionnaire Before the Game Run

At the end of session 1, after the group meeting, participants individually answered four questions on the website. The first two questions examined whether they understood the initial costs and minimum number of airplanes required to recoup the initial cost. The third question asked which task they considered to be the most difficult, to examine whether they understood the overall process' critical path. The fourth question required them to enter their estimation of their team's net profit gain.

Questionnaire

(1) Do you understand that the initial cost is ¥200,000?
(2) Can you correctly estimate the minimum number of airplanes required to recoup the initial cost?
(3) Which task do you think is the hardest? Please choose one from the following alternatives:
     Draw lines, Cut, Fold wings, Write on the wings, Fold fuselages,
     Write on the fuselages, Combine wings with fuselages, Transport materials
(4) Please estimate the net profit gain (sales minus costs) of your team.

Participants answered questions (1) and (2) by choosing from among four options: "Yes, I do/can," "Now I understand/can," "Neither yes nor no," and "I have no idea." Participants answered question (3) by choosing from among eight options. Question (4) called for a free description.

Questionnaire After the Game Run

At the end of session 2, after the game run, a debriefing sheet was distributed to each participant. Question items were as follows.

Debriefing Sheet

Q1 Please give us your feedback on this game run in two lines.
Q2-1 How much did you understand of the process of producing the airplane?
Q2-2 Which task looked the hardest?
Q3-1 How well did you understand your team's plan?
Q3-2 Please explain your team's plan.
Q4-1 Did you predict your team would end up with this result?
Q4-2 What result did you predict?
Q5-1 How satisfied are you with the result of this game?
Q5-2 Why do you think so?
Q6 What do you think should have been done better?
Q7 If you were to participate in the same game again, what would you like to do?
Q8 If you were to apply what you have learned from this game, what would it be?

Participants answered questions Q2-1, Q3-1, Q4-1, and Q5-1 on a 6-point scale ranging from 1 (never) to 6 (fully) and then described the details in a few lines to the questions Q2-2, Q3-2, Q4-2, and Q5-2. Questions Q1, Q6, Q7, and Q8 called for free description.

2.4 Hypothesis

The teams with plenty of members who understood the situation well would achieve solid results. Answers to the questionnaire prior to the game run would be the index of how well individual participants understood the situation. When a few members understood the situation well, the team would not be able to reach solid results unless the team eagerly listened to those members' voices.

3 Results

3.1 Level of Understanding Prior to the Game Run

Table 3 shows the frequency distribution of answers to questions (1) and (2). A little more than half of the participants correctly understood the initial cost and estimated the minimum number of airplanes required to recoup the initial cost. Approximately a quarter of the participants recognized them after being asked about them.

Table 3. Frequency distribution of answers to questions (1) and (2) in Group 1

	Understood	Just now	Neither	No idea	Total
(1)The initial cost	59	25	5	10	99
(2)The minimum number of airplanes required to recoup the initial cost	53	23	13	9	98

Answers to the question about the production process' hardest task were as follows. Writing on the fuselages, the bottleneck in an OPT scheduling game, was chosen by 43 participants. Transport materials was chosen by 38 participants. Other tasks were chosen by 18 participants. A little less than half the participants correctly understood the production process' critical part.

3.2 Individual Estimations Prior to the Game Run and Team's Final Profit

Table 4 and Fig. 1 show the mean and median of individual estimations prior to the game run, and the team's final profit. Teams B, C, D, and E generated a surplus; Teams A and F–K ended with a deficit.

All teams with a deficit, other than Team G, show the pattern described in Fig. 1; the mean is the highest, the median is next, and team's final profit is third. This indicates that individual estimations were optimistically biased. Since the median was lower than the average, the average was pulled by one or a few relatively optimistic members. All teams that ended with a surplus, except Team C, showed very little difference between

Table 4. The mean and median of individual estimations and team's final profit

Team	Mean (¥)	Median (¥)	Team's final profit (¥)
A	208,333	200,000	−15,000
B	448,750	400,000	303,000
C	548,889	1,000,000	132,000
D	763,333	200,000	329,000
E	228,000	200,000	284,000
F	525,000	500,000	−1,038,000
G	67,500	100,000	−50,000
H	378,889	100,000	−157,000
I	448,889	100,000	−93,000
J	1,003,333	200,000	−64,000
K	329,000	150,000	−30,000

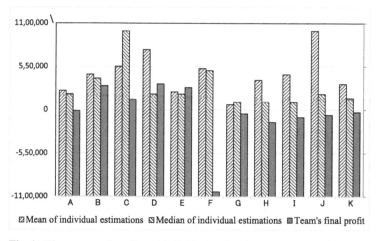

Fig. 1. The mean and median of individual estimations and team's final profit

the median and the final profit. Team C seems unique in that it has a very high median (Table 4 and Fig. 1).

Table 5 and Fig. 2 show the number of experienced members and team's final profit in the order of team's final profit. Here, an experienced member means the participant who understood the situation appropriately, that is, who answered questions (1), (2), and (3) with 1, 1, 6, respectively. When there were no experienced members, team's final profits were below zero as in Teams H, I, and K. When the number of experienced members was 4 or 5, as in Teams B, D, and E, the team's final profits were above zero. When the number of experienced members was between 1 and 3, as in Teams A, C, F,

G, and J, team's final profits were mostly below zero, with Team C as the one notable exception.

Table 5. Team result and the number of experienced members

Team	Number of experienced members	Team's final profit (¥)
H	0	−157,000
I	0	−93,000
K	0	−30,000
F	**1**	**−1,038,000**
A	**1**	**−15,000**
J	**2**	**−64,000**
C	**2**	**132,000**
G	**3**	**−50,000**
E	4	284,000
B	4	303,000
D	5	329,000

In Table 5 and Fig. 2, we see that Team C ended with a profit of ¥132,000 while Team F ended with a significant loss of -¥1,038,000. Looking deeper, the frequency distribution of answers to questions (1) to (3) in Teams C and F are shown in Tables 6, 7 and 8. According to Table 6 and 7, Team C seemed to understand the situation much

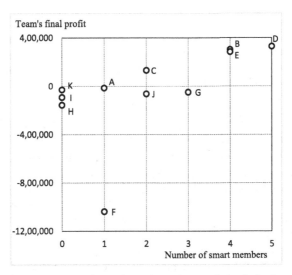

Fig. 2. The number of experienced members and team's final profit.

better than Team F. However, Table 8 shows that Team C had a lesser understanding of the critical task than Team F. With an eye on these prior understanding levels of the members in Teams C and F, let us look at the posterior results.

Table 6. Answers about the initial cost in Teams C and F

Team	Understood	Just now	Neither	No idea	No answer	Total
C	7	2	0	0	0	9
F	2	5	1	0	1	9

Table 7. Answers about the number of airplanes to recoup the initial cost in Teams F and C

Team	Estimated	Just now	Neither	No idea	No answer	Total
C	7	1	1	0	0	9
F	1	5	1	1	1	9

Table 8. Answers about the hardest task of the production process in Teams F and C

Team	Write on the fuselages	Transport	Others	No answer	Total
C	2	4	3	0	9
F	5	2	1	1	9

3.3 Answers to the Debriefing Sheet

Table 9 shows team-by-team averages of individual answers to the debriefing sheet. Q2-1 shows the level of understanding of the whole production process, Q3-1 shows the level of understanding regarding the team's strategy, Q4-1 shows the level of outcome prediction, and Q5-1 shows the level of satisfaction with the result.

Figure 3 shows the relationship of team-by-team averages between process understanding (Q2-1) and strategy understanding (Q3-1). The determination coefficient is 0.56 and the correlation coefficient is 0.75. The more members understand the entire production process, the more they understand their strategy, and vice versa.

In Fig. 3, the coordinate values of the teams that ended the game with a surplus are shown in bold squares. Four teams ended with a surplus. Three of these four teams—Teams B, D, and E—had scores that demonstrated their high understanding of the process and strategy. Although Team C also finished with a surplus, its levels of process and

Table 9. Average of answers to debriefing sheet and team's final profit

Team	Q2-1	Q3-1	Q4-1	Q5-1	Team's final profit (¥)
F	4.78	4.11	3.22	3.11	−1,038,000
H	3.89	4.11	3.78	3.56	−157,000
I	3.44	4.11	4.67	3.78	−93,000
J	4.56	3.89	2.56	2.89	−64,000
G	4.00	3.56	3.75	2.78	−50,000
K	4.50	4.33	4.22	4.56	−30,000
A	3.50	3.10	3.10	2.30	−15,000
C	3.89	4.13	3.22	4.89	132,000
E	5.30	4.60	4.10	4.00	284,000
B	5.60	4.70	3.50	4.70	303,000
D	5.20	5.20	5.00	5.50	329,000

strategy understanding were not as high as Teams B, D, and E. Moreover, Team C's level of process understanding was lower than that of Teams F, J, and K. It is noteworthy that despite an average score as high as 4.78— for the level of understanding of the production process—team F ended with a large deficit.

In sum, the hypotheses were roughly supported. The teams with plenty of members who understood the situation well achieved solid results (Teams, B, D, and E). Teams

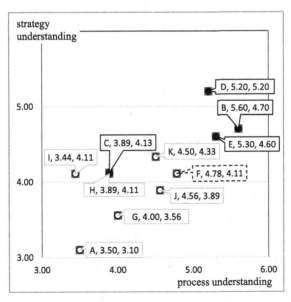

Fig. 3. The relationship between process understanding and strategy understanding.

with few or no members who understood the situation well did not reach solid results (Teams A, G, H, I, J, and K). Exceptions were Teams C and F. Team C was unique in that only two members understood the situation well and the final profit was a surplus. Team F was unique in that the levels of understanding before the game run were low and the final profit was a significant loss, yet the perceived levels of understanding after the game run were high.

4 Discussion

This study examined the following hypothesis. When a few members in a group understand a situation well, the group will be unable to reach a suitable result unless the team eagerly listens to those members' voices. As shown in Table 5, Team C ended with a profit of ¥132,000, whereas Team F ended with a significant loss of -¥1,038,000. This raises the following question—what is the difference between Teams C and F? Both teams consisted of nine members and all were males. Teams C and F had similar numbers of experienced members who understood the situation well (two and one, respectively). Prior to the game run, seven members understood the initial cost in Team C and two members in Team F (Table 6); additionally, seven members estimated the number of airplanes required to recoup the initial cost in Team C, while one member did in Team F (Table 7). Five members of Team F considered "writing on the fuselages" as the most difficult task (Table 8). Therefore, the lack of understanding of the basic conditions related to initial cost in Team F resulted in the worst outcome—increasing the number of workers for the task "writing on the fuselages." In other words, the opinions of the two members with high understanding in Team C were listened to by other members, whereas that of the one member with high understanding in Team F was not heard. An encouraging aspect is that five members in Team F seemed to understand the initial cost and estimated the number of airplanes needed to recoup the initial cost immediately after being asked about them (see Tables 6 and 7). This would be the first step in utilizing unshared knowledge.

Stasser and Titus [7] suggested that "unstructured discussion in the face of a consensus requirement may often fail as a means of combining unique informational resources." (p. 1477) It is possible that a certain structured discussion would be able to shed light on the value of unique informational resources.

Let us look at the studies on group accuracy and instructional interventions. Henry [12] and Henry, Kmet, Desrosiers, and Landa [13] used a series of quantitative estimation questions, such as the coldest temperature ever recorded in Alabama, and examined which factors affected group accuracy. Instructional interventions seem to contribute to structuring group discussion and reaching better decision-making.

Henry [12] compared two different instructional interventions: "information sharing" and "choosing." In the condition of information sharing, participants were asked to list the three most relevant pieces of information which came up in their discussion of each question. In the condition of choosing, participants were asked to determine which individual estimate was the most accurate for each question. In both conditions, simply telling groups to either share information or choose led to significantly better group performance. Henry [12] suggested that "strategic suggestions could have beneficial effects on group performance either because they identify a practical strategy or because they give groups the permission to make comparisons" (p. 195–196).

Henry, Kmet, Desrosiers, and Landa [13] used the same two interventions and examined how interpersonal cohesiveness within a group influences the effectiveness of the two techniques. Participants in the high cohesiveness condition were provided an opportunity to get to know each other before they worked on the estimation task. One of the researchers' predictions was "these cohesive groups should perform more effectively when they are given a task strategy that also fosters cooperation and positive feelings (i.e., the information sharing strategy)" (Henry, Kmet, Desrosiers, and Landa [13], p. 30). Their prediction was partially supported. The effect was limited to same-sex groups. Mixed-sex groups were simply more accurate regardless of experimental condition.

Regarding the differences between Teams C and F, Team C had plenty of members who understood the basic conditions before the game run. Thus, Team C might have been open to the voices of two members with greater understanding during group discussion. On the other hand, Team F had a few members who understood the basic conditions before the game run. Moreover, participants in Team F misperceived their levels of understanding after the game run (see Fig. 3). This indicates that Team F did not reach an understanding of the process and stuck to the worst solution. Team F must not have listened to the member with the greatest understanding.

What may have supported the participants in Team F would be to give strategic instructions to help structure their group discussion. Cozy and friendly atmospheres will not necessarily lead to a reasonably appropriate decision. Serious rather than casual discussion is required. It is important to prepare an environment in which people can have intense discussions and not be afraid of being attacked, hated, isolated, teased, and so on. Concrete instructions such as "do not use majority-rule," "pay attention to all conditions," "make an estimate of the team's outcome," or "choose the most accurate value among members' estimation," may help the group have an effective discussion and reach an appropriate decision.

For participants with high understanding, informative questions are effective for successfully achieving the game's goal and to have fruitful discussions leading to an appropriate decision. For inexperienced participants, informative questions will be too vague to be effective, resulting in a group discussion that is not fruitful for them. During the game run, therefore, they may unexpectedly encounter issues and try to cope with them, which can result in significant failure. Although important lessons can be learned from failure, if concrete instructions help such participants shift their focus, they may be able to have fruitful discussions similar to participants with high understanding. Additional strategic instructions would allow participants to change their mindset and spark a serious conversation, resulting in participants searching for information regardless of whether it is shared by the majority. Suitable triggers include informative questions for experienced members and strategic instructions for inexperienced members.

References

1. Buehler, R., Messervey, D., Griffin, D.: Collaborative planning and prediction: does group discussion affect optimistic biases in time estimation? Organ. Behav. Hum. Decision Processes **97**, 47–63 (2005)
2. Kahneman, D., Tversky, A.: Intuitive prediction biases and corrective procedures. Technical report. McLean, VA: Decisions and Designs Inc. (1977). https://apps.dtic.mil/dtic/tr/fulltext/u2/a047747.pdf. Accessed 8 Mar 2020
3. Buehler, R., Griffin, D., Ross, M. It's about time: optimistic predictions in work and love. European Review of Social Psychology **6**(1), 1–32 (1995). Republished on line 04 March 2011 https://doi.org/10.1080/14792779343000112. Accessed 8 Mar 2020
4. Kruger, J., Evans, M.: If you don't want to be late, enumerate: Unpacking reduces the planning fallacy. J. Exper. Psychol. **40**, 586–598 (2004)
5. Moss, S.: The planning fallacy. SICOTESTS. https://www.sicotests.com/psyarticle.asp?id=385. Accessed 8 Mar 2020
6. Nakamura, M.: Unpacking and overconfidence in a production management game. In: 50th ISAGA Conference Proceedings, Poland (2019)
7. Stasser, G., Titus, W.: Pooling of unshared information in group decision making: Biased information sampling during discussion. J. Personality Soc. Psychol. **48**(6), 1467–1478 (1985)
8. Stasser, G., Stewart, D.: Discovery of hidden profiles by decision-making groups: solving a problem versus making a judgment. J. Personal. Soc. Psychol. **63**(3), 426–434 (1992)
9. Legg, L.: Planes or bust: an OPT scheduling game. In: Armstrong, R., Percival, F., Saunders, D. (eds.) The Simulation and Gaming Yearbook Volume 2: Interactive Learning, pp. 209–219. Kogan Page, London (1994)
10. Goldratt, E.M., Fox, R.E.: The Goal: A Process of Ongoing Improvement Third Revised. North River Press, Great Barrington (2004)
11. Nakamura, M.: Japanese translation of Legg's "Planes or bust: an OPT scheduling game". J. Ryutsu Keizai Univ. **31**(1), 57–65 (1996)
12. Henry, R.: Improving group judgement accuracy: information sharing and determining the best member. Organizational Behav. Human Decision Processes **62**, 190–197 (1995)
13. Henry, R., Kmet, J., Desrosiers, E., Landa, A.: Examining the impact of interpersonal cohesiveness on group accuracy interventions: the importance of matching versus buffering. Organ. Behav. Human Decision Processes **87**, 25–43 (2002)

Author Index